FTB

THE RECORD OF A
FALLEN VAMPIRE

D1500673

I've become fascinated by a mineral called labradorite. It looks like a gray stone, but if you shine light on it, it glitters, changing color as you move it around. It makes me remember that not all things are as they appear to be.

–Yuri Kimura

Artist Yuri Kimura debuted two short stories in Japan's *Gangan Powered* after winning the Enix Manga Award. Shortly thereafter, she began *The Record of a Fallen Vampire*, which was serialized in Japan's *Monthly Shonen Gangan* through March 2007.

Author Kyo Shirodaira is from Nara prefecture. In addition to *The Record of a Fallen Vampire*, Shirodaira has scripted the manga *Spiral: The Bonds of Reasoning*. Shirodaira's novel *Meitantei ni Hana wo* was nominated for the 8th Annual Ayukawa Tetsuya Award in 1997.

THE RECORD OF A

FALLEN VAMPIRE

STORY BY: KYO SHIRODAIRA ART BY: YURI KIMURA

5

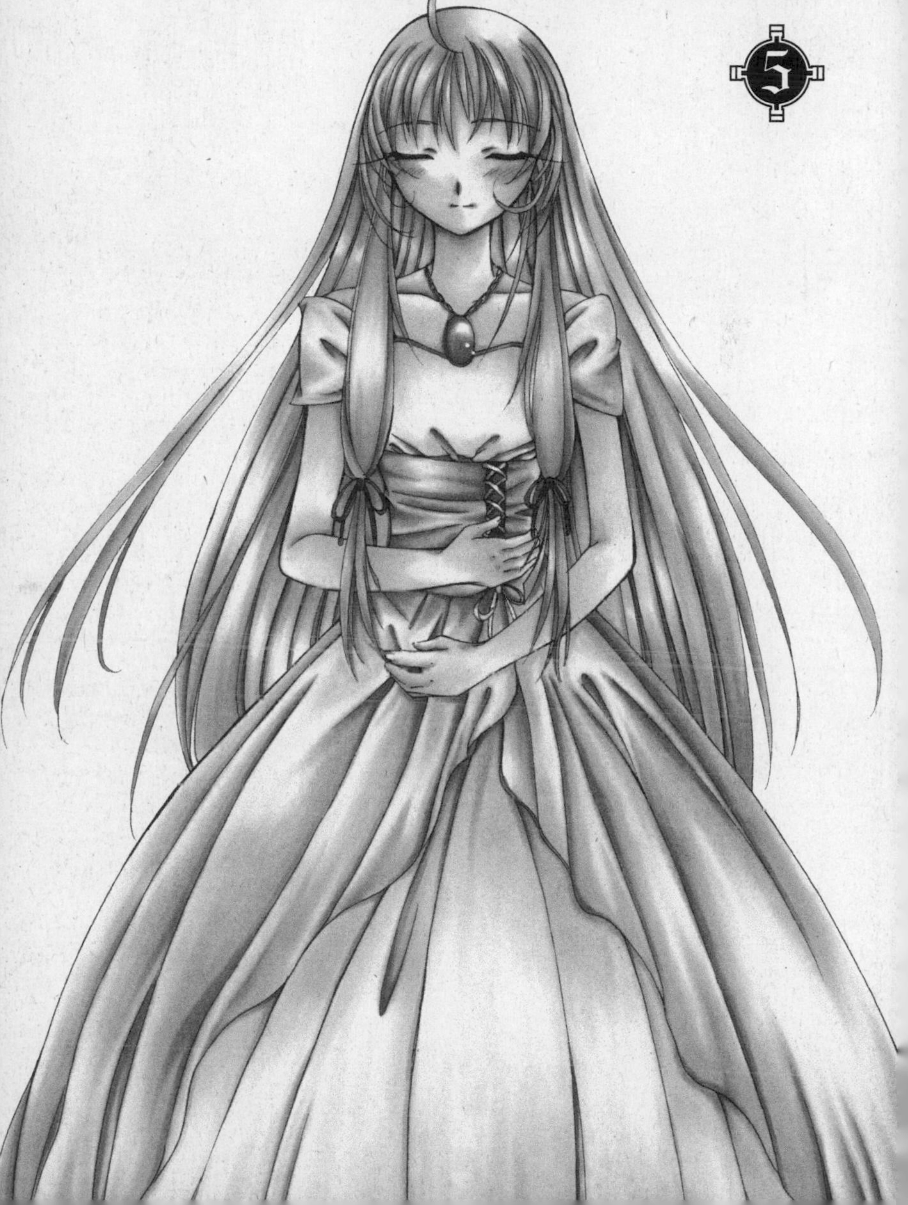

of vampires,
"Night Monarchy"
ty.

beginning of

This is the legend the history of the and its last Majes A story about the vampires' agony...

Story : Kyo Shirodaira
Art : Yuri Kimura

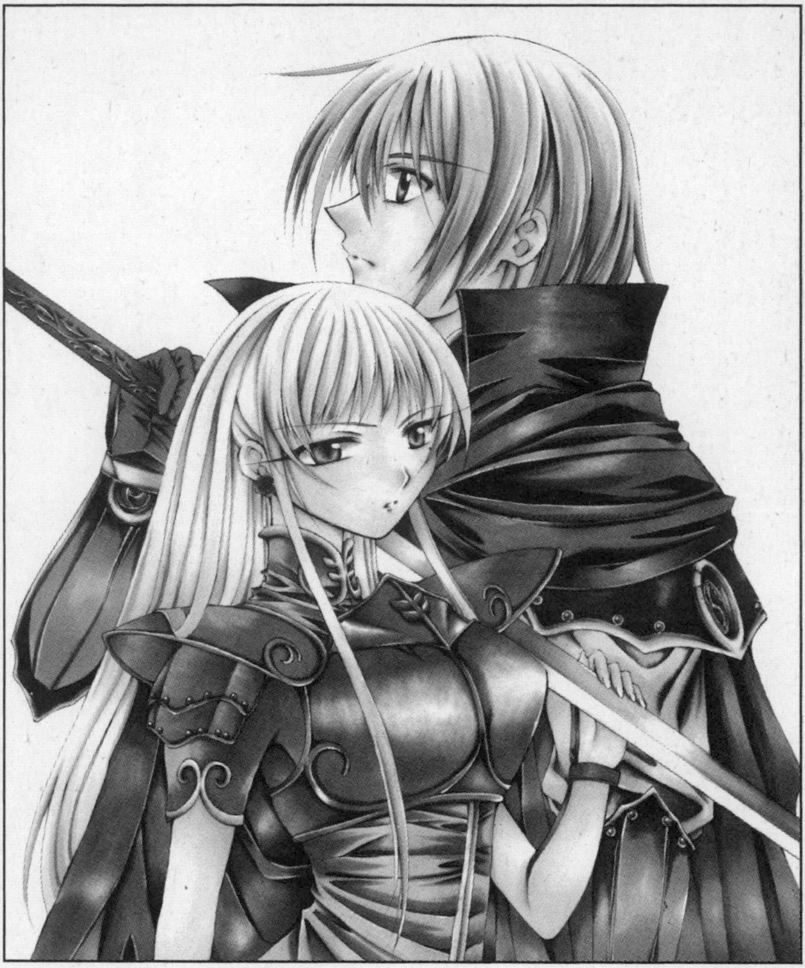

CONTENTS

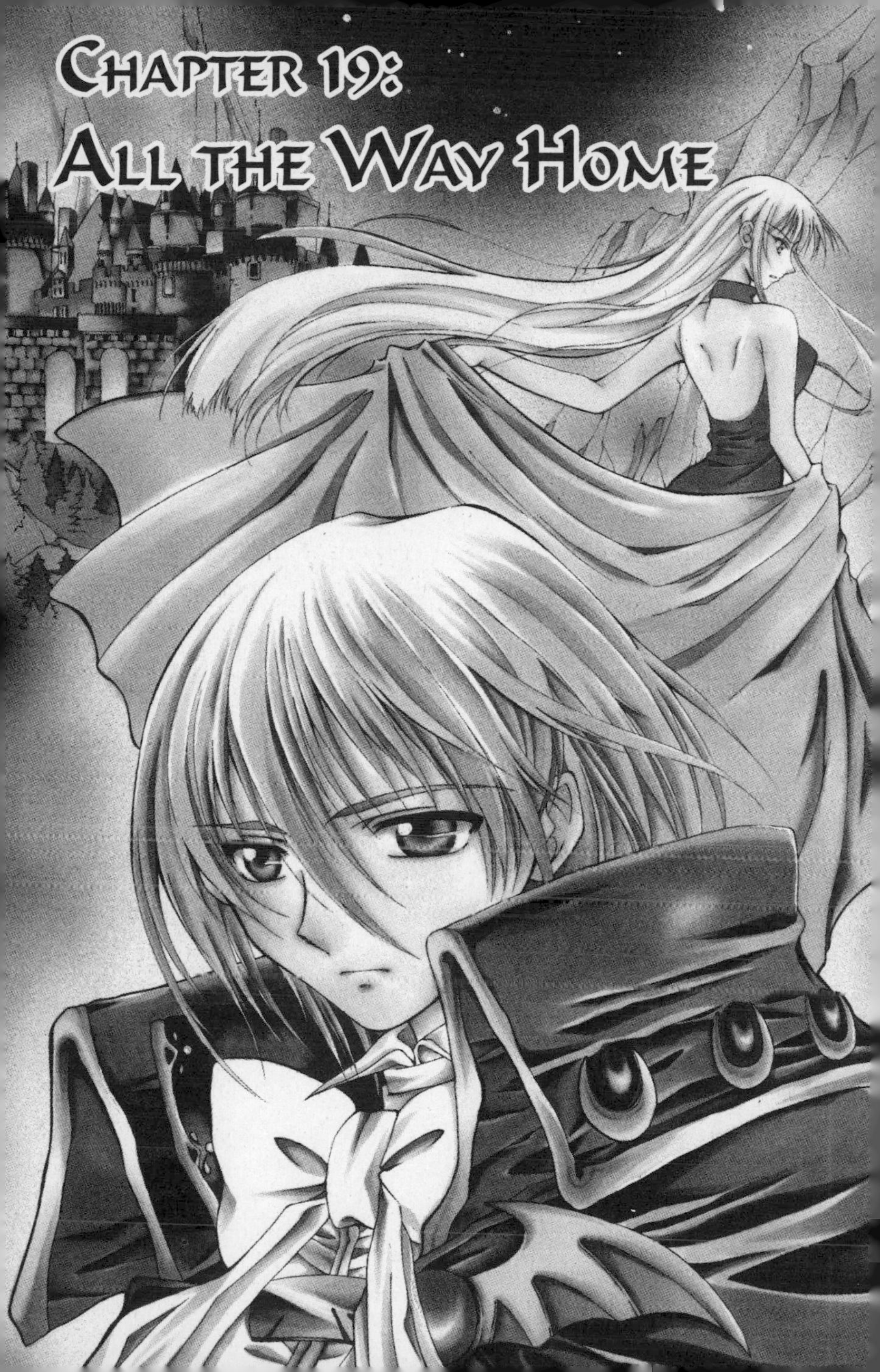
Chapter 19:
All the Way Home

THE RECORD OF A FALLEN VAMPIRE

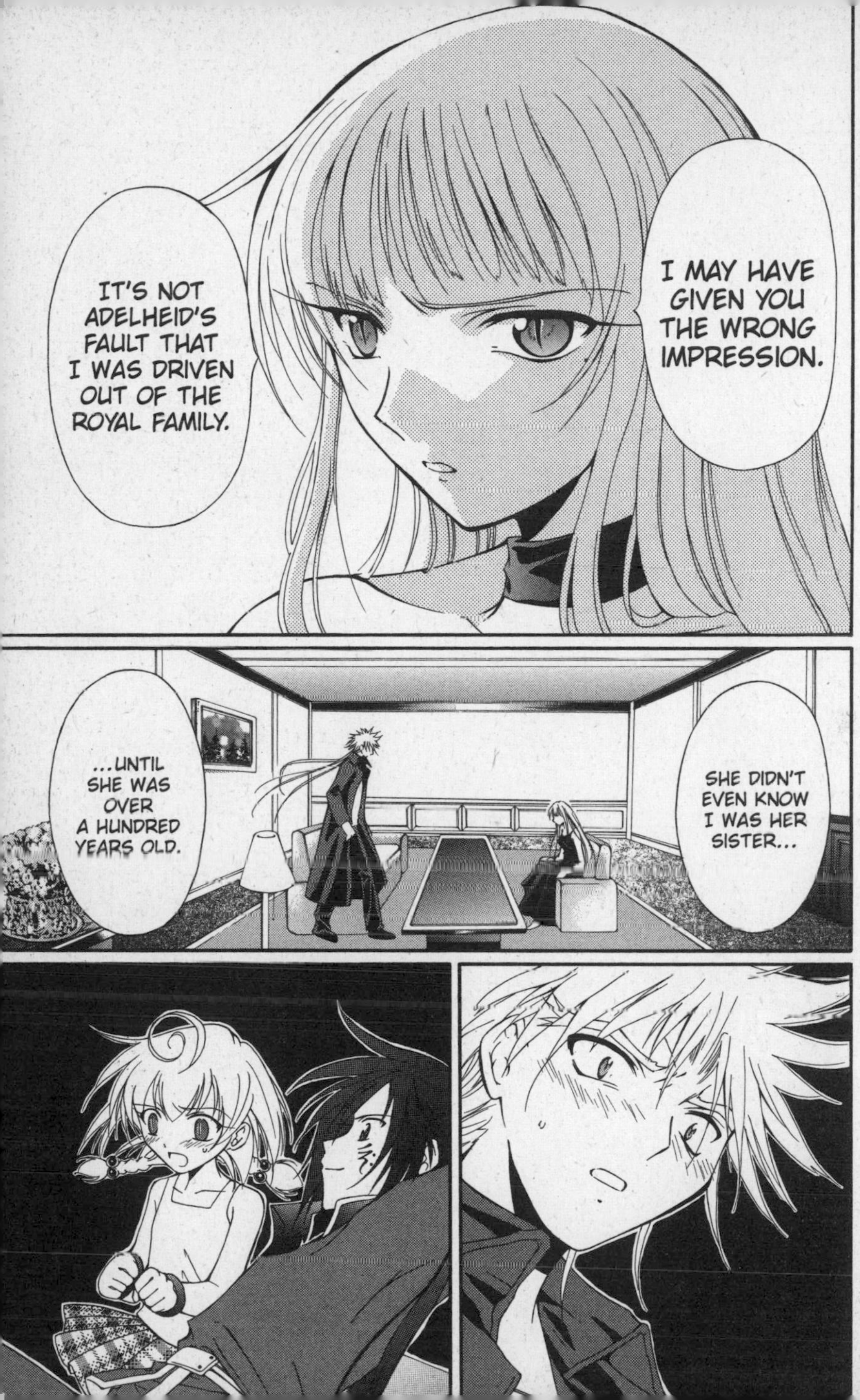
I MAY HAVE GIVEN YOU THE WRONG IMPRESSION.
IT'S NOT ADELHEID'S FAULT THAT I WAS DRIVEN OUT OF THE ROYAL FAMILY.
SHE DIDN'T EVEN KNOW I WAS HER SISTER...
...UNTIL SHE WAS OVER A HUNDRED YEARS OLD.

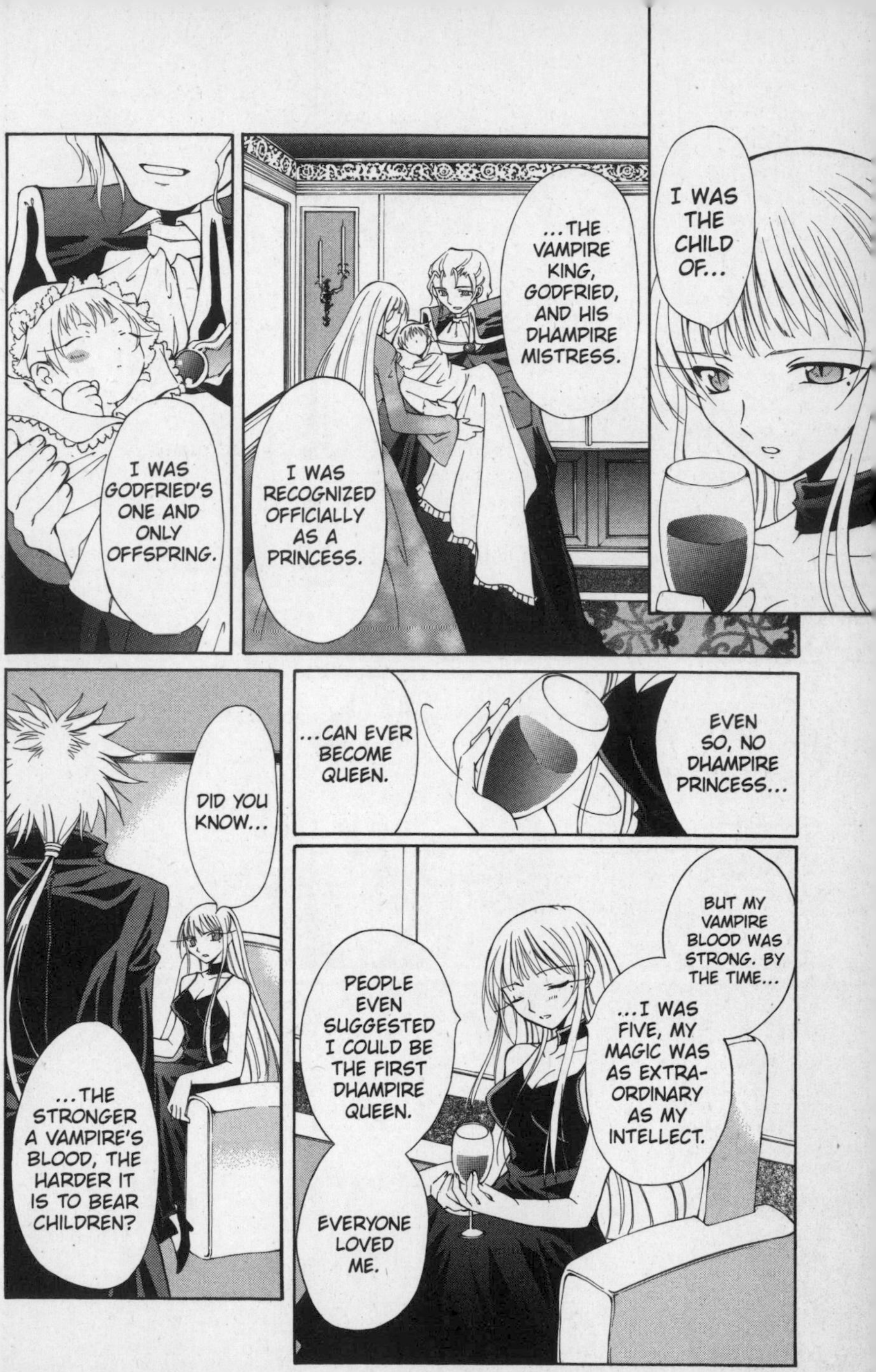
I WAS THE CHILD OF...
...THE VAMPIRE KING, GODFRIED, AND HIS DHAMPIRE MISTRESS.
I WAS RECOGNIZED OFFICIALLY AS A PRINCESS.
I WAS GODFRIED'S ONE AND ONLY OFFSPRING.
EVEN SO, NO DHAMPIRE PRINCESS...
...CAN EVER BECOME QUEEN.
BUT MY VAMPIRE BLOOD WAS STRONG. BY THE TIME...
...I WAS FIVE, MY MAGIC WAS AS EXTRA-ORDINARY AS MY INTELLECT.
PEOPLE EVEN SUGGESTED I COULD BE THE FIRST DHAMPIRE QUEEN.
EVERYONE LOVED ME.
DID YOU KNOW...
...THE STRONGER A VAMPIRE'S BLOOD, THE HARDER IT IS TO BEAR CHILDREN?

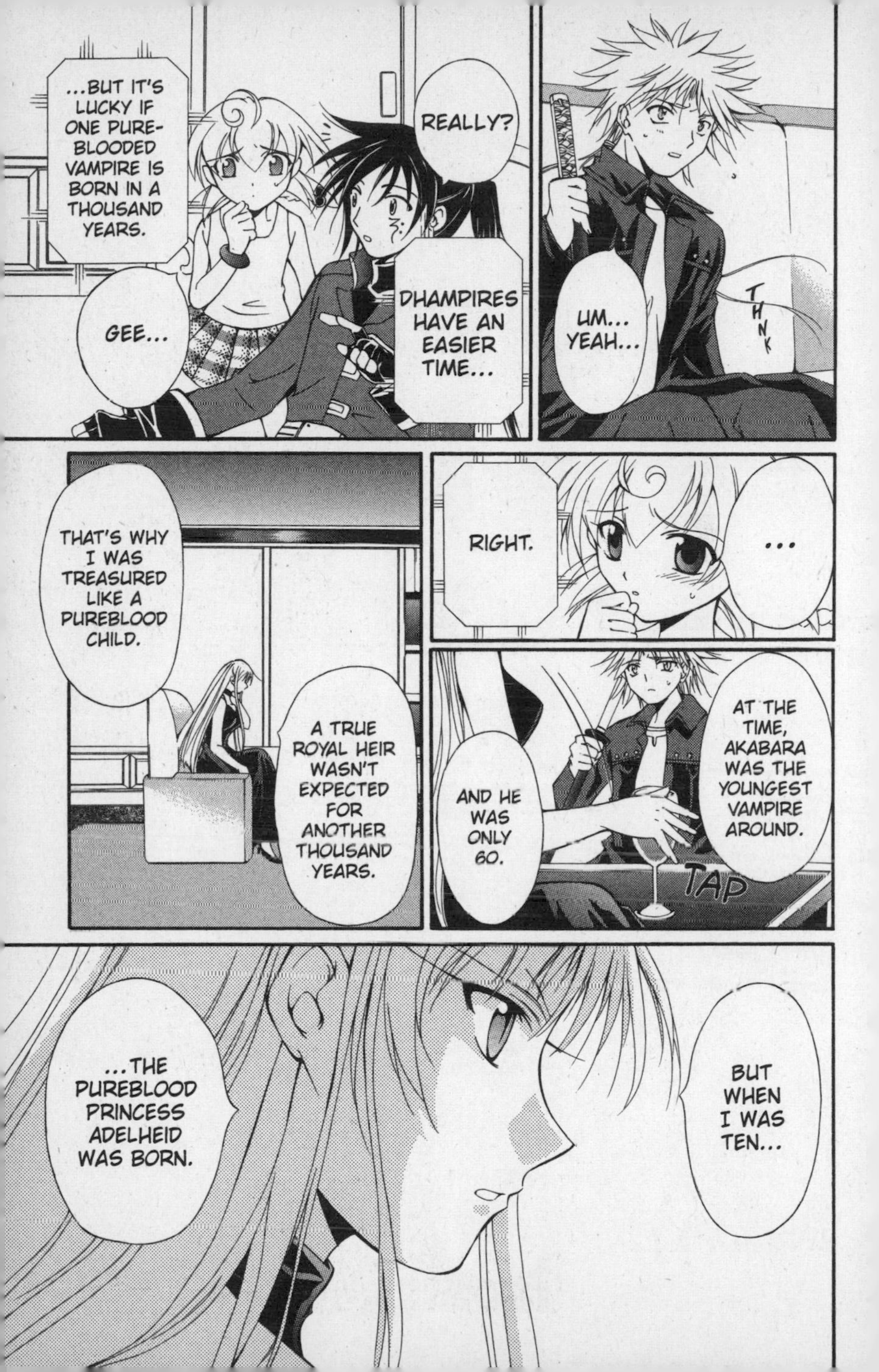
UM... YEAH...
THNK
REALLY?
DHAMPIRES HAVE AN EASIER TIME...
...BUT IT'S LUCKY IF ONE PURE-BLOODED VAMPIRE IS BORN IN A THOUSAND YEARS.
GEE...
...
RIGHT.
AT THE TIME, AKABARA WAS THE YOUNGEST VAMPIRE AROUND.
AND HE WAS ONLY 60.
TAP
A TRUE ROYAL HEIR WASN'T EXPECTED FOR ANOTHER THOUSAND YEARS.
THAT'S WHY I WAS TREASURED LIKE A PUREBLOOD CHILD.
BUT WHEN I WAS TEN...
...THE PUREBLOOD PRINCESS ADELHEID WAS BORN.

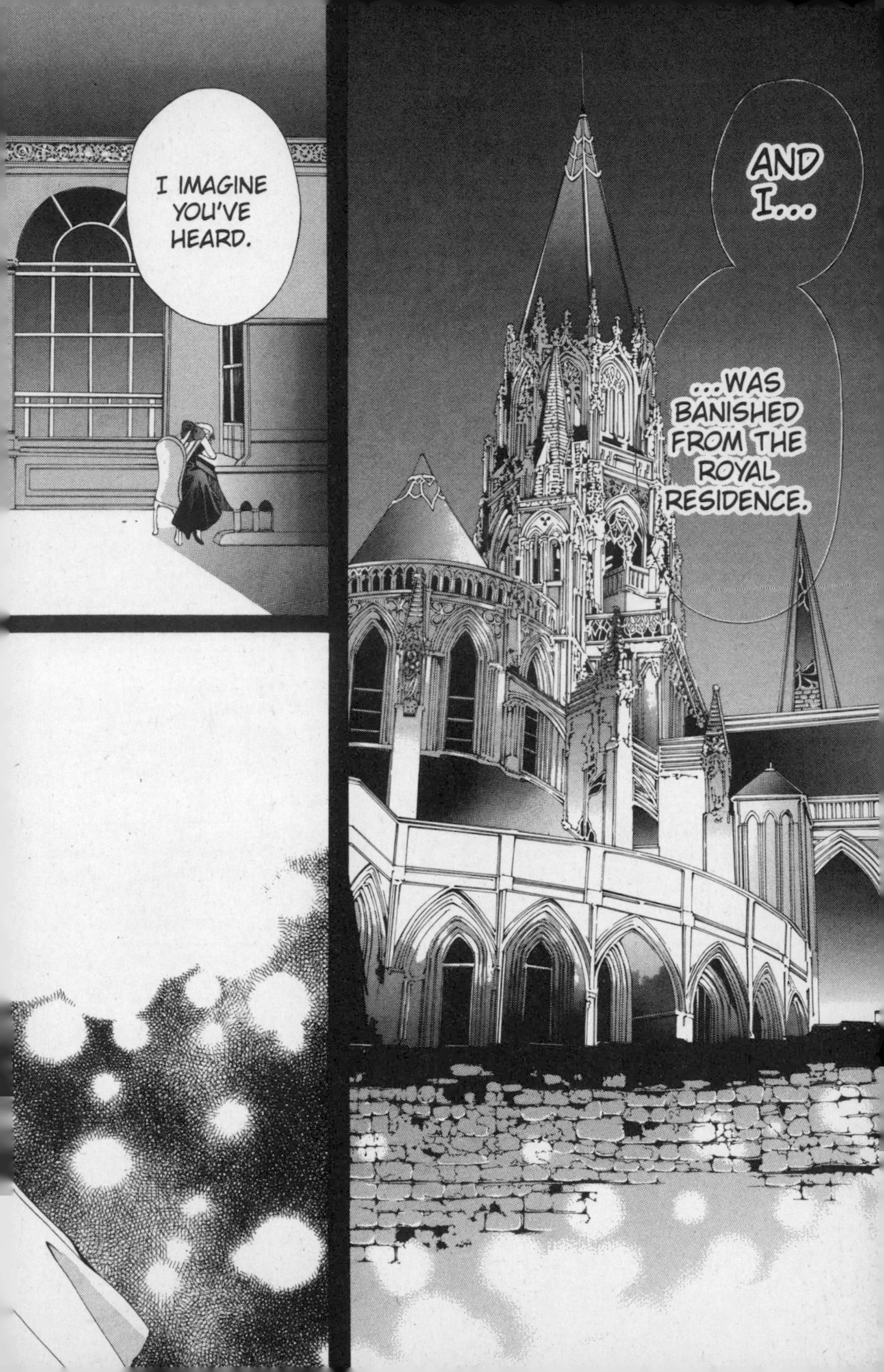
AND I...
...WAS BANISHED FROM THE ROYAL RESIDENCE.
I IMAGINE YOU'VE HEARD.

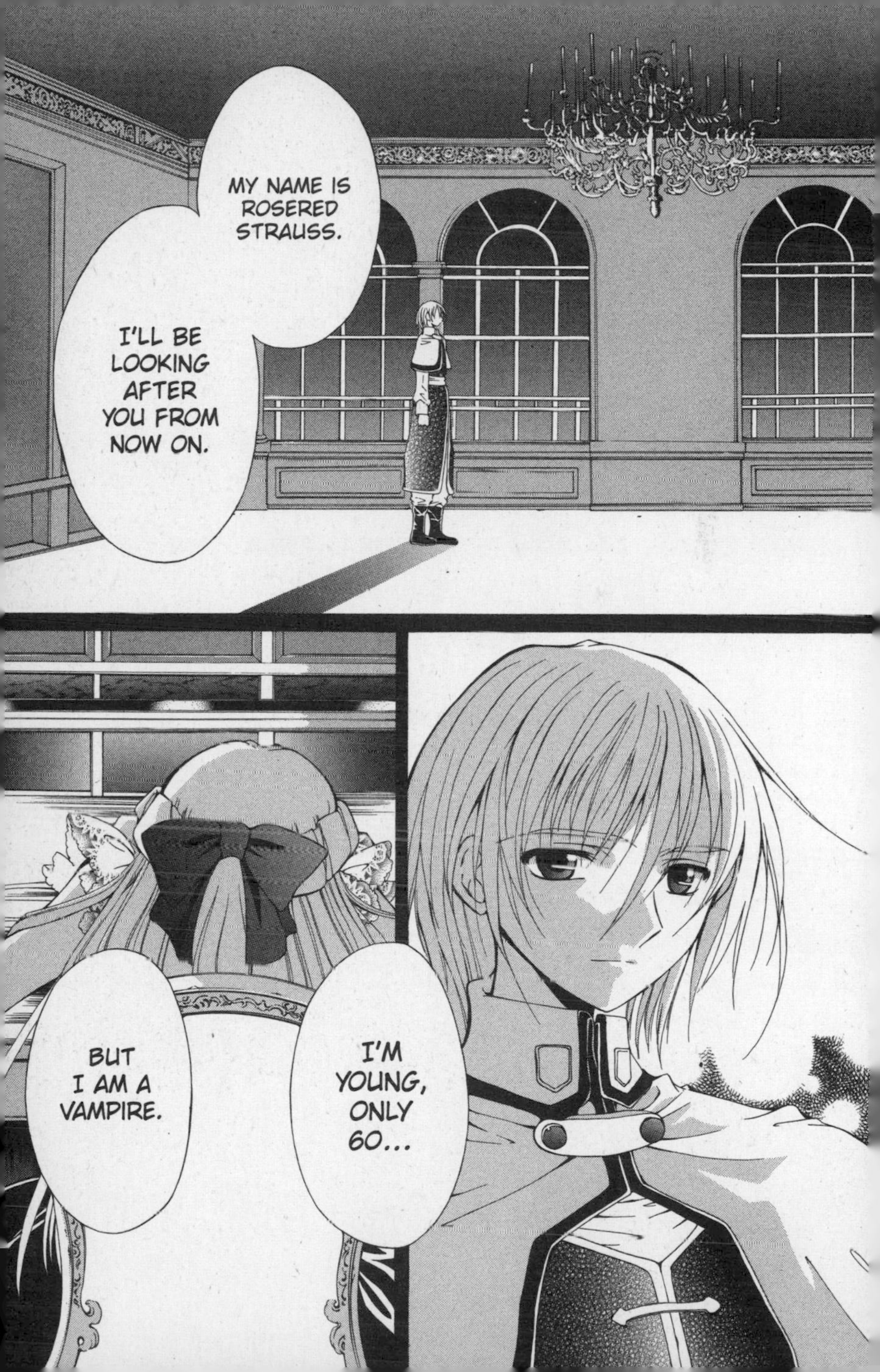
MY NAME IS ROSERED STRAUSS.
I'LL BE LOOKING AFTER YOU FROM NOW ON.
I'M YOUNG, ONLY 60...
BUT I AM A VAMPIRE.

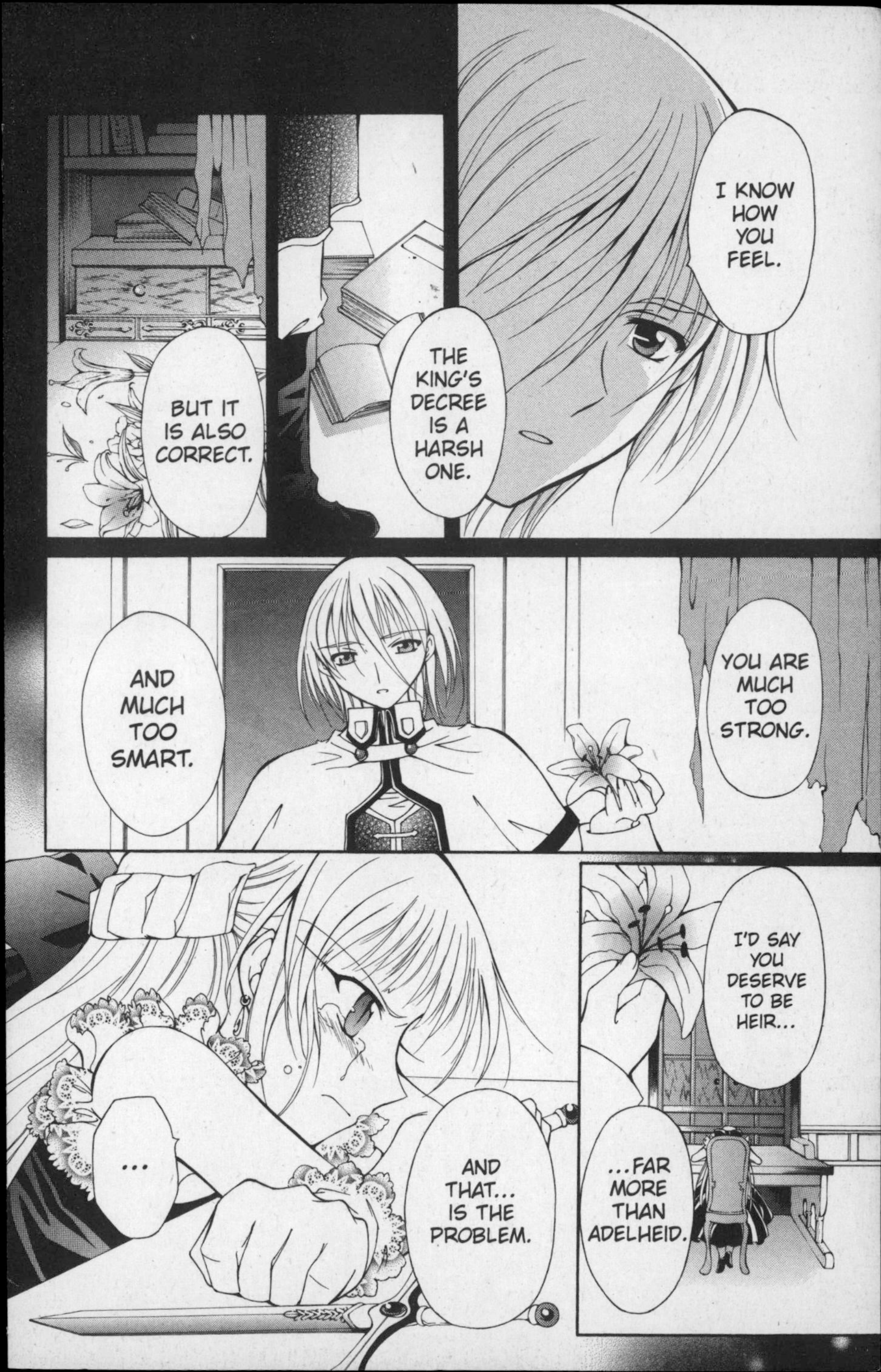
I KNOW HOW YOU FEEL.
THE KING'S DECREE IS A HARSH ONE.
BUT IT IS ALSO CORRECT.
YOU ARE MUCH TOO STRONG.
AND MUCH TOO SMART.
I'D SAY YOU DESERVE TO BE HEIR...
...FAR MORE THAN ADELHEID.
AND THAT... IS THE PROBLEM.
...

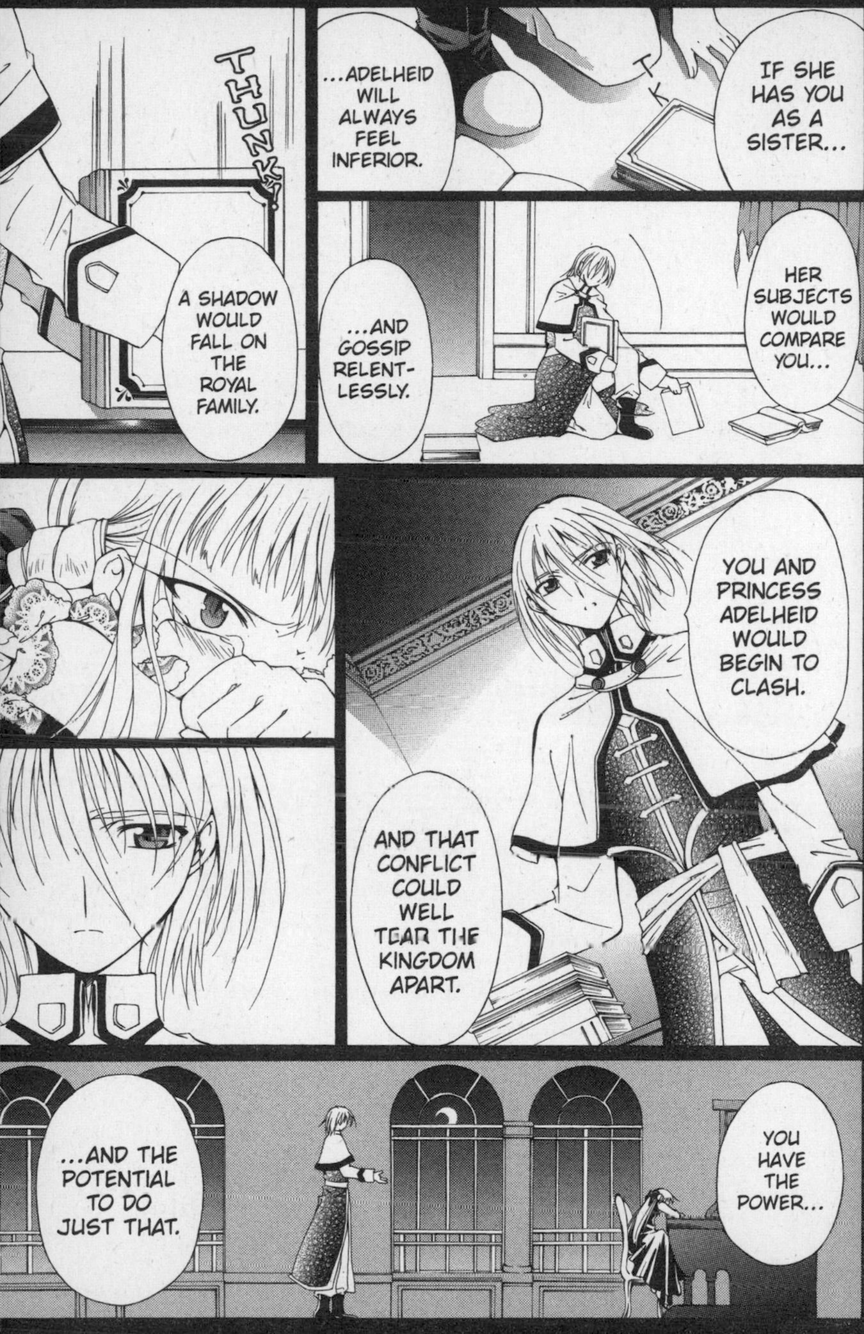
IF SHE HAS YOU AS A SISTER...
TK
...ADELHEID WILL ALWAYS FEEL INFERIOR.
HER SUBJECTS WOULD COMPARE YOU...
...AND GOSSIP RELENTLESSLY.
THUNK!
A SHADOW WOULD FALL ON THE ROYAL FAMILY.
YOU AND PRINCESS ADELHEID WOULD BEGIN TO CLASH.
AND THAT CONFLICT COULD WELL TEAR THE KINGDOM APART.
YOU HAVE THE POWER...
...AND THE POTENTIAL TO DO JUST THAT.

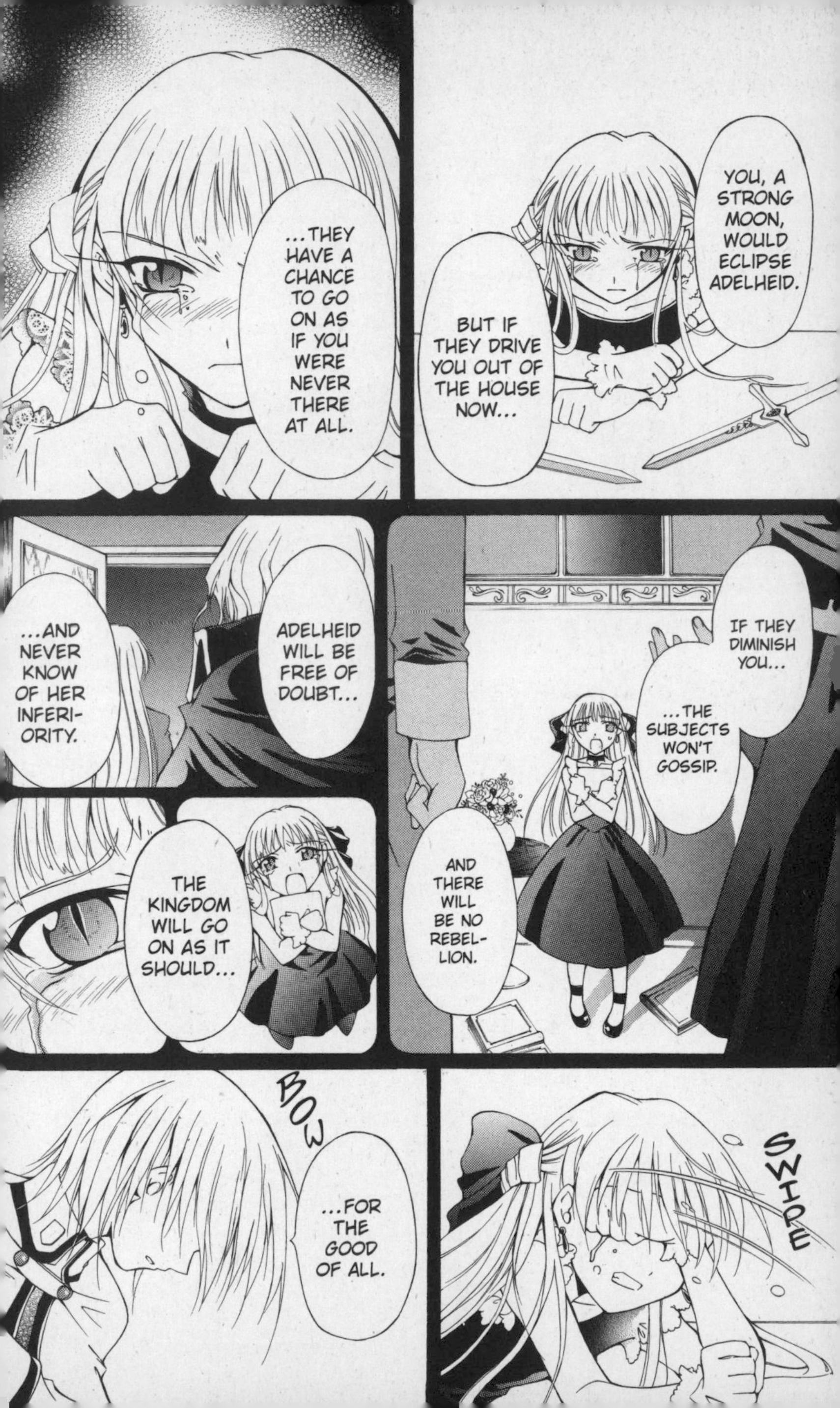
YOU, A STRONG MOON, WOULD ECLIPSE ADELHEID.
BUT IF THEY DRIVE YOU OUT OF THE HOUSE NOW...
...THEY HAVE A CHANCE TO GO ON AS IF YOU WERE NEVER THERE AT ALL.
IF THEY DIMINISH YOU...
...THE SUBJECTS WON'T GOSSIP.
AND THERE WILL BE NO REBEL-LION.
ADELHEID WILL BE FREE OF DOUBT...
...AND NEVER KNOW OF HER INFERI-ORITY.
THE KINGDOM WILL GO ON AS IT SHOULD...
SWIPE
BOW
...FOR THE GOOD OF ALL.

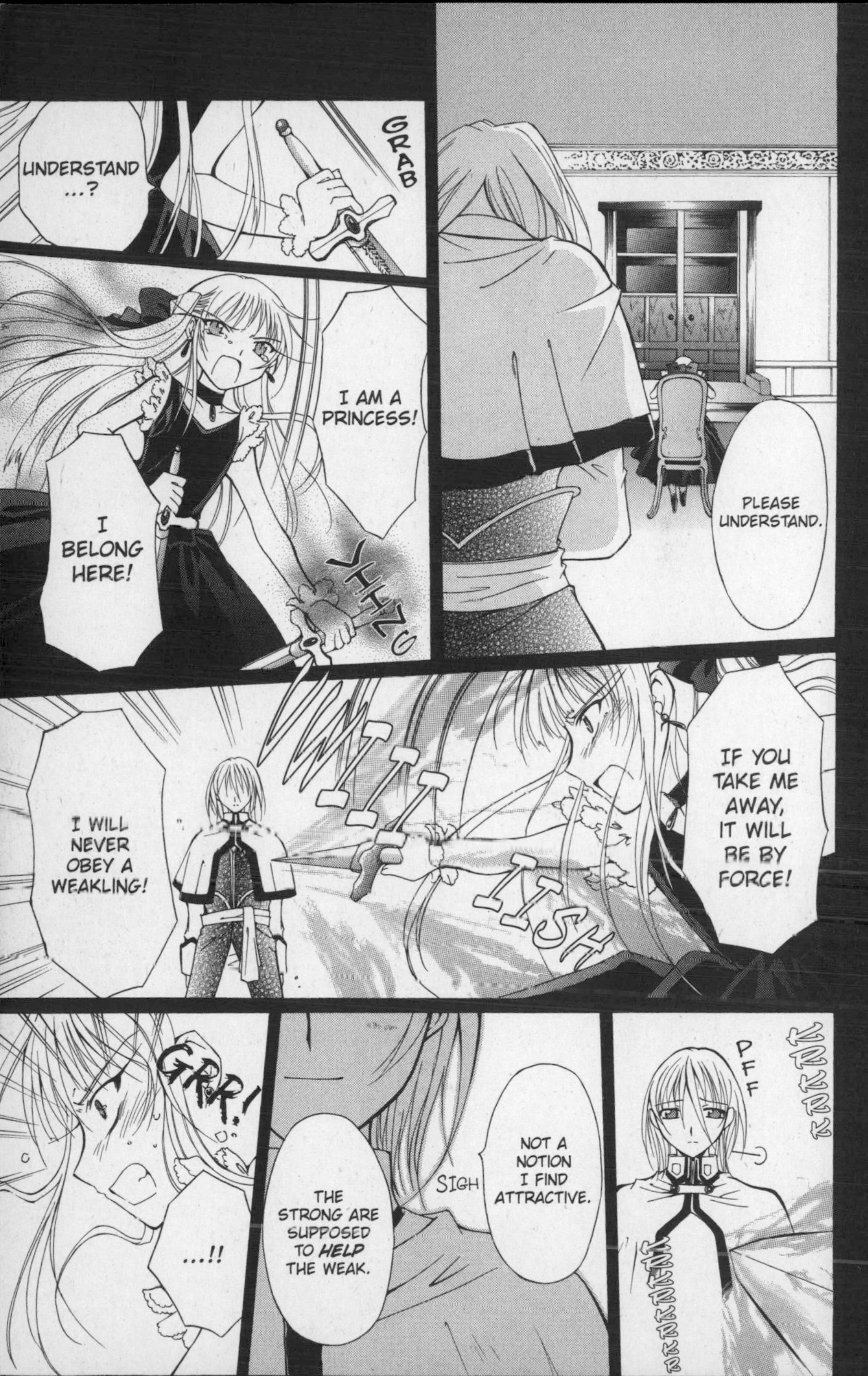
PLEASE UNDERSTAND.
GRAB
UNDERSTAND ...?
I AM A PRINCESS!
I BELONG HERE!
IF YOU TAKE ME AWAY, IT WILL BE BY FORCE!
I WILL NEVER OBEY A WEAKLING!
PFF
NOT A NOTION I FIND ATTRACTIVE.
SIGH
THE STRONG ARE SUPPOSED TO *HELP* THE WEAK.
GRR!
...!!

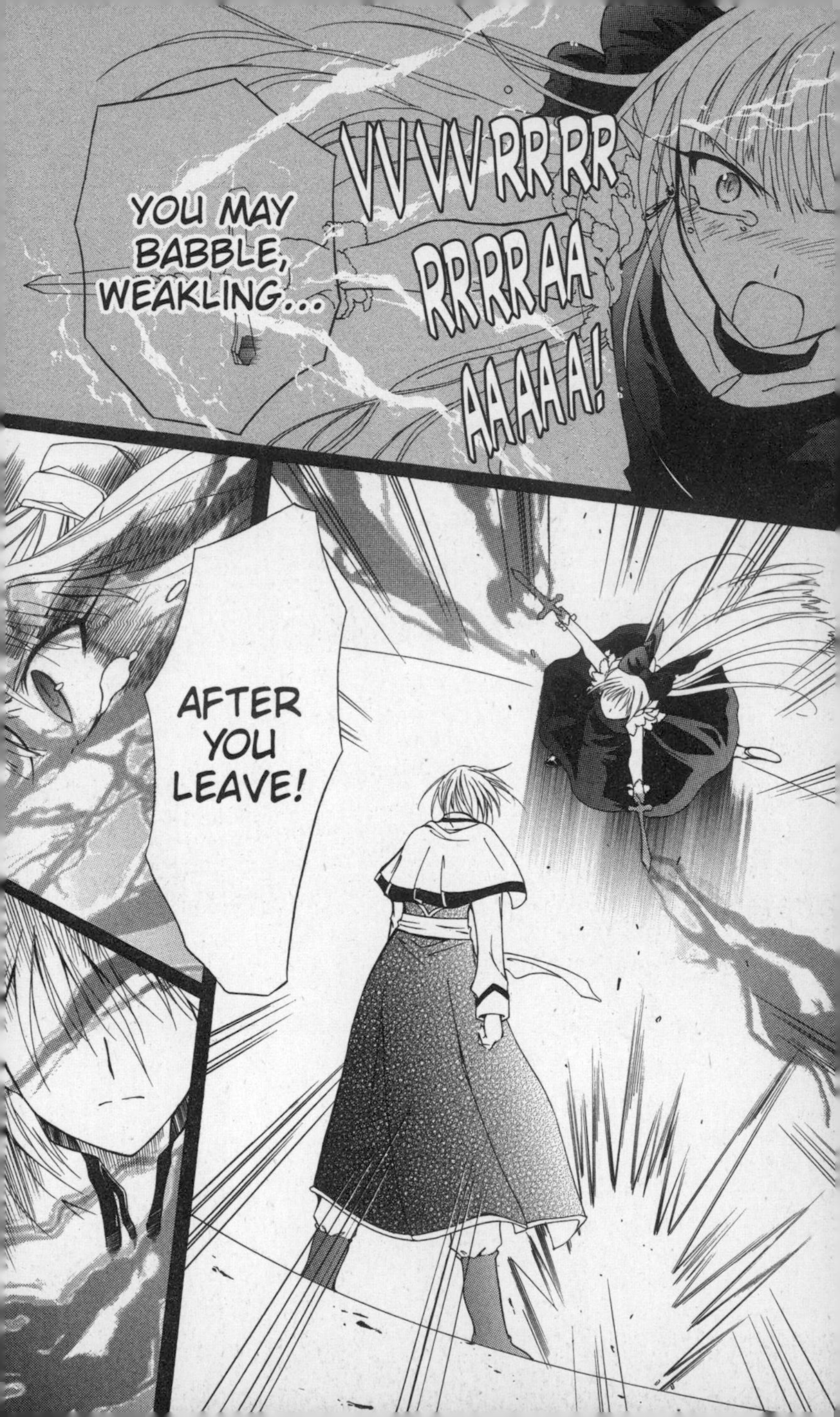
VVVVRRRR
RRRRAA
AAAAA!
YOU MAY BABBLE, WEAKLING...
AFTER YOU LEAVE!

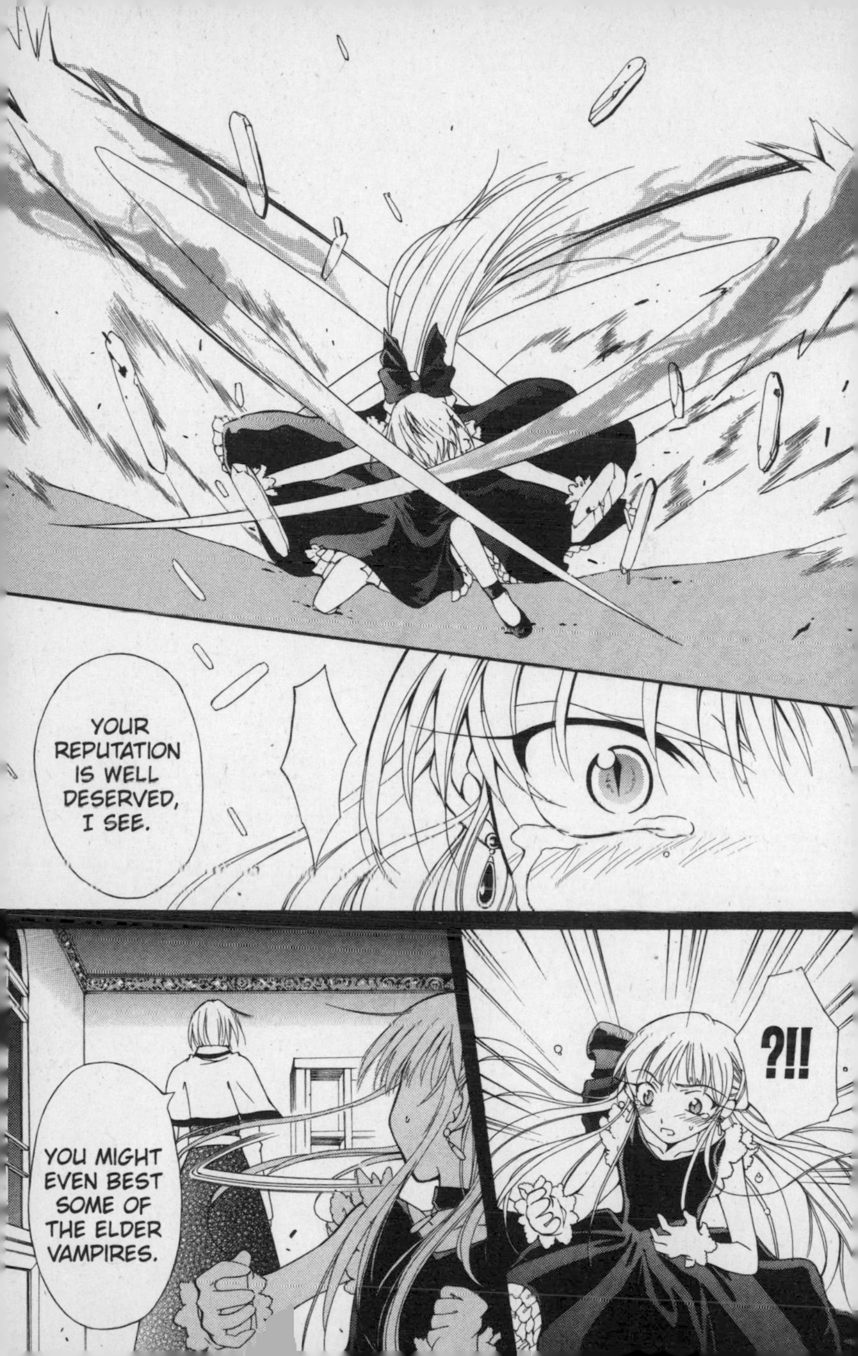
YOUR REPUTATION IS WELL DESERVED, I SEE.
?!!
YOU MIGHT EVEN BEST SOME OF THE ELDER VAMPIRES.

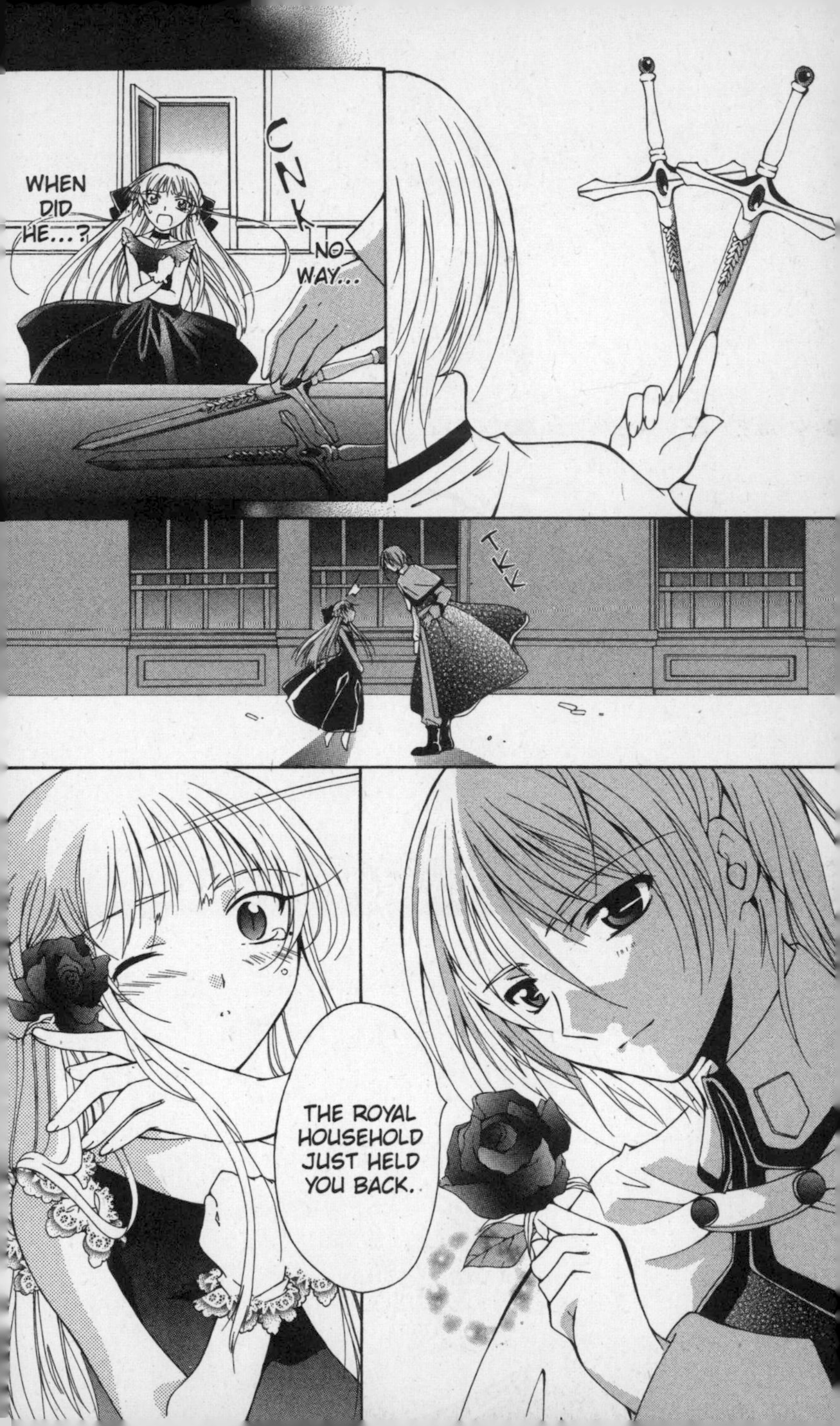
CNK
NO WAY...
WHEN DID HE...?
TKK
THE ROYAL HOUSEHOLD JUST HELD YOU BACK.

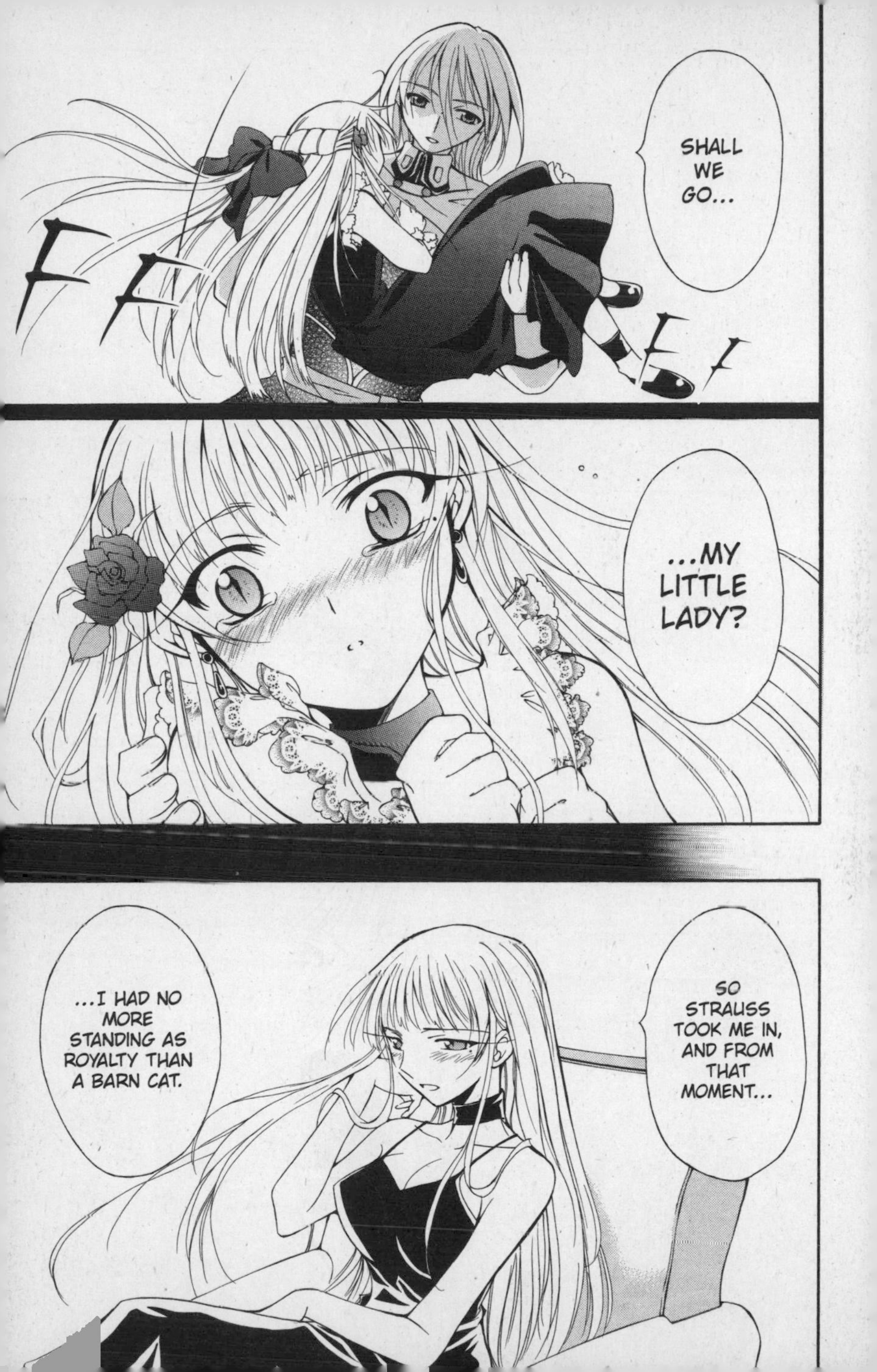
FF
E!
SHALL WE GO...
...MY LITTLE LADY?
SO STRAUSS TOOK ME IN, AND FROM THAT MOMENT...
...I HAD NO MORE STANDING AS ROYALTY THAN A BARN CAT.

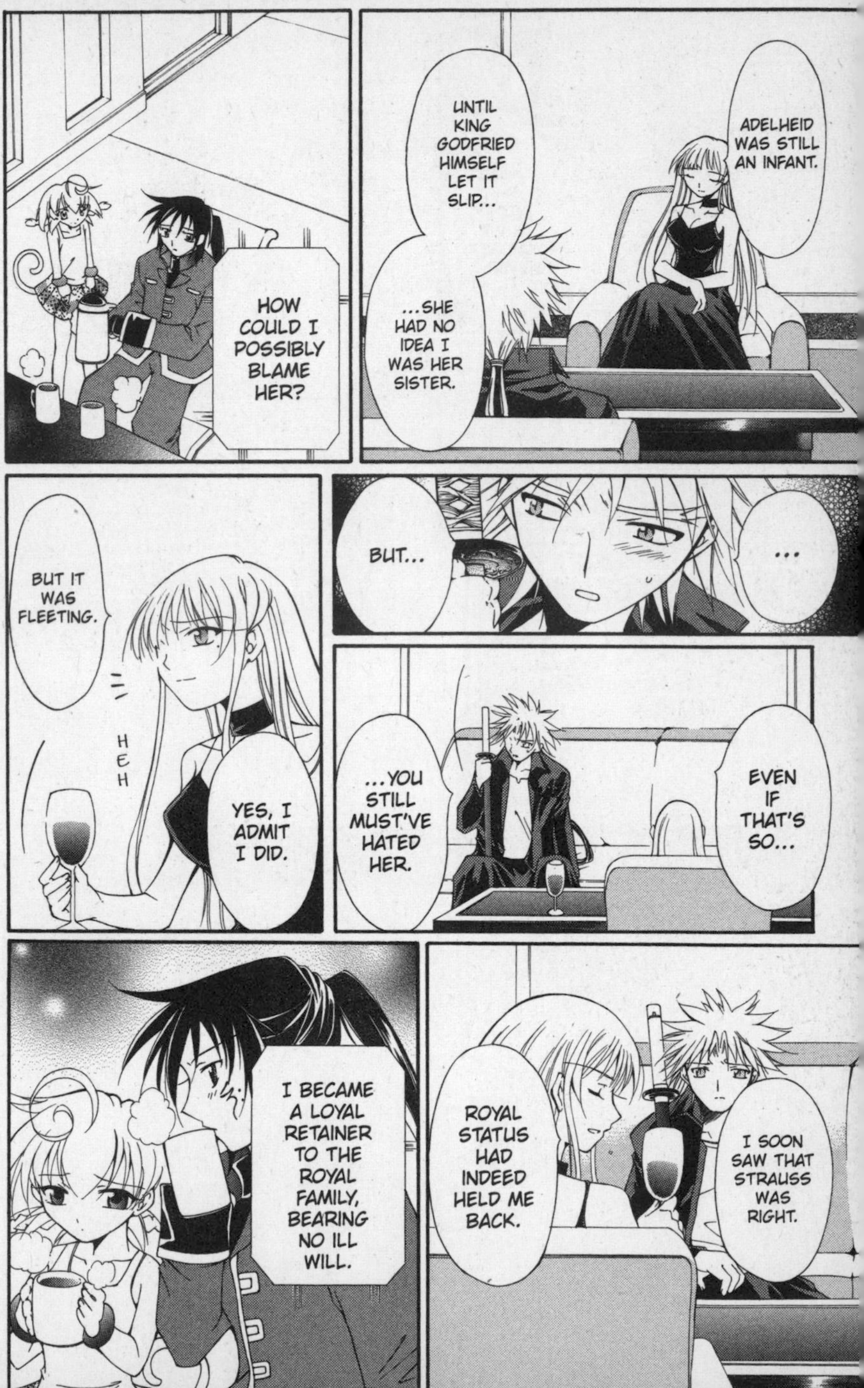
ADELHEID WAS STILL AN INFANT.
UNTIL KING GODFRIED HIMSELF LET IT SLIP...
...SHE HAD NO IDEA I WAS HER SISTER.
HOW COULD I POSSIBLY BLAME HER?
...
BUT...
EVEN IF THAT'S SO...
...YOU STILL MUST'VE HATED HER.
YES, I ADMIT I DID.
HEH
BUT IT WAS FLEETING.
I SOON SAW THAT STRAUSS WAS RIGHT.
ROYAL STATUS HAD INDEED HELD ME BACK.
I BECAME A LOYAL RETAINER TO THE ROYAL FAMILY, BEARING NO ILL WILL.

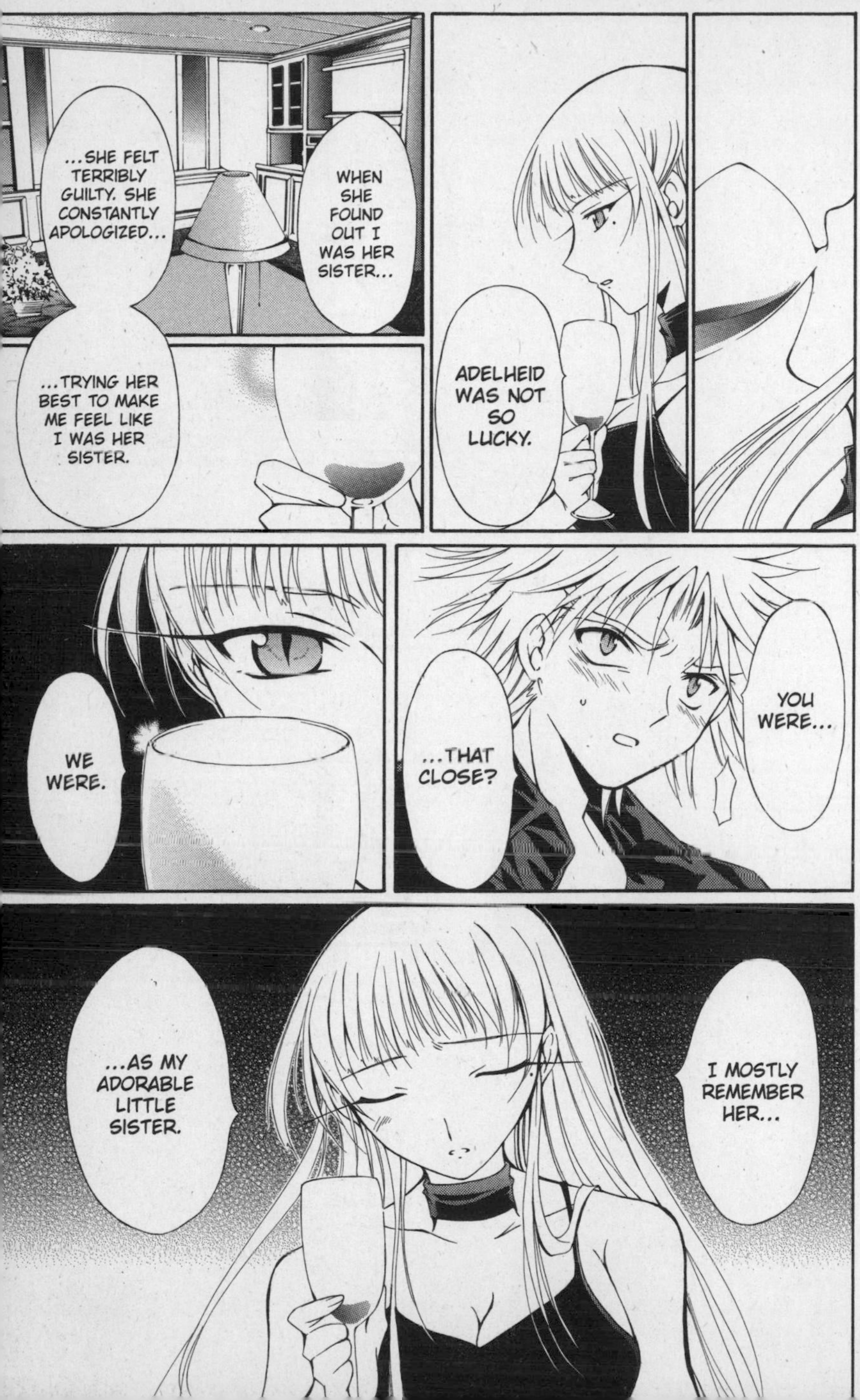
ADELHEID WAS NOT SO LUCKY.
WHEN SHE FOUND OUT I WAS HER SISTER...
...SHE FELT TERRIBLY GUILTY. SHE CONSTANTLY APOLOGIZED...
...TRYING HER BEST TO MAKE ME FEEL LIKE I WAS HER SISTER.
YOU WERE...
...THAT CLOSE?
WE WERE.
I MOSTLY REMEMBER HER...
...AS MY ADORABLE LITTLE SISTER.

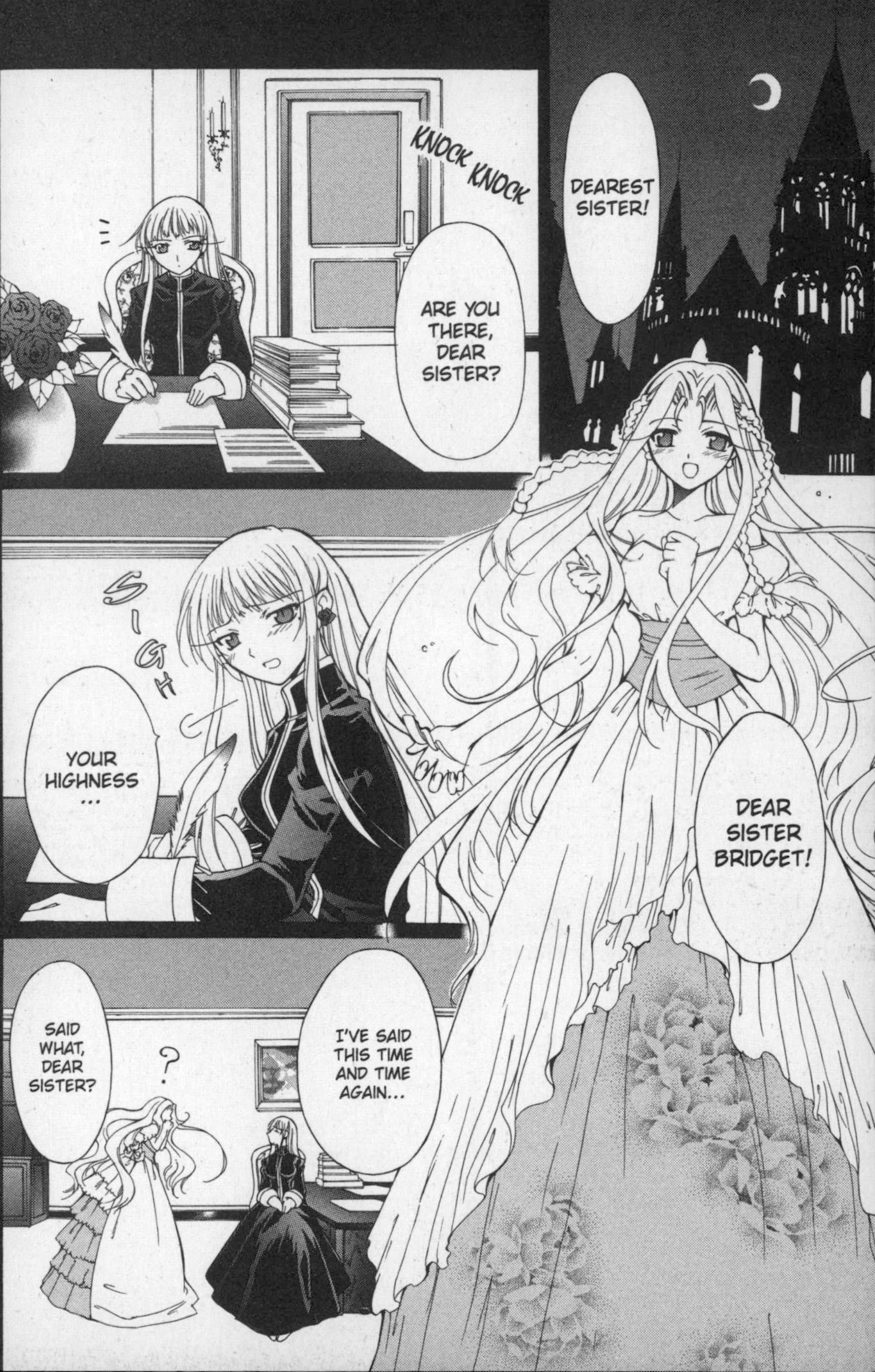
DEAREST SISTER!
DEAR SISTER BRIDGET!
KNOCK KNOCK
ARE YOU THERE, DEAR SISTER?
SIGH
YOUR HIGHNESS ...
I'VE SAID THIS TIME AND TIME AGAIN...
SAID WHAT, DEAR SISTER?
?

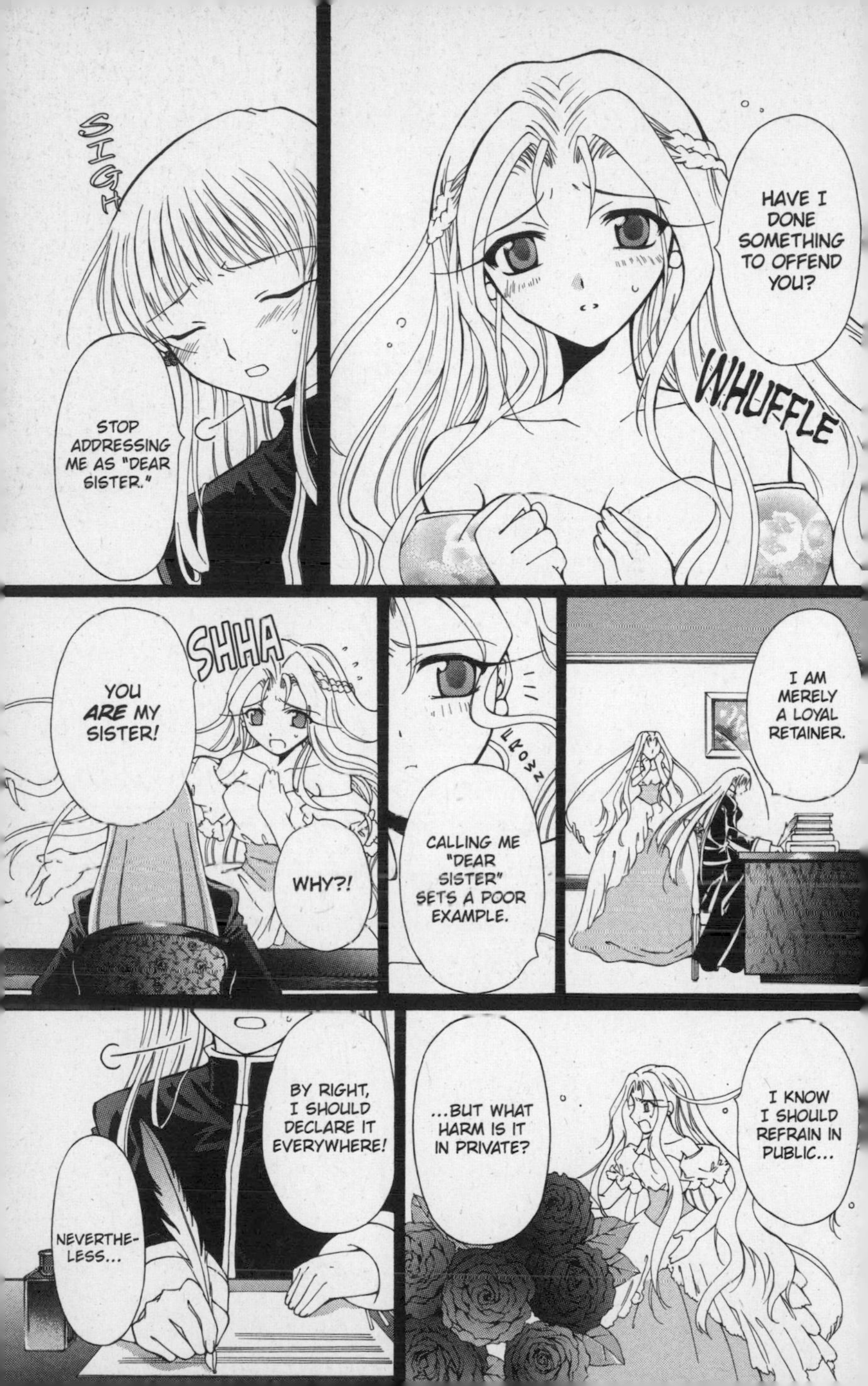
HAVE I DONE SOMETHING TO OFFEND YOU?
WHUFFLE
SIGH
STOP ADDRESSING ME AS "DEAR SISTER."
I AM MERELY A LOYAL RETAINER.
CALLING ME "DEAR SISTER" SETS A POOR EXAMPLE.
SHHA
YOU **ARE** MY SISTER!
WHY?!
I KNOW I SHOULD REFRAIN IN PUBLIC...
...BUT WHAT HARM IS IT IN PRIVATE?
BY RIGHT, I SHOULD DECLARE IT EVERYWHERE!
NEVERTHE-LESS...

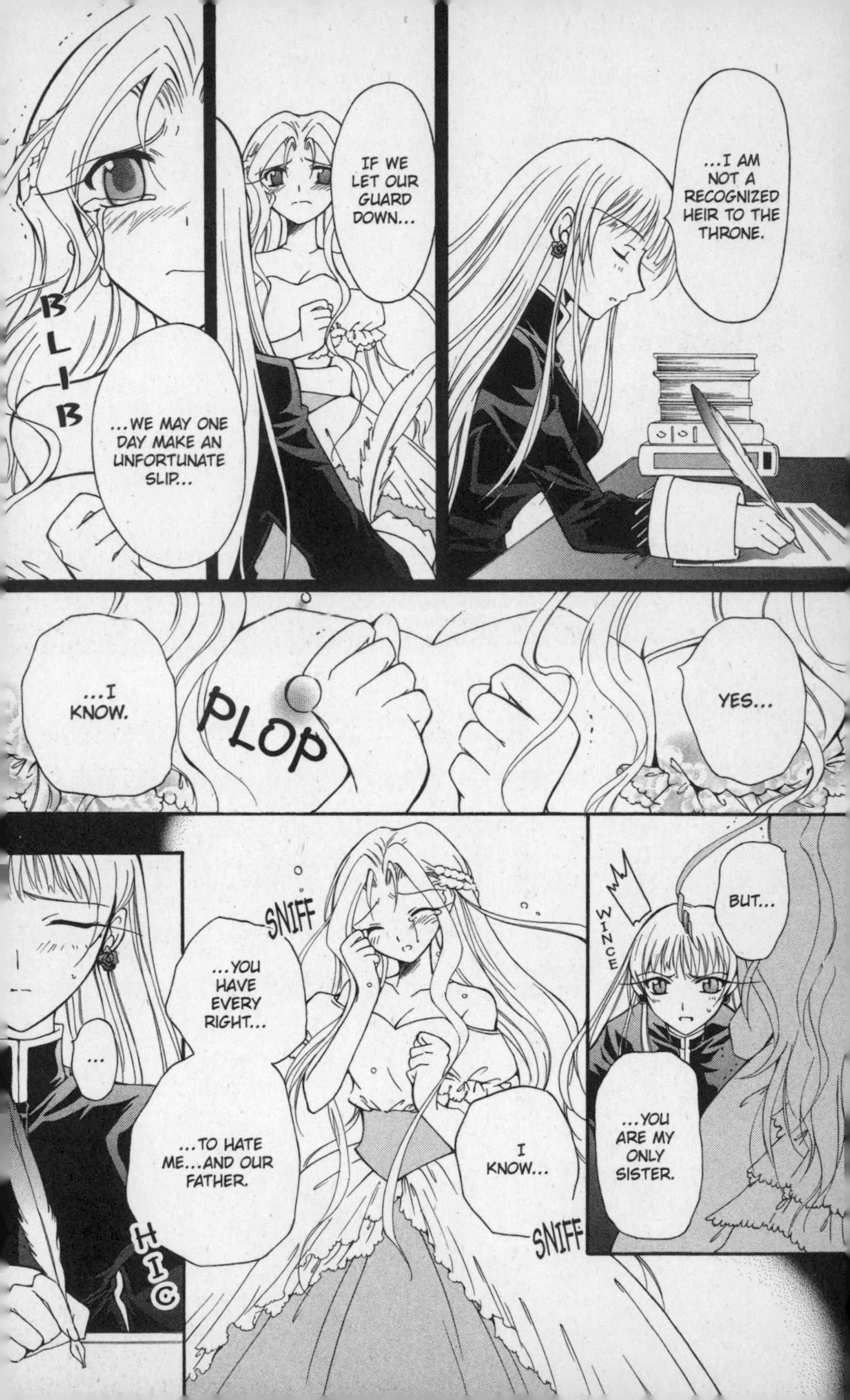
...I AM NOT A RECOGNIZED HEIR TO THE THRONE.
IF WE LET OUR GUARD DOWN...
BLIB
...WE MAY ONE DAY MAKE AN UNFORTUNATE SLIP...
YES...
PLOP
...I KNOW.
WINCE
BUT...
...YOU ARE MY ONLY SISTER.
SNIFF
...YOU HAVE EVERY RIGHT...
...TO HATE ME...AND OUR FATHER.
I KNOW...
SNIFF
...
HIC

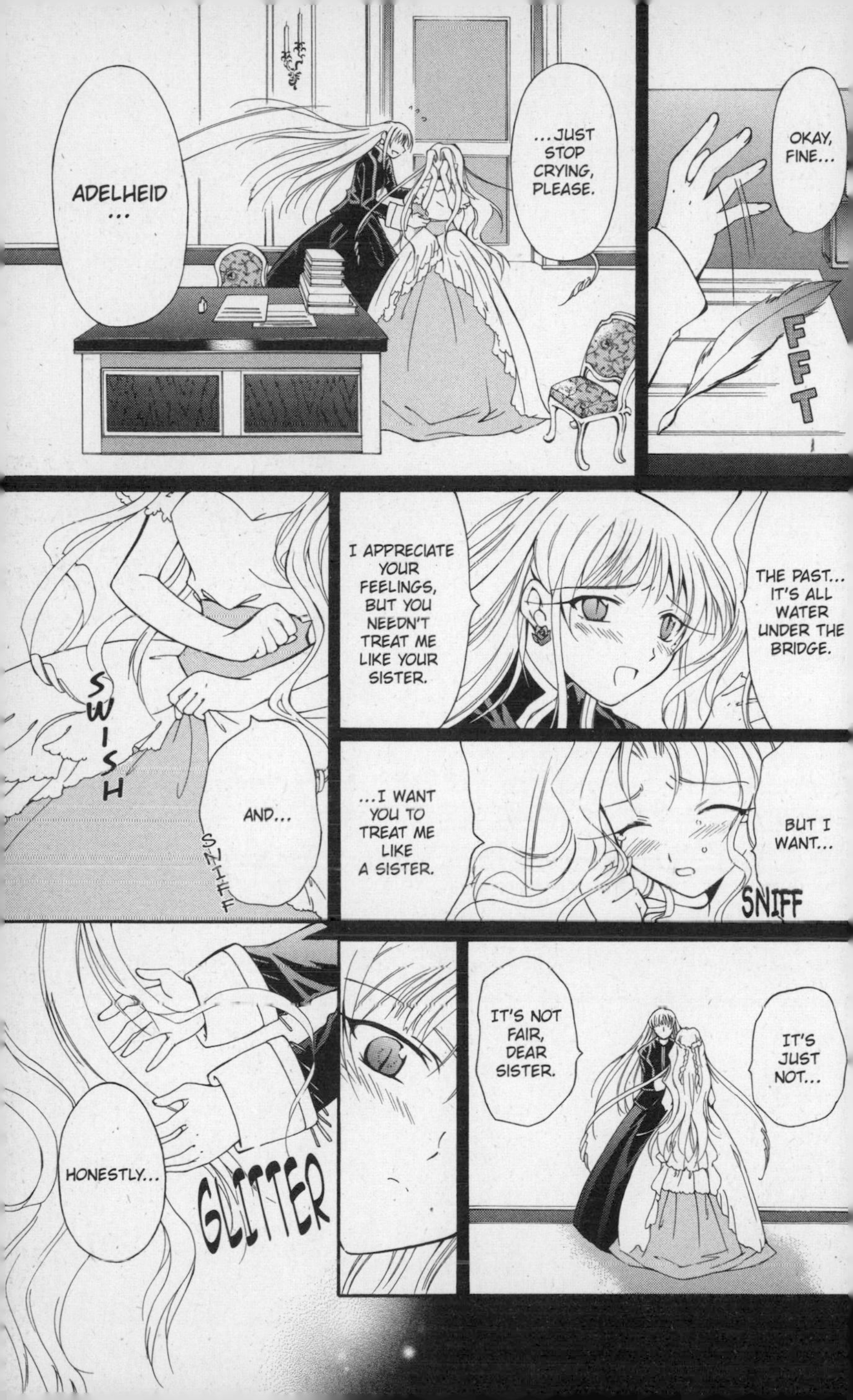

OKAY, FINE...
FFT
...JUST STOP CRYING, PLEASE.
ADELHEID ...
THE PAST... IT'S ALL WATER UNDER THE BRIDGE.
I APPRECIATE YOUR FEELINGS, BUT YOU NEEDN'T TREAT ME LIKE YOUR SISTER.
BUT I WANT...
SNIFF
...I WANT YOU TO TREAT ME LIKE A SISTER.
AND...
SNIFF
SWISH
IT'S JUST NOT...
IT'S NOT FAIR, DEAR SISTER.
GLITTER
HONESTLY...

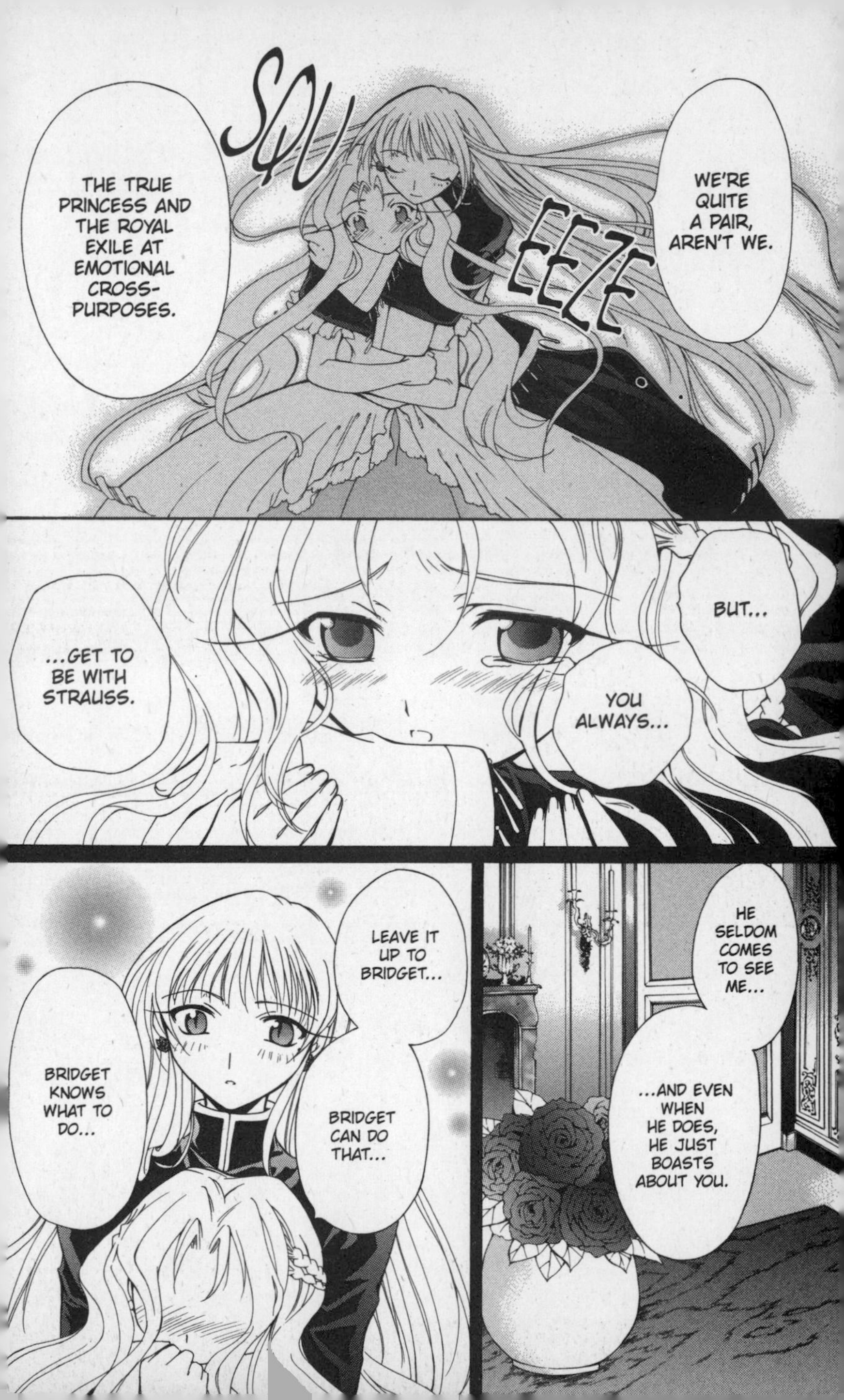
WE'RE QUITE A PAIR, AREN'T WE.
SQU
EEZE
THE TRUE PRINCESS AND THE ROYAL EXILE AT EMOTIONAL CROSS-PURPOSES.
BUT...
YOU ALWAYS...
...GET TO BE WITH STRAUSS.
HE SELDOM COMES TO SEE ME...
...AND EVEN WHEN HE DOES, HE JUST BOASTS ABOUT YOU.
LEAVE IT UP TO BRIDGET...
BRIDGET CAN DO THAT...
BRIDGET KNOWS WHAT TO DO...

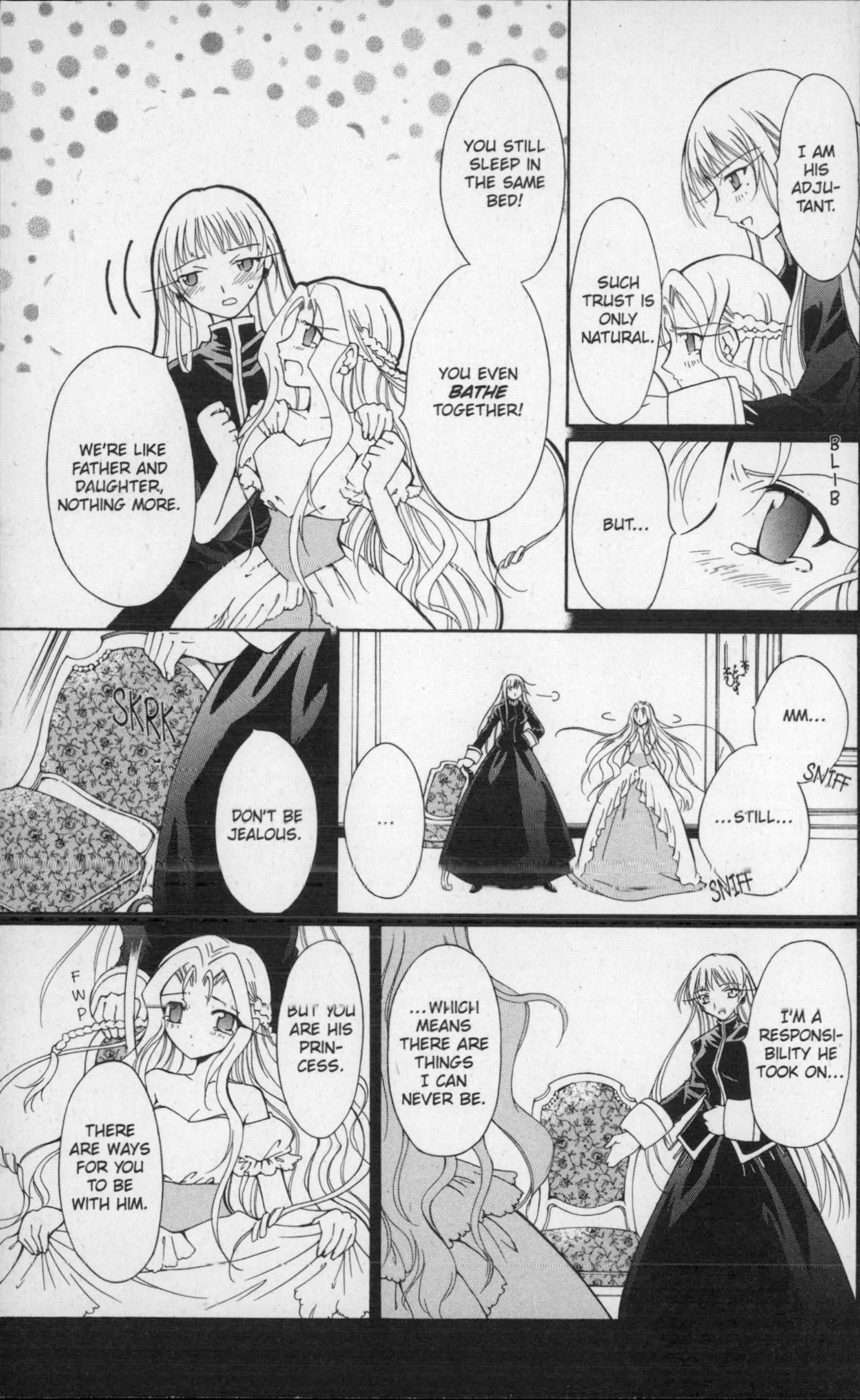
I AM HIS ADJUTANT.
SUCH TRUST IS ONLY NATURAL.
BLIB
BUT...
YOU STILL SLEEP IN THE SAME BED!
YOU EVEN *BATHE* TOGETHER!
WE'RE LIKE FATHER AND DAUGHTER, NOTHING MORE.
MM...
SNIFF
...STILL...
SNIFF
...
SKRK
DON'T BE JEALOUS.
I'M A RESPONSIBILITY HE TOOK ON...
...WHICH MEANS THERE ARE THINGS I CAN NEVER BE.
BUT YOU ARE HIS PRINCESS.
FWP
THERE ARE WAYS FOR YOU TO BE WITH HIM.

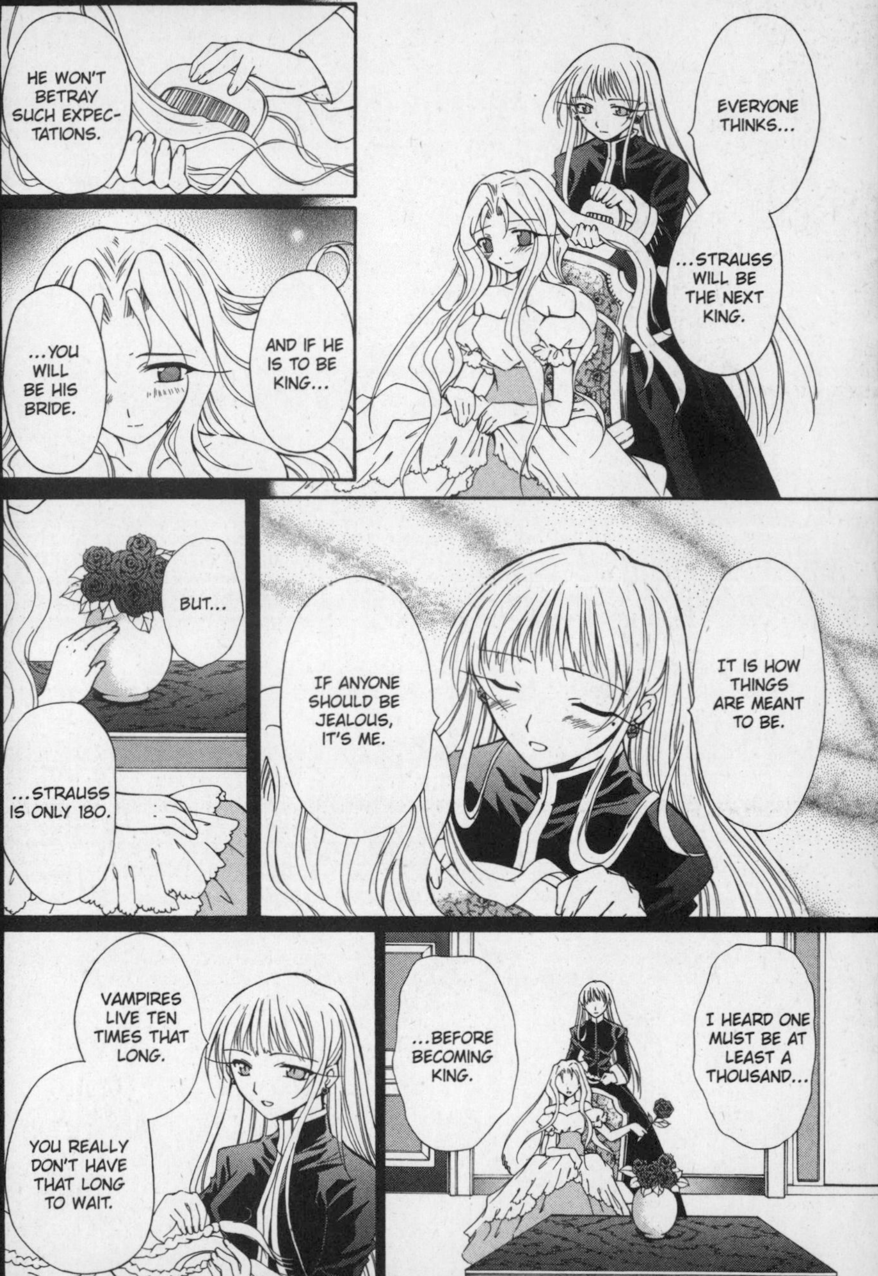
EVERYONE THINKS...
...STRAUSS WILL BE THE NEXT KING.
HE WON'T BETRAY SUCH EXPECTATIONS.
AND IF HE IS TO BE KING...
...YOU WILL BE HIS BRIDE.
IT IS HOW THINGS ARE MEANT TO BE.
IF ANYONE SHOULD BE JEALOUS, IT'S ME.
BUT...
...STRAUSS IS ONLY 180.
I HEARD ONE MUST BE AT LEAST A THOUSAND...
...BEFORE BECOMING KING.
VAMPIRES LIVE TEN TIMES THAT LONG.
YOU REALLY DON'T HAVE THAT LONG TO WAIT.

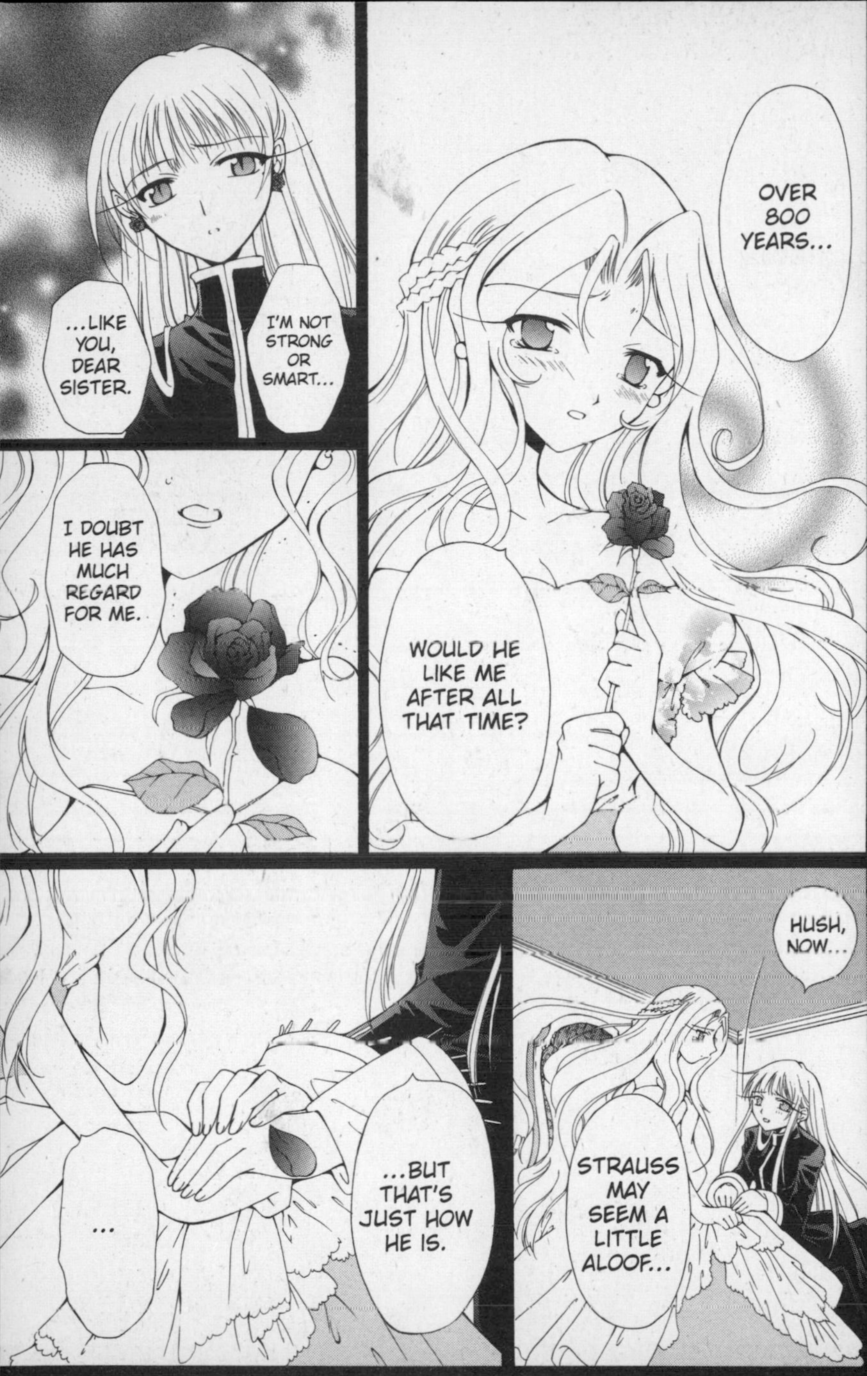
OVER 800 YEARS...
WOULD HE LIKE ME AFTER ALL THAT TIME?
I'M NOT STRONG OR SMART...
...LIKE YOU, DEAR SISTER.
I DOUBT HE HAS MUCH REGARD FOR ME.
HUSH, NOW...
STRAUSS MAY SEEM A LITTLE ALOOF...
...BUT THAT'S JUST HOW HE IS.
...

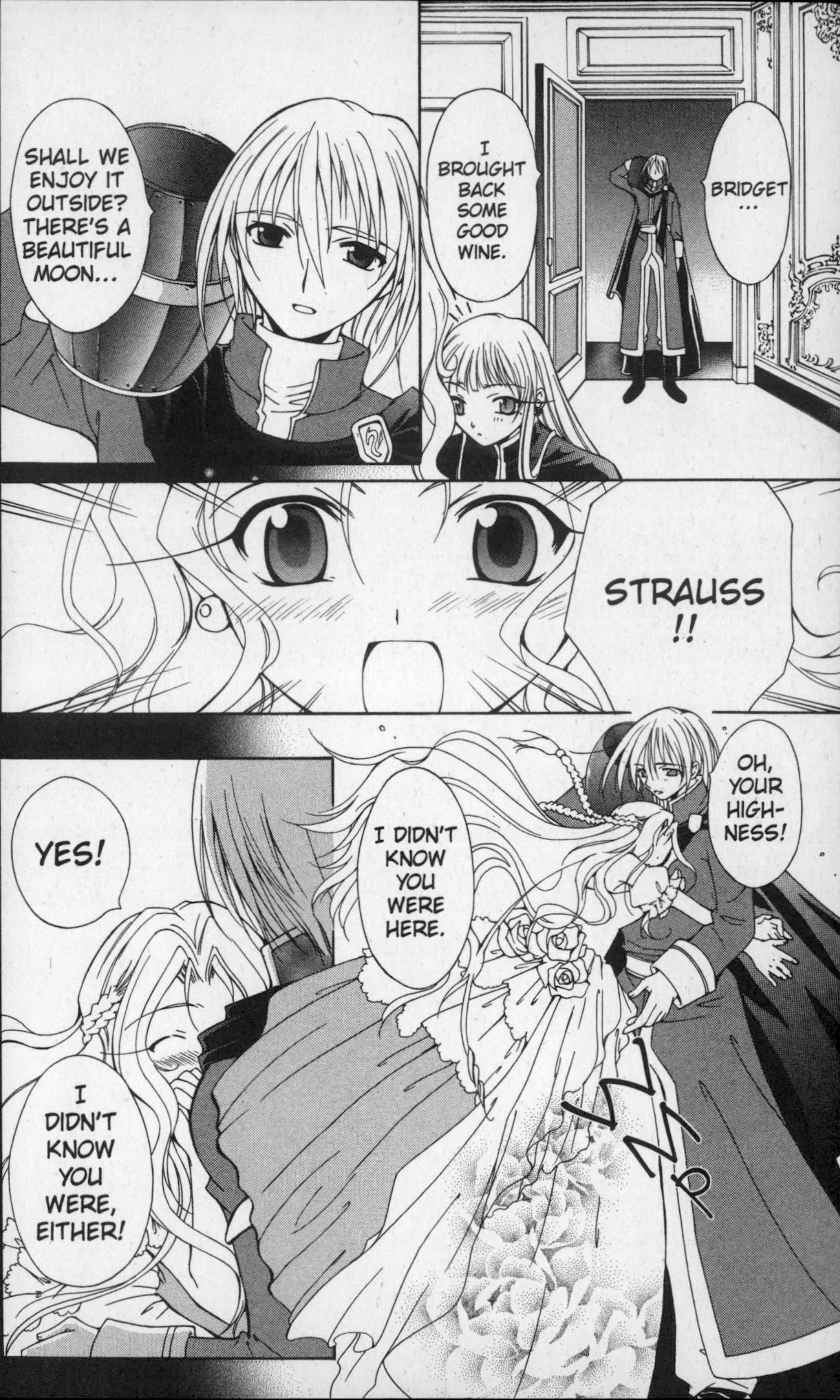
BRIDGET...
I BROUGHT BACK SOME GOOD WINE.
SHALL WE ENJOY IT OUTSIDE? THERE'S A BEAUTIFUL MOON...
STRAUSS!!
OH, YOUR HIGH-NESS!
I DIDN'T KNOW YOU WERE HERE.
YES!
I DIDN'T KNOW YOU WERE, EITHER!

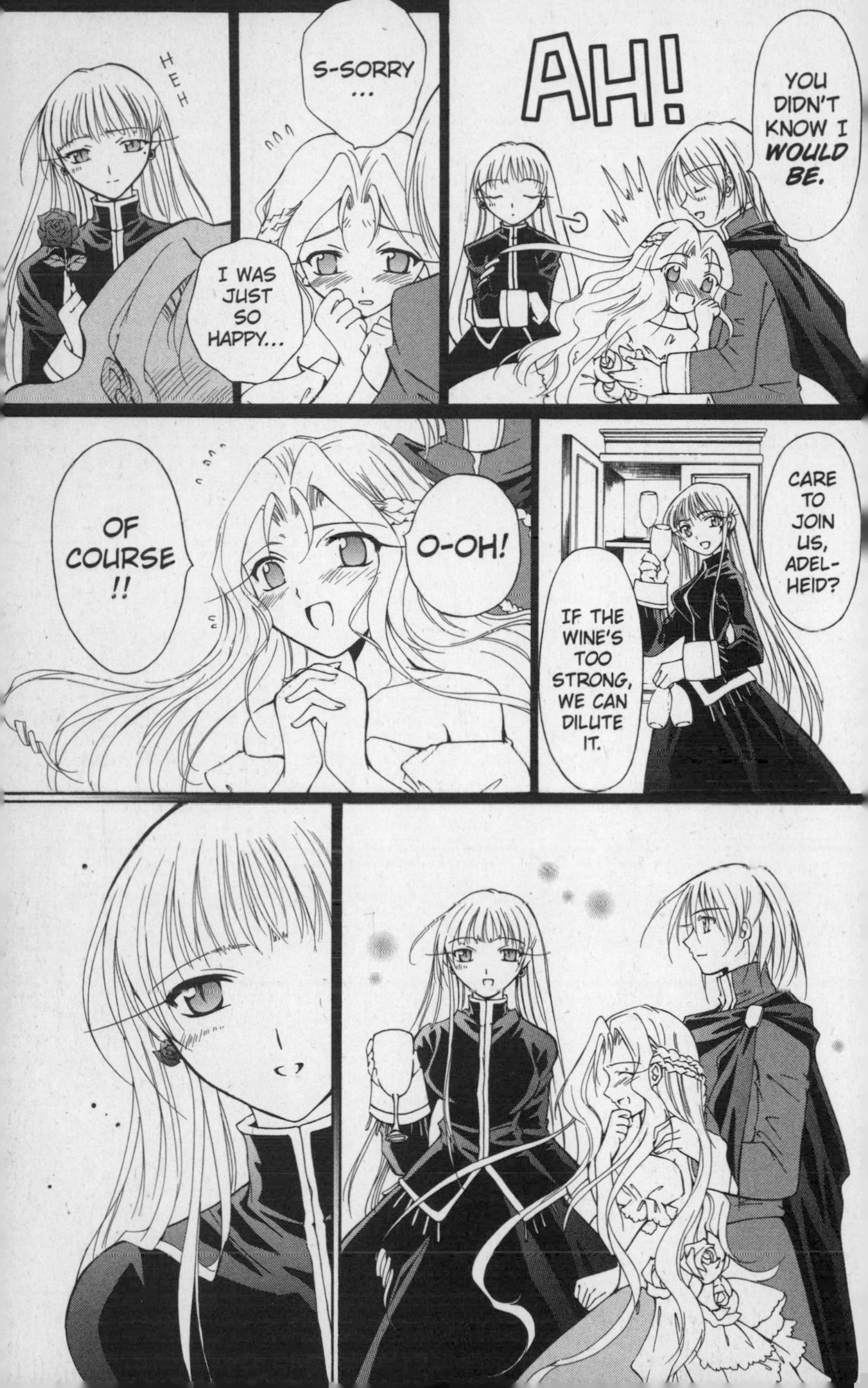
AH!
YOU DIDN'T KNOW I *WOULD* BE.
S-SORRY ...
I WAS JUST SO HAPPY...
HEH
CARE TO JOIN US, ADEL-HEID?
IF THE WINE'S TOO STRONG, WE CAN DILUTE IT.
O-OH!
OF COURSE !!

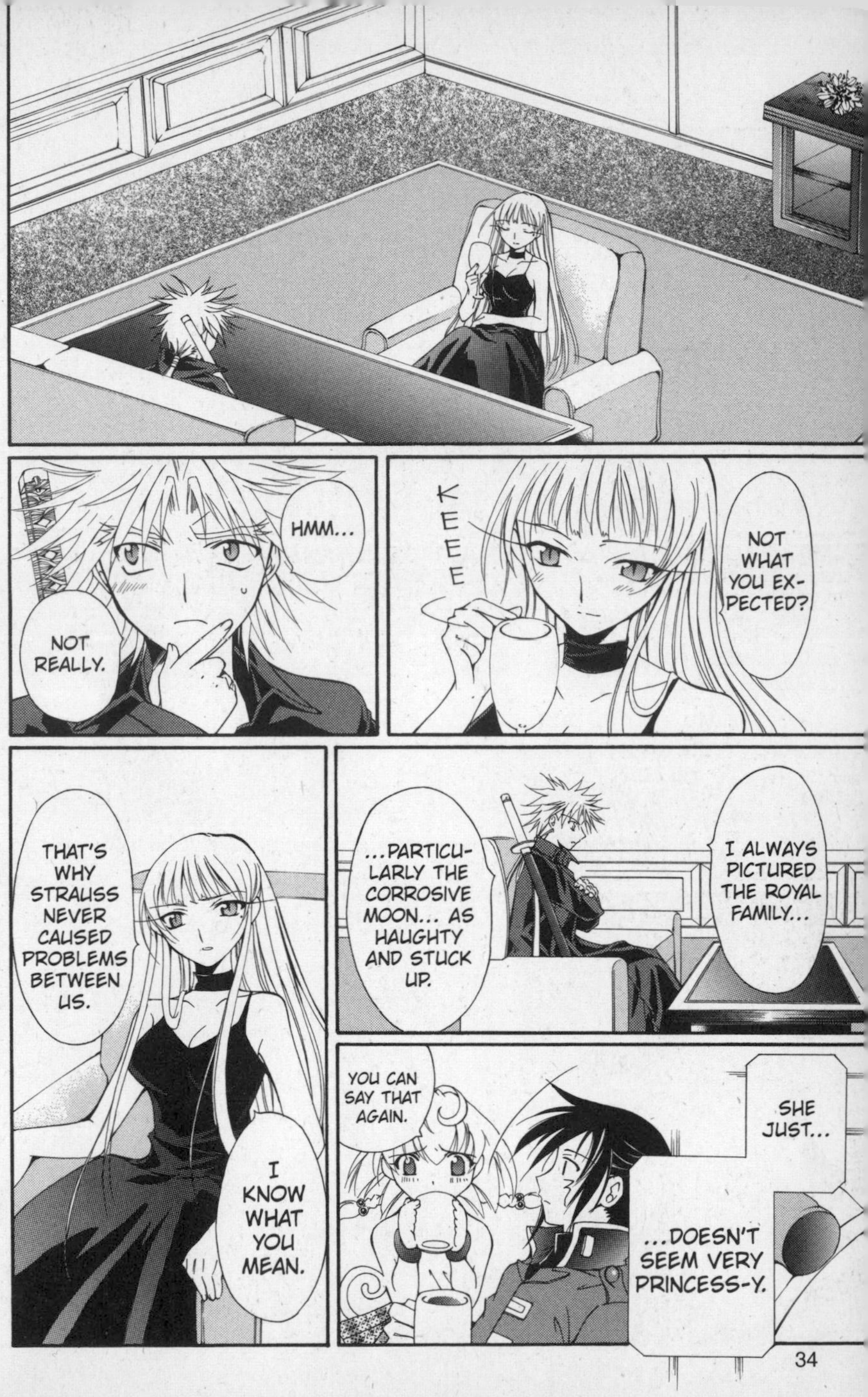
KEEE
NOT WHAT YOU EXPECTED?
HMM...
NOT REALLY.
I ALWAYS PICTURED THE ROYAL FAMILY...
...PARTICULARLY THE CORROSIVE MOON... AS HAUGHTY AND STUCK UP.
SHE JUST...
...DOESN'T SEEM VERY PRINCESS-Y.
YOU CAN SAY THAT AGAIN.
I KNOW WHAT YOU MEAN.
THAT'S WHY STRAUSS NEVER CAUSED PROBLEMS BETWEEN US.

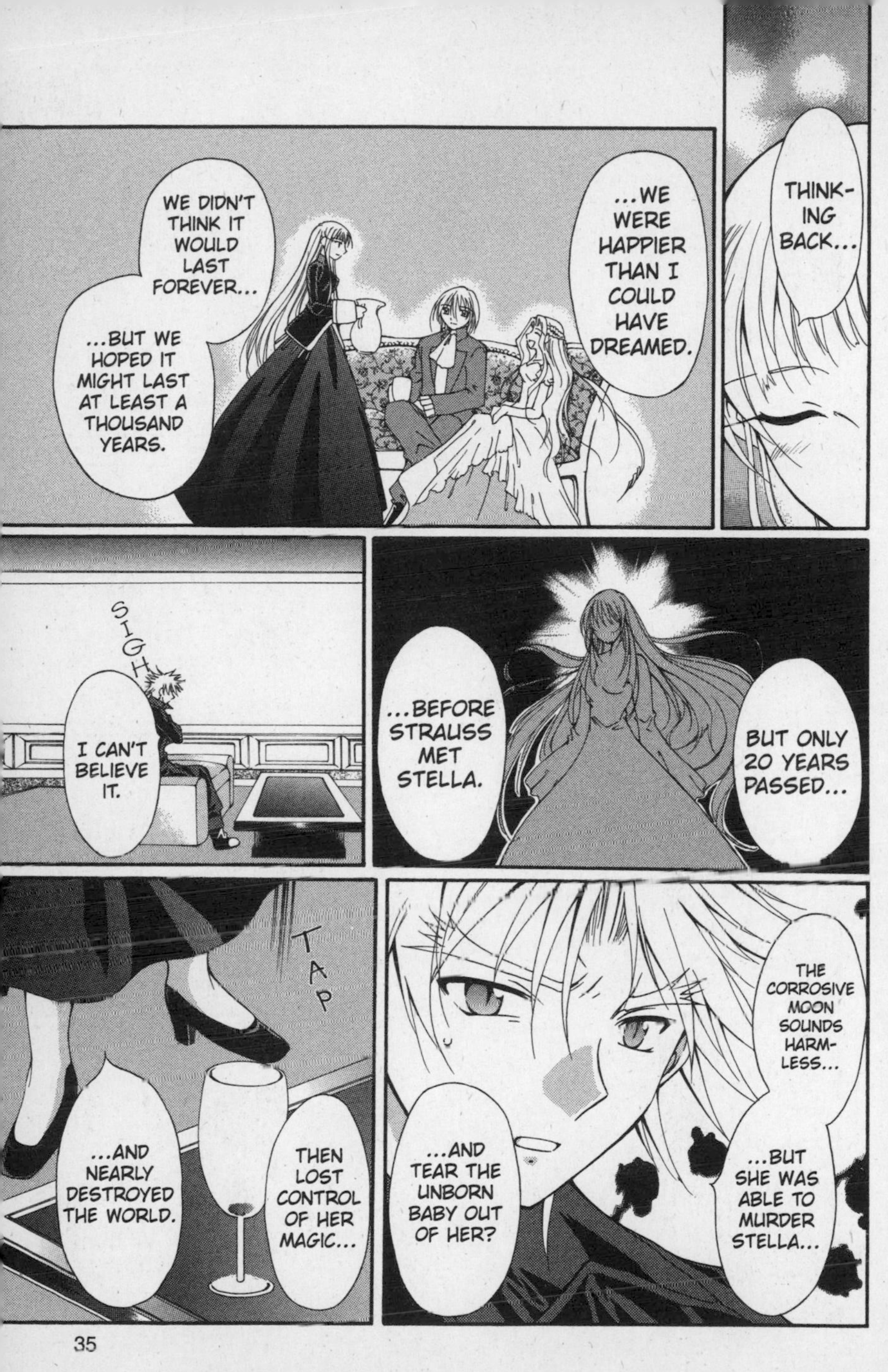
THINKING BACK...
...WE WERE HAPPIER THAN I COULD HAVE DREAMED.
WE DIDN'T THINK IT WOULD LAST FOREVER...
...BUT WE HOPED IT MIGHT LAST AT LEAST A THOUSAND YEARS.
BUT ONLY 20 YEARS PASSED...
...BEFORE STRAUSS MET STELLA.
SIGH
I CAN'T BELIEVE IT.
THE CORROSIVE MOON SOUNDS HARMLESS...
...BUT SHE WAS ABLE TO MURDER STELLA...
...AND TEAR THE UNBORN BABY OUT OF HER?
TAP
THEN LOST CONTROL OF HER MAGIC...
...AND NEARLY DESTROYED THE WORLD.

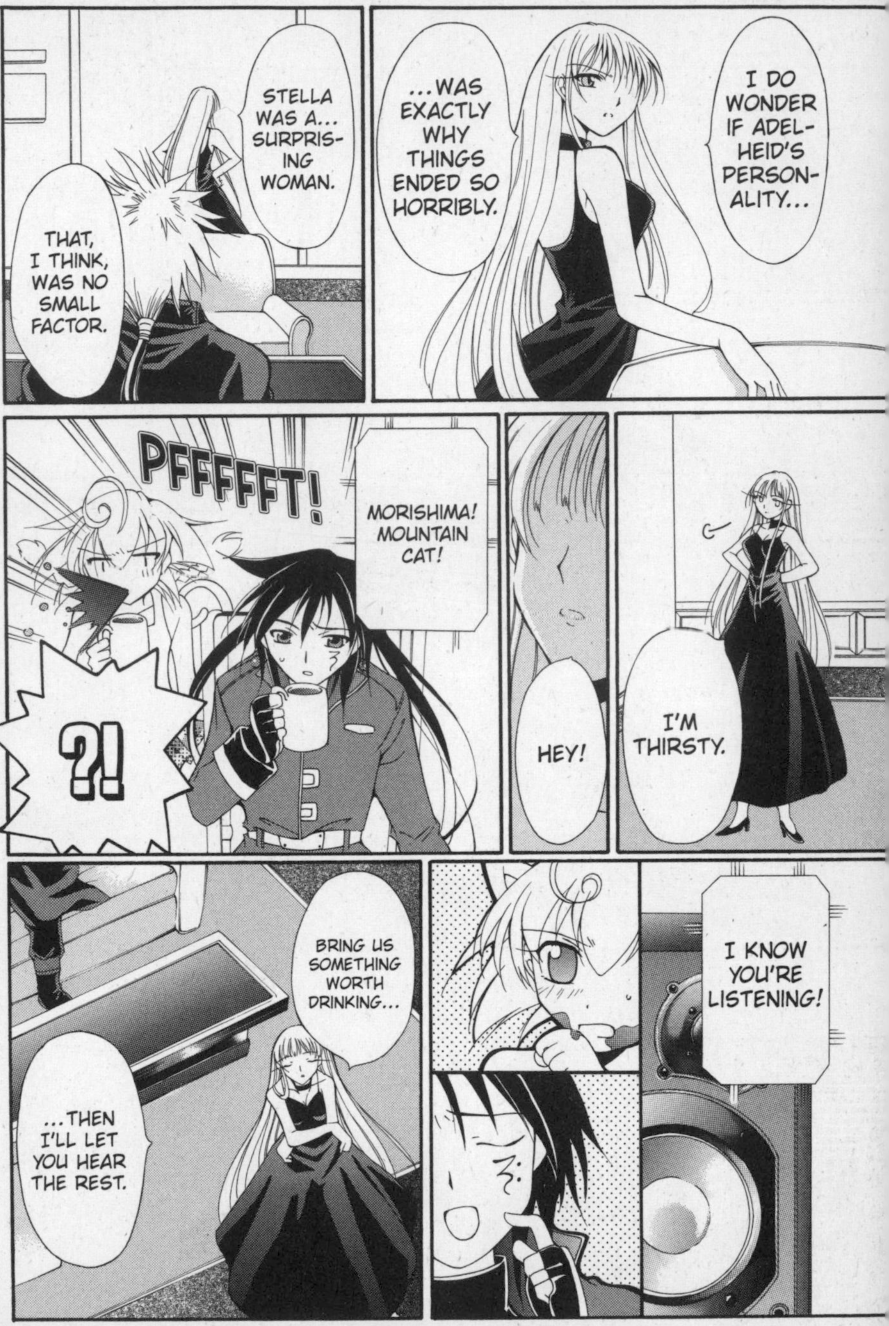
I DO WONDER IF ADELHEID'S PERSONALITY...
...WAS EXACTLY WHY THINGS ENDED SO HORRIBLY.
STELLA WAS A... SURPRISING WOMAN.
THAT, I THINK, WAS NO SMALL FACTOR.
I'M THIRSTY.
HEY!
MORISHIMA! MOUNTAIN CAT!
PFFFFFT!
?!
I KNOW YOU'RE LISTENING!
BRING US SOMETHING WORTH DRINKING...
...THEN I'LL LET YOU HEAR THE REST.

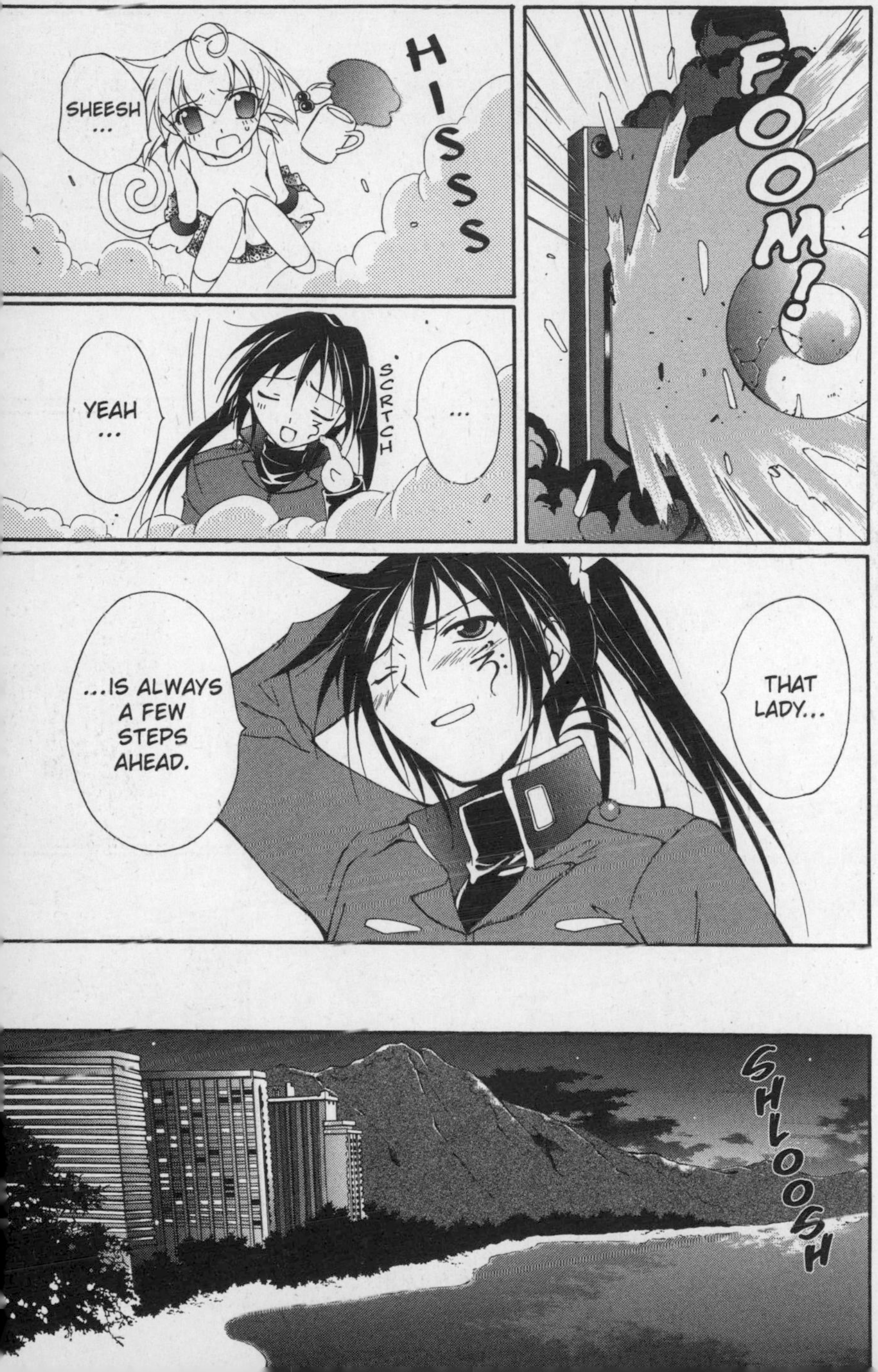
FOOM!
HISSS
SHEESH...
...
SCRTCH
YEAH...
THAT LADY...
...IS ALWAYS A FEW STEPS AHEAD.
SHLOOSH

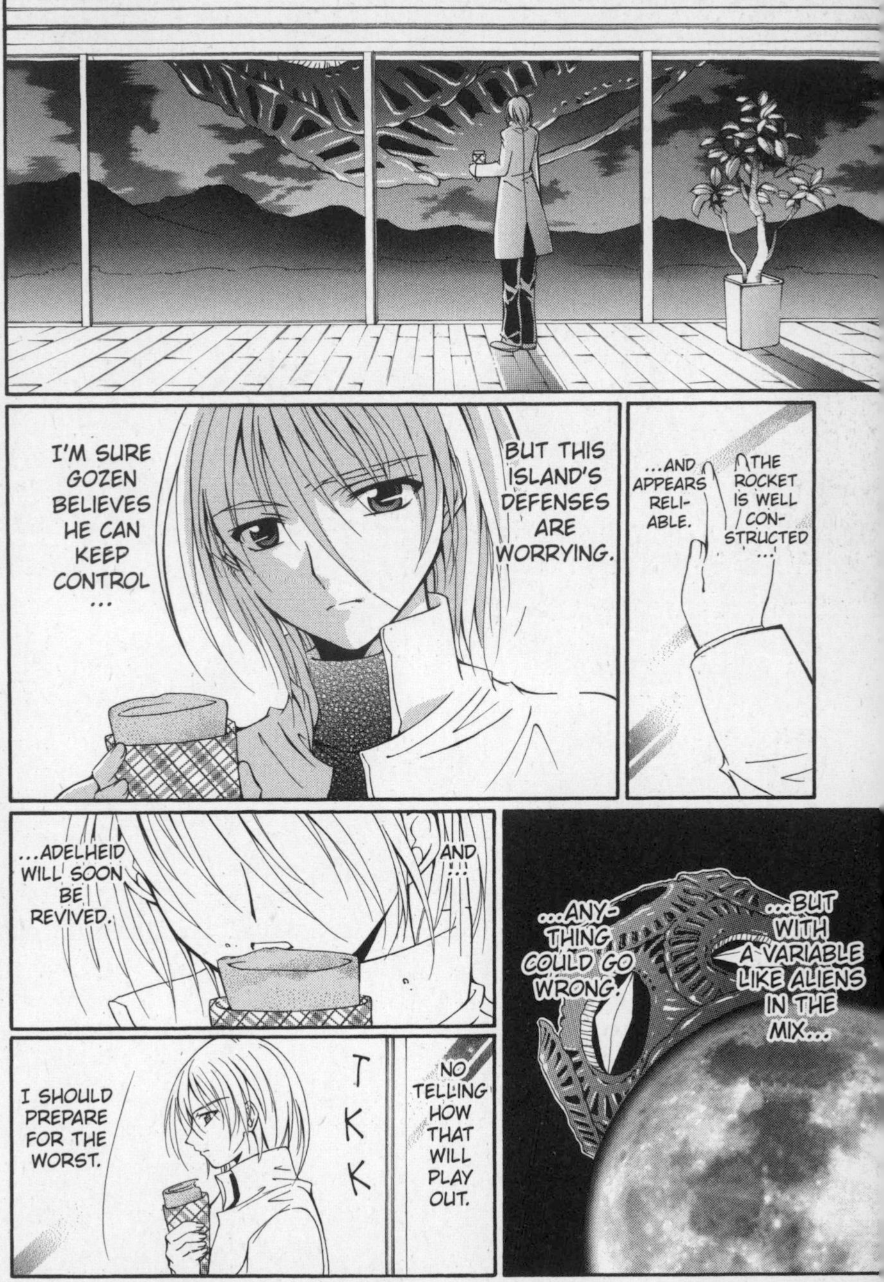
THE ROCKET IS WELL CONSTRUCTED...
...AND APPEARS RELIABLE.
BUT THIS ISLAND'S DEFENSES ARE WORRYING.
I'M SURE GOZEN BELIEVES HE CAN KEEP CONTROL...
...BUT WITH A VARIABLE LIKE ALIENS IN THE MIX...
...ANYTHING COULD GO WRONG.
AND...
...ADELHEID WILL SOON BE REVIVED.
NO TELLING HOW THAT WILL PLAY OUT.
TKK
I SHOULD PREPARE FOR THE WORST.

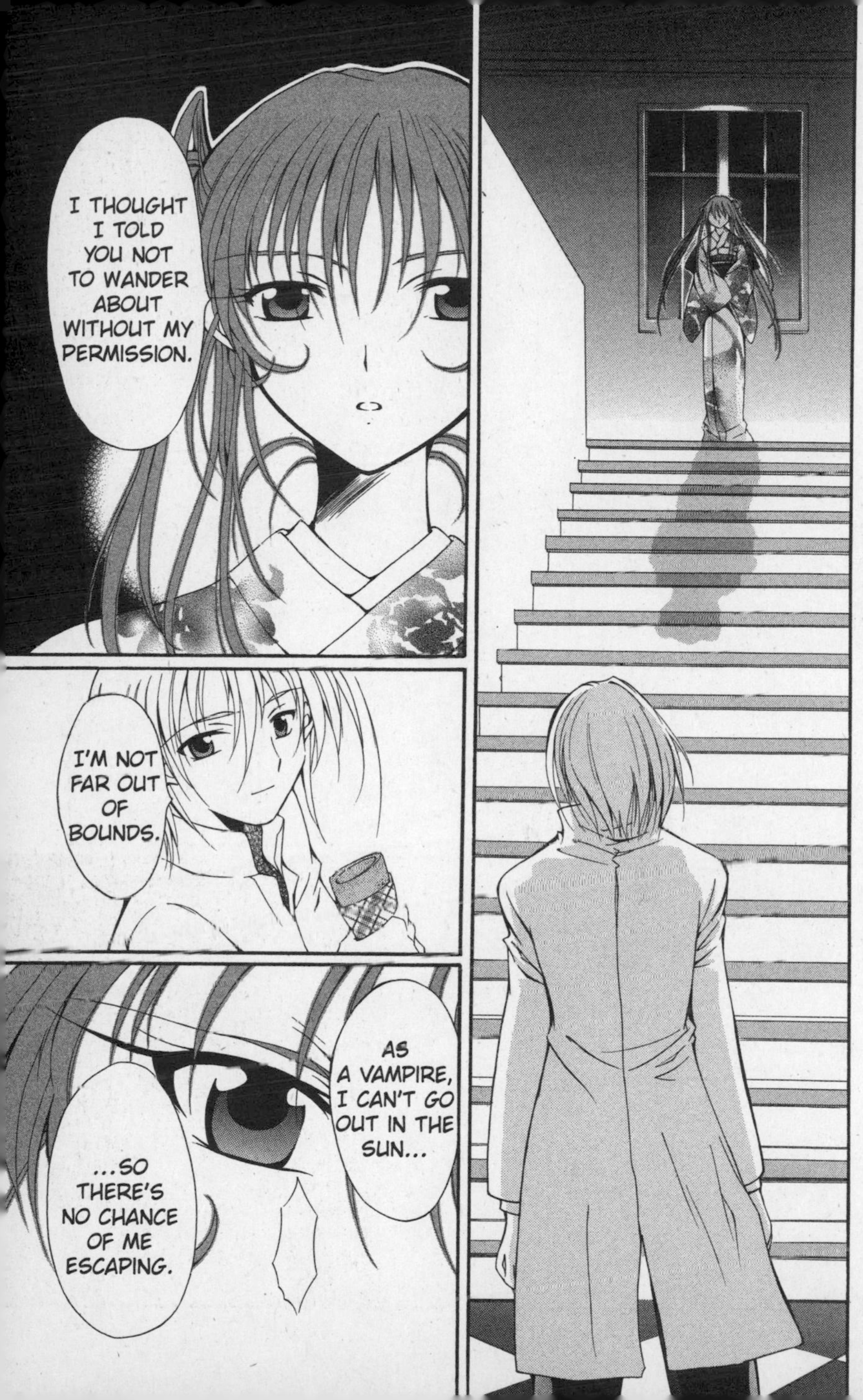
I THOUGHT I TOLD YOU NOT TO WANDER ABOUT WITHOUT MY PERMISSION.
I'M NOT FAR OUT OF BOUNDS.
AS A VAMPIRE, I CAN'T GO OUT IN THE SUN...
...SO THERE'S NO CHANCE OF ME ESCAPING.

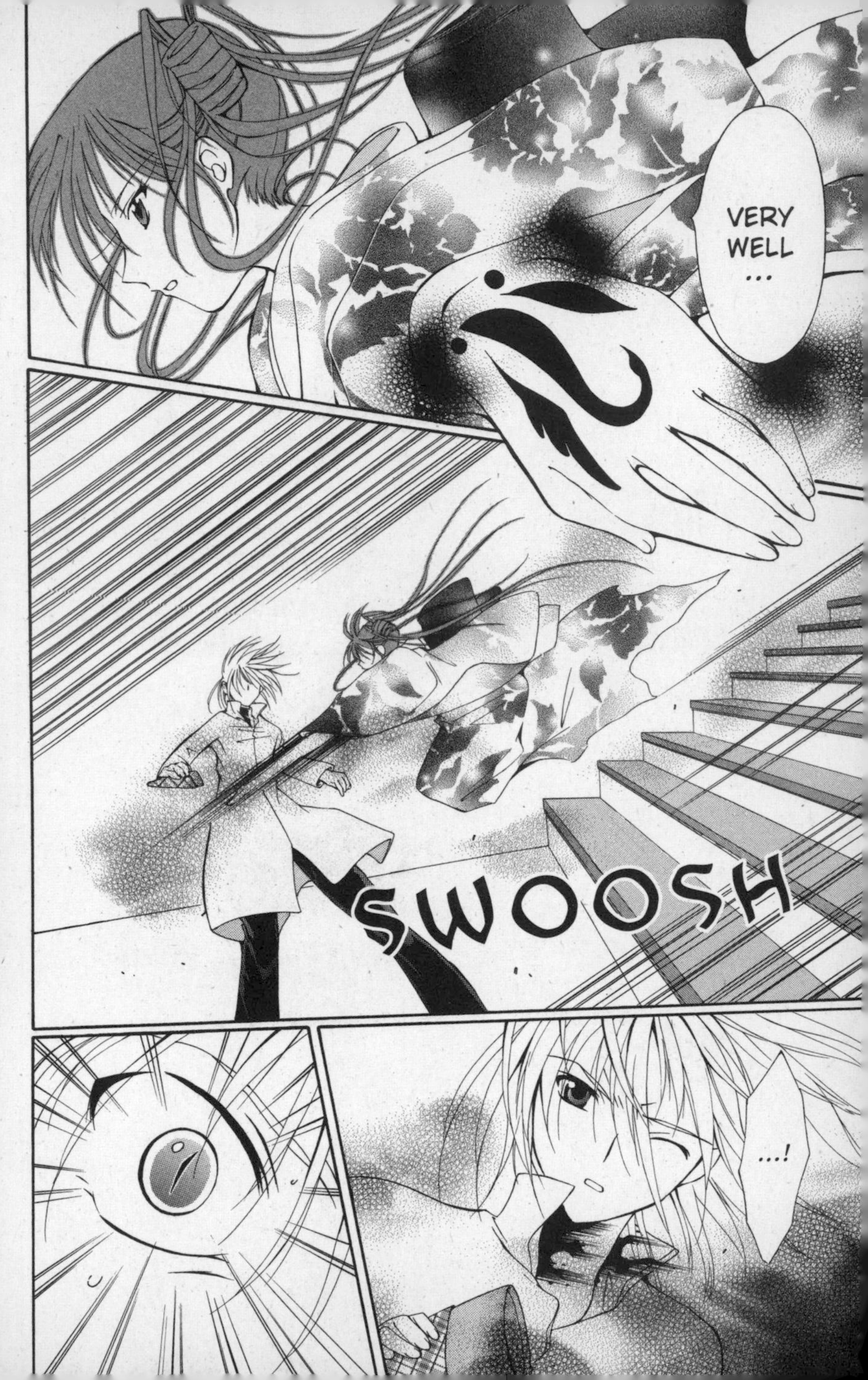
VERY WELL ...
SWOOSH
...!

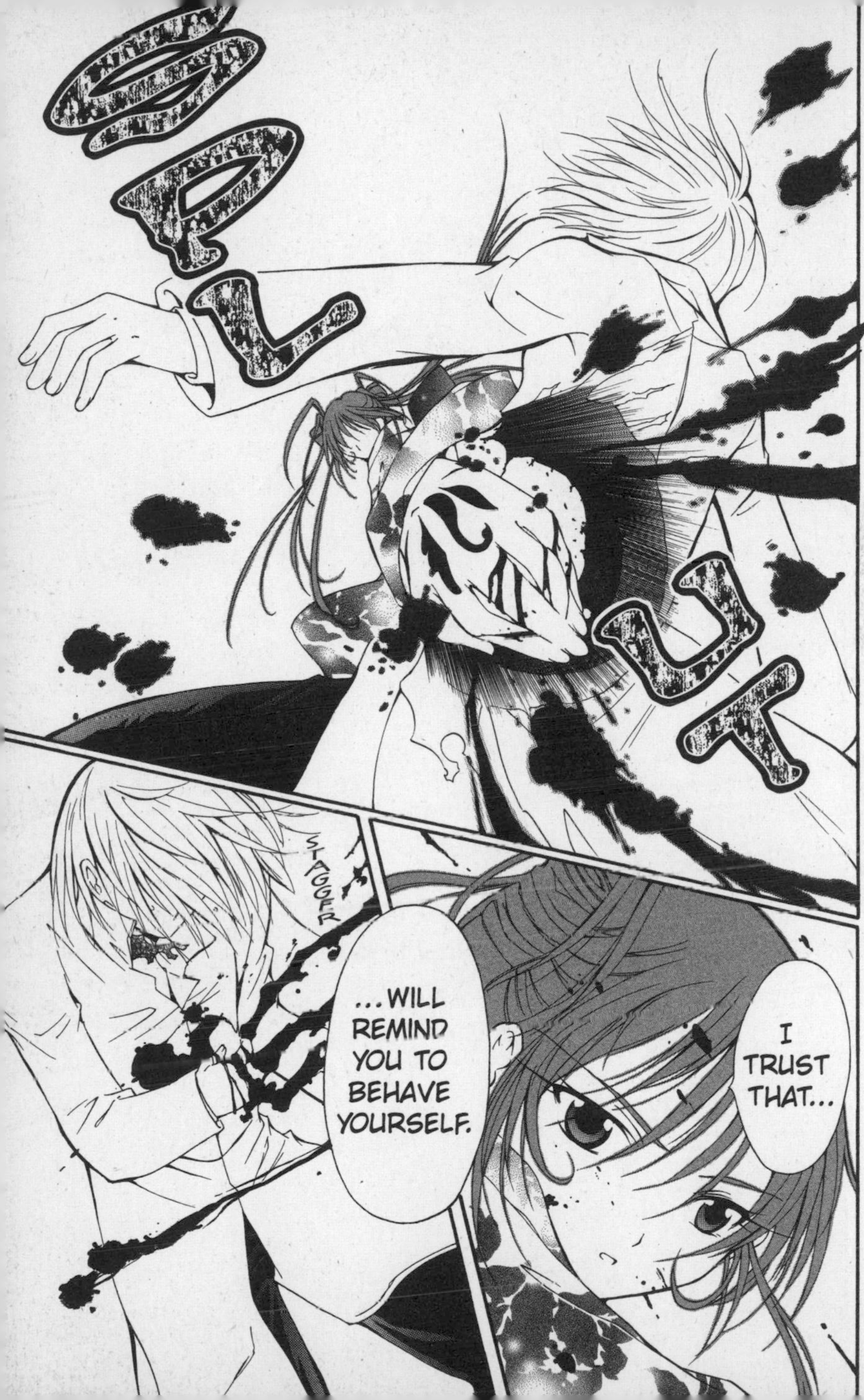
SPLUT
I TRUST THAT...
...WILL REMIND YOU TO BEHAVE YOURSELF.
STAGGER

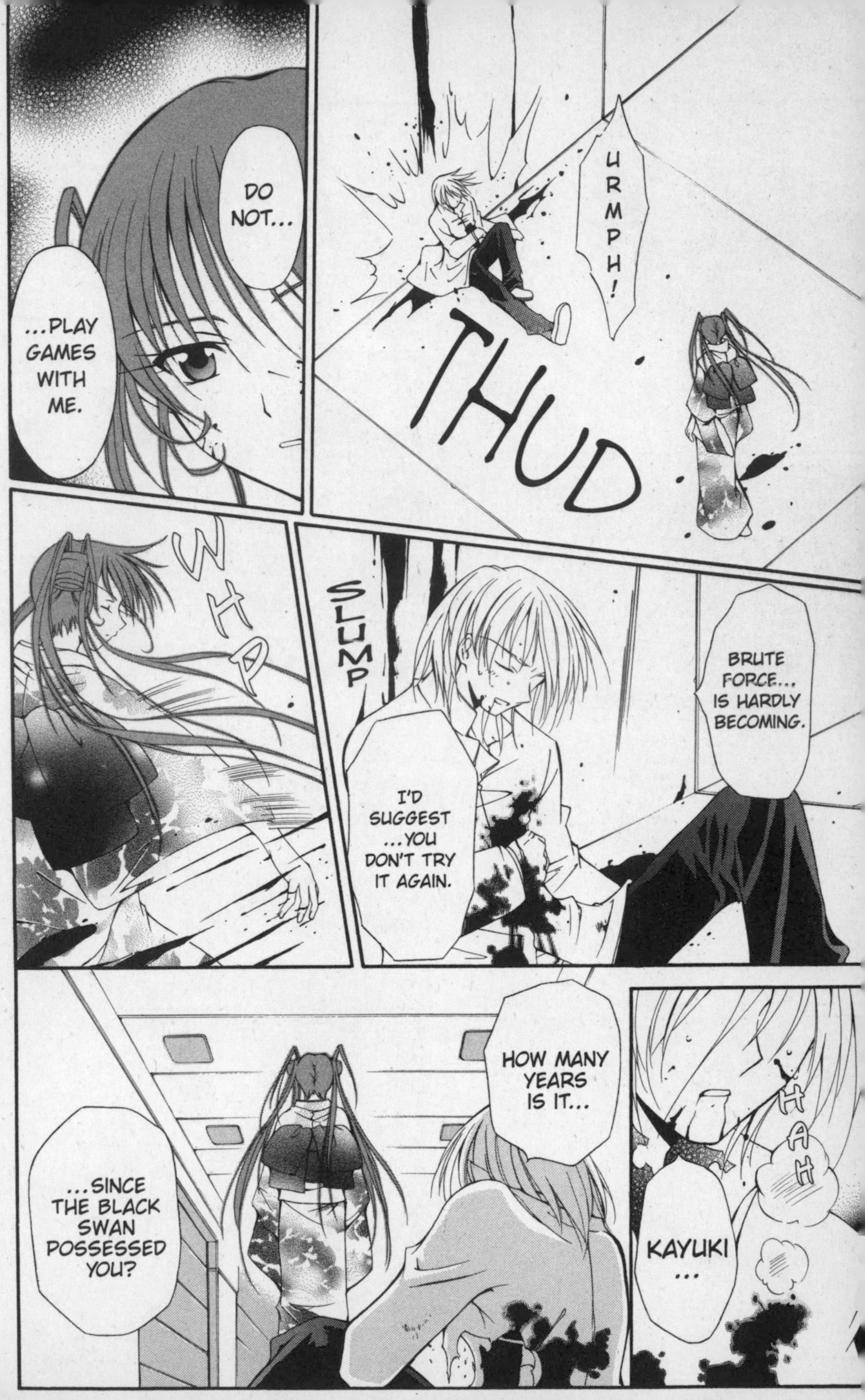
URMPH!
THUD
DO NOT...
...PLAY GAMES WITH ME.
BRUTE FORCE... IS HARDLY BECOMING.
SLUMP
I'D SUGGEST ...YOU DON'T TRY IT AGAIN.
WHA
HAH
KAYUKI...
HOW MANY YEARS IS IT...
...SINCE THE BLACK SWAN POSSESSED YOU?

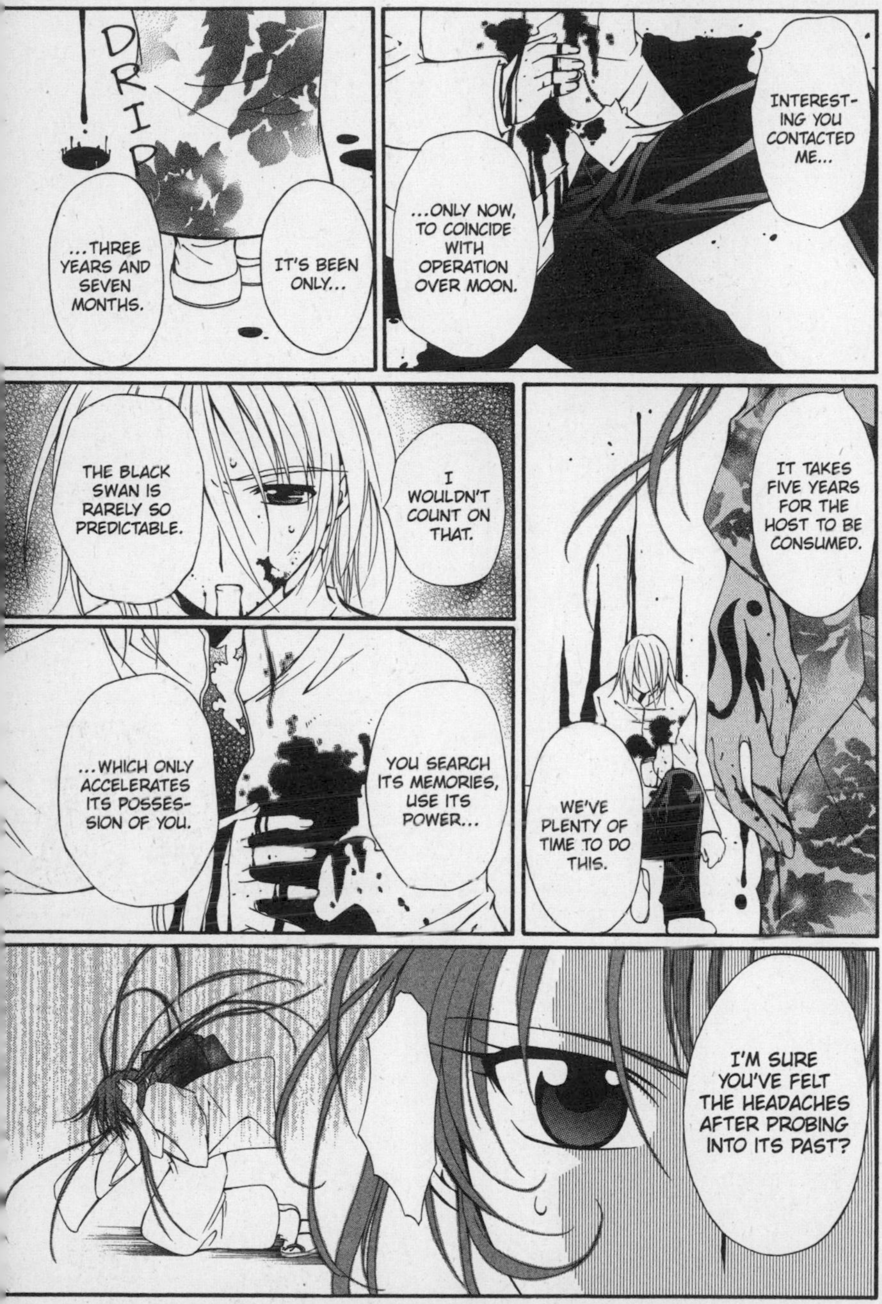
INTEREST-ING YOU CONTACTED ME...
...ONLY NOW, TO COINCIDE WITH OPERATION OVER MOON.
DRIP
IT'S BEEN ONLY...
...THREE YEARS AND SEVEN MONTHS.
IT TAKES FIVE YEARS FOR THE HOST TO BE CONSUMED.
WE'VE PLENTY OF TIME TO DO THIS.
I WOULDN'T COUNT ON THAT.
THE BLACK SWAN IS RARELY SO PREDICTABLE.
YOU SEARCH ITS MEMORIES, USE ITS POWER...
...WHICH ONLY ACCELERATES ITS POSSES-SION OF YOU.
I'M SURE YOU'VE FELT THE HEADACHES AFTER PROBING INTO ITS PAST?

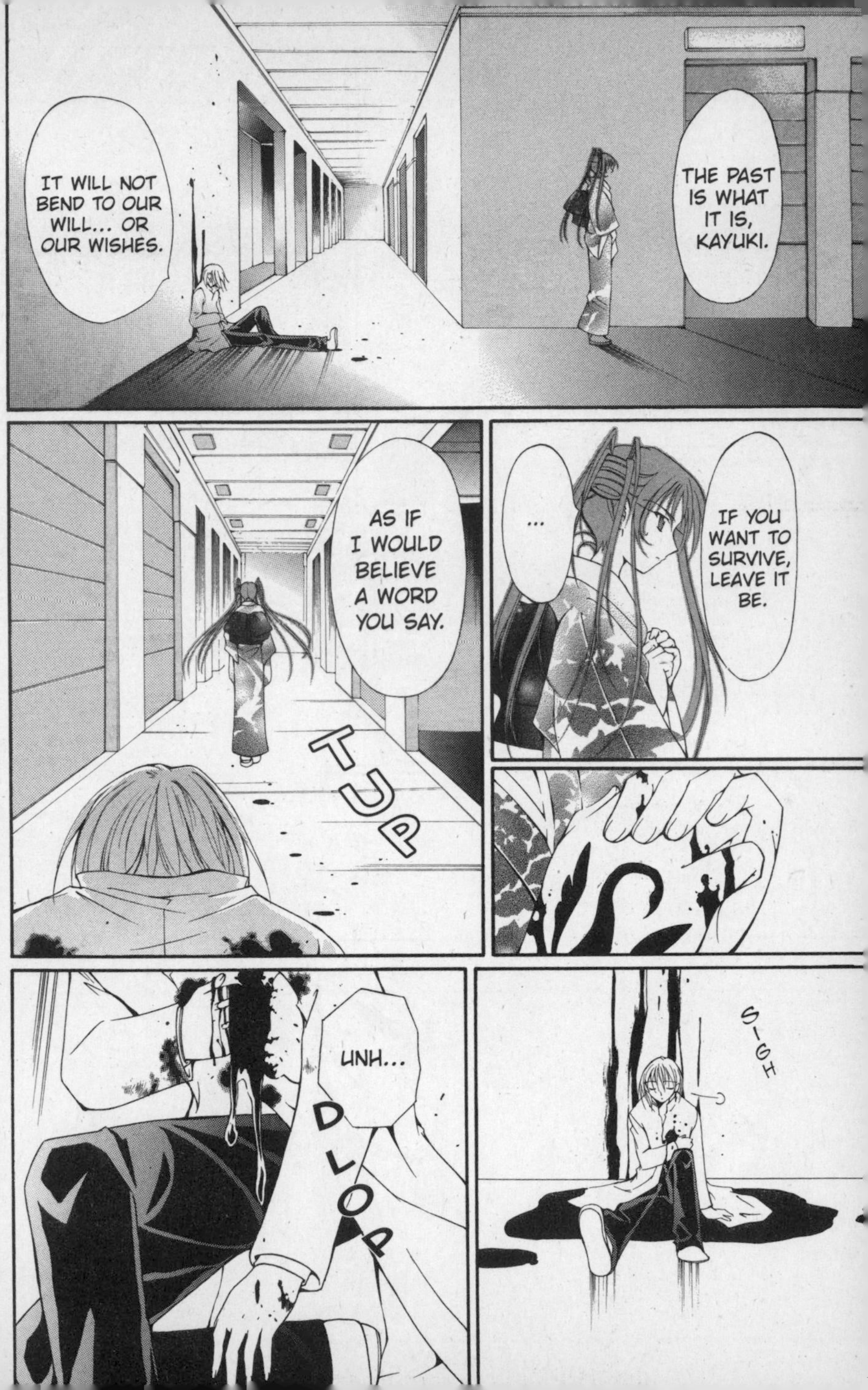
THE PAST IS WHAT IT IS, KAYUKI.
IT WILL NOT BEND TO OUR WILL... OR OUR WISHES.
IF YOU WANT TO SURVIVE, LEAVE IT BE.
...
AS IF I WOULD BELIEVE A WORD YOU SAY.
TUP
SIGH
UNH...
DLOP

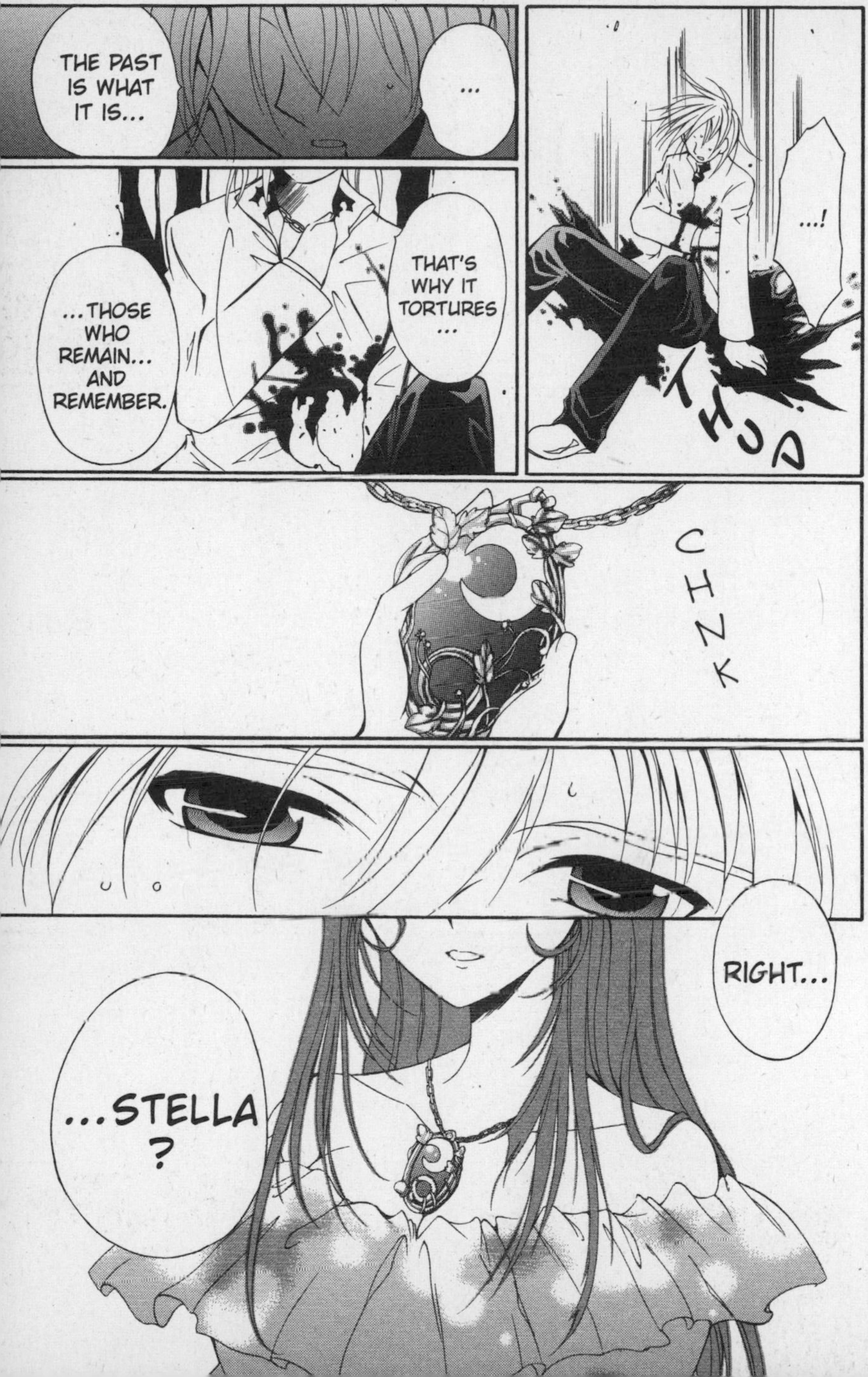
...!
THUD
THE PAST IS WHAT IT IS...
...
THAT'S WHY IT TORTURES...
...THOSE WHO REMAIN... AND REMEMBER.
CHNK
RIGHT...
...STELLA?

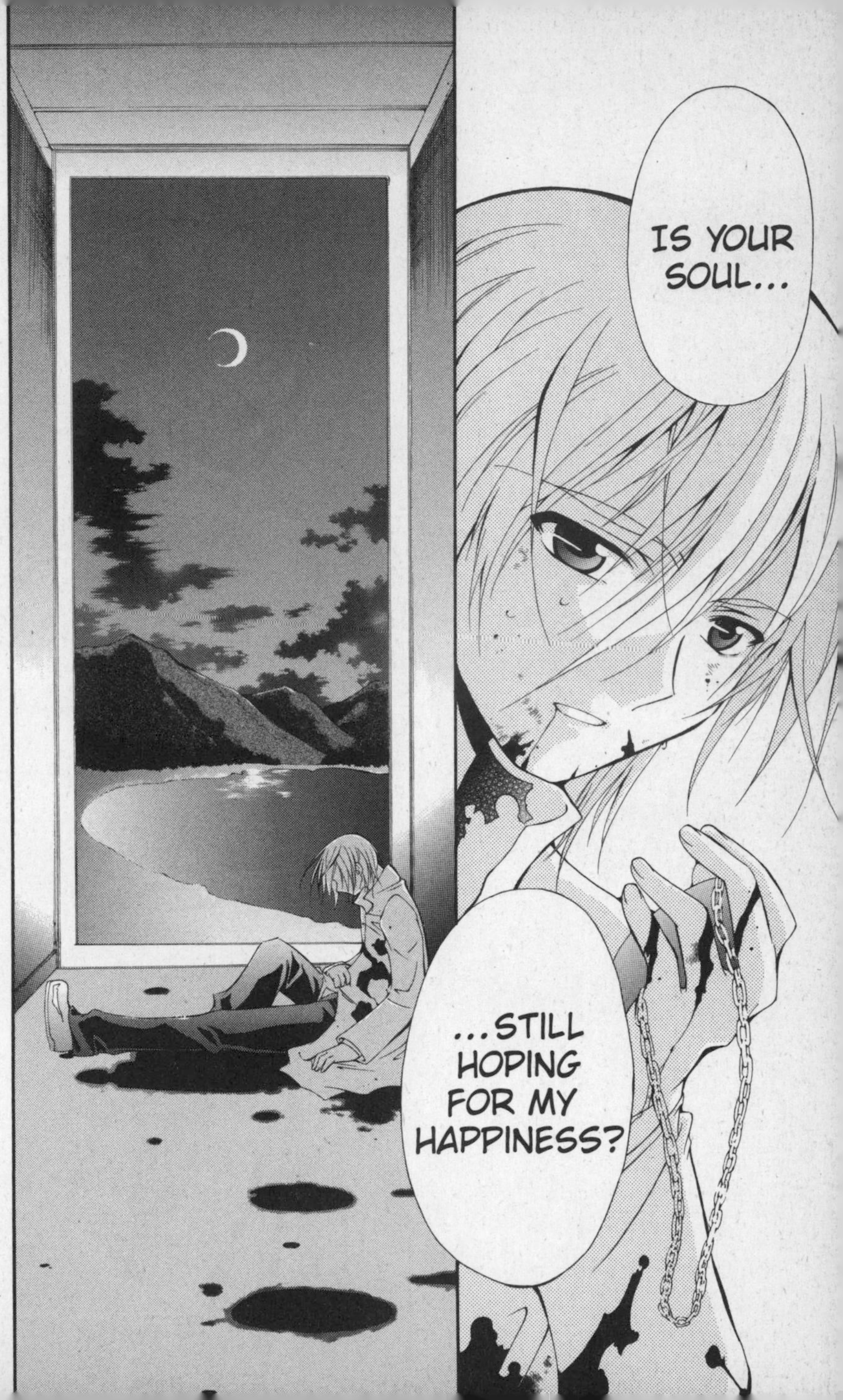
IS YOUR SOUL...
...STILL HOPING FOR MY HAPPINESS?

THE RECORD OF A

FALLEN VAMPIRE

THE RECORD OF A

FALLEN VAMPIRE

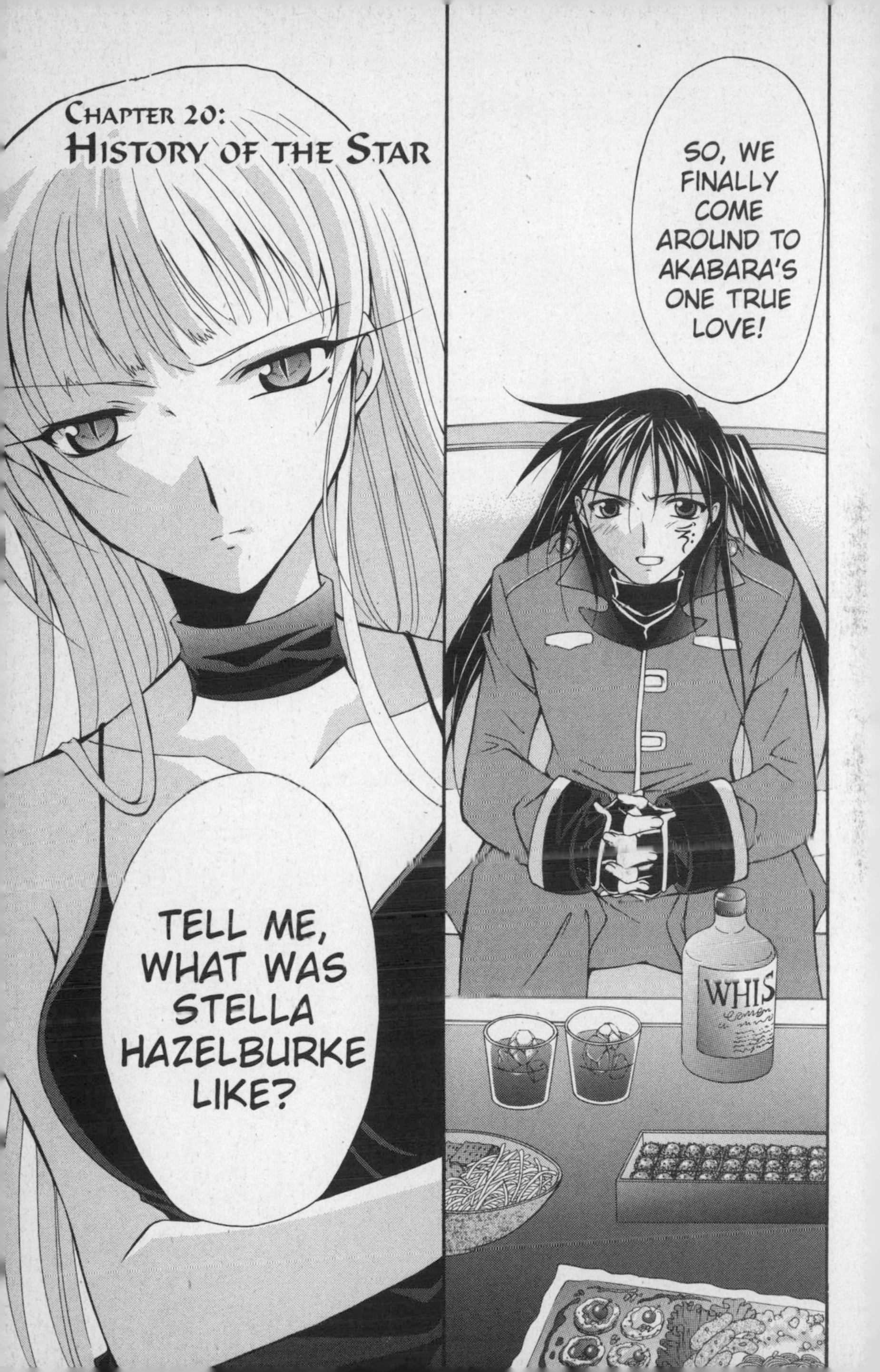
SO, WE FINALLY COME AROUND TO AKABARA'S ONE TRUE LOVE!
CHAPTER 20: HISTORY OF THE STAR
TELL ME, WHAT WAS STELLA HAZELBURKE LIKE?
WHIS

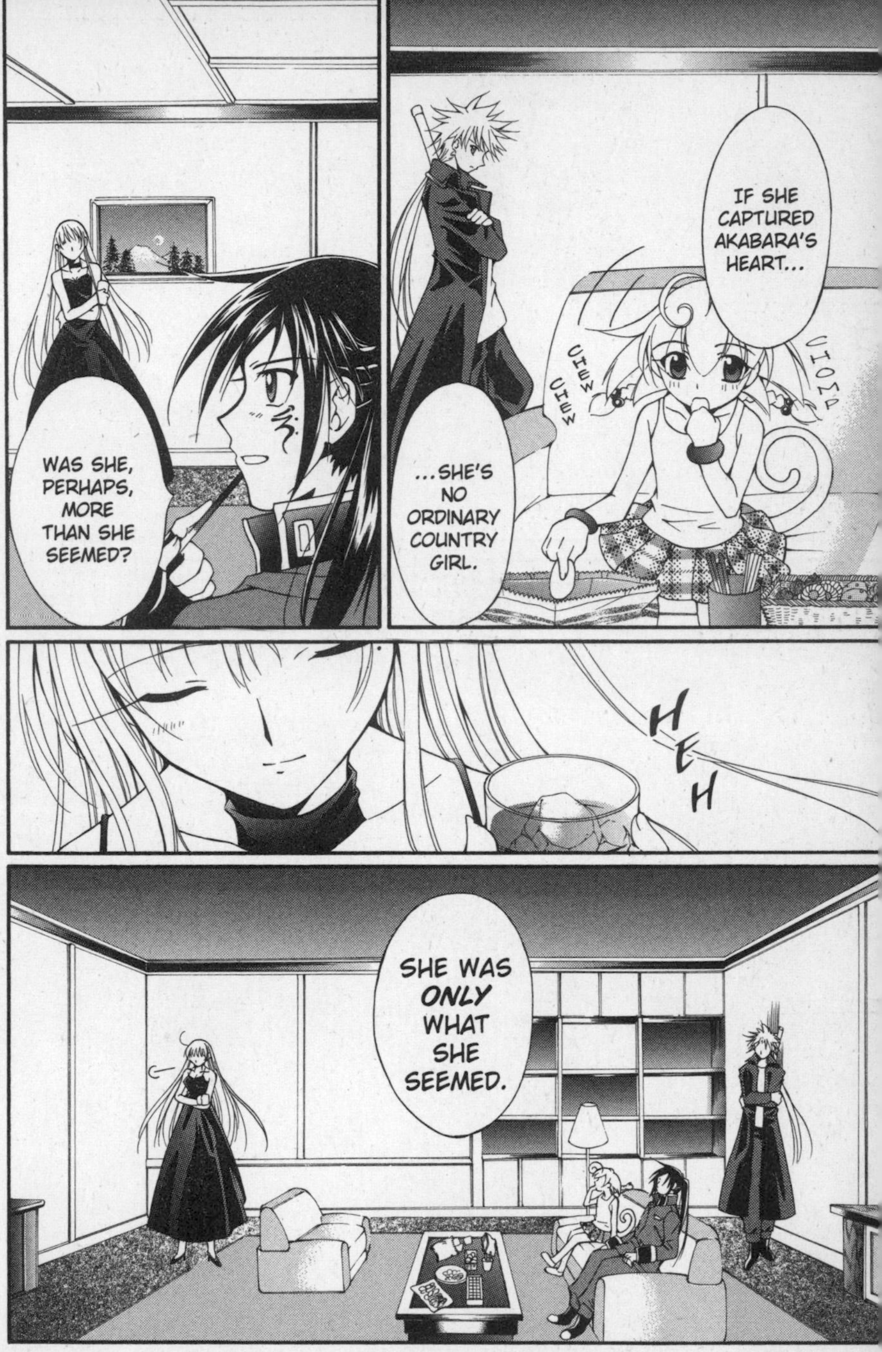
IF SHE CAPTURED AKABARA'S HEART...
CHOMP
CHEW CHEW
...SHE'S NO ORDINARY COUNTRY GIRL.
WAS SHE, PERHAPS, MORE THAN SHE SEEMED?
HEH HEH
SHE WAS *ONLY* WHAT SHE SEEMED.

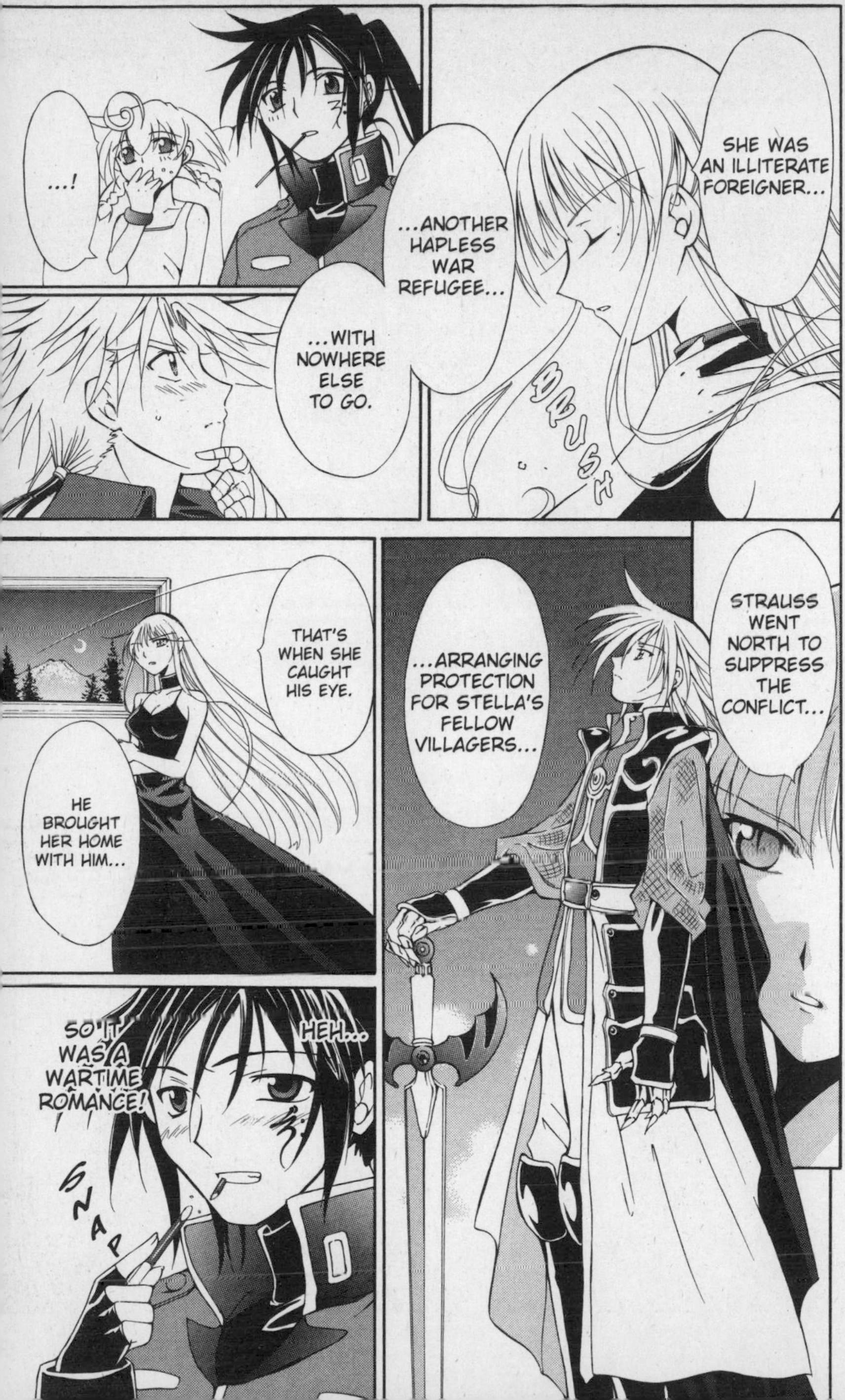
SHE WAS AN ILLITERATE FOREIGNER...
...ANOTHER HAPLESS WAR REFUGEE...
...WITH NOWHERE ELSE TO GO.
BRUSH
...!
STRAUSS WENT NORTH TO SUPPRESS THE CONFLICT...
...ARRANGING PROTECTION FOR STELLA'S FELLOW VILLAGERS...
THAT'S WHEN SHE CAUGHT HIS EYE.
HE BROUGHT HER HOME WITH HIM...
HEH...
SO IT WAS A WARTIME ROMANCE!
SNAP

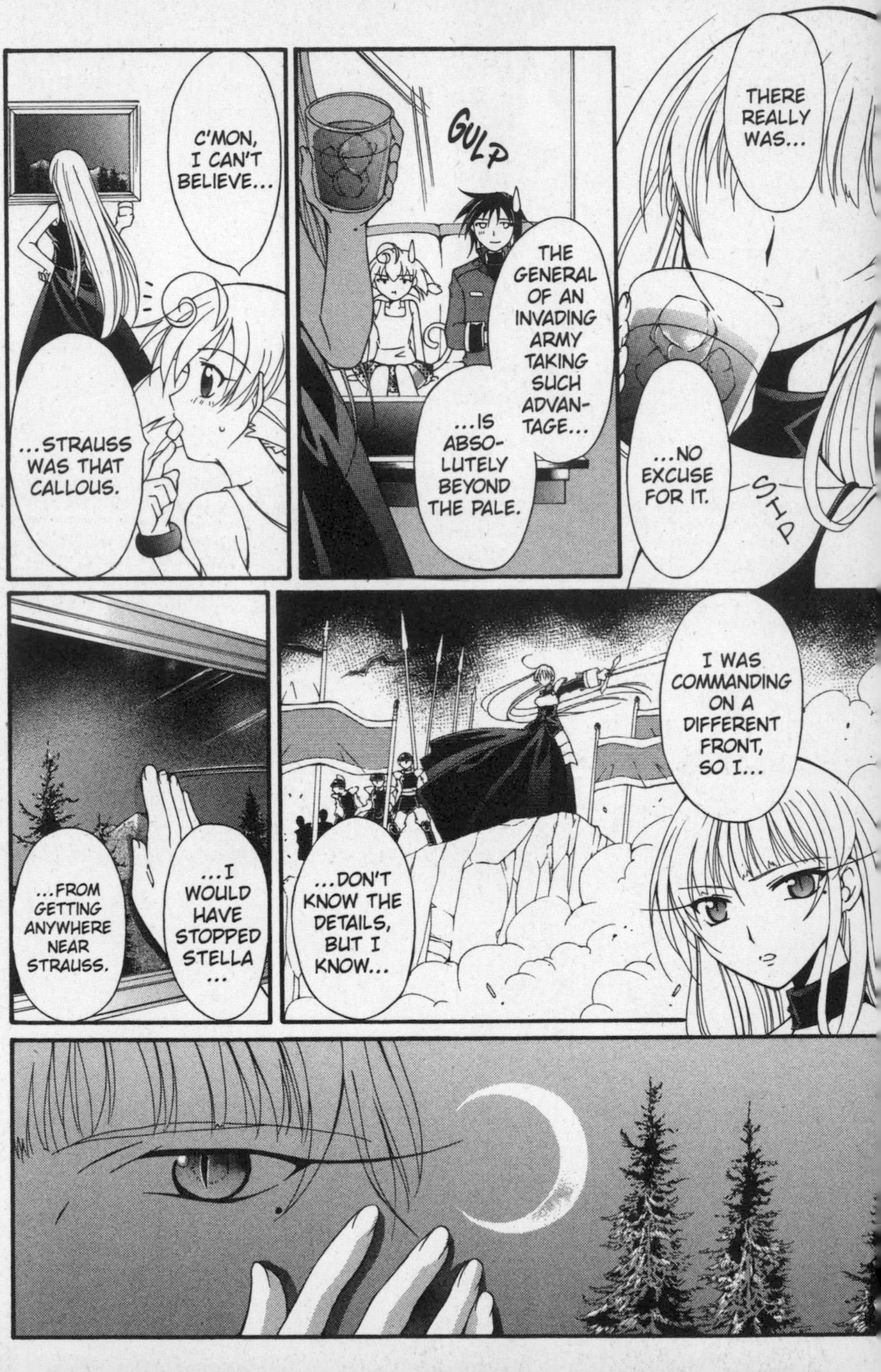
THERE REALLY WAS...
...NO EXCUSE FOR IT.
SIP
GULP
THE GENERAL OF AN INVADING ARMY TAKING SUCH ADVANTAGE...
...IS ABSOLUTELY BEYOND THE PALE.
C'MON, I CAN'T BELIEVE...
...STRAUSS WAS THAT CALLOUS.
I WAS COMMANDING ON A DIFFERENT FRONT, SO I...
...DON'T KNOW THE DETAILS, BUT I KNOW...
...I WOULD HAVE STOPPED STELLA...
...FROM GETTING ANYWHERE NEAR STRAUSS.

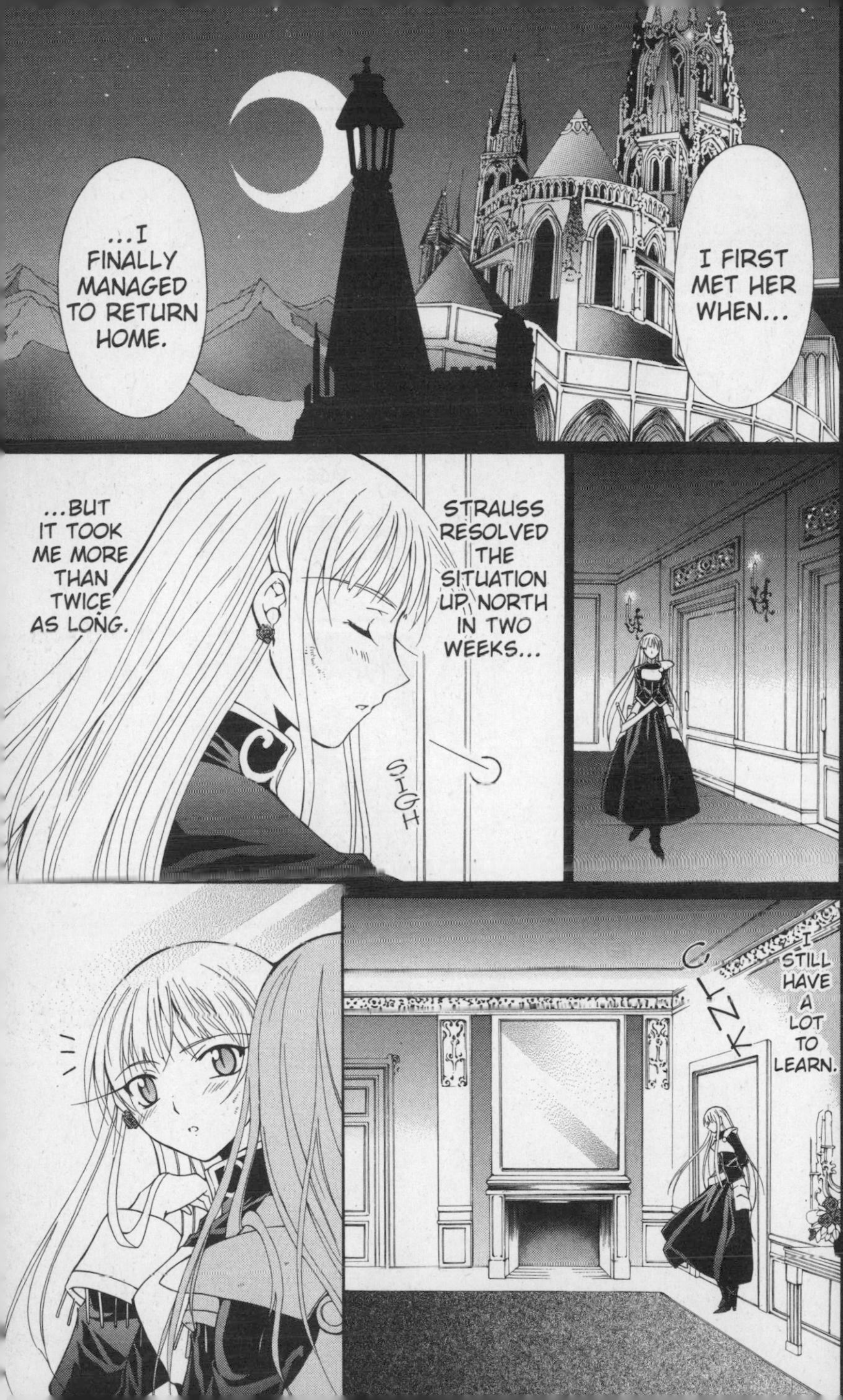
I FIRST MET HER WHEN...
...I FINALLY MANAGED TO RETURN HOME.
STRAUSS RESOLVED THE SITUATION UP NORTH IN TWO WEEKS...
...BUT IT TOOK ME MORE THAN TWICE AS LONG.
SIGH
I STILL HAVE A LOT TO LEARN.
CLINK

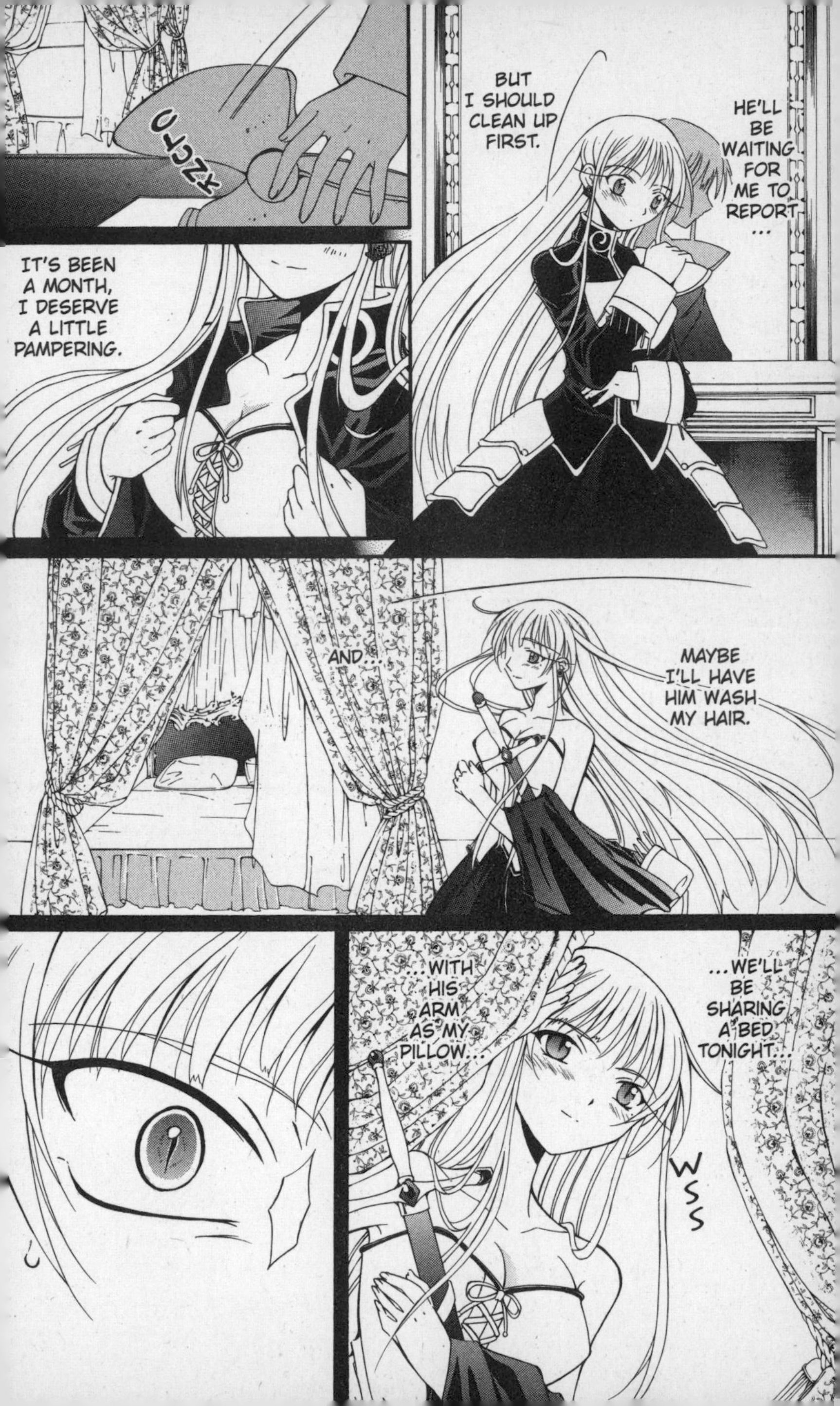
HE'LL BE WAITING FOR ME TO REPORT...
BUT I SHOULD CLEAN UP FIRST.
IT'S BEEN A MONTH, I DESERVE A LITTLE PAMPERING.
MAYBE I'LL HAVE HIM WASH MY HAIR.
AND...
...WE'LL BE SHARING A BED TONIGHT...
...WITH HIS ARM AS MY PILLOW...
WSS

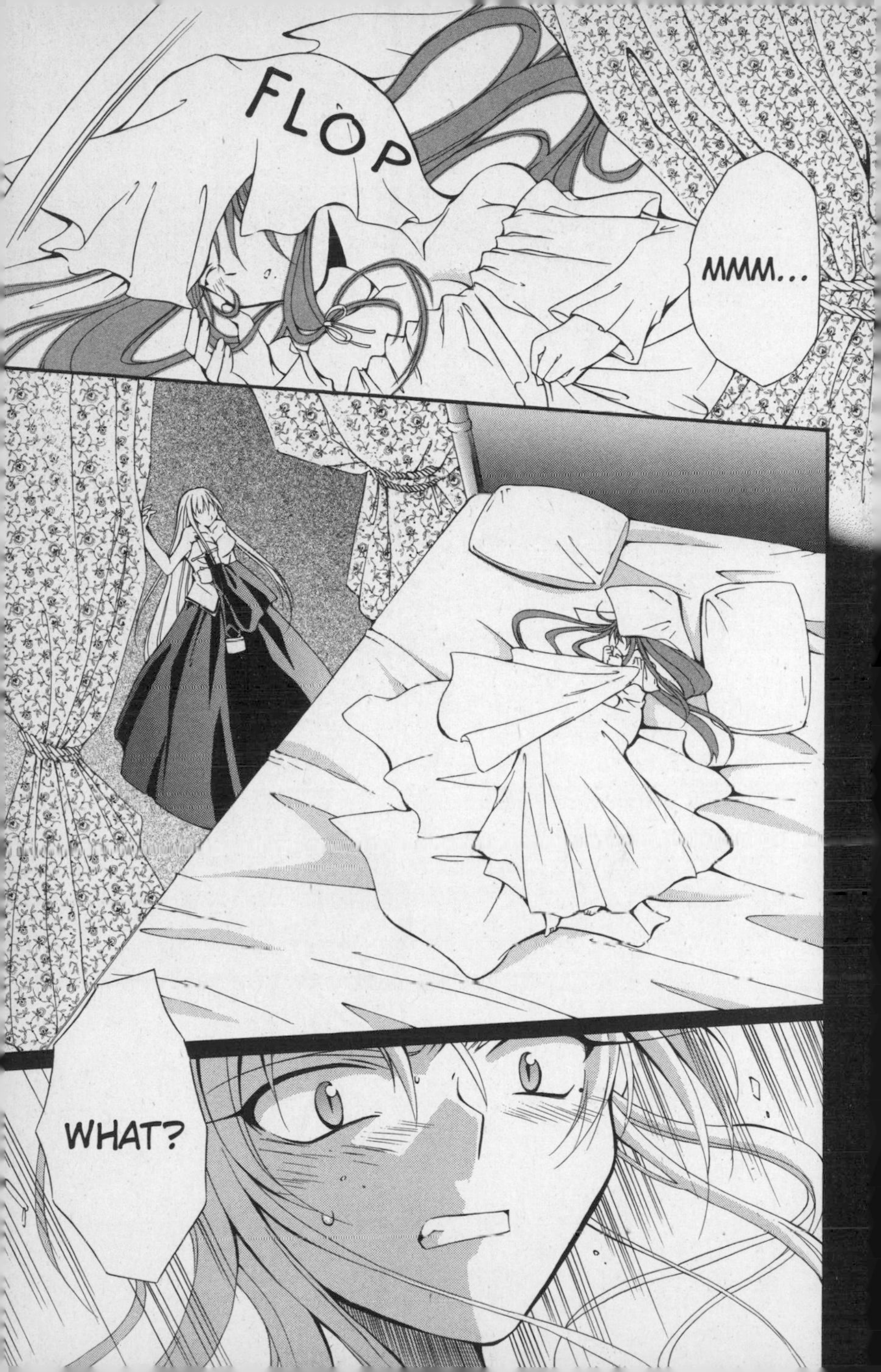
MMM...
FLOP
WHAT?

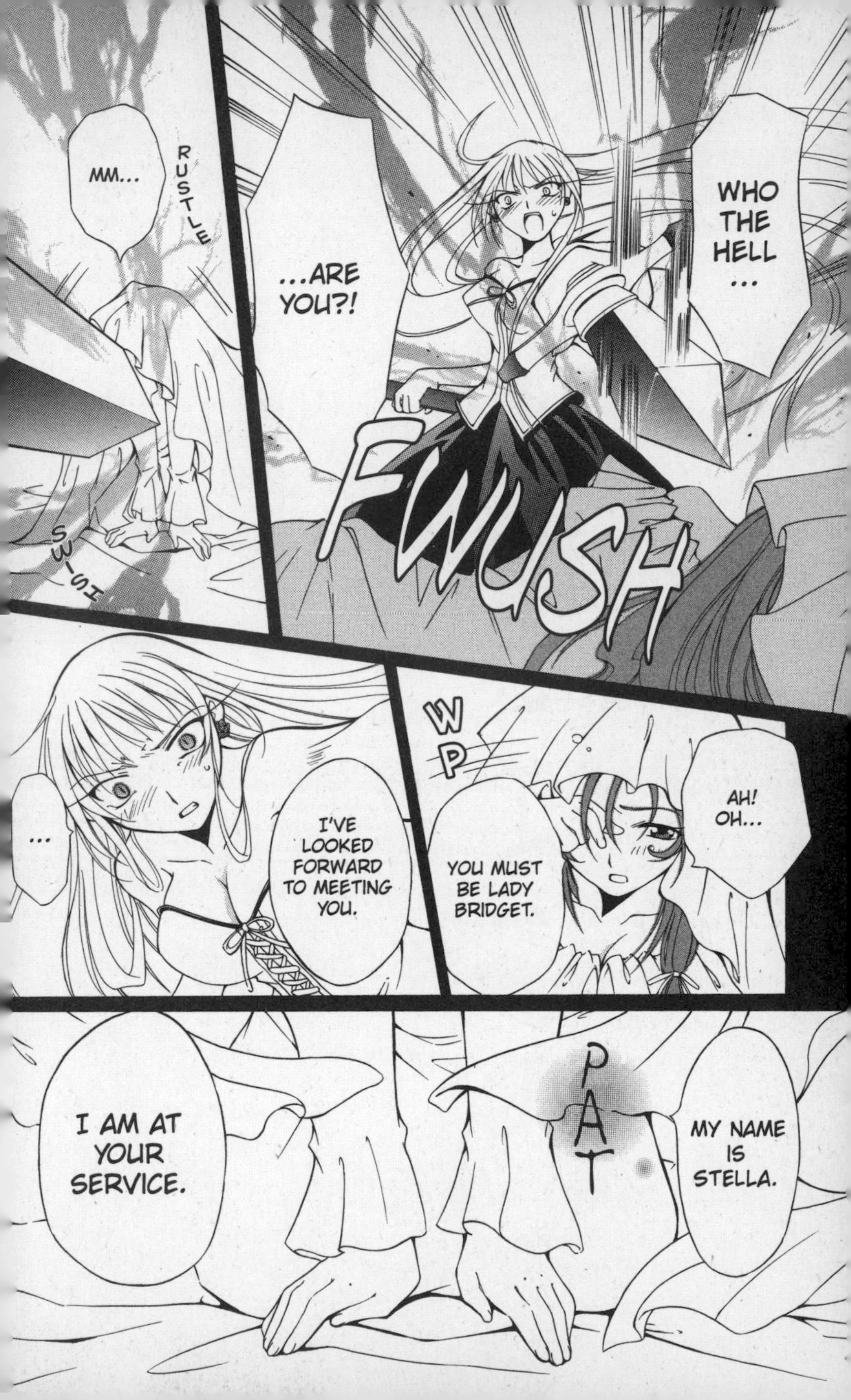
WHO THE HELL...
...ARE YOU?!
FWUSH
MM...
RUSTLE
SWISH
AH! OH...
WP
YOU MUST BE LADY BRIDGET.
I'VE LOOKED FORWARD TO MEETING YOU.
...
MY NAME IS STELLA.
PAT
I AM AT YOUR SERVICE.

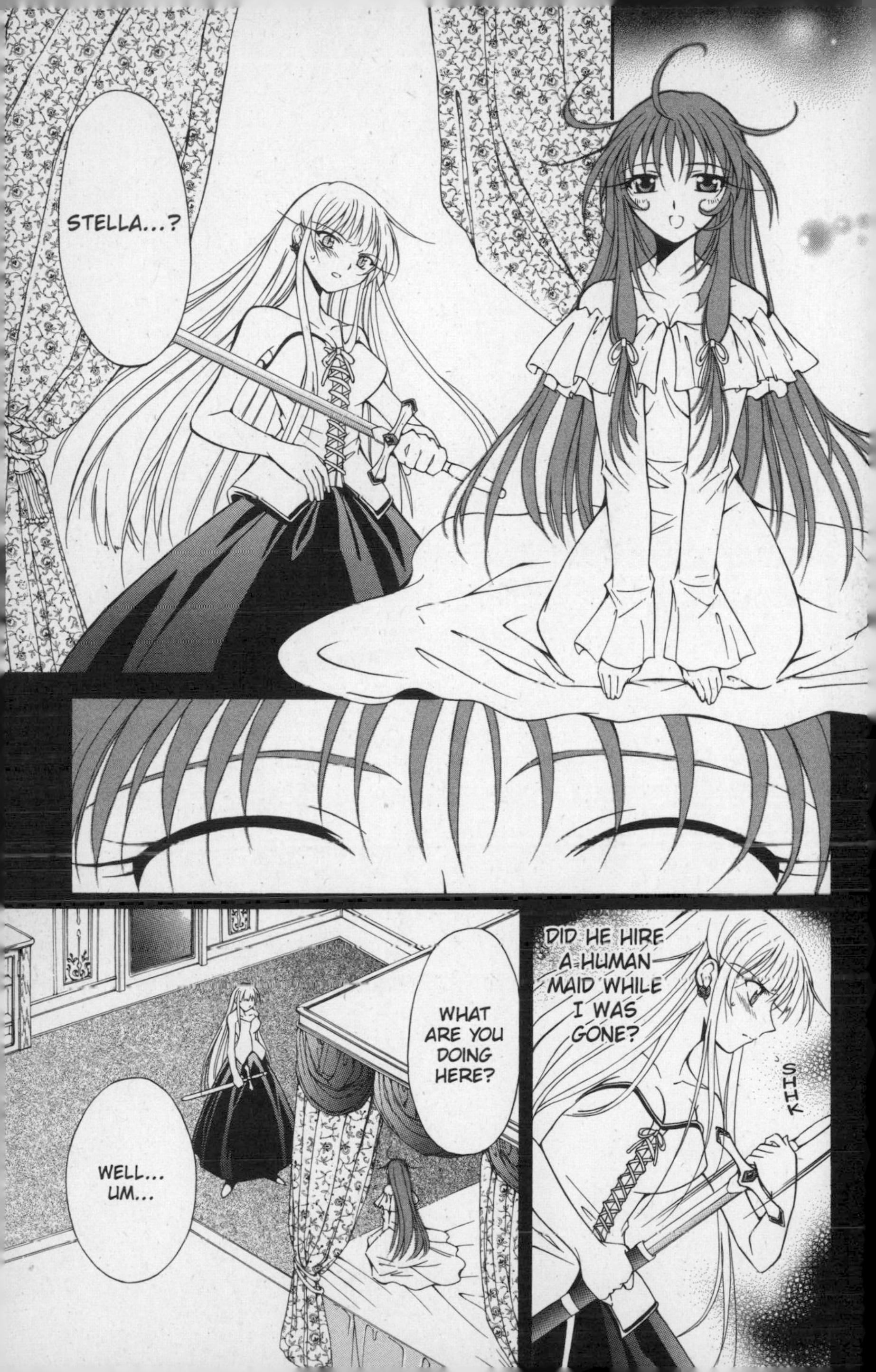
STELLA...?
DID HE HIRE A HUMAN MAID WHILE I WAS GONE?
SHHK
WHAT ARE YOU DOING HERE?
WELL... UM...

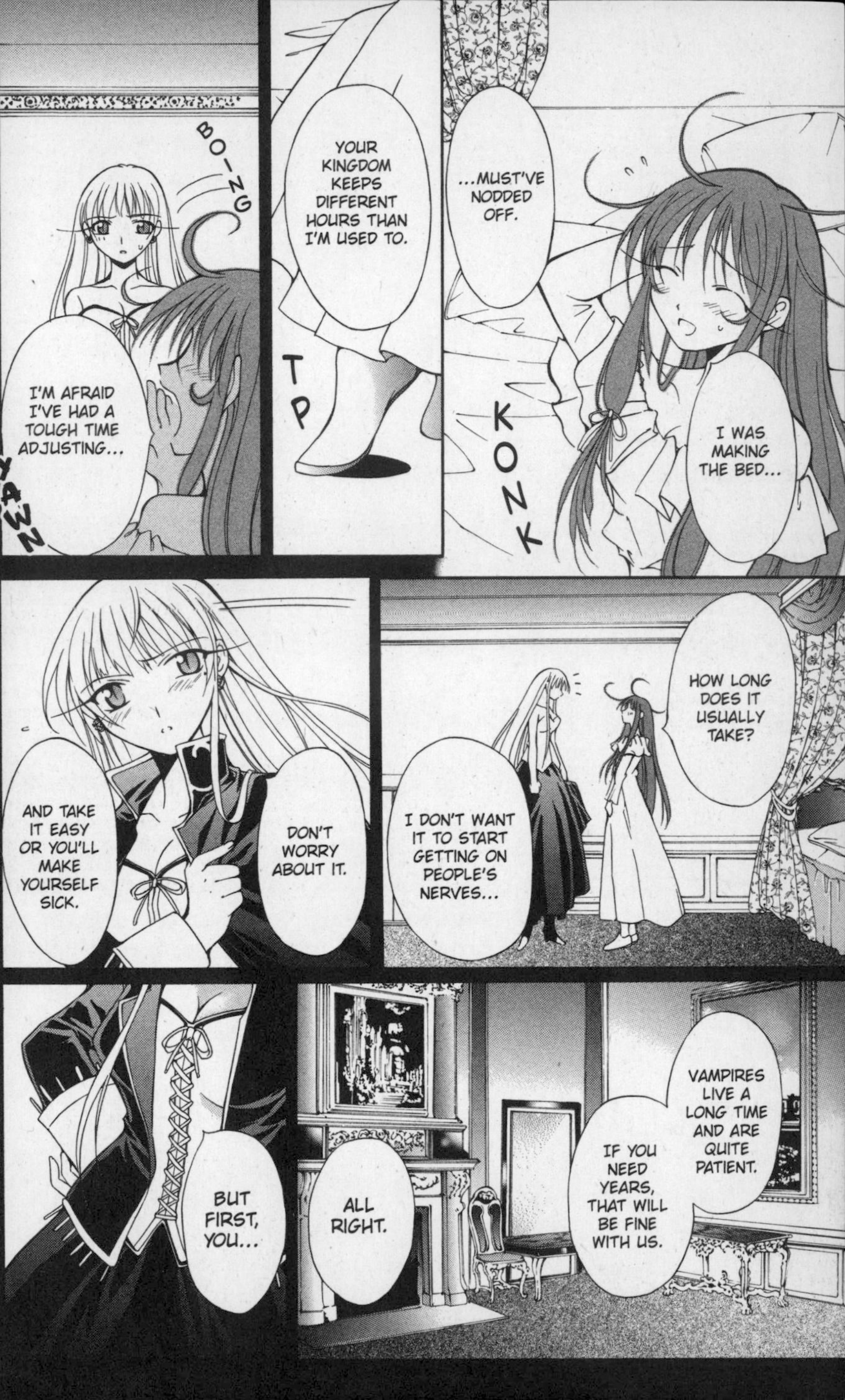
I WAS MAKING THE BED...
...MUST'VE NODDED OFF.
KONK
YOUR KINGDOM KEEPS DIFFERENT HOURS THAN I'M USED TO.
TP
BOING
I'M AFRAID I'VE HAD A TOUGH TIME ADJUSTING...
YAWN
HOW LONG DOES IT USUALLY TAKE?
I DON'T WANT IT TO START GETTING ON PEOPLE'S NERVES...
DON'T WORRY ABOUT IT.
AND TAKE IT EASY OR YOU'LL MAKE YOURSELF SICK.
VAMPIRES LIVE A LONG TIME AND ARE QUITE PATIENT.
IF YOU NEED YEARS, THAT WILL BE FINE WITH US.
ALL RIGHT.
BUT FIRST, YOU...

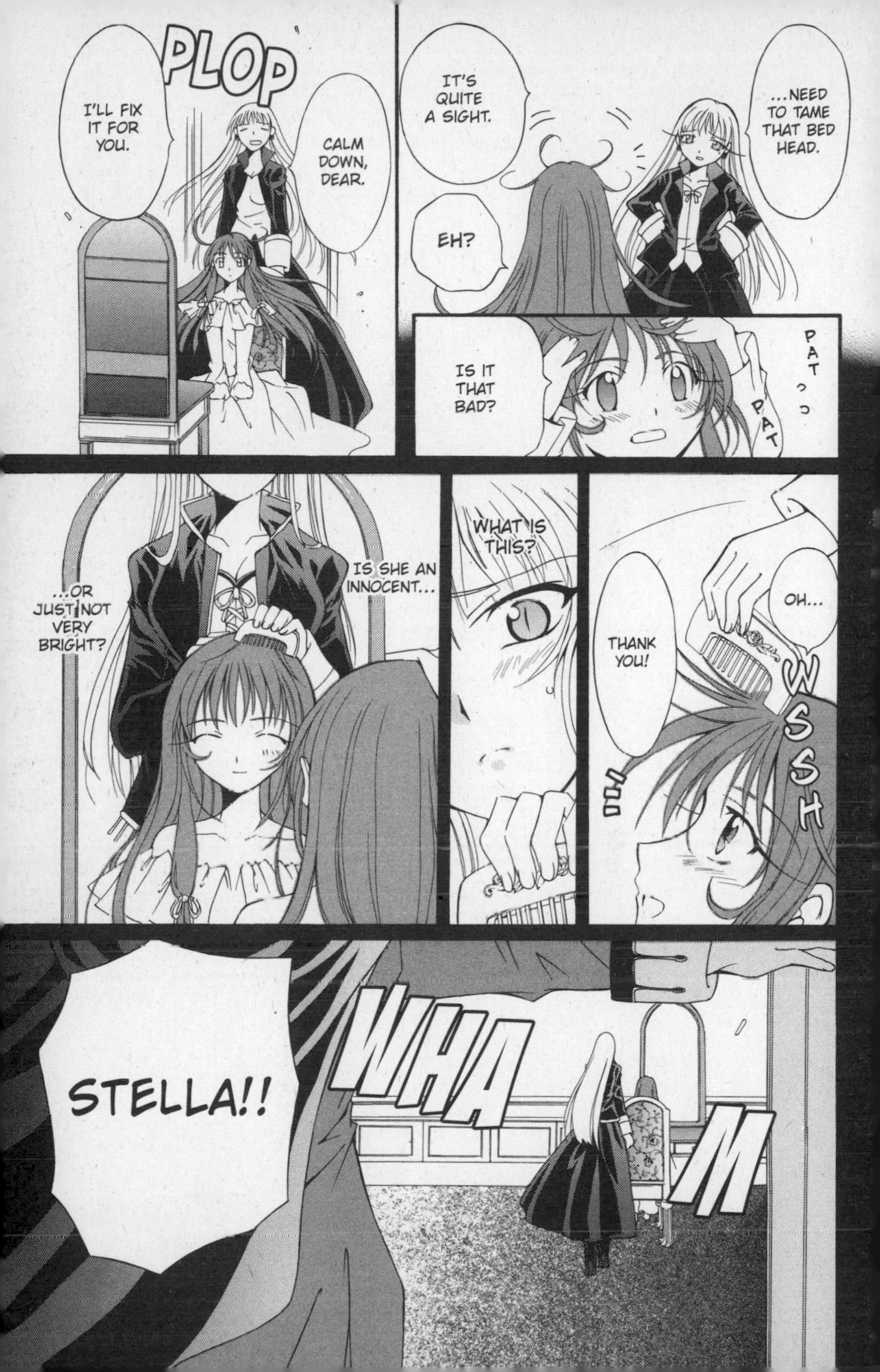
...NEED TO TAME THAT BED HEAD.
IT'S QUITE A SIGHT.
EH?
PAT PAT
IS IT THAT BAD?
PLOP
CALM DOWN, DEAR.
I'LL FIX IT FOR YOU.
WSSH
OH...
THANK YOU!
WHAT IS THIS?
IS SHE AN INNOCENT...
...OR JUST NOT VERY BRIGHT?
WHAM
STELLA!!

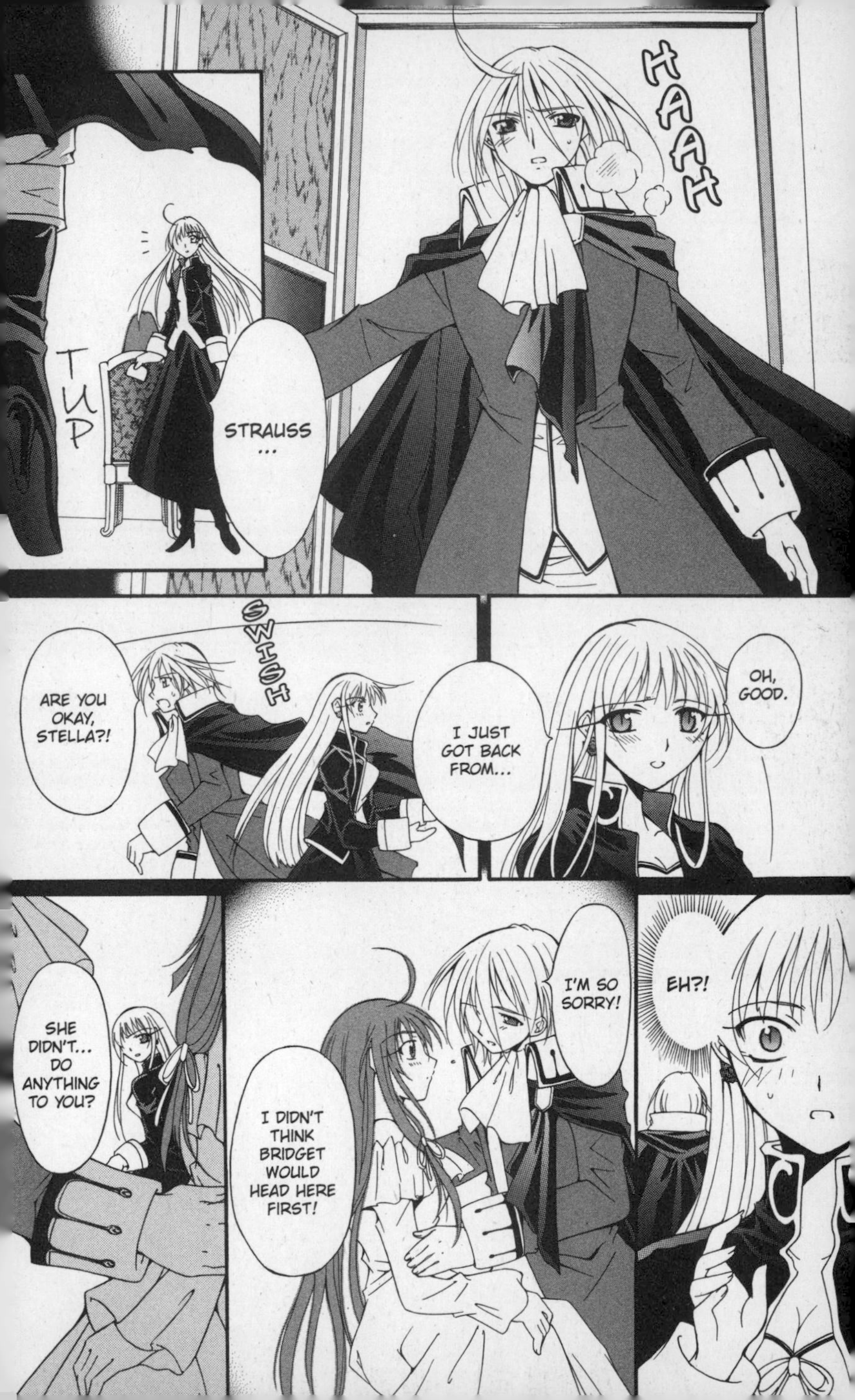
HAAAH
STRAUSS ...
TUP
OH, GOOD.
I JUST GOT BACK FROM...
SWISH
ARE YOU OKAY, STELLA?!
EH?!
I'M SO SORRY!
I DIDN'T THINK BRIDGET WOULD HEAD HERE FIRST!
SHE DIDN'T... DO ANYTHING TO YOU?

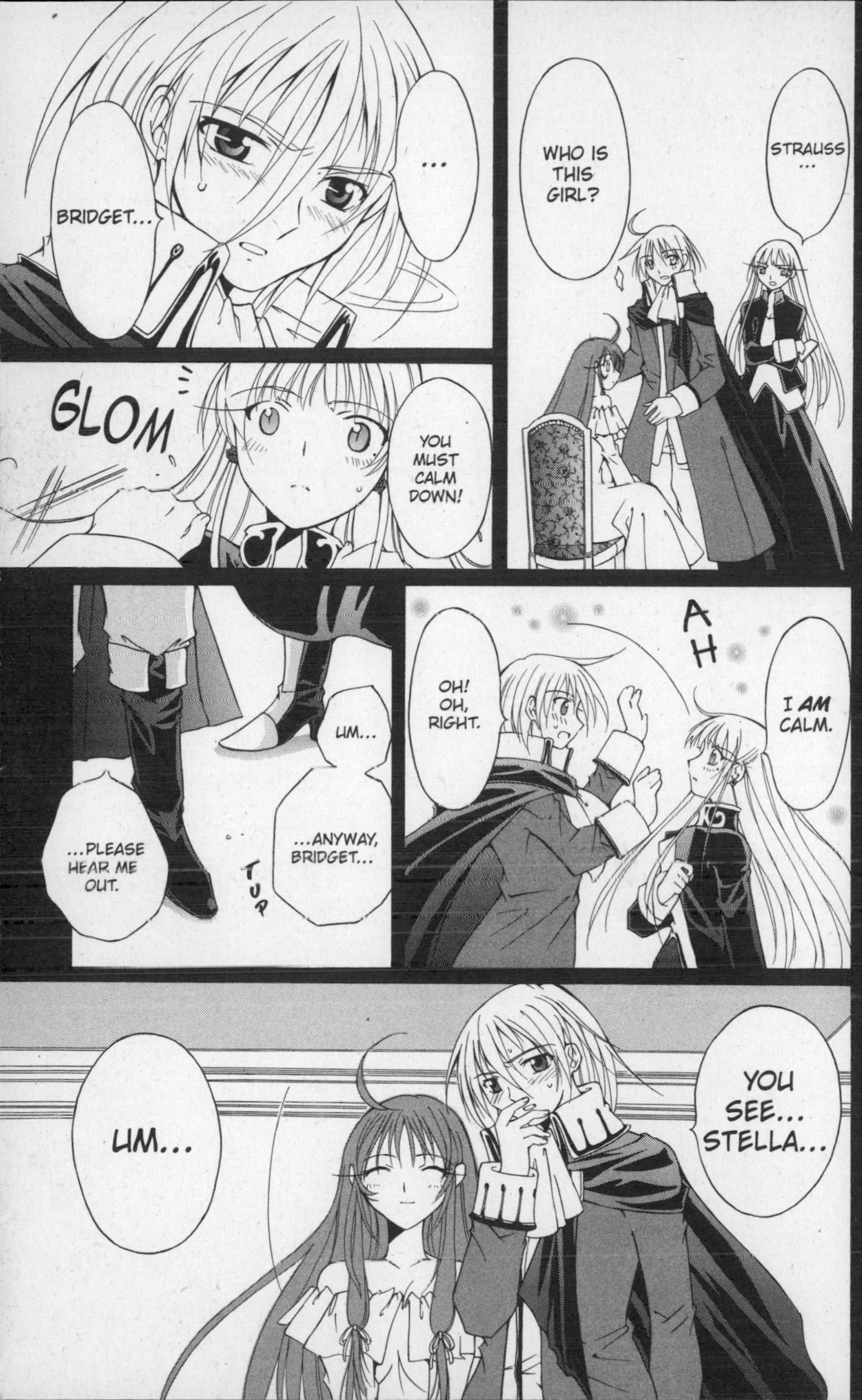
STRAUSS...
WHO IS THIS GIRL?
...
BRIDGET...
YOU MUST CALM DOWN!
GLOM
I AM CALM.
AH
OH! OH, RIGHT.
UM...
...ANYWAY, BRIDGET...
TUP
...PLEASE HEAR ME OUT.
YOU SEE... STELLA...
UM...

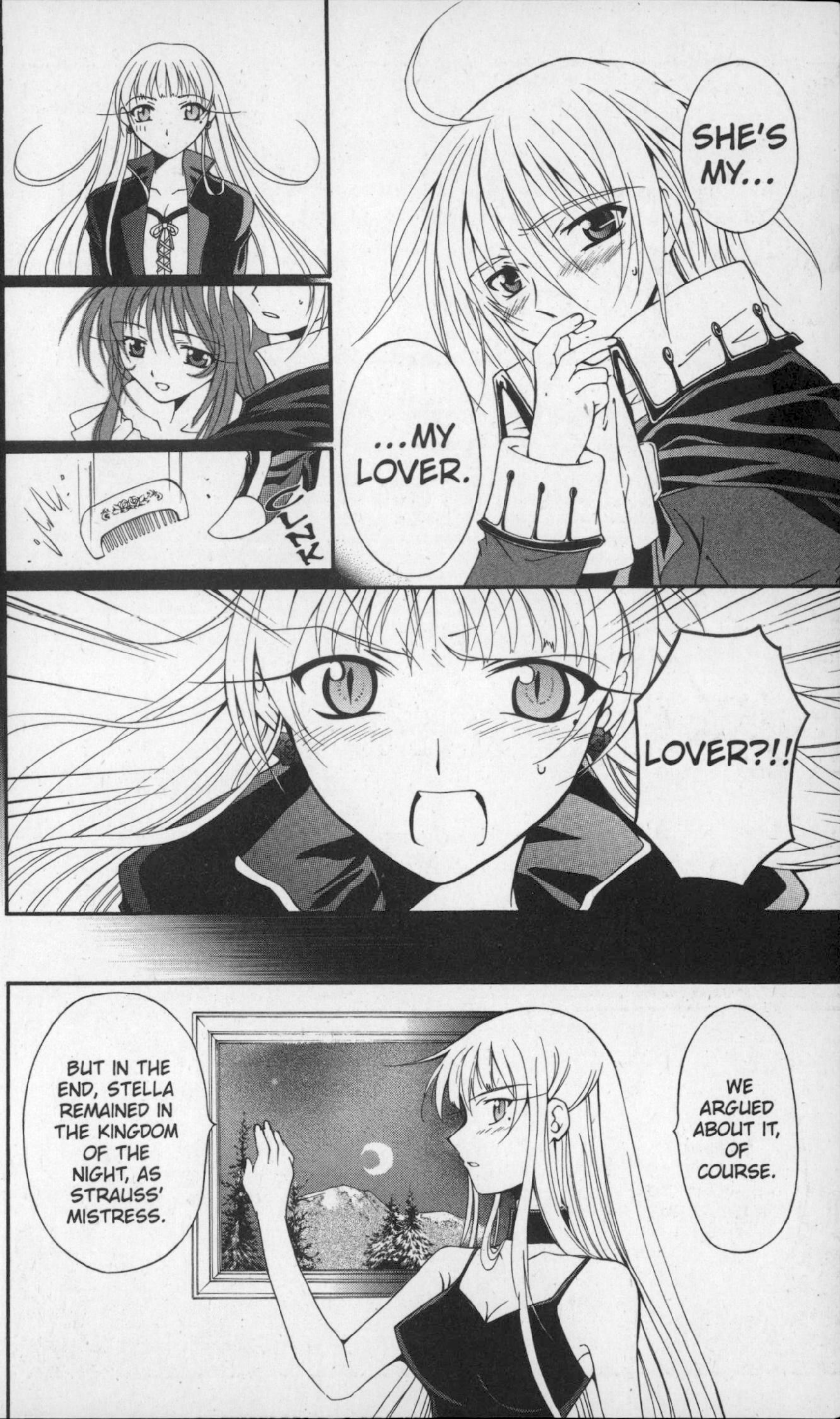
SHE'S MY...
...MY LOVER.
CLNK
LOVER?!!
WE ARGUED ABOUT IT, OF COURSE.
BUT IN THE END, STELLA REMAINED IN THE KINGDOM OF THE NIGHT, AS STRAUSS' MISTRESS.

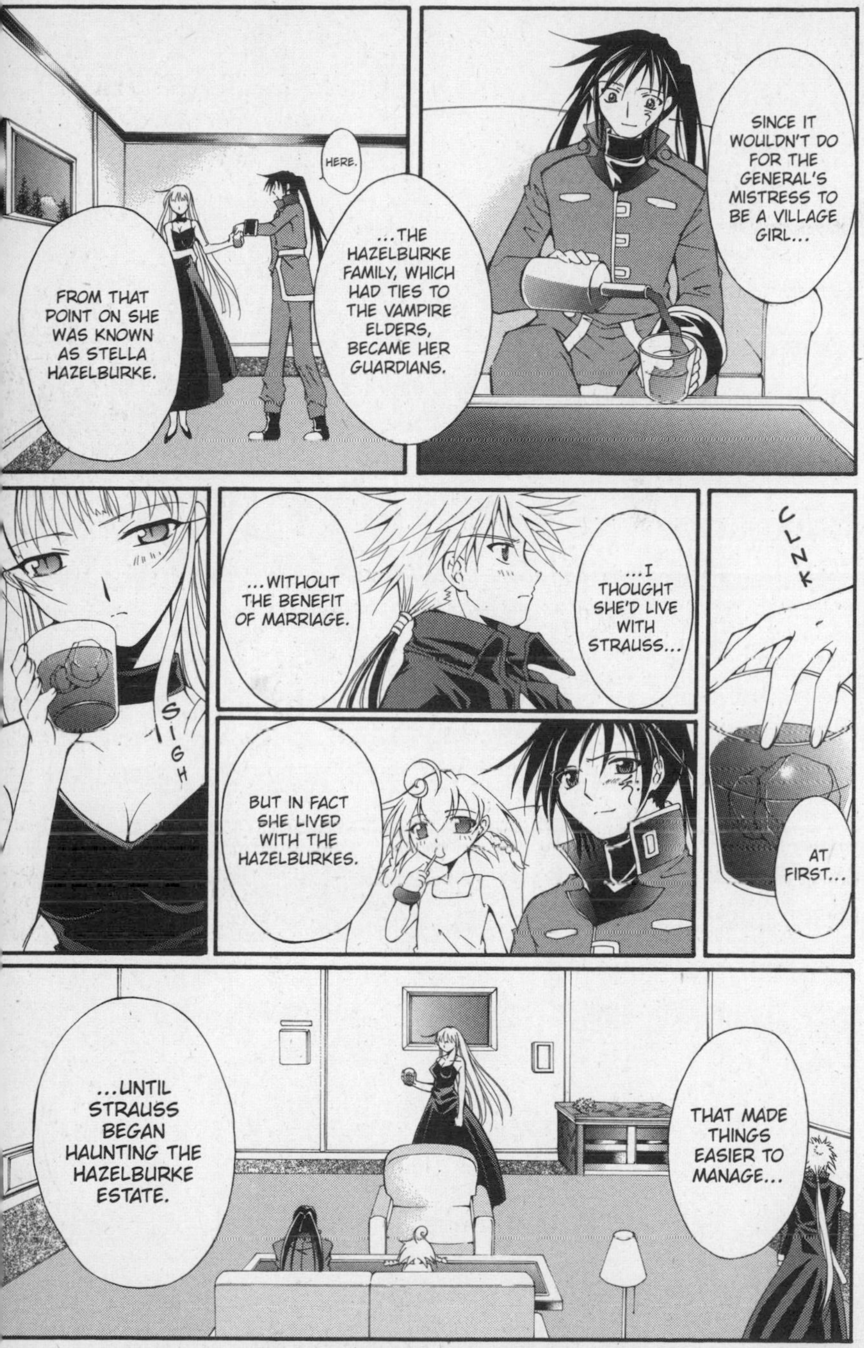
SINCE IT WOULDN'T DO FOR THE GENERAL'S MISTRESS TO BE A VILLAGE GIRL...
...THE HAZELBURKE FAMILY, WHICH HAD TIES TO THE VAMPIRE ELDERS, BECAME HER GUARDIANS.
HERE.
FROM THAT POINT ON SHE WAS KNOWN AS STELLA HAZELBURKE.
CLNK
AT FIRST...
...I THOUGHT SHE'D LIVE WITH STRAUSS...
...WITHOUT THE BENEFIT OF MARRIAGE.
BUT IN FACT SHE LIVED WITH THE HAZELBURKES.
SIGH
THAT MADE THINGS EASIER TO MANAGE...
...UNTIL STRAUSS BEGAN HAUNTING THE HAZELBURKE ESTATE.

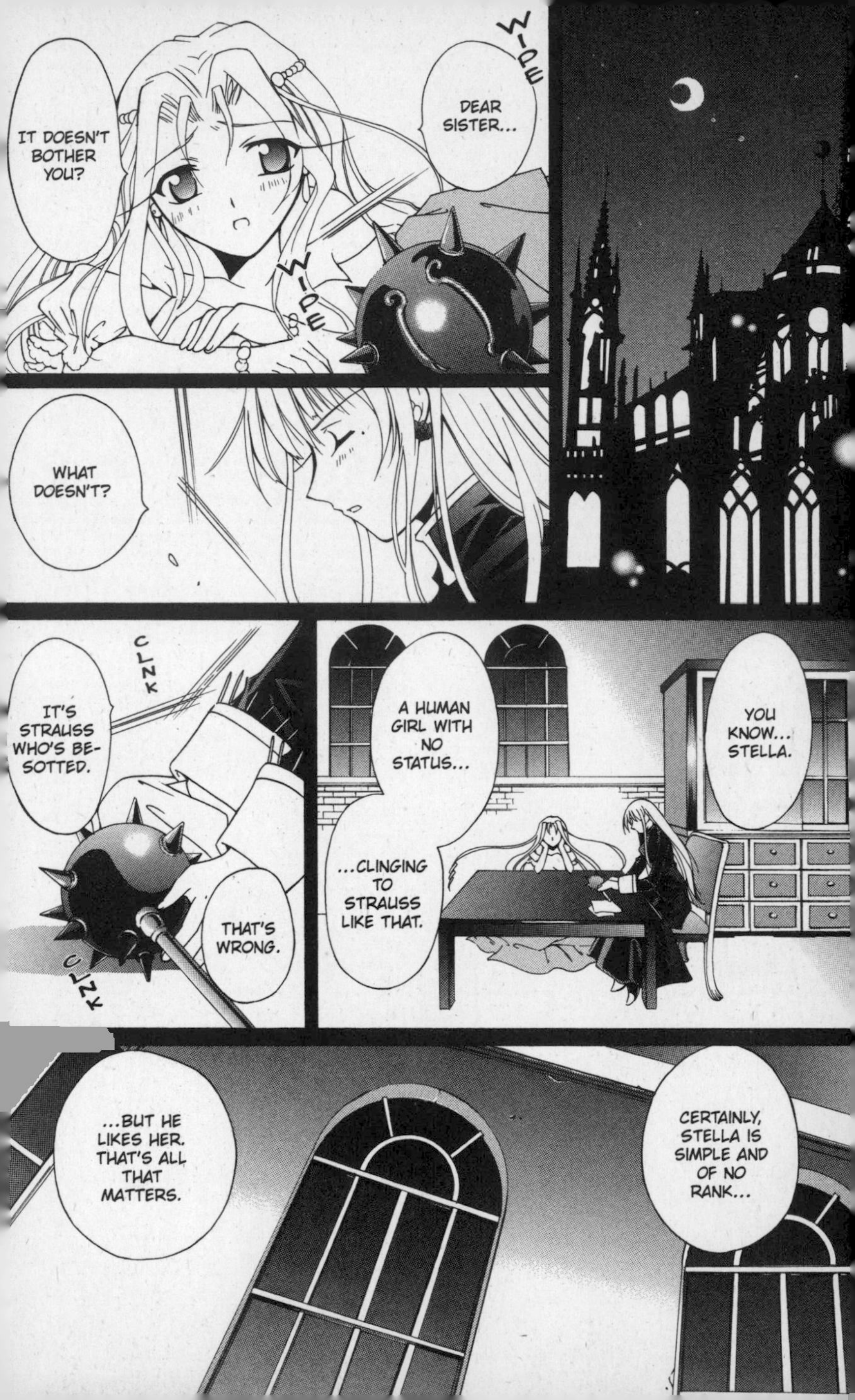
WIPE
DEAR SISTER...
IT DOESN'T BOTHER YOU?
WIPE
WHAT DOESN'T?
YOU KNOW... STELLA.
A HUMAN GIRL WITH NO STATUS...
...CLINGING TO STRAUSS LIKE THAT.
CLNK
IT'S STRAUSS WHO'S BE-SOTTED.
THAT'S WRONG.
CLNK
CERTAINLY, STELLA IS SIMPLE AND OF NO RANK...
...BUT HE LIKES HER. THAT'S ALL THAT MATTERS.

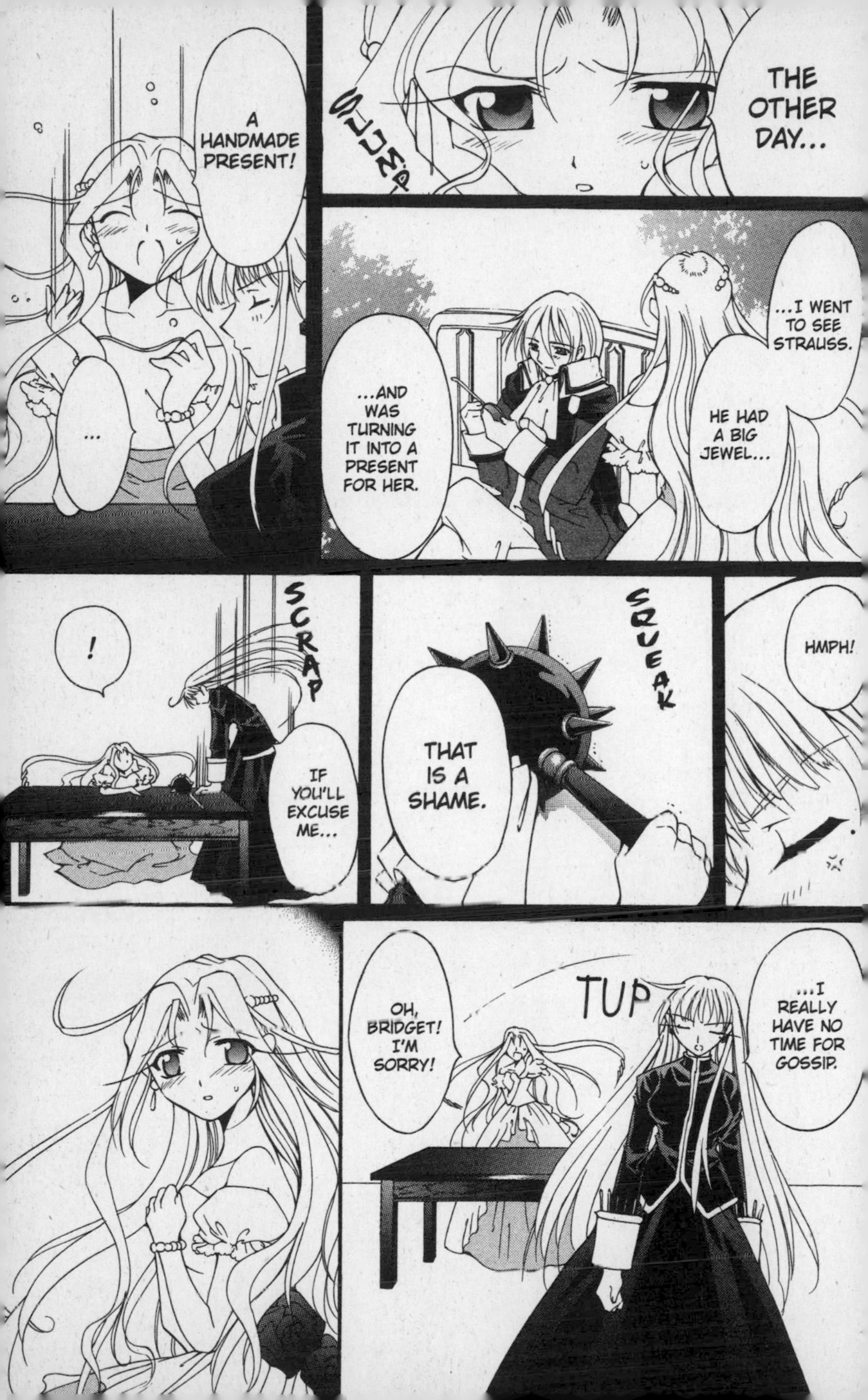

THE OTHER DAY...
SLUMP
...I WENT TO SEE STRAUSS.
HE HAD A BIG JEWEL...
...AND WAS TURNING IT INTO A PRESENT FOR HER.
A HANDMADE PRESENT!
...
HMPH!
SQUEAK
THAT IS A SHAME.
SCRAP
!
IF YOU'LL EXCUSE ME...
...I REALLY HAVE NO TIME FOR GOSSIP.
TUP
OH, BRIDGET! I'M SORRY!

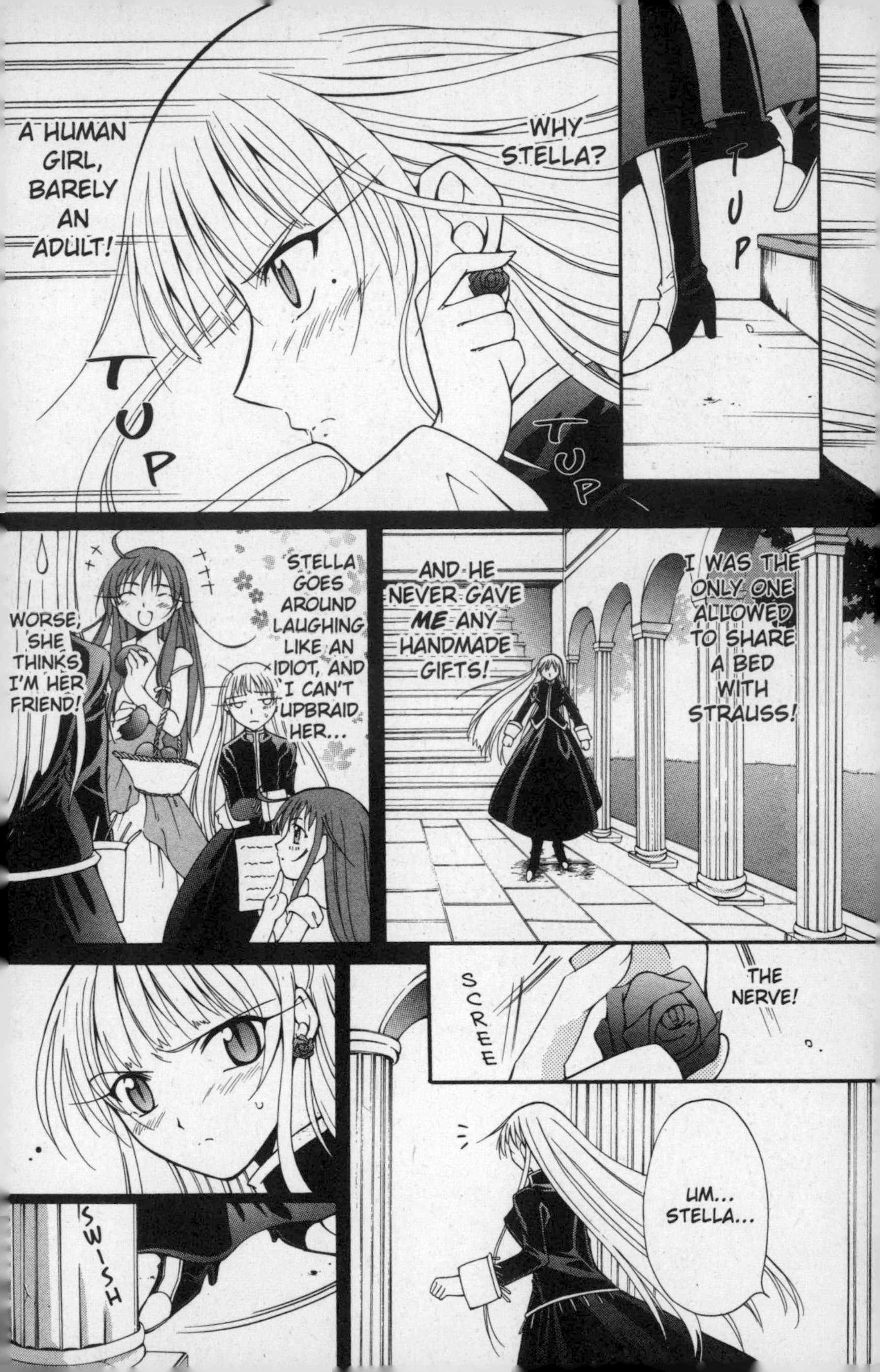
TUP
WHY STELLA?
TUP
A HUMAN GIRL, BARELY AN ADULT!
TUP
I WAS THE ONLY ONE ALLOWED TO SHARE A BED WITH STRAUSS!
AND HE NEVER GAVE ME ANY HANDMADE GIFTS!
STELLA GOES AROUND LAUGHING LIKE AN IDIOT, AND I CAN'T UPBRAID HER...
WORSE, SHE THINKS I'M HER FRIEND!
THE NERVE!
SCREE
UM... STELLA...
SWISH

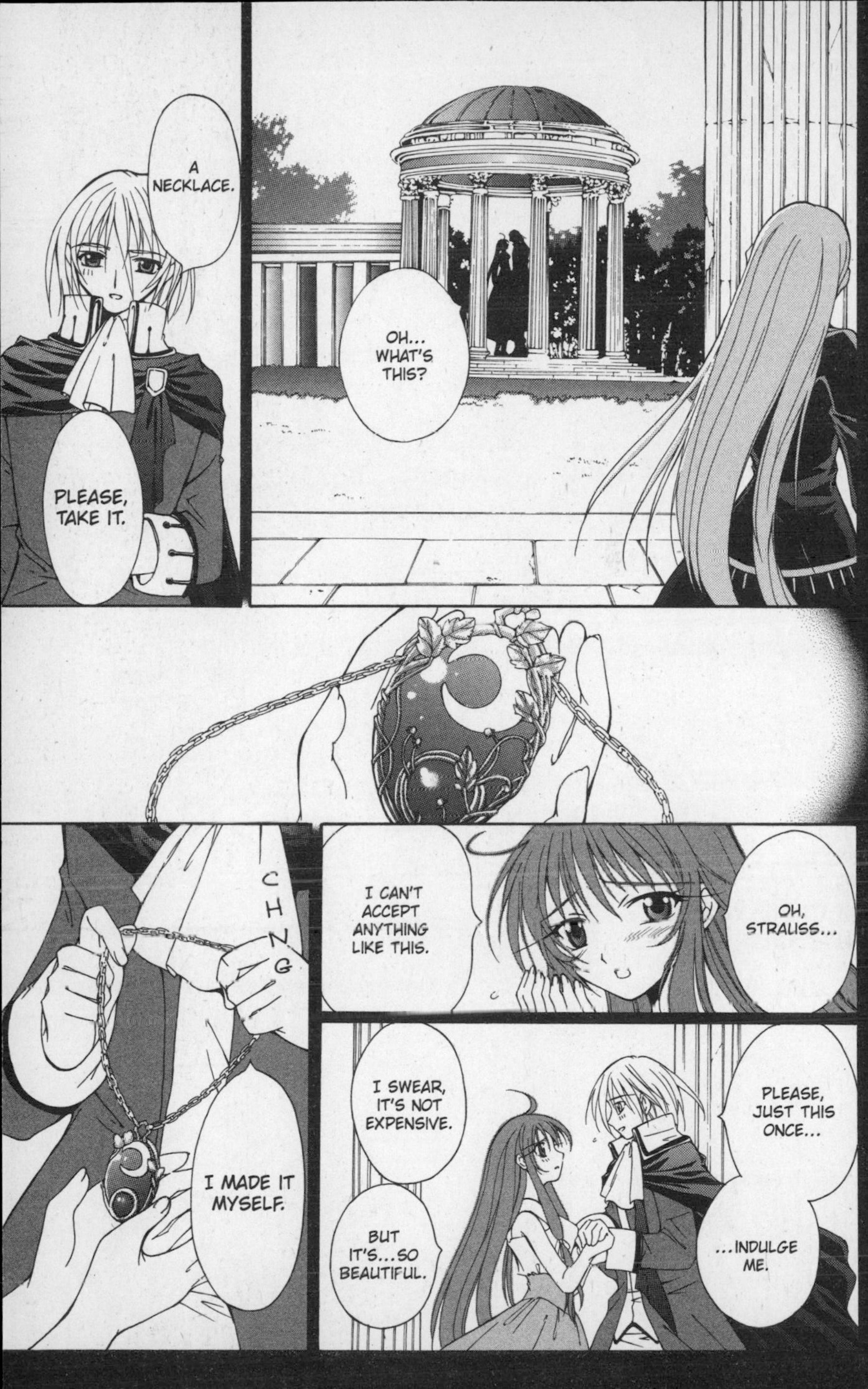
OH... WHAT'S THIS?
A NECKLACE.
PLEASE, TAKE IT.
OH, STRAUSS...
I CAN'T ACCEPT ANYTHING LIKE THIS.
PLEASE, JUST THIS ONCE...
I SWEAR, IT'S NOT EXPENSIVE.
...INDULGE ME.
BUT IT'S...SO BEAUTIFUL.
CHNG
I MADE IT MYSELF.

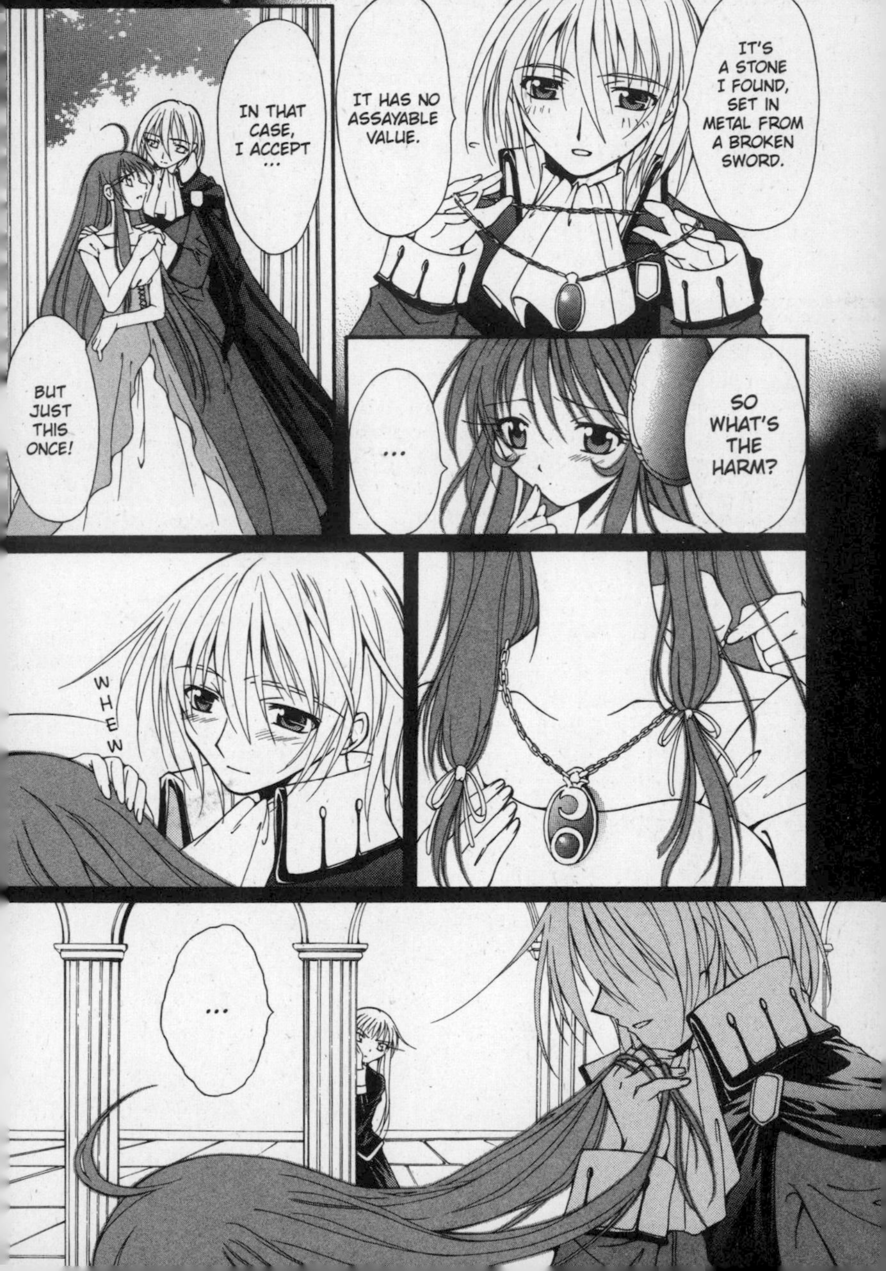
IT'S A STONE I FOUND, SET IN METAL FROM A BROKEN SWORD.
IT HAS NO ASSAYABLE VALUE.
SO WHAT'S THE HARM?
...
IN THAT CASE, I ACCEPT ...
BUT JUST THIS ONCE!
WHEW
...

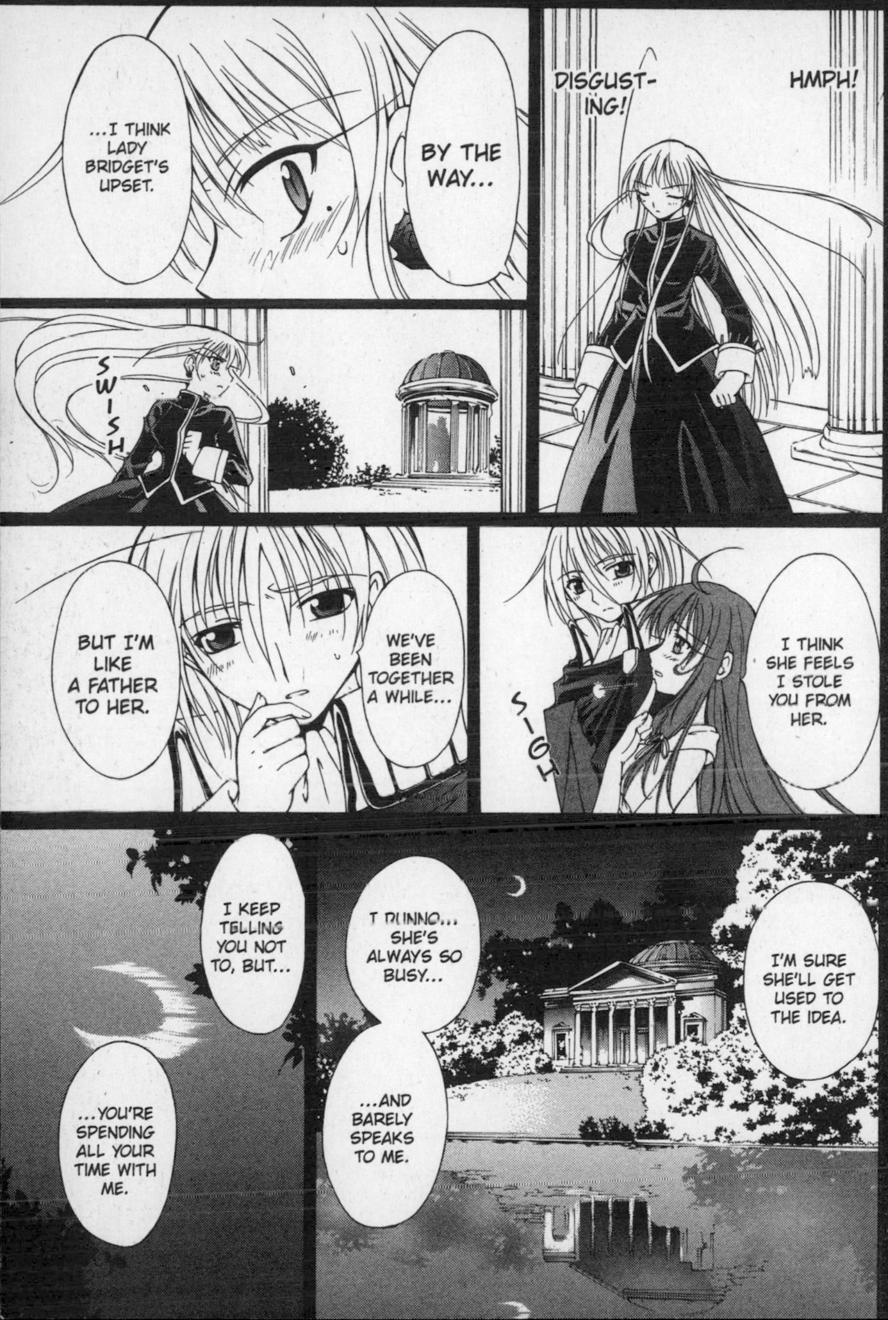
HMPH!
DISGUST-ING!
BY THE WAY...
...I THINK LADY BRIDGET'S UPSET.
SWISH
I THINK SHE FEELS I STOLE YOU FROM HER.
SIGH
WE'VE BEEN TOGETHER A WHILE...
BUT I'M LIKE A FATHER TO HER.
I'M SURE SHE'LL GET USED TO THE IDEA.
I DUNNO... SHE'S ALWAYS SO BUSY...
...AND BARELY SPEAKS TO ME.
I KEEP TELLING YOU NOT TO, BUT...
...YOU'RE SPENDING ALL YOUR TIME WITH ME.

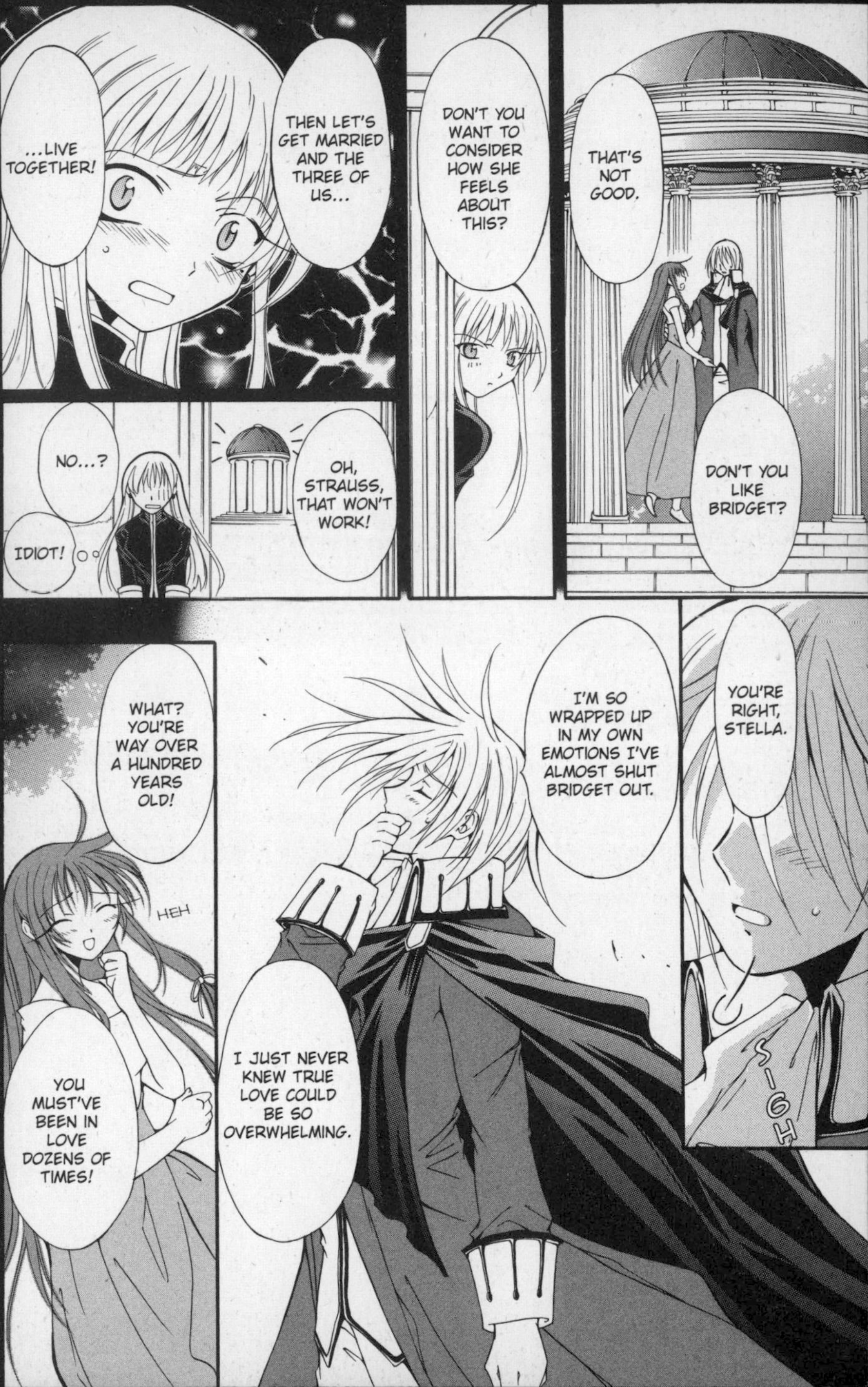
THAT'S NOT GOOD.
DON'T YOU LIKE BRIDGET?
DON'T YOU WANT TO CONSIDER HOW SHE FEELS ABOUT THIS?
THEN LET'S GET MARRIED AND THE THREE OF US...
...LIVE TOGETHER!
OH, STRAUSS, THAT WON'T WORK!
NO...?
IDIOT!
YOU'RE RIGHT, STELLA.
S-I-G-H
I'M SO WRAPPED UP IN MY OWN EMOTIONS I'VE ALMOST SHUT BRIDGET OUT.
I JUST NEVER KNEW TRUE LOVE COULD BE SO OVERWHELMING.
WHAT? YOU'RE WAY OVER A HUNDRED YEARS OLD!
HEH
YOU MUST'VE BEEN IN LOVE DOZENS OF TIMES!

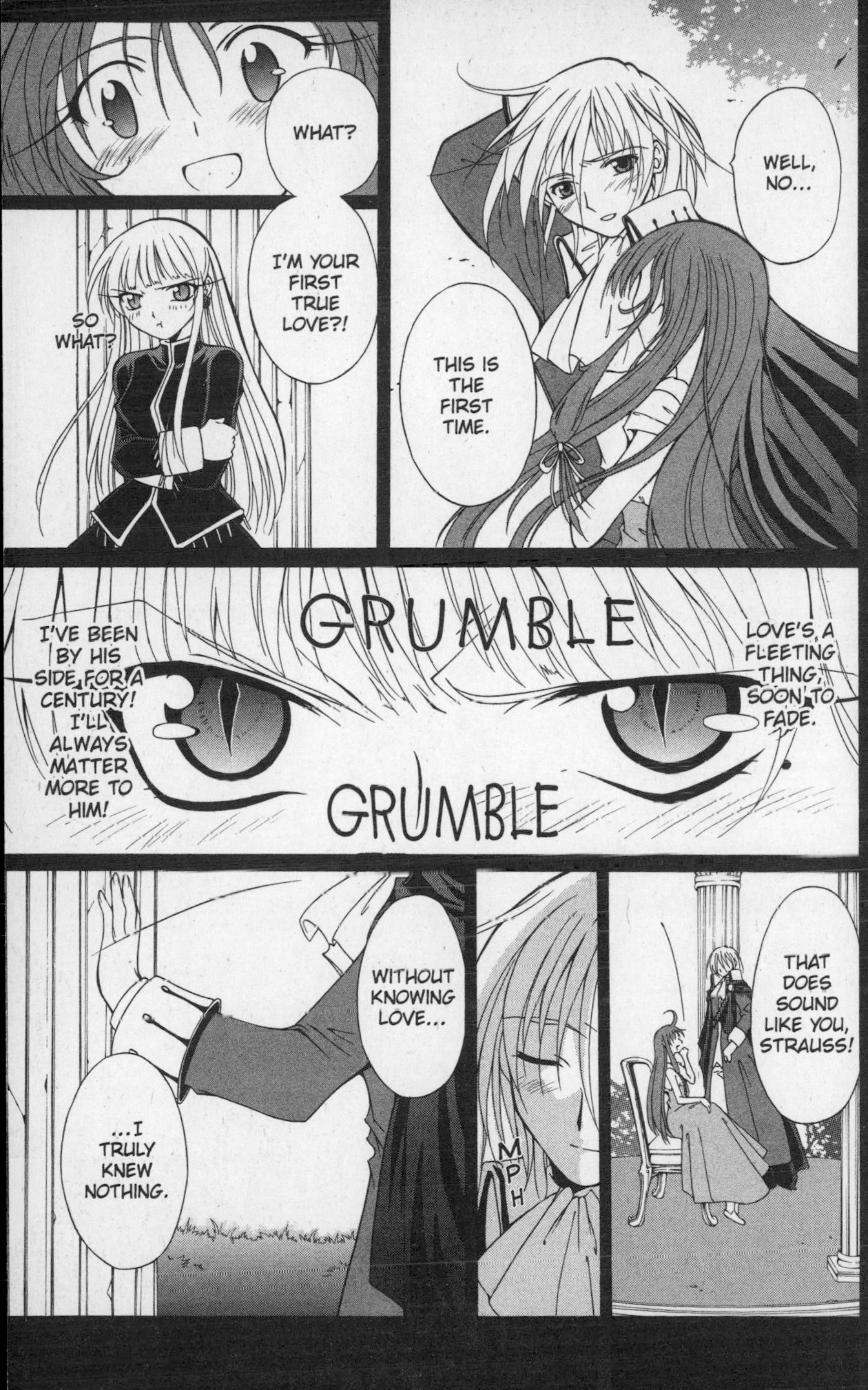
WELL, NO...
THIS IS THE FIRST TIME.
WHAT?
I'M YOUR FIRST TRUE LOVE?!
SO WHAT?
GRUMBLE
LOVE'S A FLEETING THING, SOON TO FADE.
I'VE BEEN BY HIS SIDE FOR A CENTURY! I'LL ALWAYS MATTER MORE TO HIM!
GRUMBLE
THAT DOES SOUND LIKE YOU, STRAUSS!
MPH
WITHOUT KNOWING LOVE...
...I TRULY KNEW NOTHING.

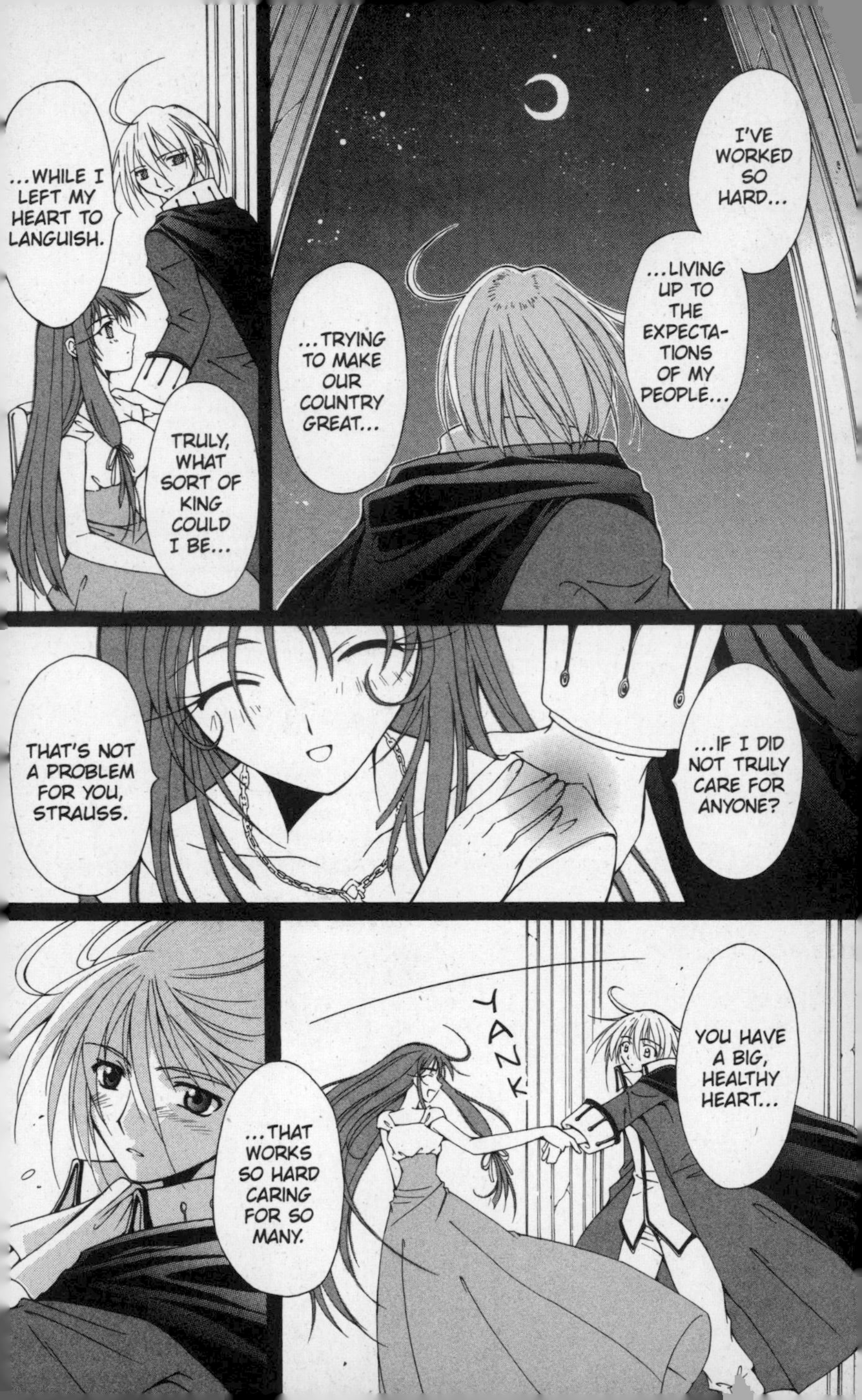
I'VE WORKED SO HARD...
...LIVING UP TO THE EXPECTATIONS OF MY PEOPLE...
...TRYING TO MAKE OUR COUNTRY GREAT...
...WHILE I LEFT MY HEART TO LANGUISH.
TRULY, WHAT SORT OF KING COULD I BE...
...IF I DID NOT TRULY CARE FOR ANYONE?
THAT'S NOT A PROBLEM FOR YOU, STRAUSS.
YOU HAVE A BIG, HEALTHY HEART...
YANK
...THAT WORKS SO HARD CARING FOR SO MANY.

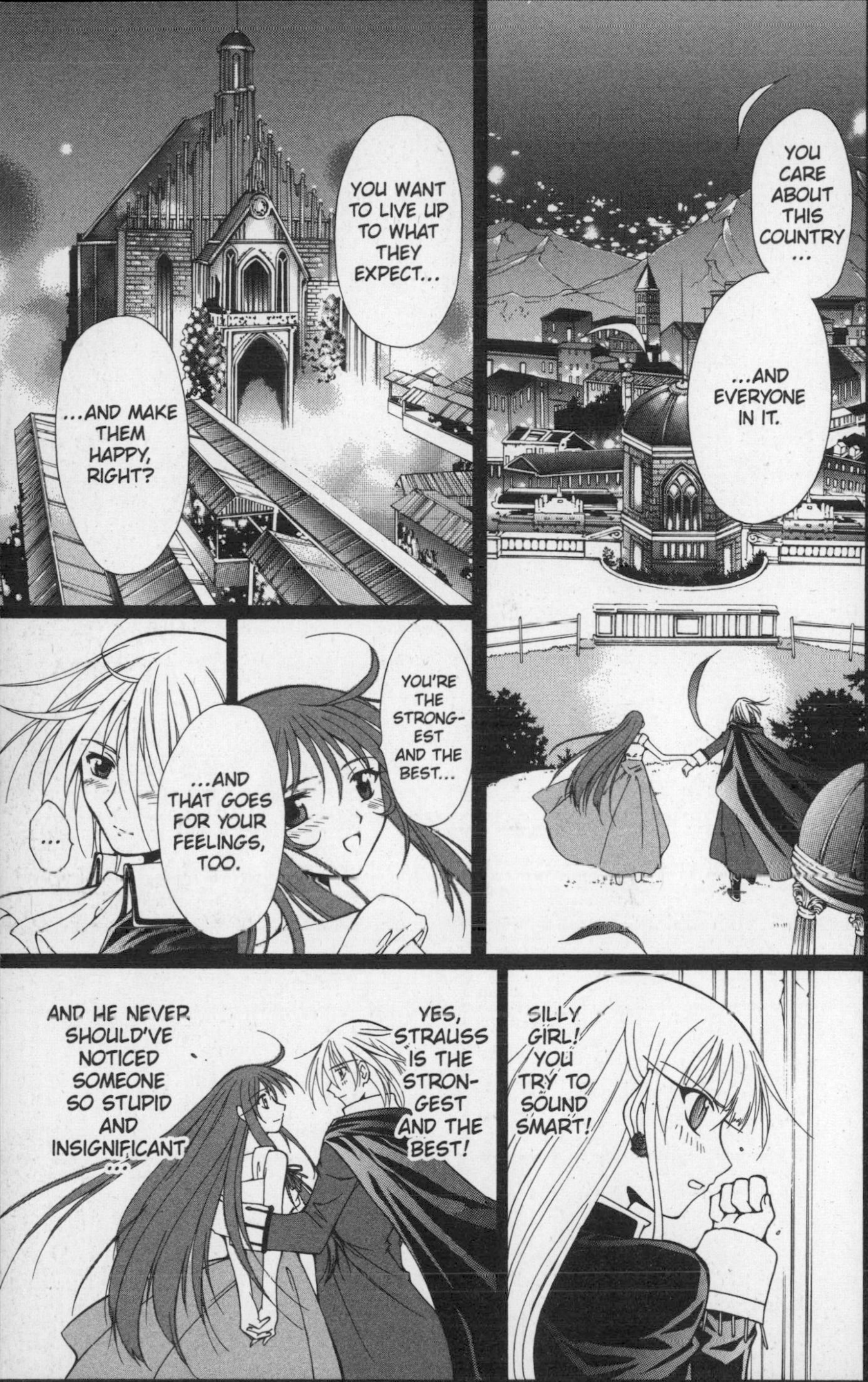

YOU CARE ABOUT THIS COUNTRY...
...AND EVERYONE IN IT.
YOU WANT TO LIVE UP TO WHAT THEY EXPECT...
...AND MAKE THEM HAPPY, RIGHT?
YOU'RE THE STRONG-EST AND THE BEST...
...AND THAT GOES FOR YOUR FEELINGS, TOO.
...
SILLY GIRL! YOU TRY TO SOUND SMART!
YES, STRAUSS IS THE STRON-GEST AND THE BEST!
AND HE NEVER SHOULD'VE NOTICED SOMEONE SO STUPID AND INSIGNIFICANT...

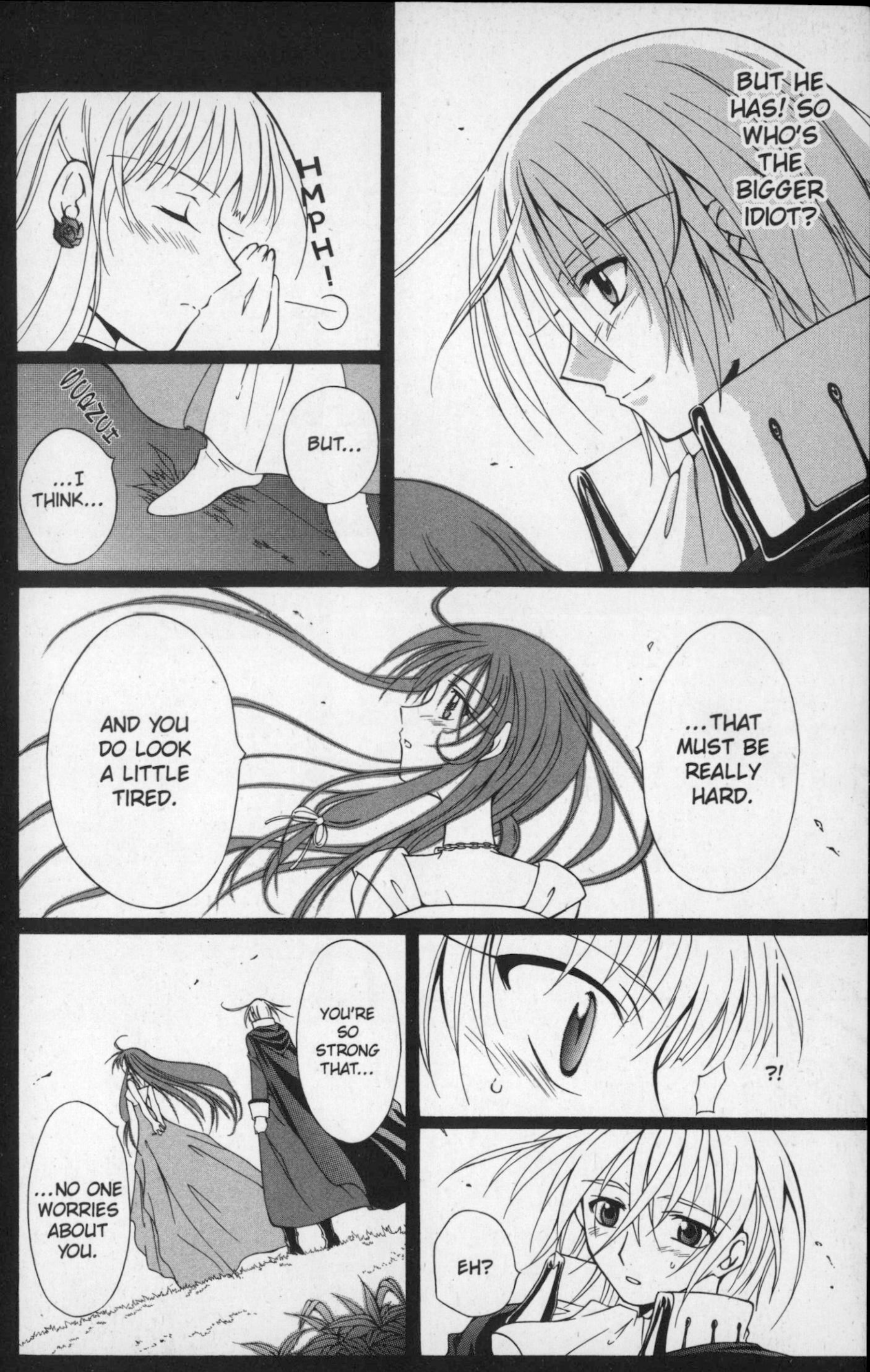
BUT HE HAS! SO WHO'S THE BIGGER IDIOT?
HMPH!
BUT...
...I THINK...
...THAT MUST BE REALLY HARD.
AND YOU DO LOOK A LITTLE TIRED.
?!
EH?
YOU'RE SO STRONG THAT...
...NO ONE WORRIES ABOUT YOU.

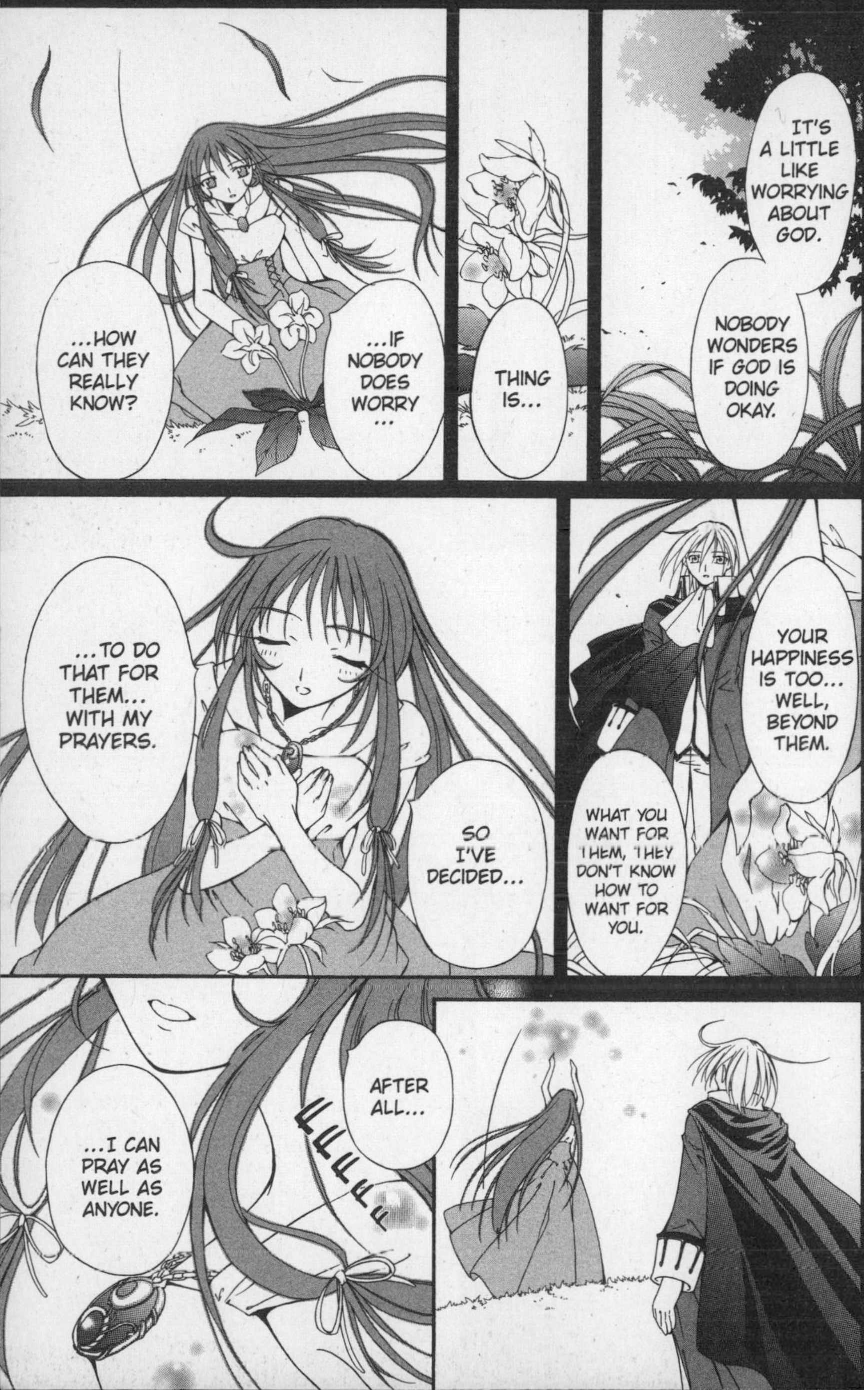
IT'S A LITTLE LIKE WORRYING ABOUT GOD.
NOBODY WONDERS IF GOD IS DOING OKAY.
THING IS...
...IF NOBODY DOES WORRY ...
...HOW CAN THEY REALLY KNOW?
YOUR HAPPINESS IS TOO... WELL, BEYOND THEM.
WHAT YOU WANT FOR THEM, THEY DON'T KNOW HOW TO WANT FOR YOU.
SO I'VE DECIDED...
...TO DO THAT FOR THEM... WITH MY PRAYERS.
AFTER ALL...
...I CAN PRAY AS WELL AS ANYONE.

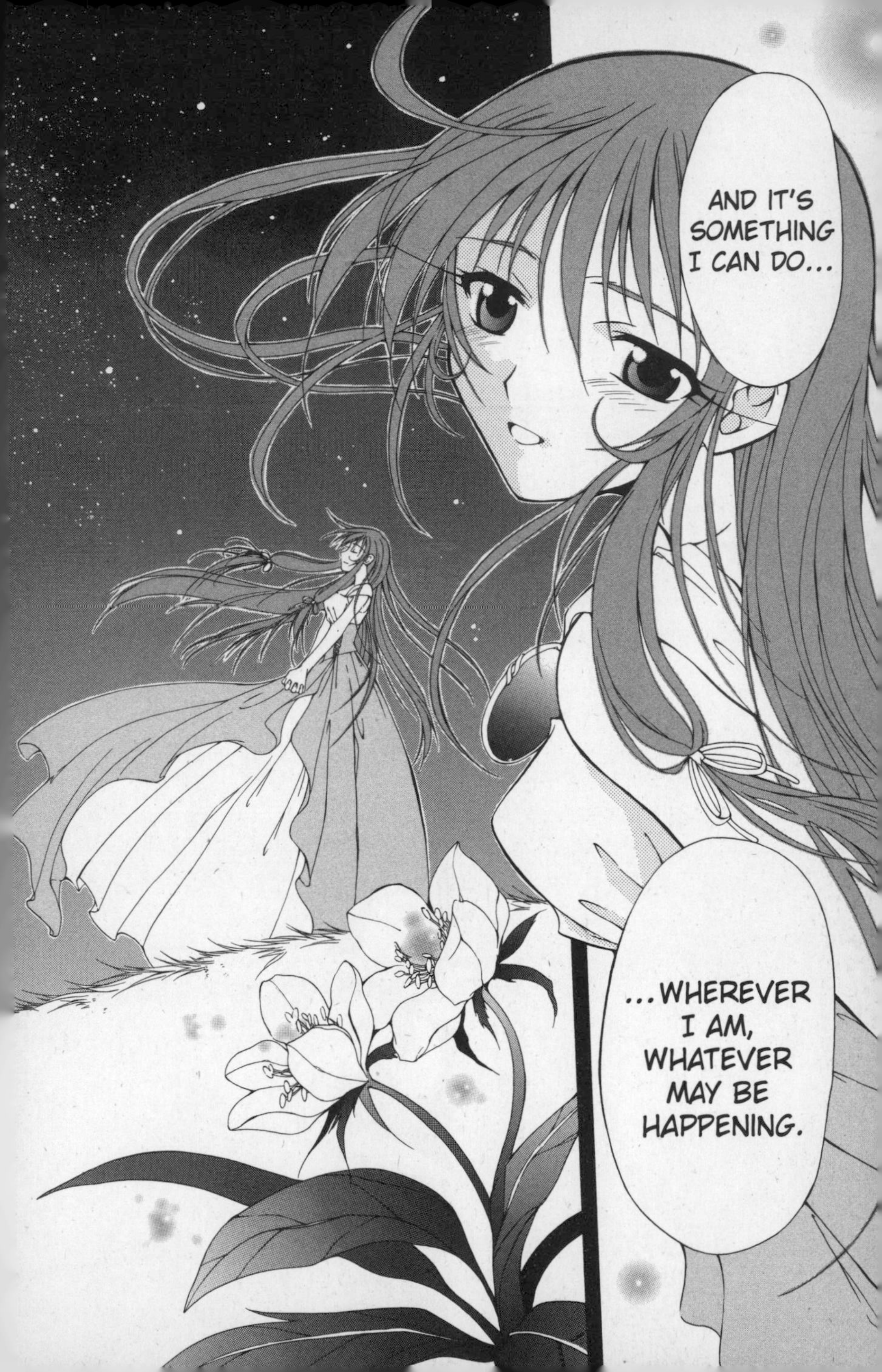
AND IT'S SOMETHING I CAN DO...
...WHEREVER I AM, WHATEVER MAY BE HAPPENING.

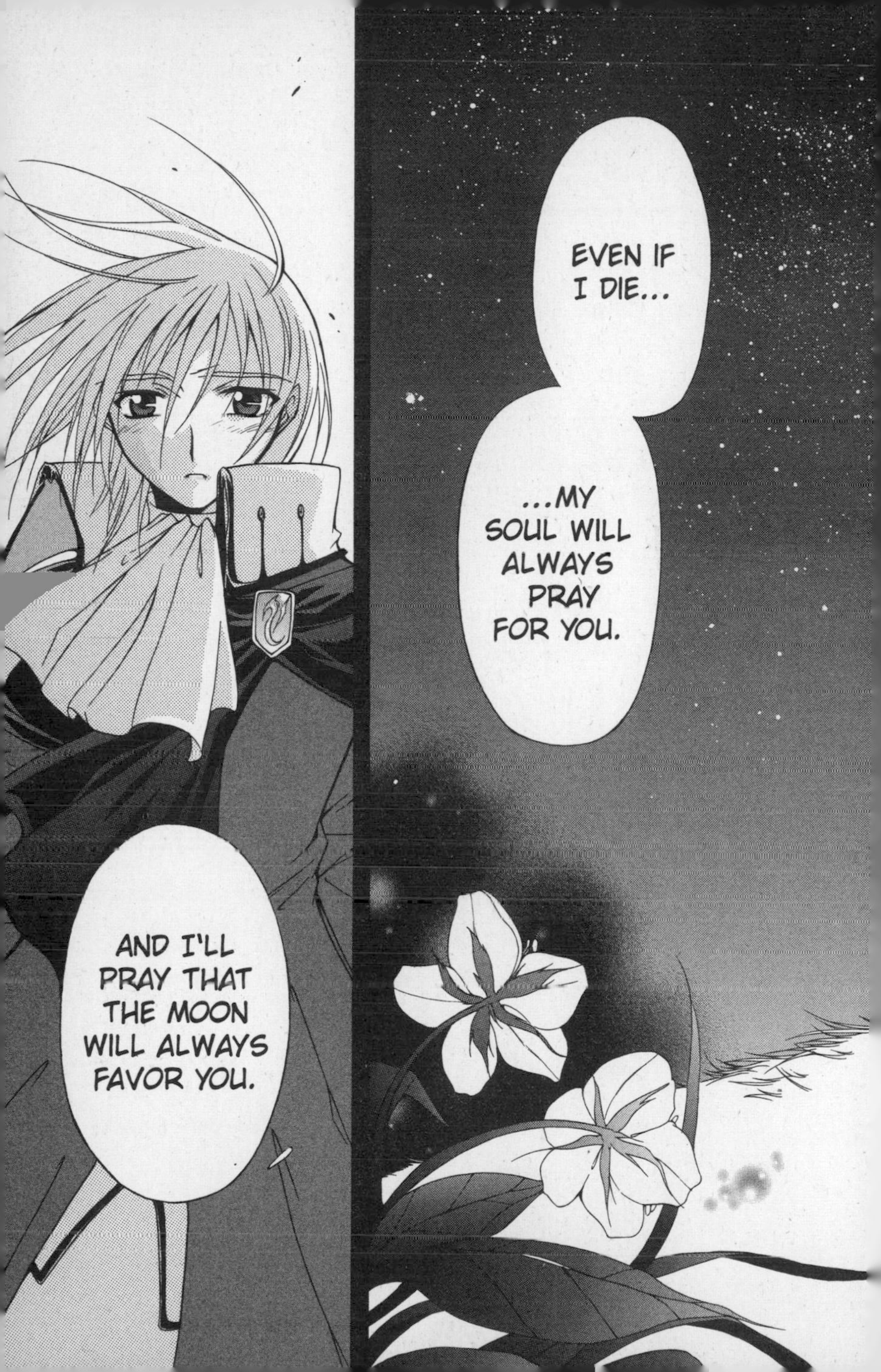
EVEN IF I DIE...
...MY SOUL WILL ALWAYS PRAY FOR YOU.
AND I'LL PRAY THAT THE MOON WILL ALWAYS FAVOR YOU.

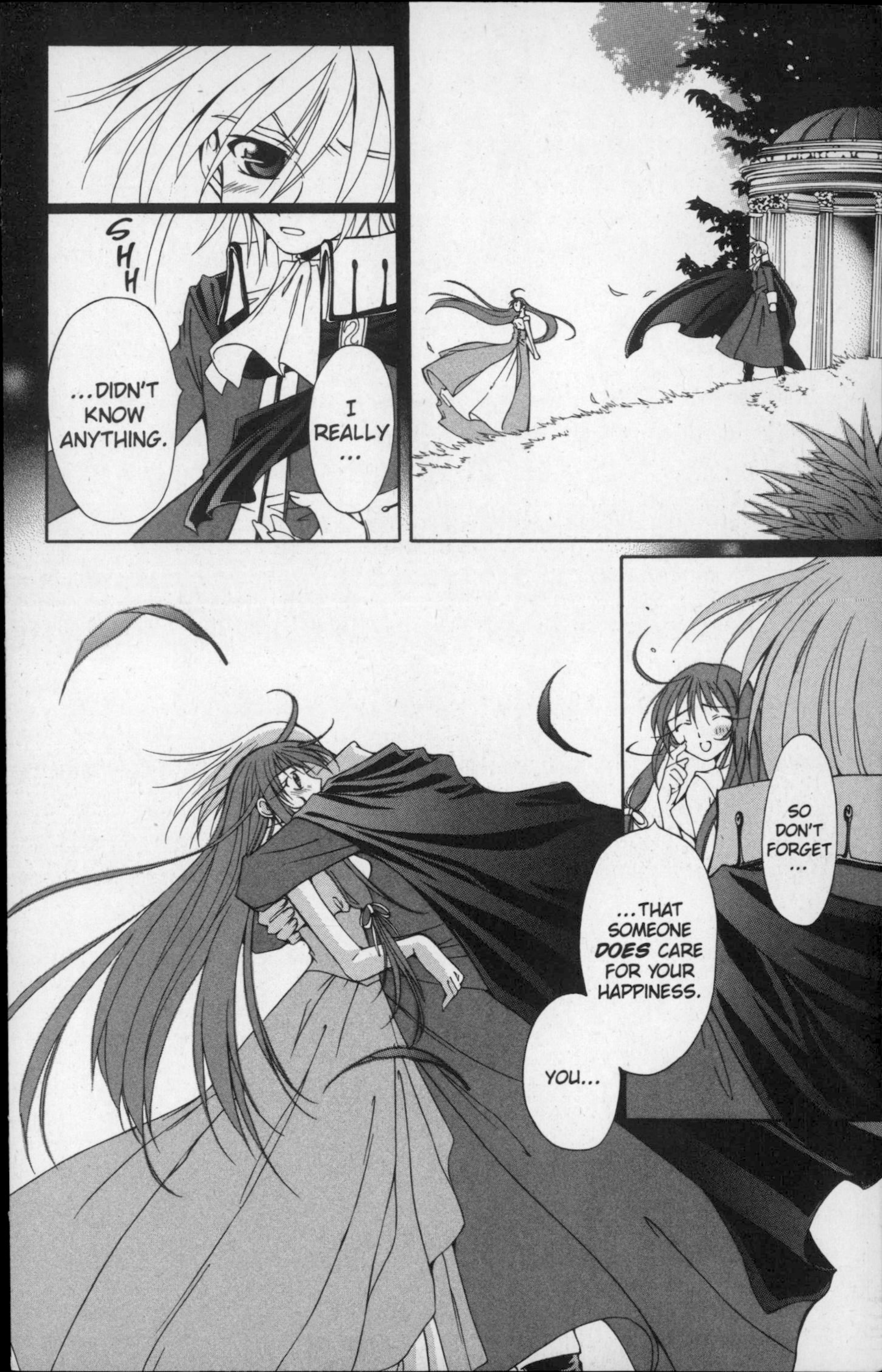
I REALLY...
...DIDN'T KNOW ANYTHING.
SHH
SO DON'T FORGET...
...THAT SOMEONE DOES CARE FOR YOUR HAPPINESS.
YOU...

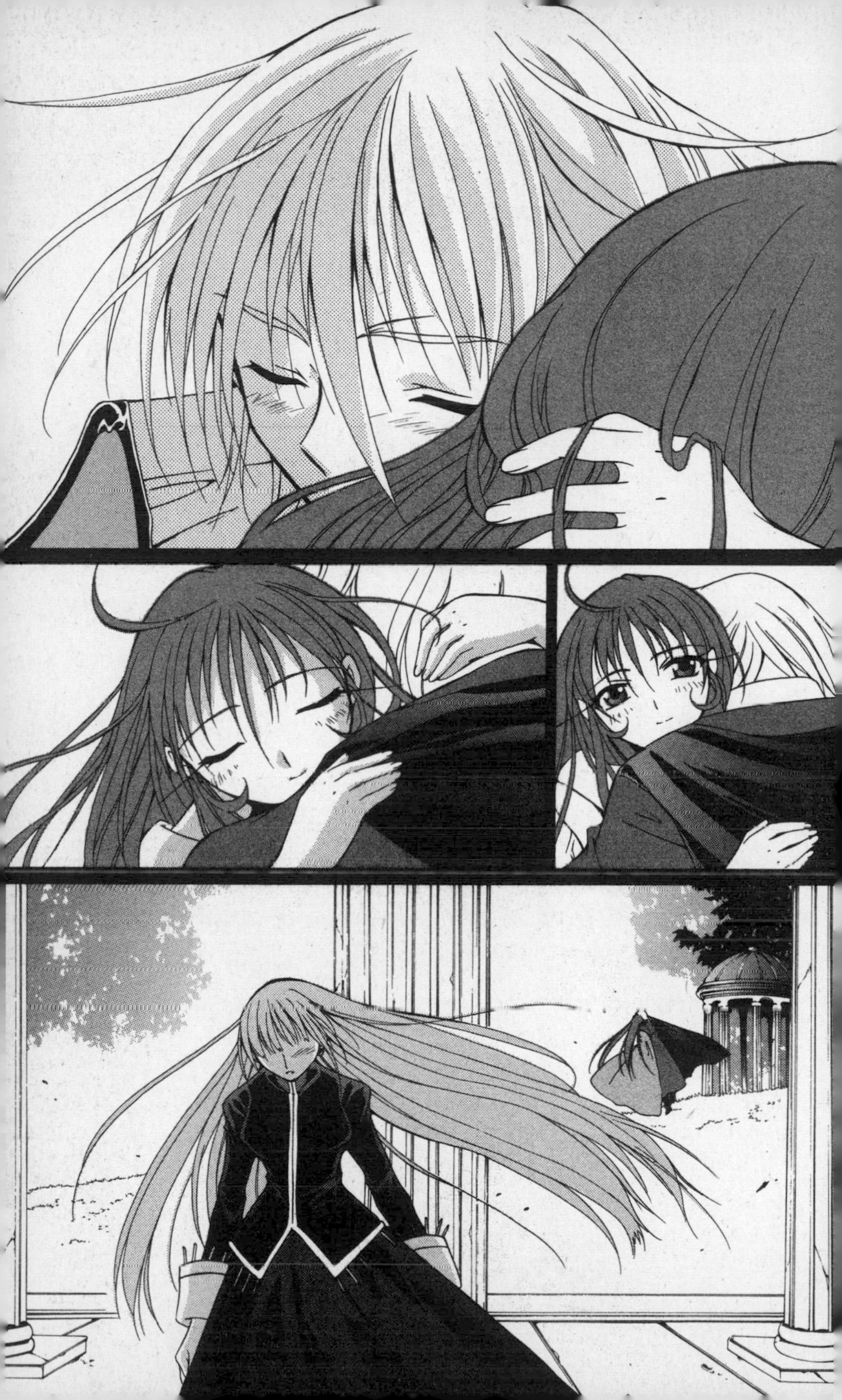

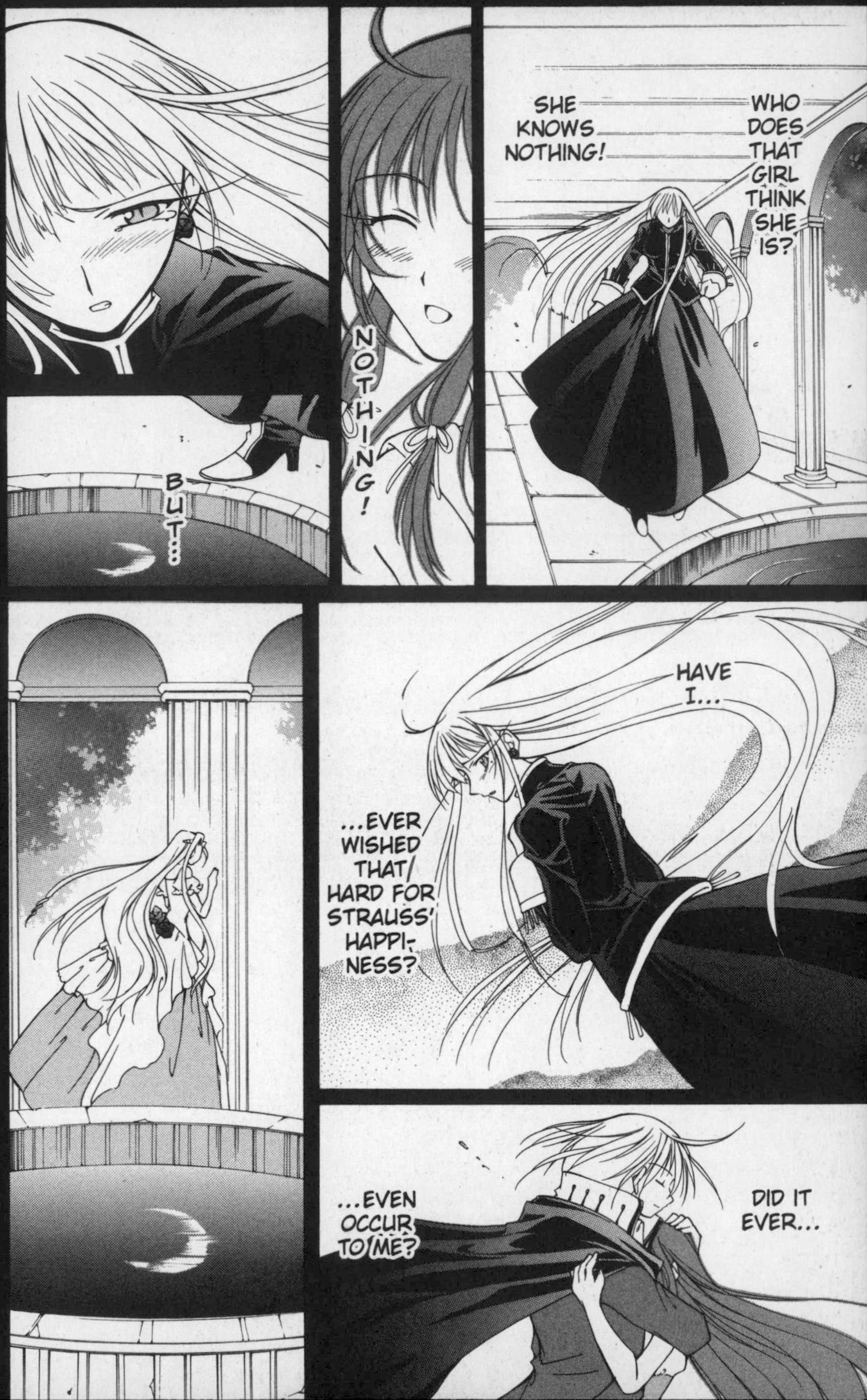
WHO DOES THAT GIRL THINK SHE IS?
SHE KNOWS NOTHING!
NOTHING!
BUT...
HAVE I...
...EVER WISHED THAT HARD FOR STRAUSS' HAPPINESS?
DID IT EVER...
...EVEN OCCUR TO ME?

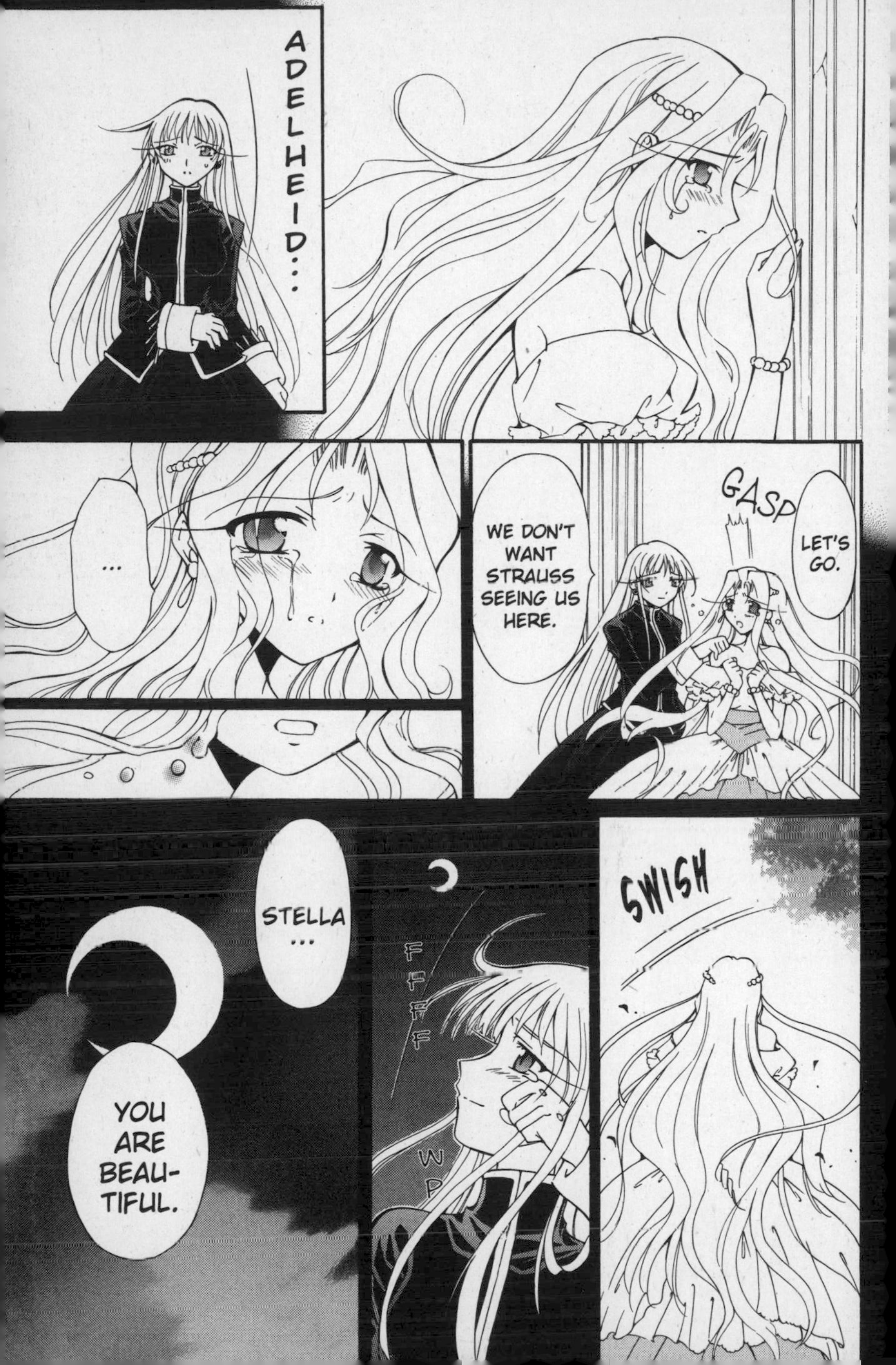
ADELHEID...
GASP
LET'S GO.
WE DON'T WANT STRAUSS SEEING US HERE.
...
SWISH
FFFF
WP
STELLA...
YOU ARE BEAUTIFUL.

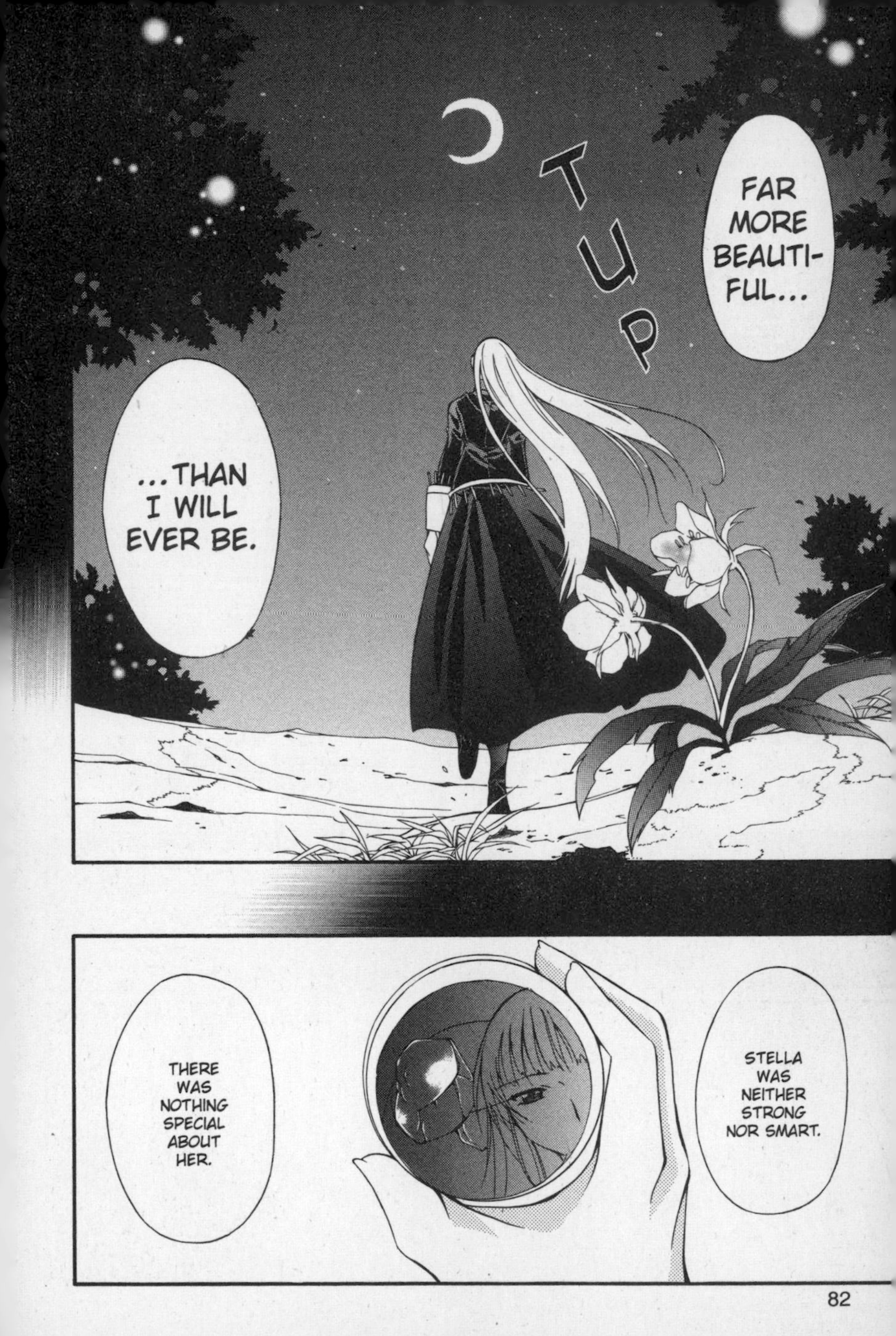
FAR MORE BEAUTIFUL...
TUP
...THAN I WILL EVER BE.
STELLA WAS NEITHER STRONG NOR SMART.
THERE WAS NOTHING SPECIAL ABOUT HER.

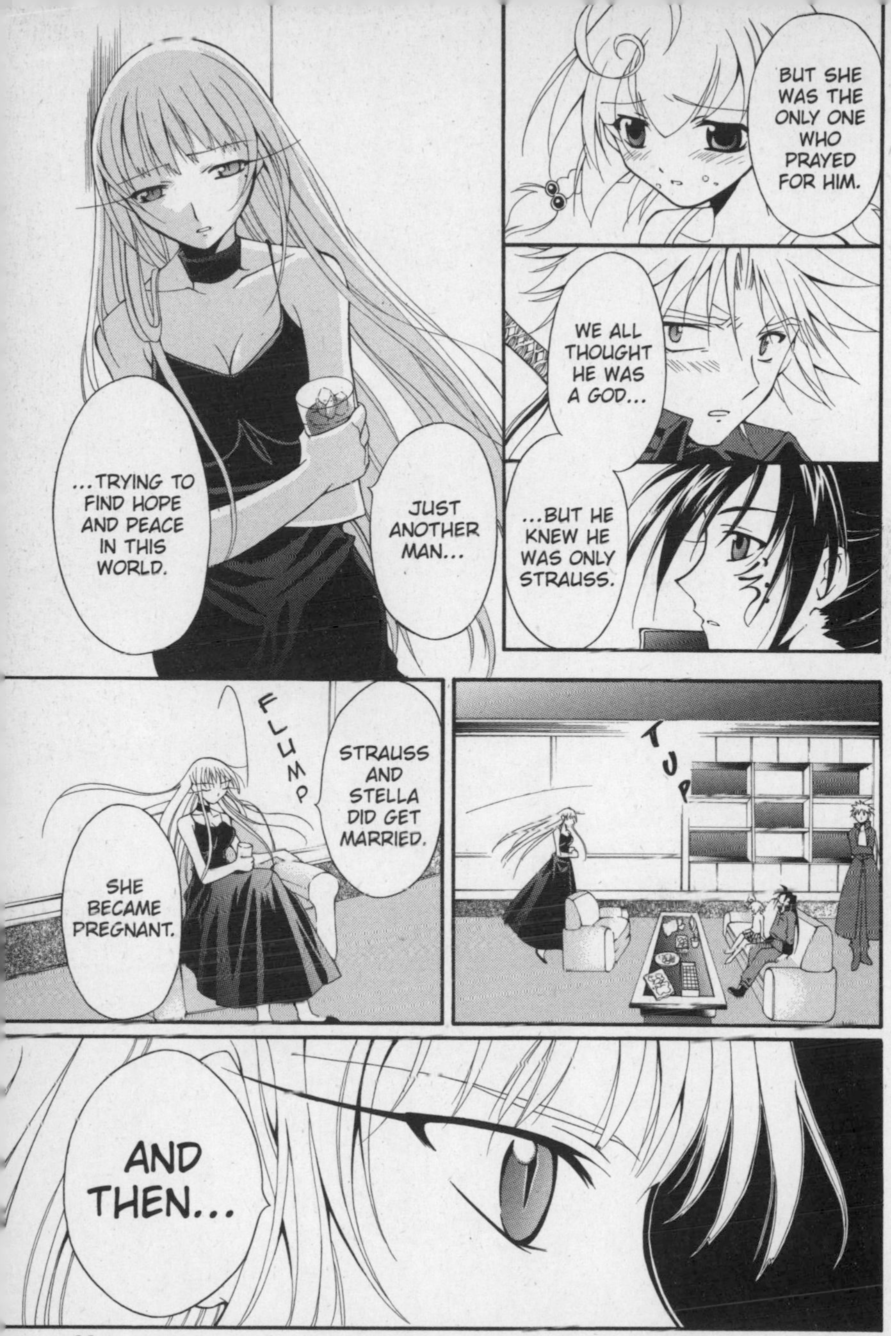
BUT SHE WAS THE ONLY ONE WHO PRAYED FOR HIM.
WE ALL THOUGHT HE WAS A GOD...
...BUT HE KNEW HE WAS ONLY STRAUSS.
JUST ANOTHER MAN...
...TRYING TO FIND HOPE AND PEACE IN THIS WORLD.
TUP
FLUMP
STRAUSS AND STELLA DID GET MARRIED.
SHE BECAME PREGNANT.
AND THEN...

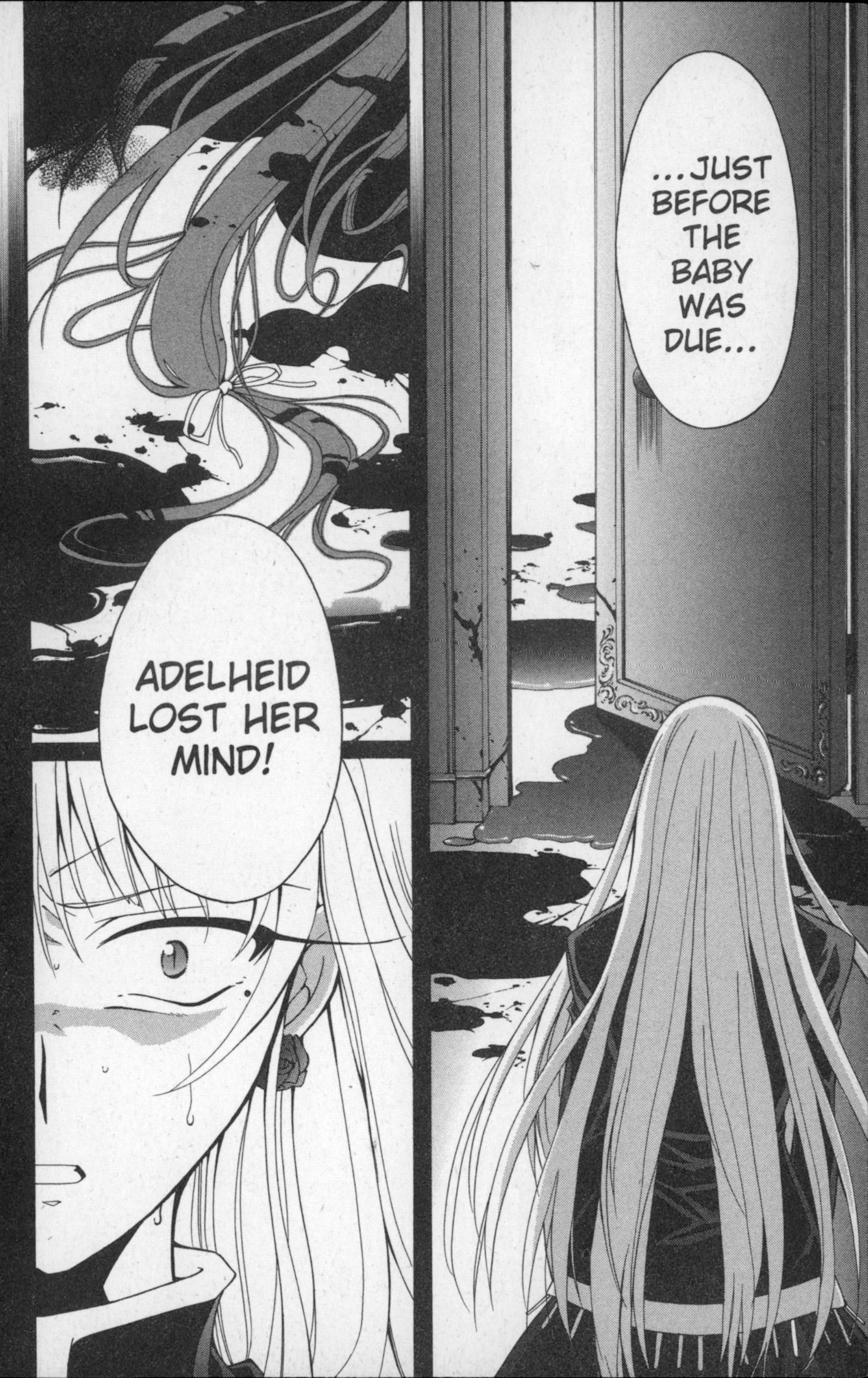
...JUST BEFORE THE BABY WAS DUE...
ADELHEID LOST HER MIND!

THE RECORD OF A

FALLEN VAMPIRE

THE RECORD OF A

FALLEN VAMPIRE

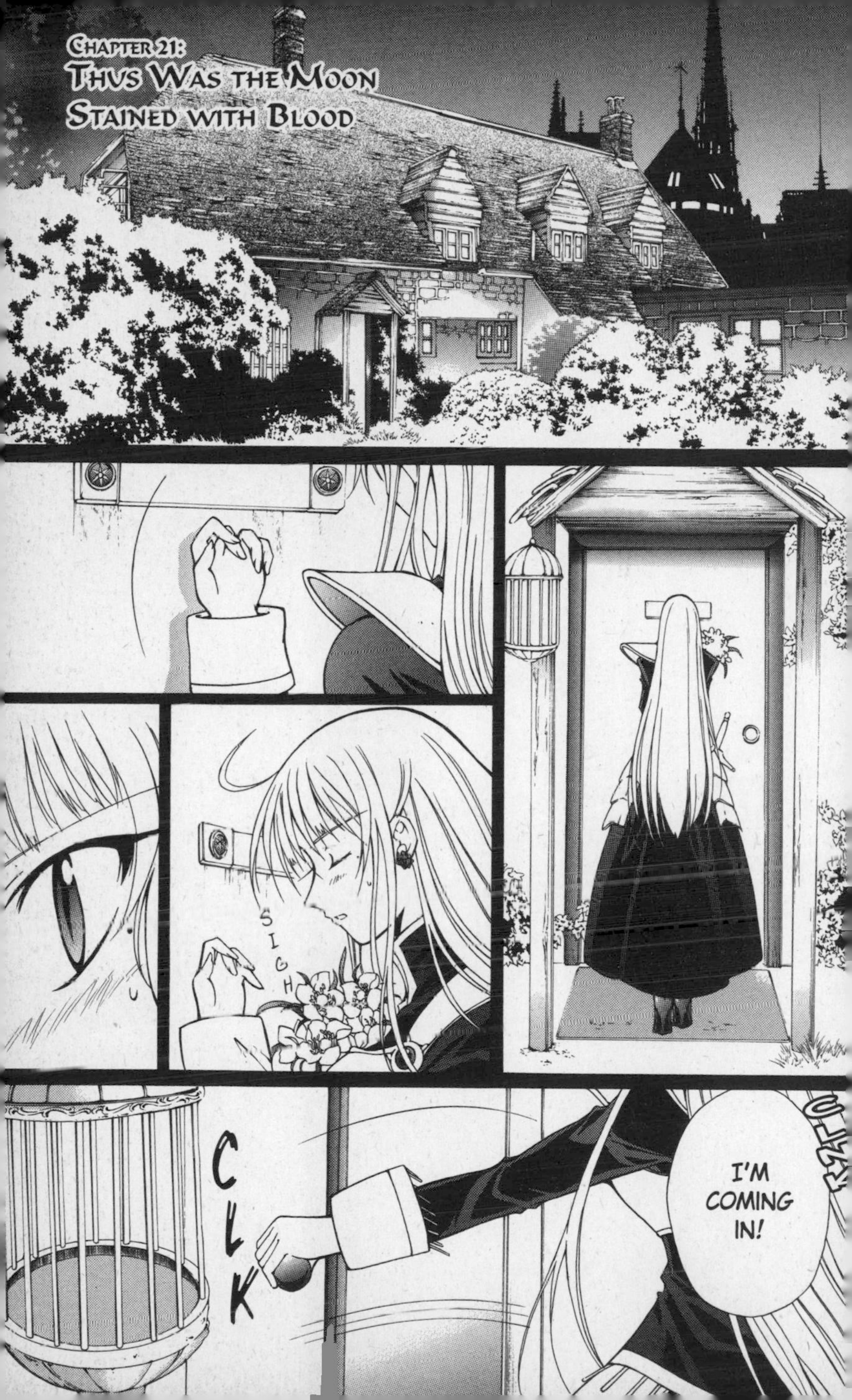
Chapter 21:
Thus Was the Moon Stained with Blood
SIGH
I'M COMING IN!
CLK

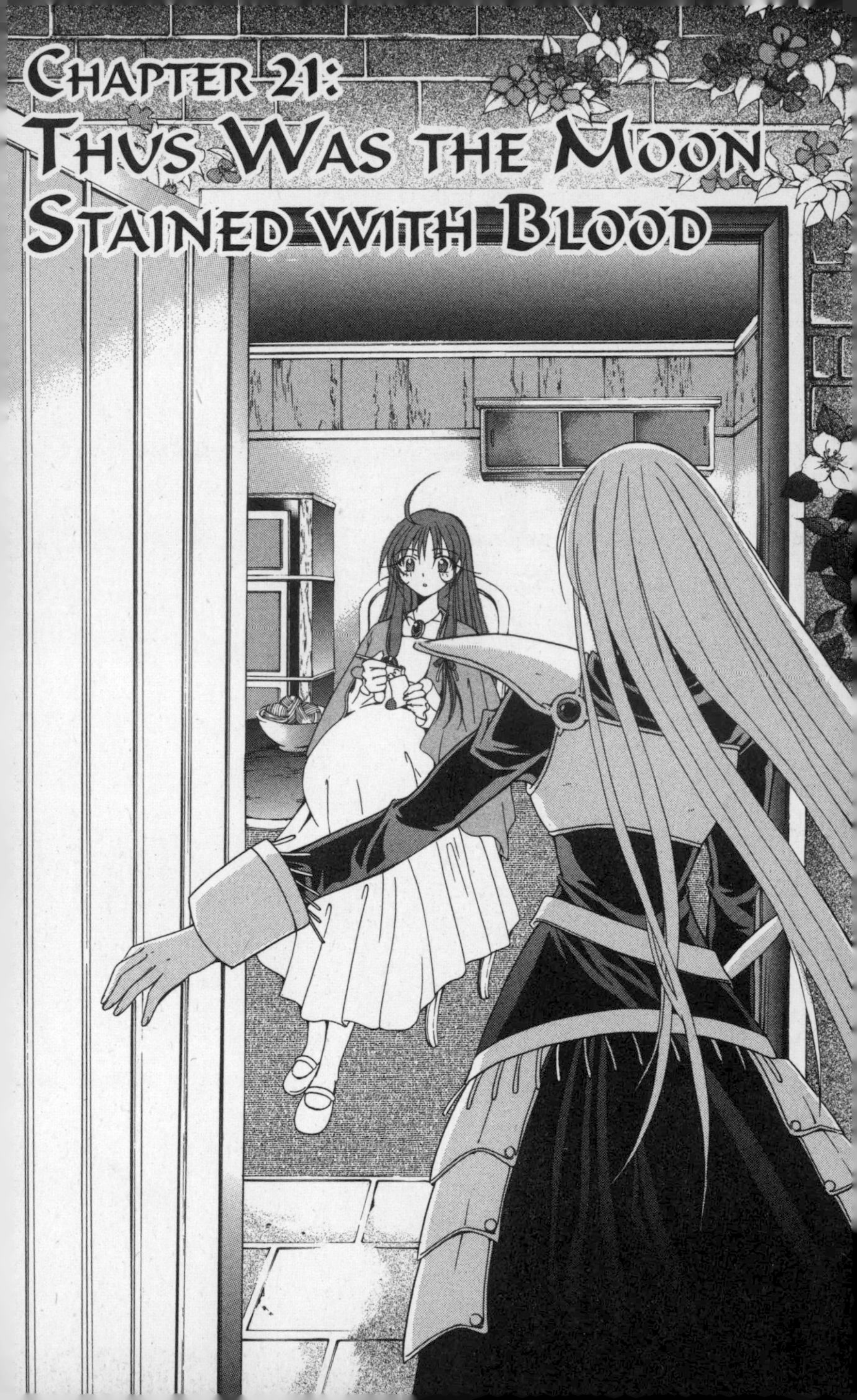
Chapter 21:
Thus Was the Moon Stained with Blood

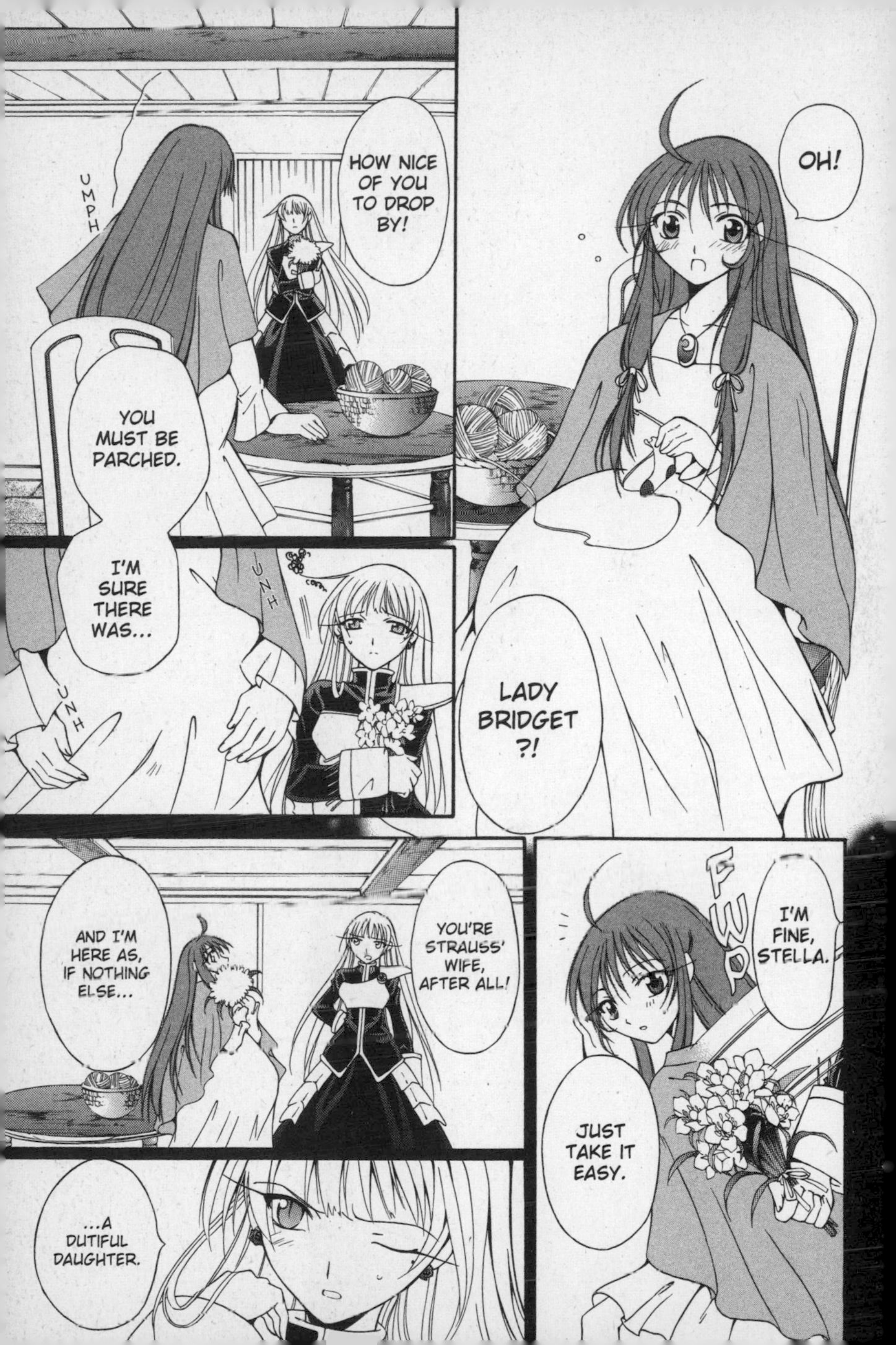
OH!
LADY BRIDGET ?!
HOW NICE OF YOU TO DROP BY!
UMPH
YOU MUST BE PARCHED.
UNH
I'M SURE THERE WAS...
UNH
FWAP
I'M FINE, STELLA.
JUST TAKE IT EASY.
YOU'RE STRAUSS' WIFE, AFTER ALL!
AND I'M HERE AS, IF NOTHING ELSE...
...A DUTIFUL DAUGHTER.

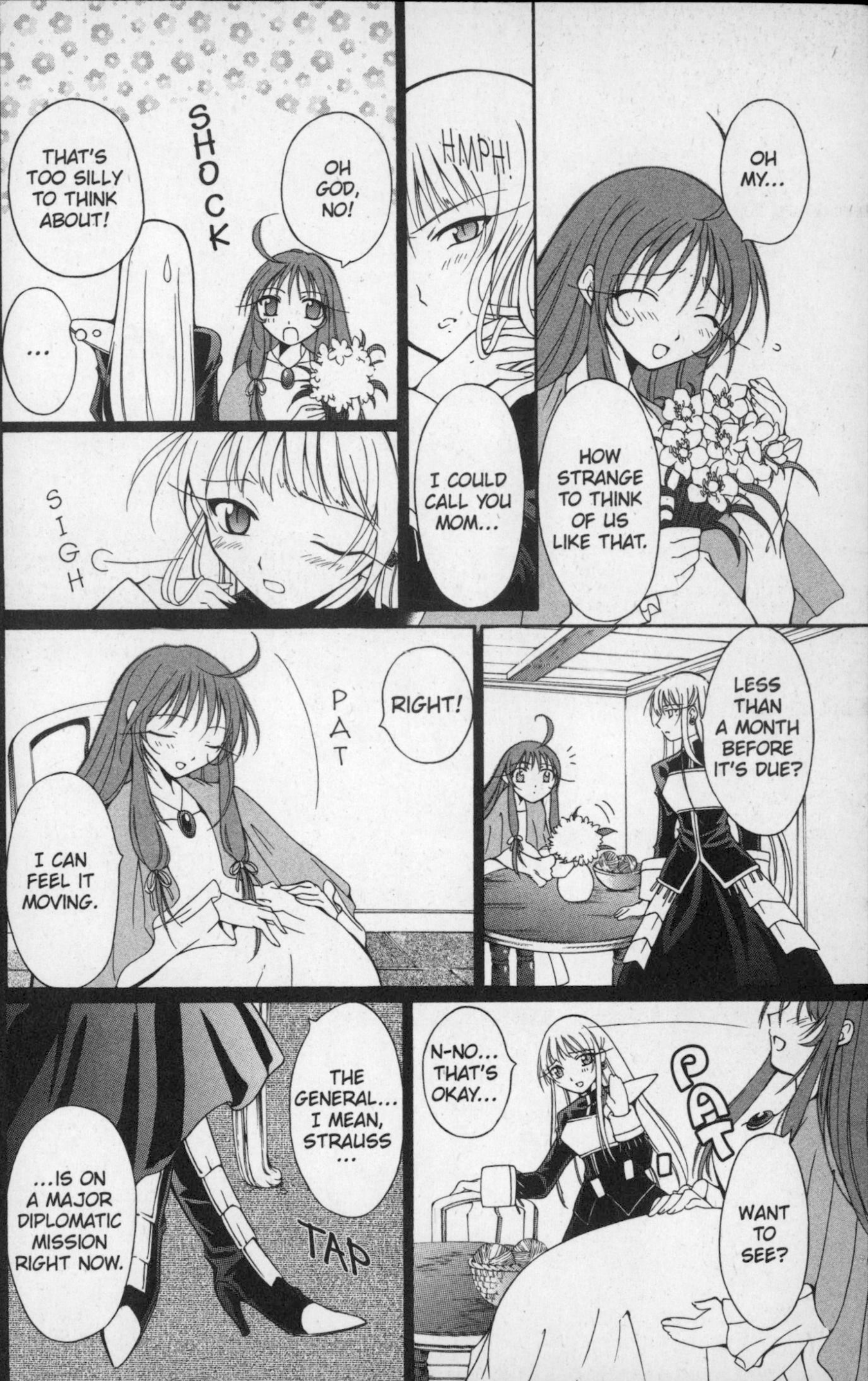

OH MY...
HOW STRANGE TO THINK OF US LIKE THAT.
HMPH!
I COULD CALL YOU MOM...
OH GOD, NO!
SHOCK
THAT'S TOO SILLY TO THINK ABOUT!
...
SIGH
LESS THAN A MONTH BEFORE IT'S DUE?
RIGHT!
PAT
I CAN FEEL IT MOVING.
PAT
WANT TO SEE?
N-NO... THAT'S OKAY...
THE GENERAL... I MEAN, STRAUSS...
...IS ON A MAJOR DIPLOMATIC MISSION RIGHT NOW.
TAP

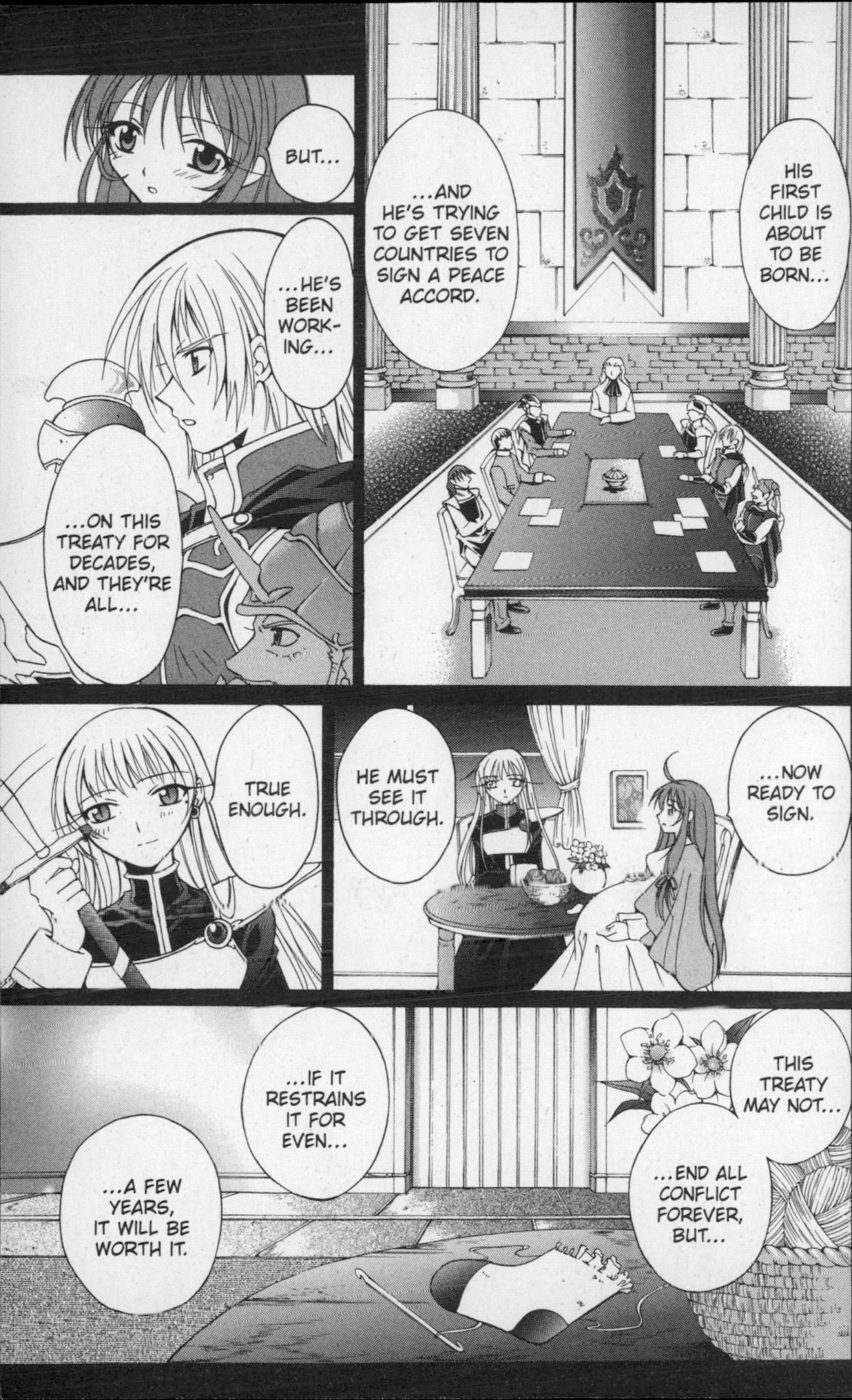
HIS FIRST CHILD IS ABOUT TO BE BORN...
...AND HE'S TRYING TO GET SEVEN COUNTRIES TO SIGN A PEACE ACCORD.
BUT...
...HE'S BEEN WORK-ING...
...ON THIS TREATY FOR DECADES, AND THEY'RE ALL...
...NOW READY TO SIGN.
HE MUST SEE IT THROUGH.
TRUE ENOUGH.
THIS TREATY MAY NOT...
...END ALL CONFLICT FOREVER, BUT...
...IF IT RESTRAINS IT FOR EVEN...
...A FEW YEARS, IT WILL BE WORTH IT.

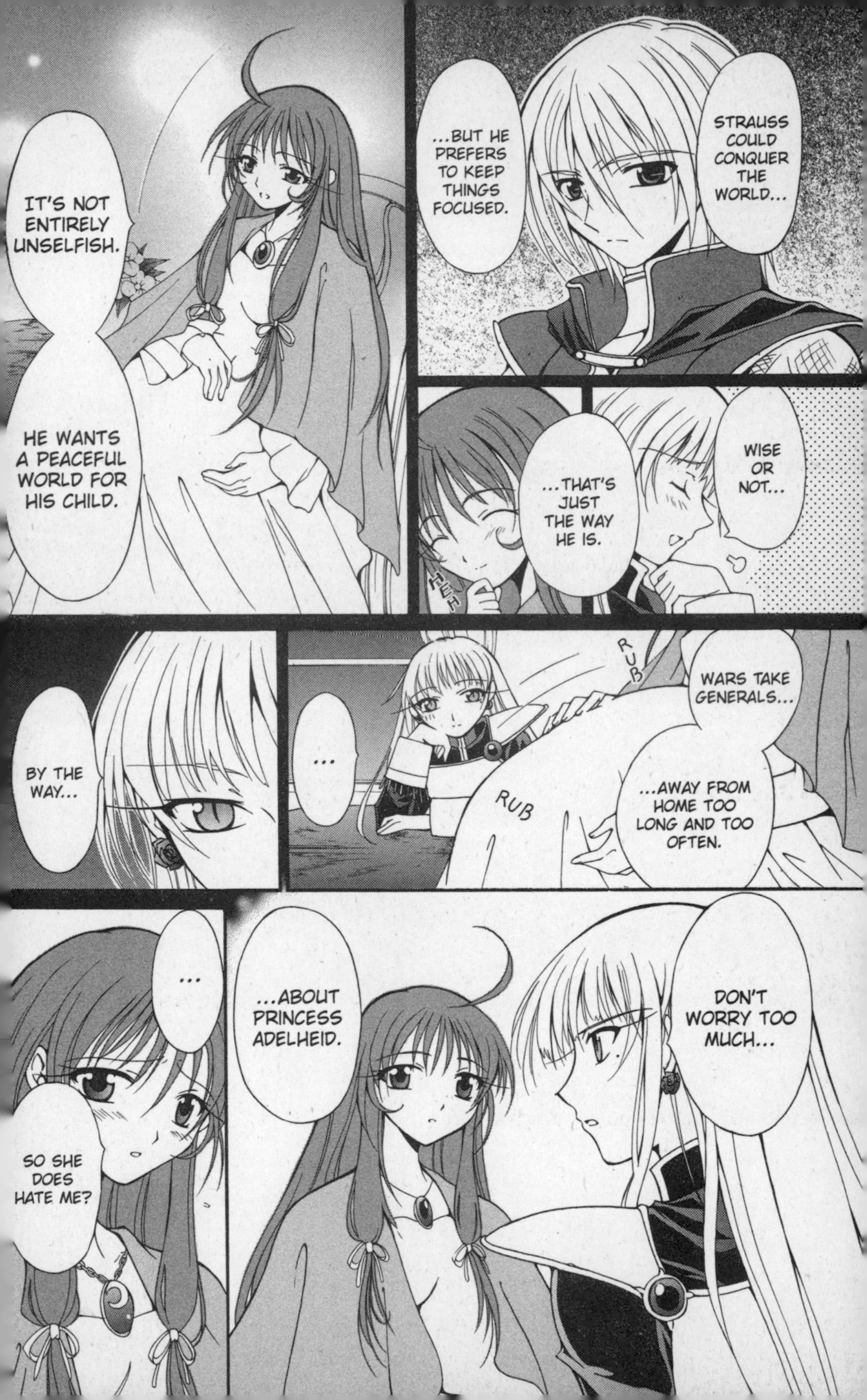
STRAUSS COULD CONQUER THE WORLD...
...BUT HE PREFERS TO KEEP THINGS FOCUSED.
WISE OR NOT...
...THAT'S JUST THE WAY HE IS.
HEH
IT'S NOT ENTIRELY UNSELFISH.
HE WANTS A PEACEFUL WORLD FOR HIS CHILD.
RUB
WARS TAKE GENERALS...
RUB
...AWAY FROM HOME TOO LONG AND TOO OFTEN.
...
BY THE WAY...
DON'T WORRY TOO MUCH...
...ABOUT PRINCESS ADELHEID.
...
SO SHE DOES HATE ME?

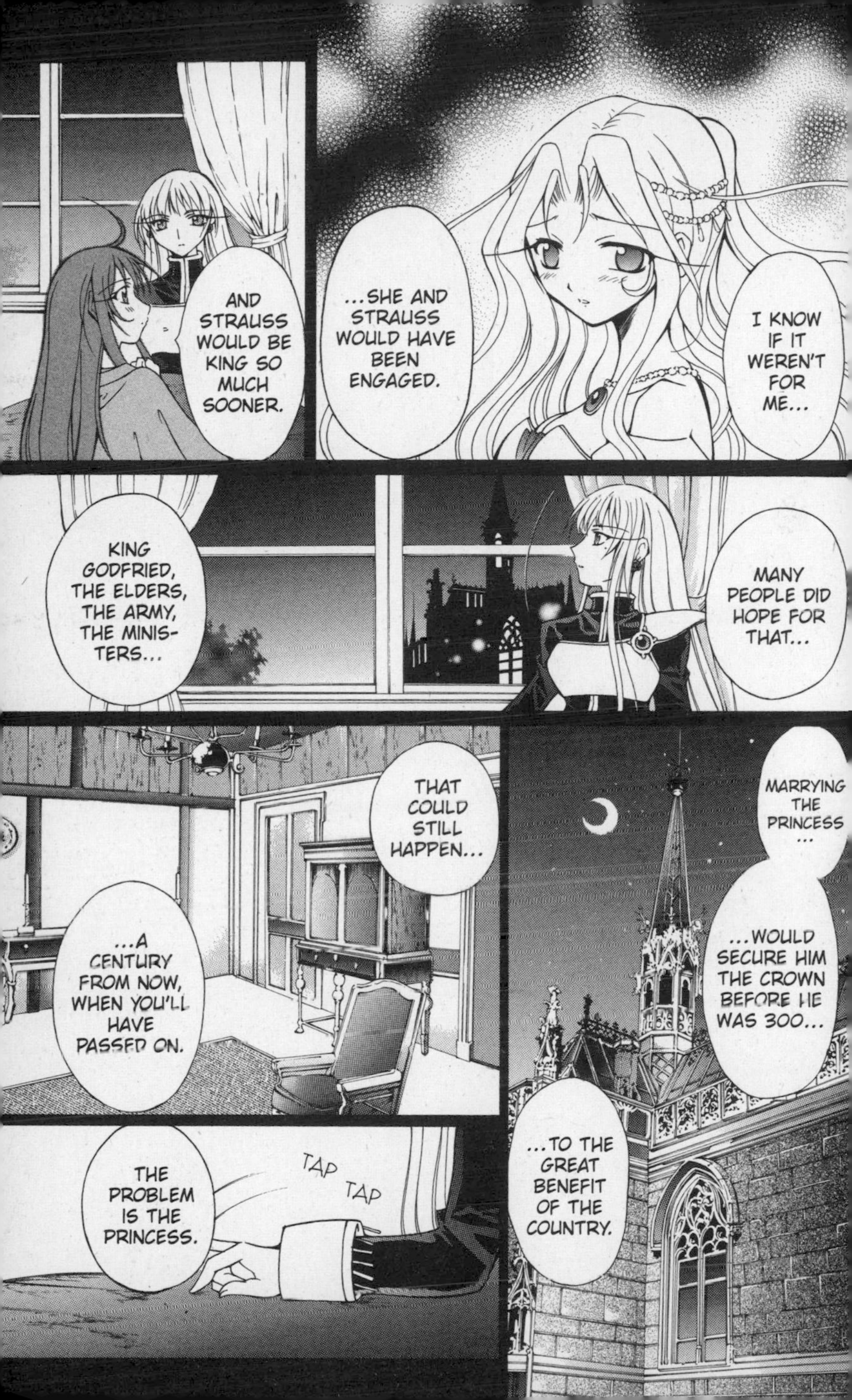
I KNOW IF IT WEREN'T FOR ME...
...SHE AND STRAUSS WOULD HAVE BEEN ENGAGED.
AND STRAUSS WOULD BE KING SO MUCH SOONER.
MANY PEOPLE DID HOPE FOR THAT...
KING GODFRIED, THE ELDERS, THE ARMY, THE MINIS-TERS...
MARRYING THE PRINCESS...
...WOULD SECURE HIM THE CROWN BEFORE HE WAS 300...
...TO THE GREAT BENEFIT OF THE COUNTRY.
THAT COULD STILL HAPPEN...
...A CENTURY FROM NOW, WHEN YOU'LL HAVE PASSED ON.
TAP TAP
THE PROBLEM IS THE PRINCESS.

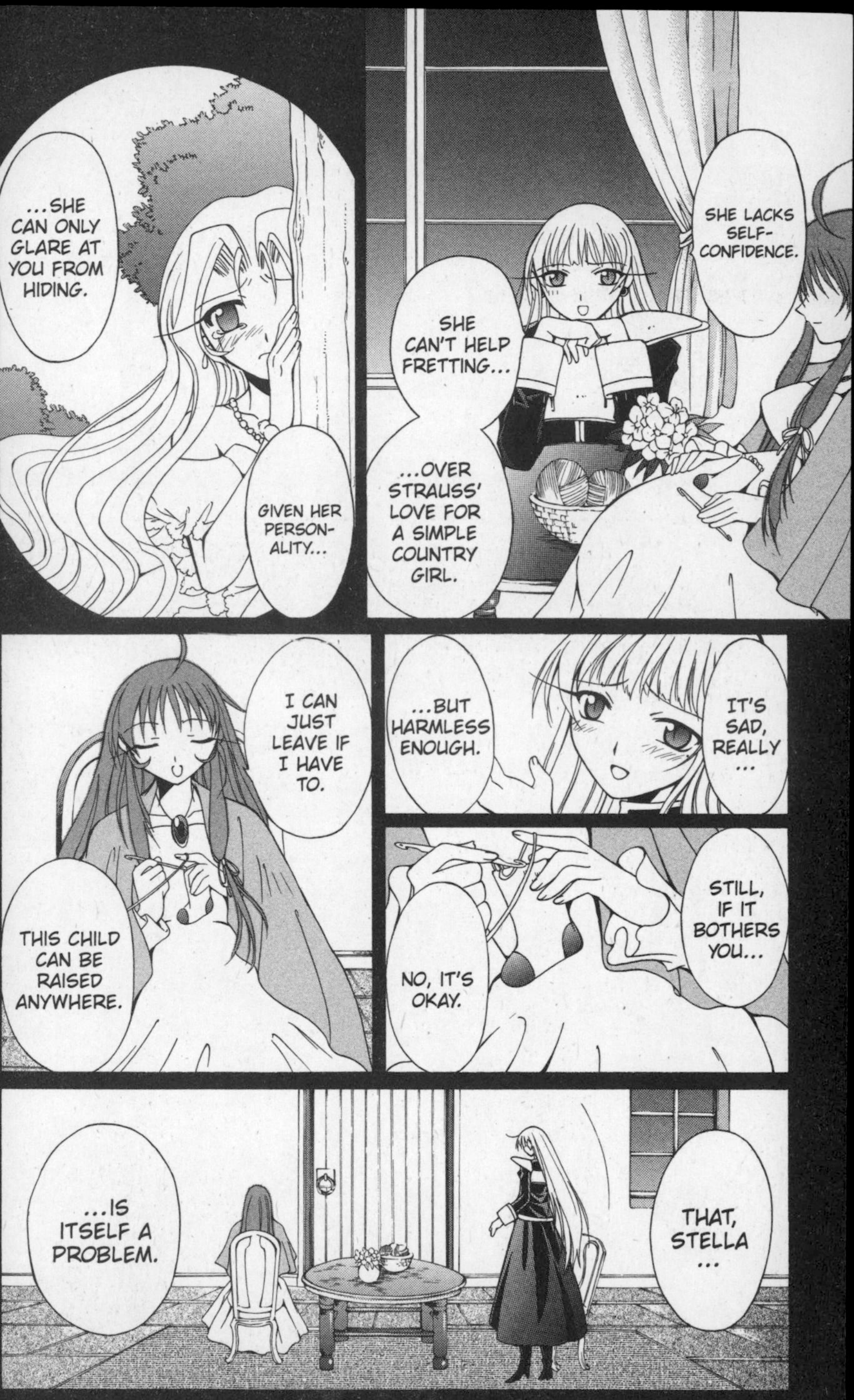
SHE LACKS SELF-CONFIDENCE.
SHE CAN'T HELP FRETTING...
...OVER STRAUSS' LOVE FOR A SIMPLE COUNTRY GIRL.
GIVEN HER PERSON-ALITY...
...SHE CAN ONLY GLARE AT YOU FROM HIDING.
IT'S SAD, REALLY...
...BUT HARMLESS ENOUGH.
STILL, IF IT BOTHERS YOU...
NO, IT'S OKAY.
I CAN JUST LEAVE IF I HAVE TO.
THIS CHILD CAN BE RAISED ANYWHERE.
THAT, STELLA...
...IS ITSELF A PROBLEM.

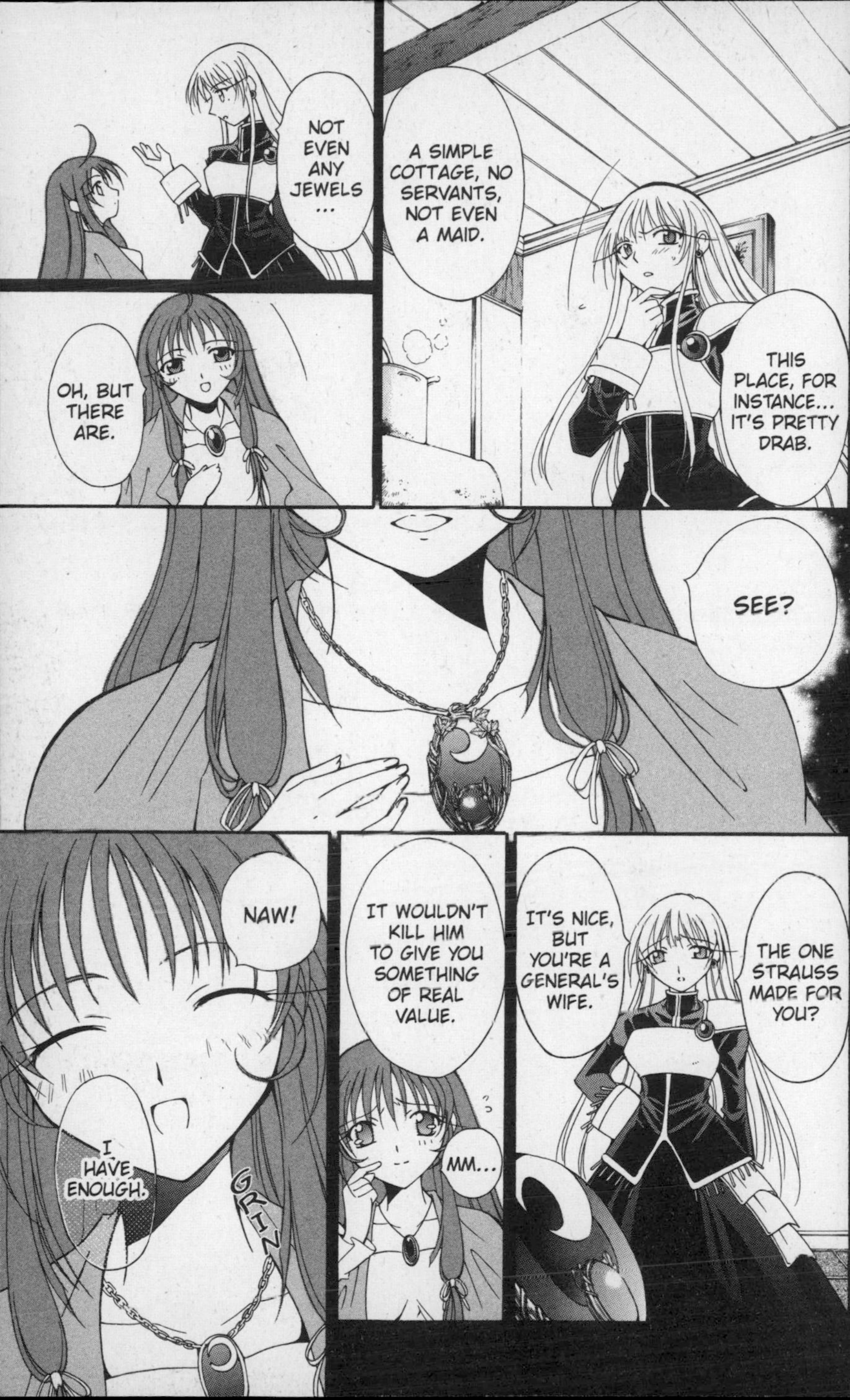
THIS PLACE, FOR INSTANCE... IT'S PRETTY DRAB.
A SIMPLE COTTAGE, NO SERVANTS, NOT EVEN A MAID.
NOT EVEN ANY JEWELS ...
OH, BUT THERE ARE.
SEE?
THE ONE STRAUSS MADE FOR YOU?
IT'S NICE, BUT YOU'RE A GENERAL'S WIFE.
IT WOULDN'T KILL HIM TO GIVE YOU SOMETHING OF REAL VALUE.
MM...
NAW!
I HAVE ENOUGH.
GRIN

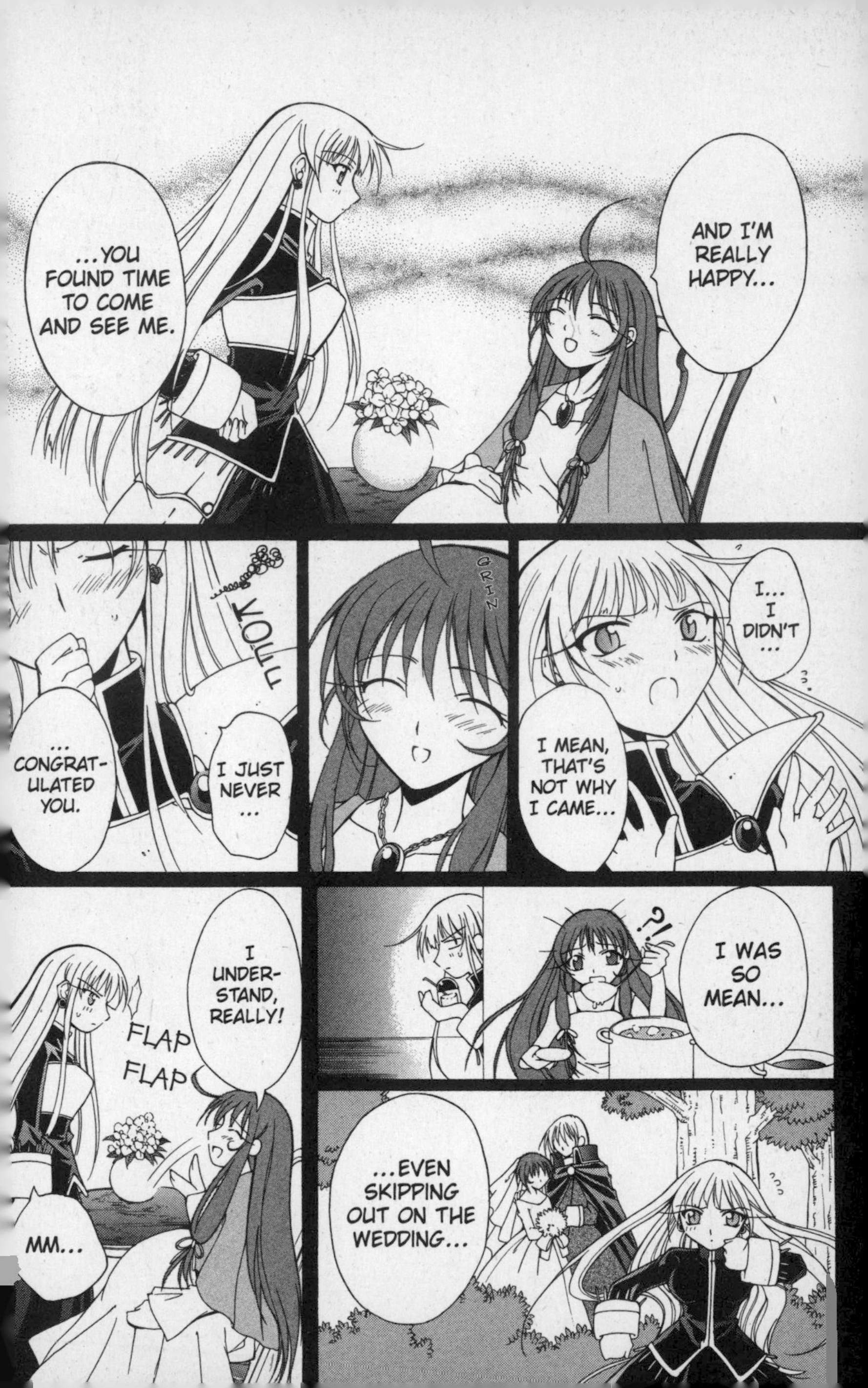
AND I'M REALLY HAPPY...
...YOU FOUND TIME TO COME AND SEE ME.
I... I DIDN'T ...
I MEAN, THAT'S NOT WHY I CAME...
GRIN
I JUST NEVER ...
... CONGRATULATED YOU.
?!
I WAS SO MEAN...
...EVEN SKIPPING OUT ON THE WEDDING...
I UNDERSTAND, REALLY!
FLAP
FLAP
MM...

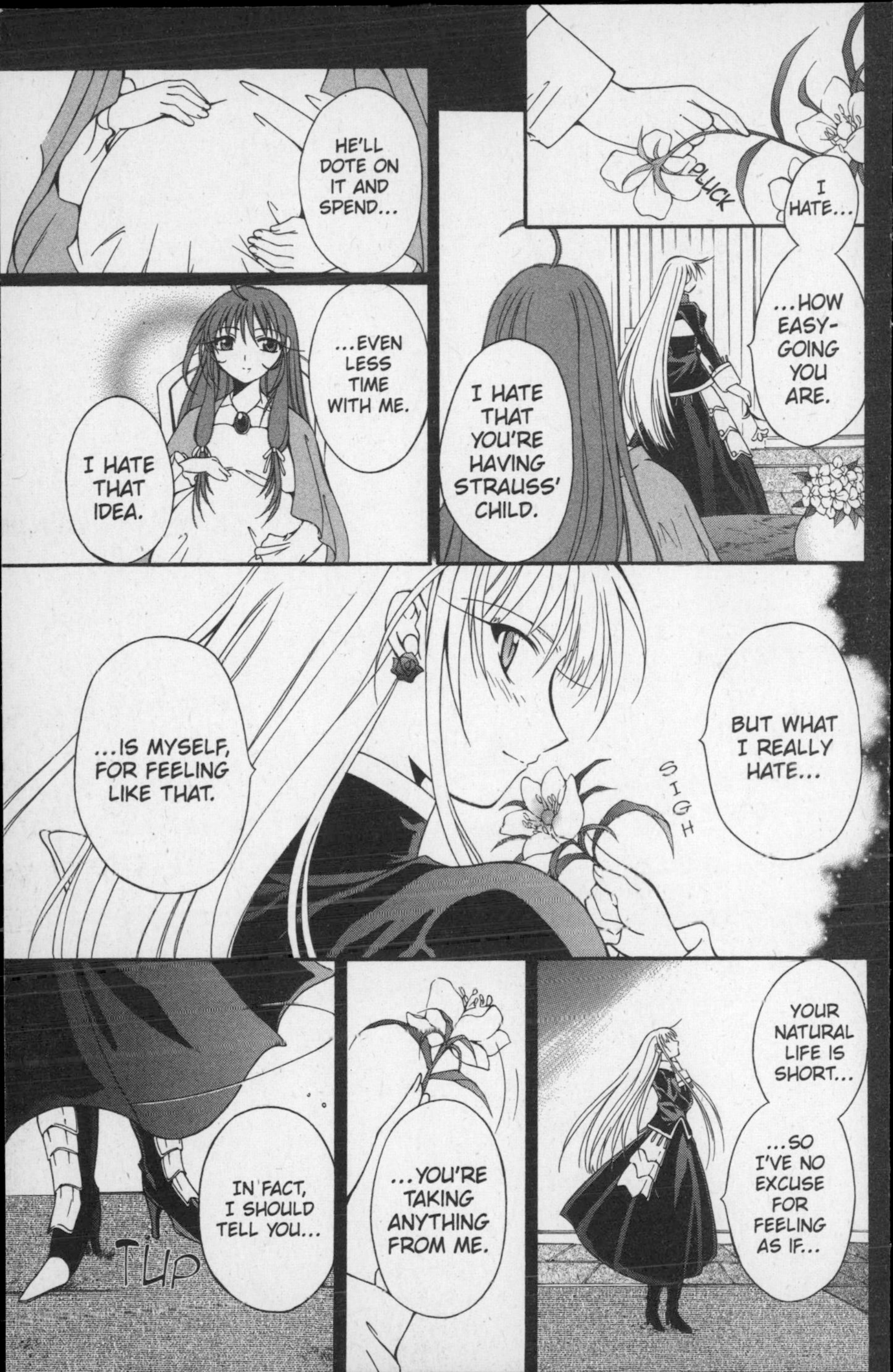
PLUCK
I HATE...
...HOW EASY-GOING YOU ARE.
I HATE THAT YOU'RE HAVING STRAUSS' CHILD.
HE'LL DOTE ON IT AND SPEND...
...EVEN LESS TIME WITH ME.
I HATE THAT IDEA.
BUT WHAT I REALLY HATE...
SIGH
...IS MYSELF, FOR FEELING LIKE THAT.
YOUR NATURAL LIFE IS SHORT...
...SO I'VE NO EXCUSE FOR FEELING AS IF...
...YOU'RE TAKING ANYTHING FROM ME.
IN FACT, I SHOULD TELL YOU...
TUP

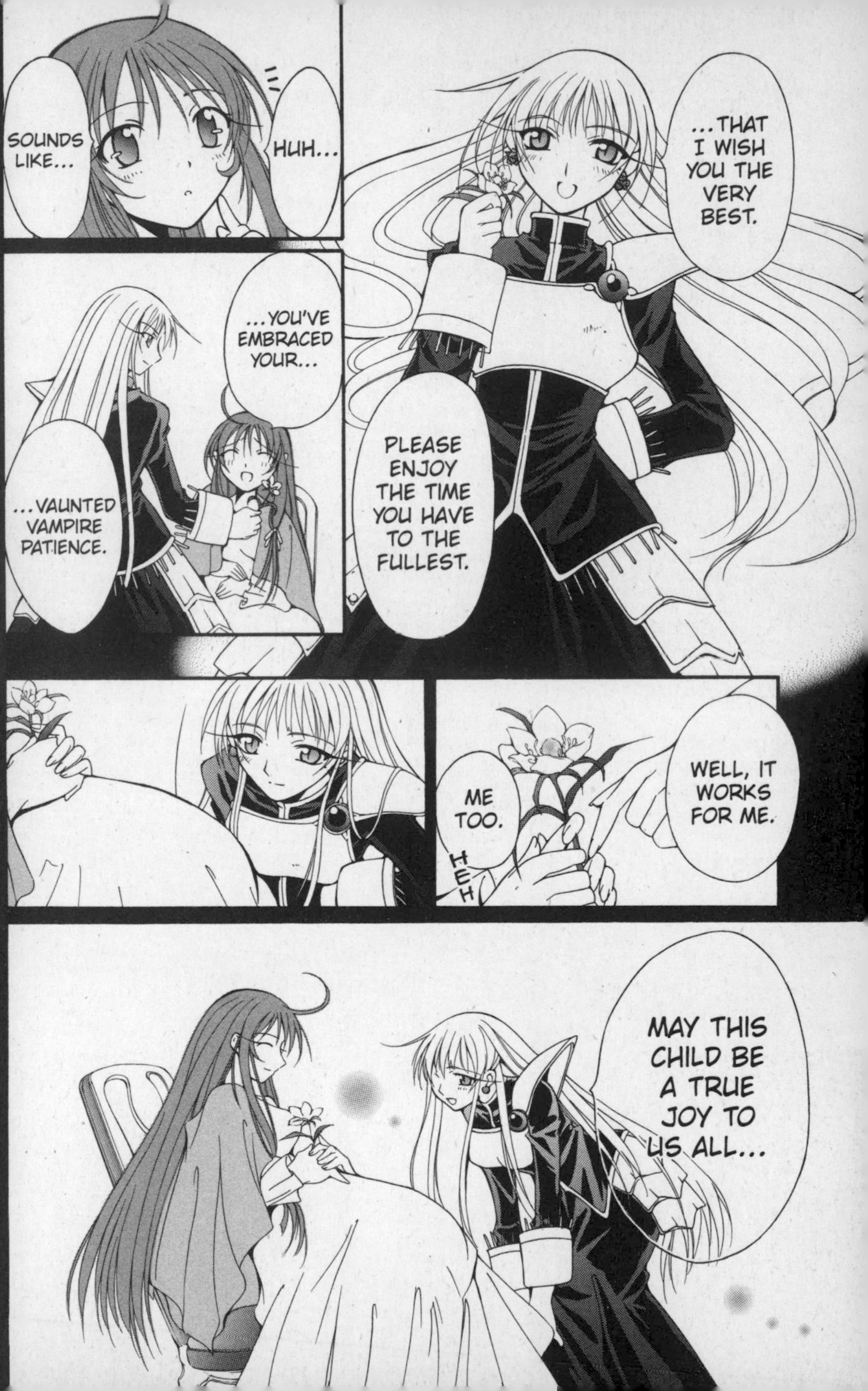
...THAT I WISH YOU THE VERY BEST.
PLEASE ENJOY THE TIME YOU HAVE TO THE FULLEST.
HUH...
SOUNDS LIKE...
...YOU'VE EMBRACED YOUR...
...VAUNTED VAMPIRE PATIENCE.
WELL, IT WORKS FOR ME.
ME TOO.
HEH
MAY THIS CHILD BE A TRUE JOY TO US ALL...

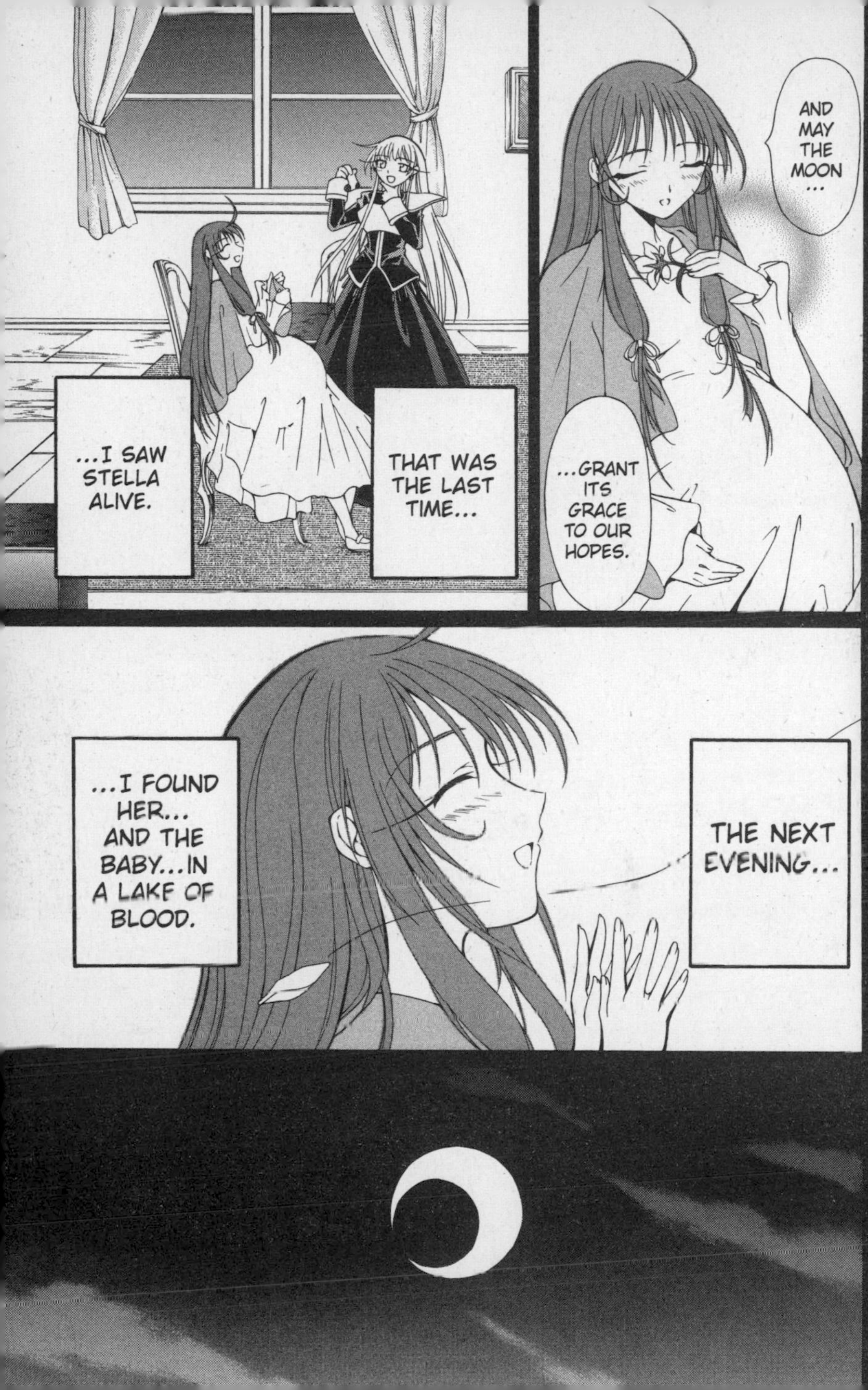
AND MAY THE MOON...
...GRANT ITS GRACE TO OUR HOPES.
THAT WAS THE LAST TIME...
...I SAW STELLA ALIVE.
THE NEXT EVENING...
...I FOUND HER... AND THE BABY...IN A LAKE OF BLOOD.

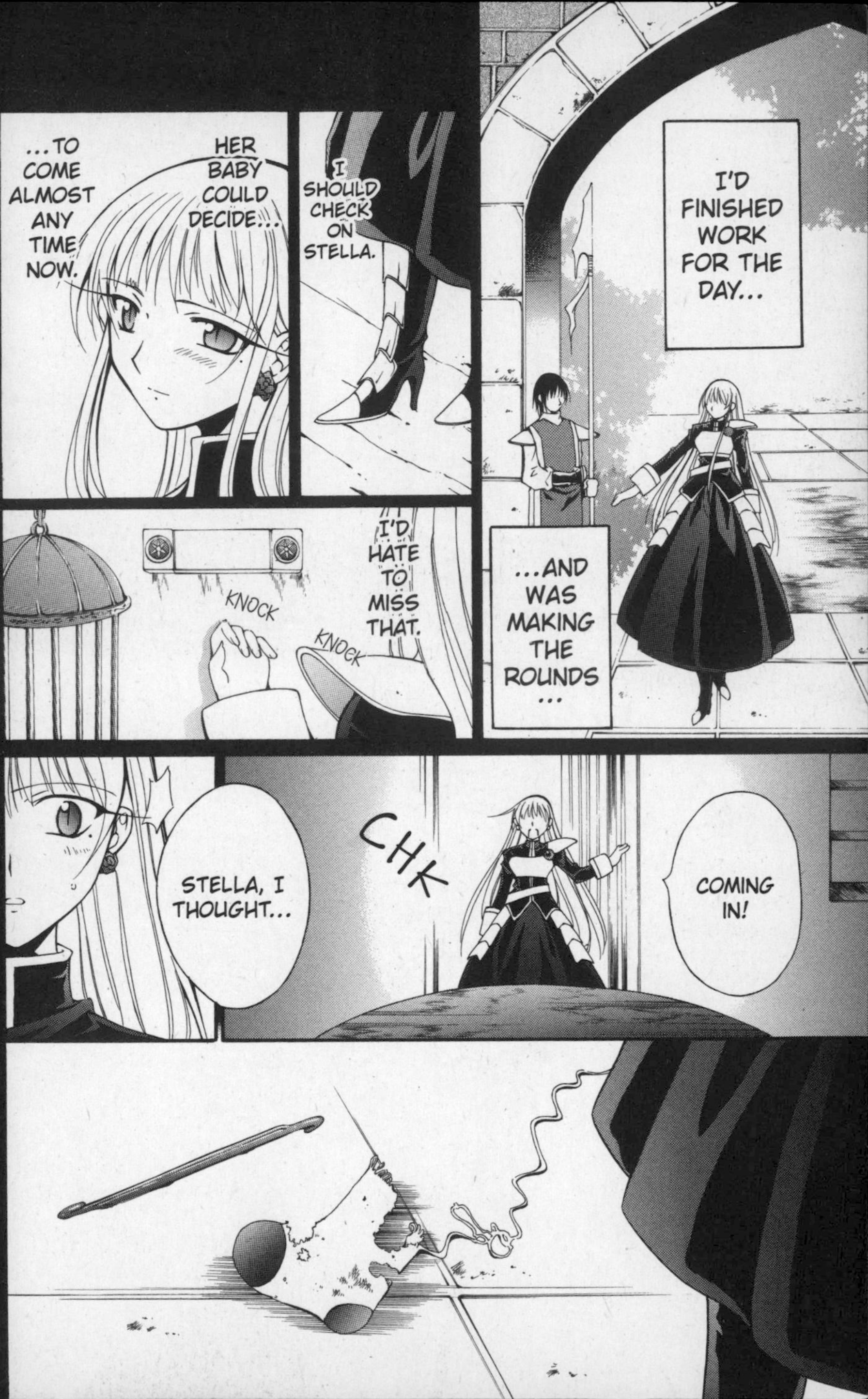
I'D FINISHED WORK FOR THE DAY...
...AND WAS MAKING THE ROUNDS...
I SHOULD CHECK ON STELLA.
HER BABY COULD DECIDE...
...TO COME ALMOST ANY TIME NOW.
I'D HATE TO MISS THAT.
KNOCK
KNOCK
COMING IN!
CHK
STELLA, I THOUGHT...

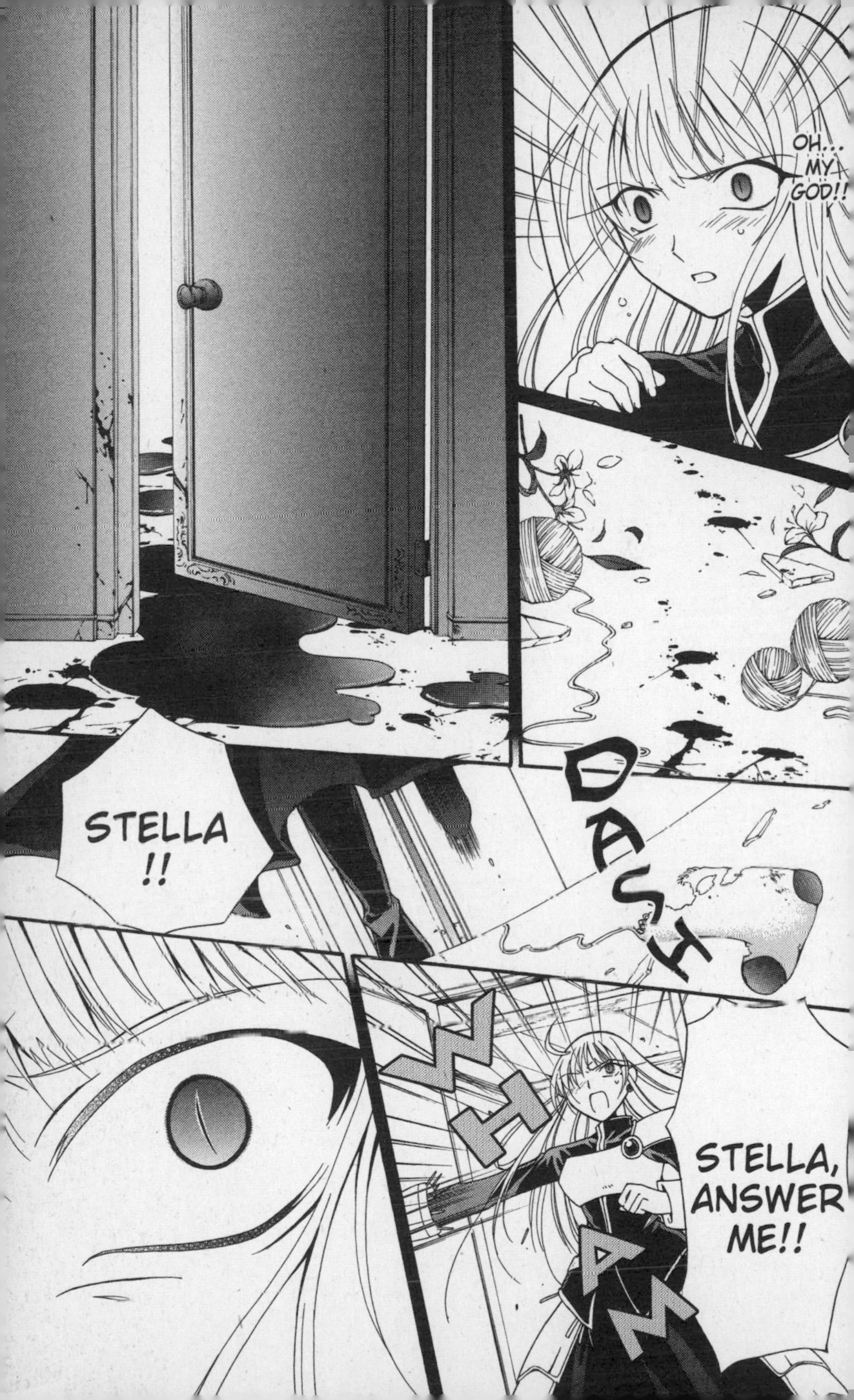
OH... MY GOD!!
STELLA !!
DASH
WHAM
STELLA, ANSWER ME!!

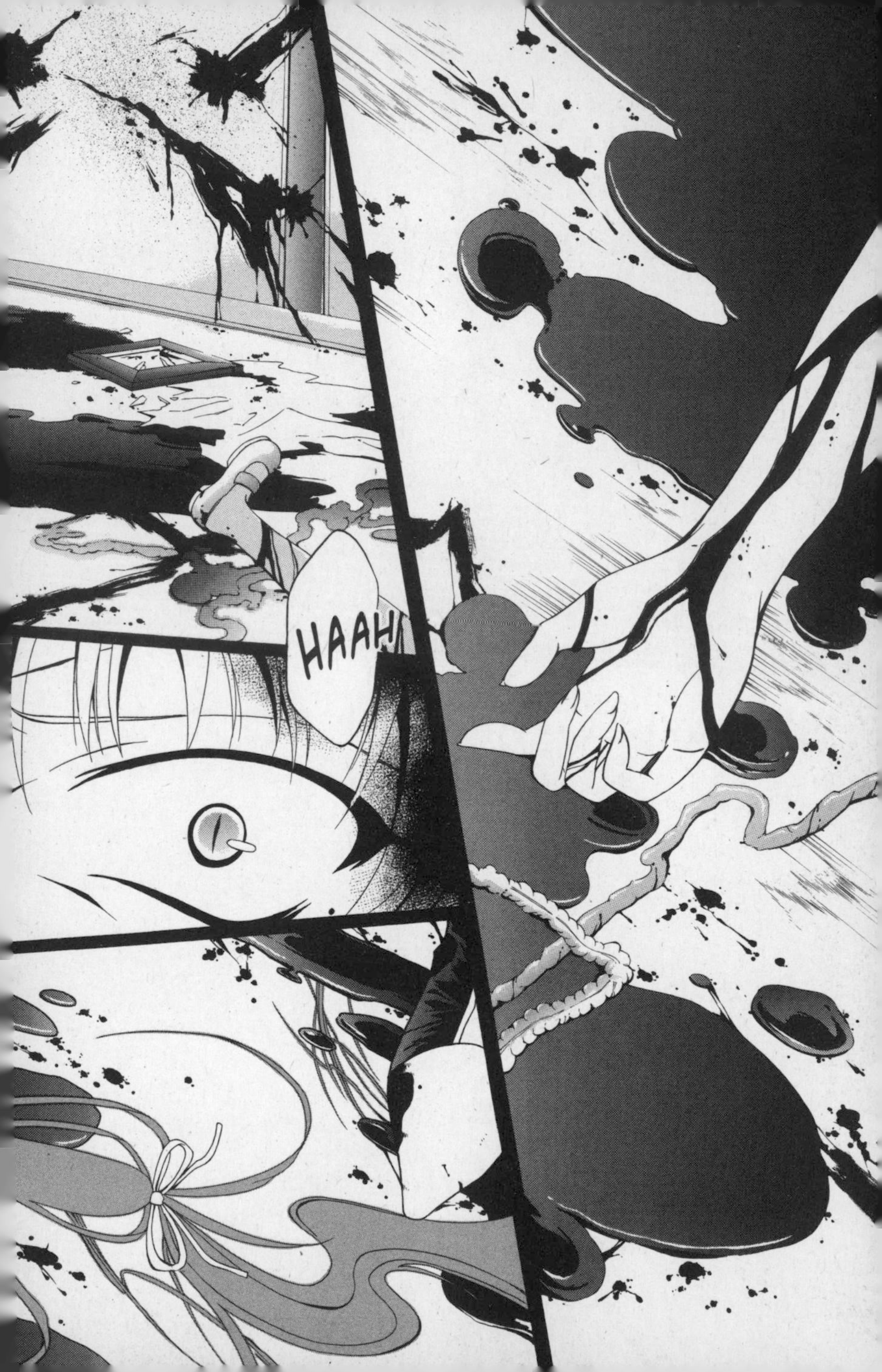
HAAH

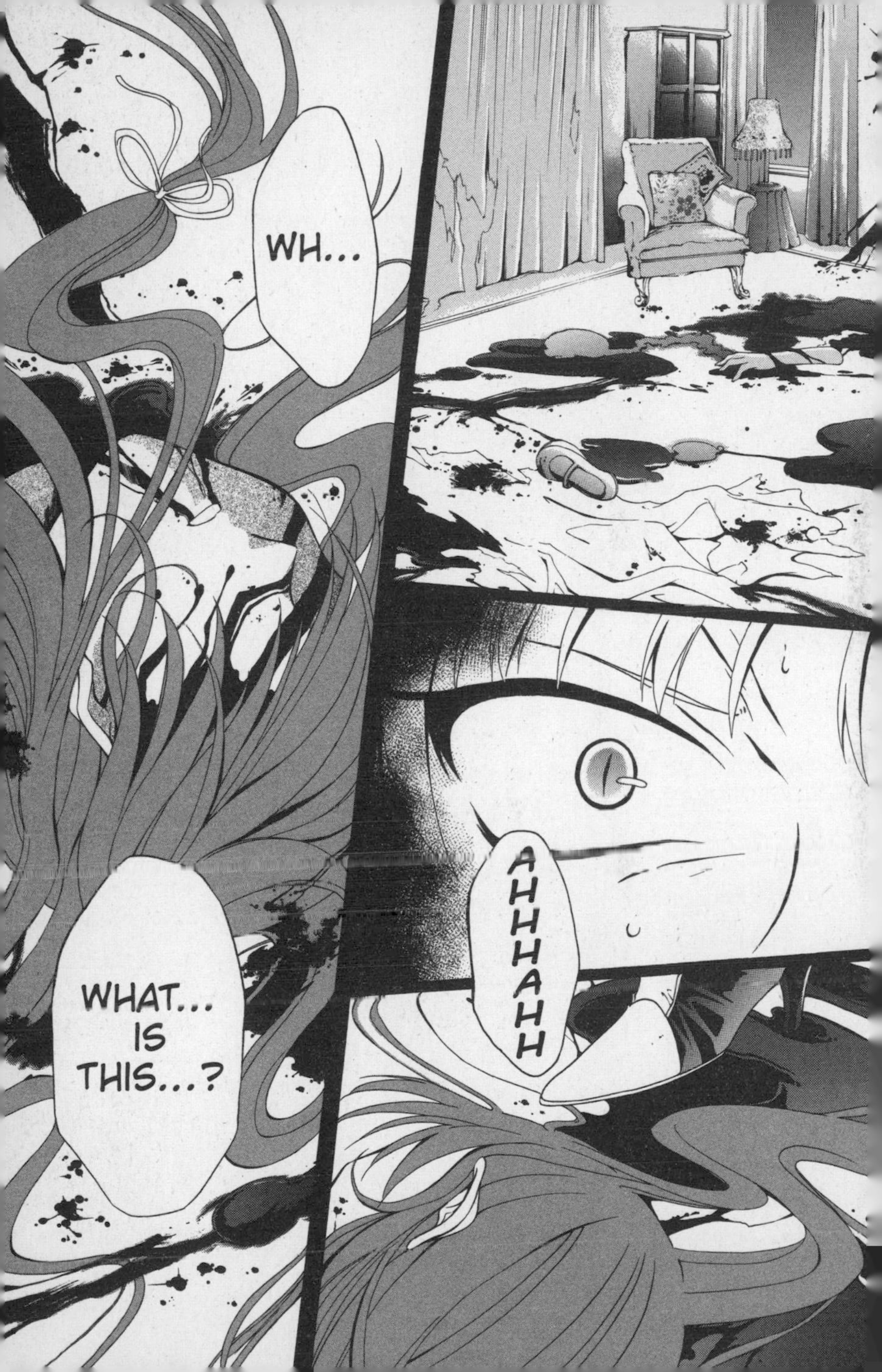
AHHHAHH
WH...
WHAT... IS THIS...?

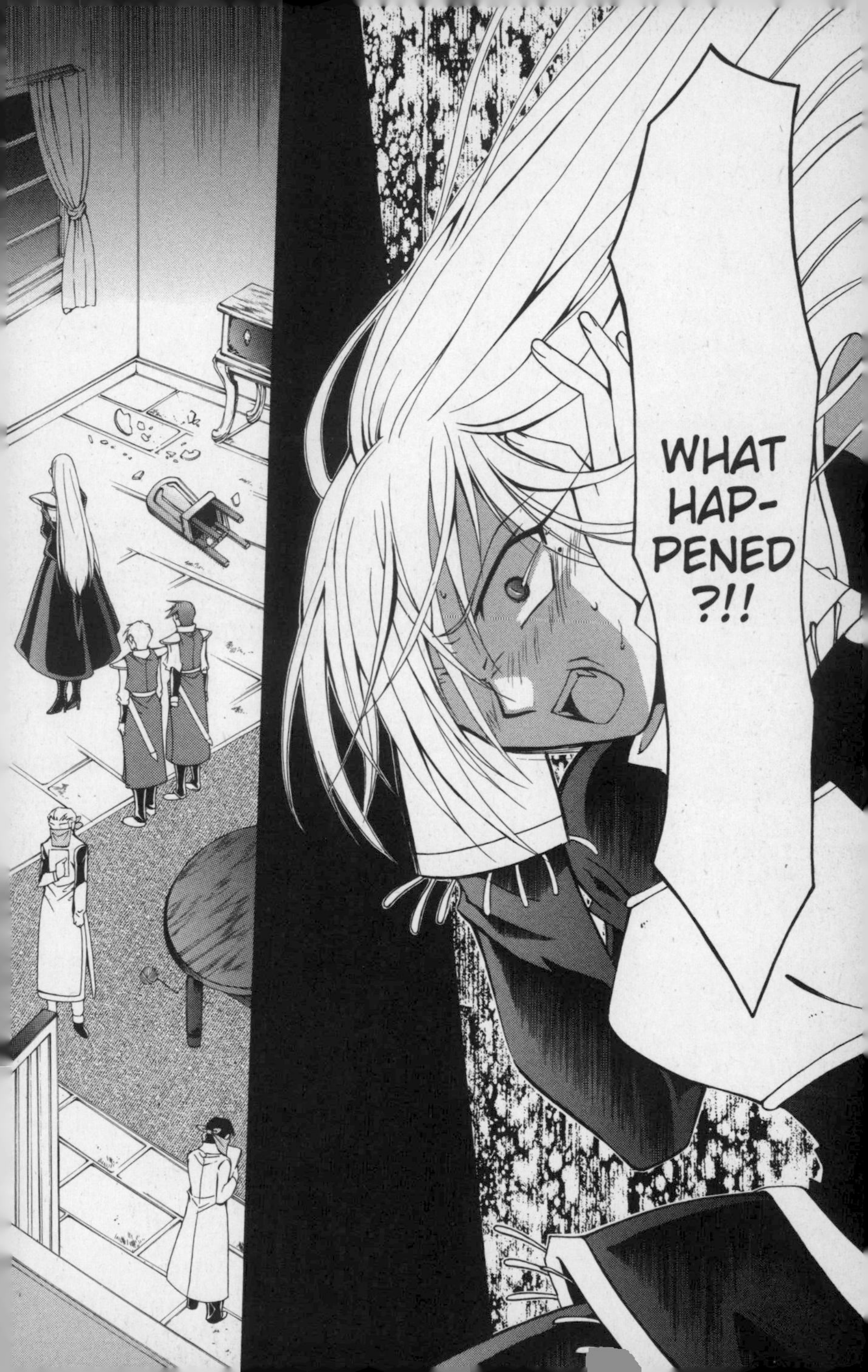
WHAT HAP-PENED ?!!

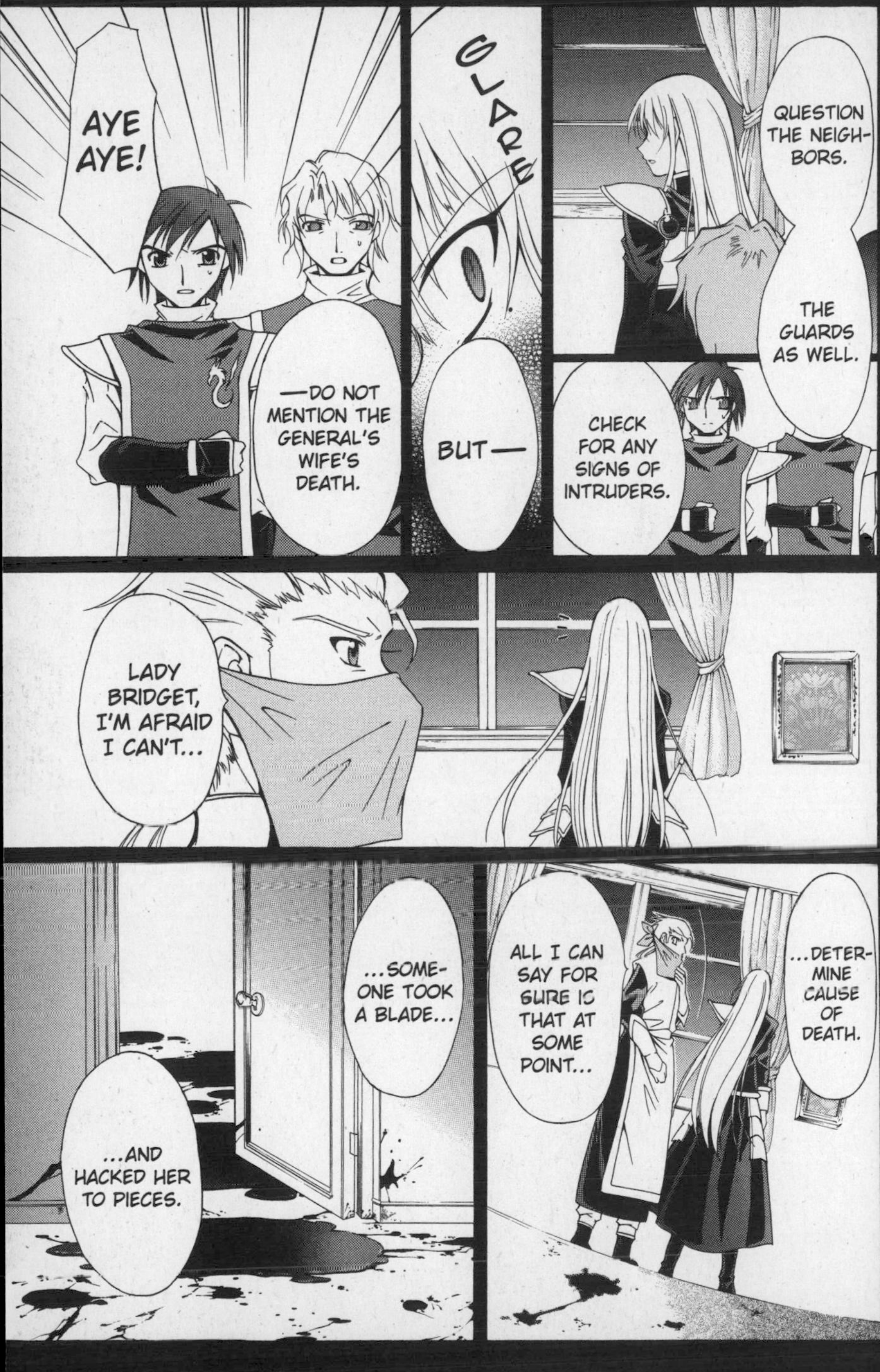
QUESTION THE NEIGH-BORS.
THE GUARDS AS WELL.
CHECK FOR ANY SIGNS OF INTRUDERS.
GLARE
BUT—
—DO NOT MENTION THE GENERAL'S WIFE'S DEATH.
AYE AYE!
LADY BRIDGET, I'M AFRAID I CAN'T...
...DETER-MINE CAUSE OF DEATH.
ALL I CAN SAY FOR SURE IS THAT AT SOME POINT...
...SOME-ONE TOOK A BLADE...
...AND HACKED HER TO PIECES.

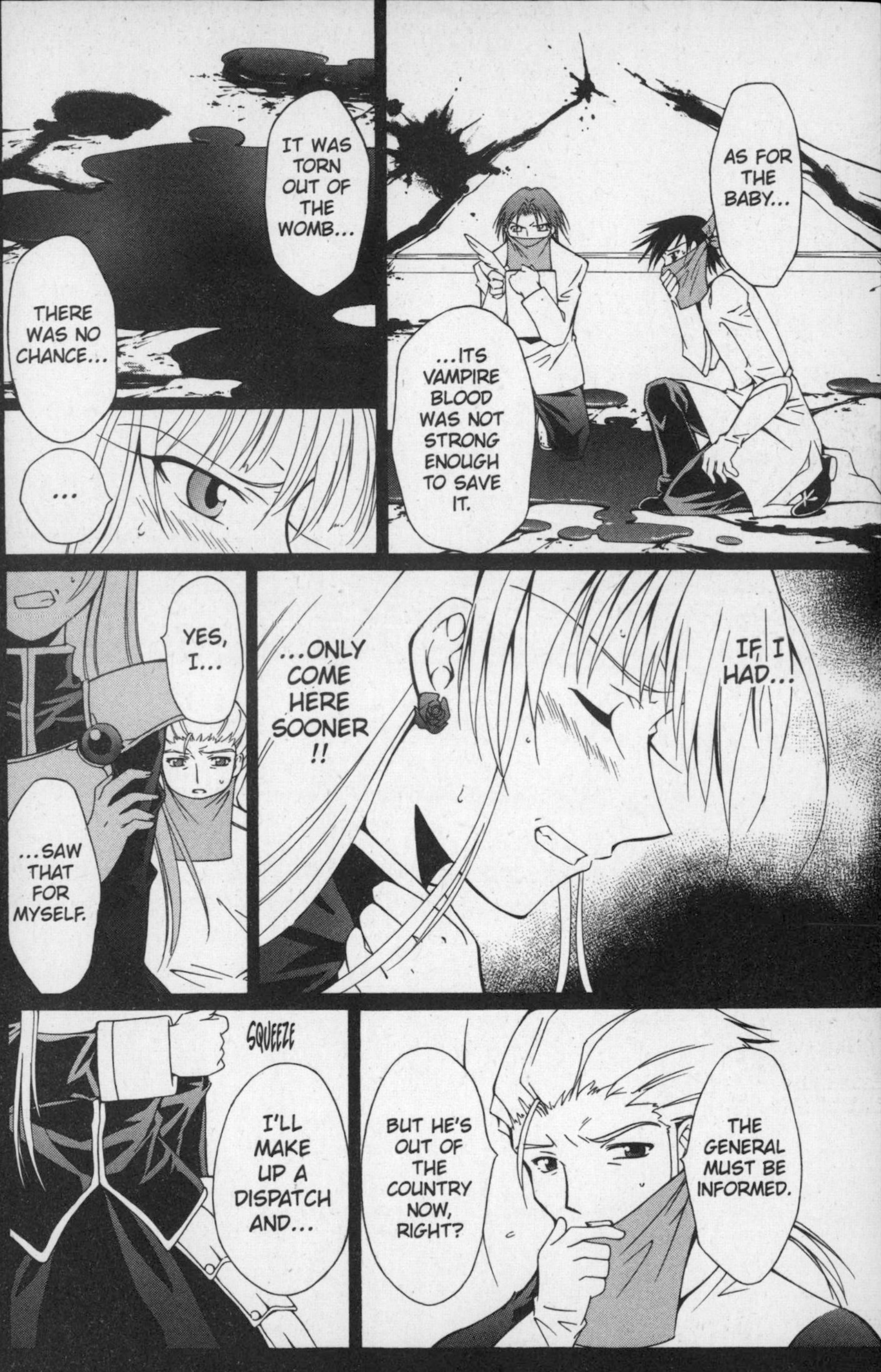
AS FOR THE BABY...
...ITS VAMPIRE BLOOD WAS NOT STRONG ENOUGH TO SAVE IT.
IT WAS TORN OUT OF THE WOMB...
THERE WAS NO CHANCE...
...
IF I HAD...
...ONLY COME HERE SOONER!!
YES, I...
...SAW THAT FOR MYSELF.
THE GENERAL MUST BE INFORMED.
BUT HE'S OUT OF THE COUNTRY NOW, RIGHT?
SQUEEZE
I'LL MAKE UP A DISPATCH AND...

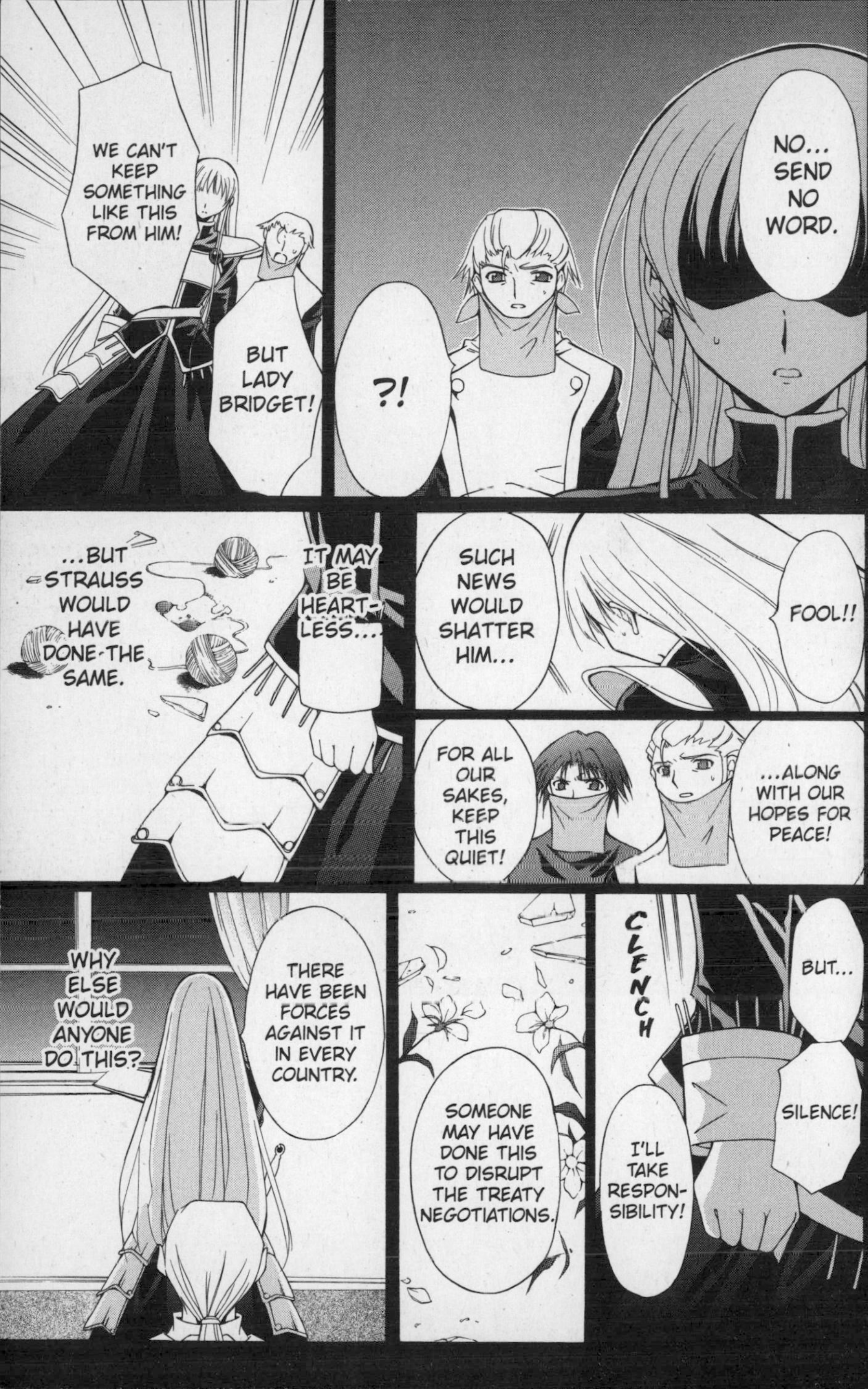
NO... SEND NO WORD.
?!
WE CAN'T KEEP SOMETHING LIKE THIS FROM HIM!
BUT LADY BRIDGET!
FOOL!!
SUCH NEWS WOULD SHATTER HIM...
...ALONG WITH OUR HOPES FOR PEACE!
FOR ALL OUR SAKES, KEEP THIS QUIET!
IT MAY BE HEART-LESS...
...BUT STRAUSS WOULD HAVE DONE THE SAME.
BUT...
SILENCE!
CLENCH
I'LL TAKE RESPON-SIBILITY!
SOMEONE MAY HAVE DONE THIS TO DISRUPT THE TREATY NEGOTIATIONS.
THERE HAVE BEEN FORCES AGAINST IT IN EVERY COUNTRY.
WHY ELSE WOULD ANYONE DO THIS?

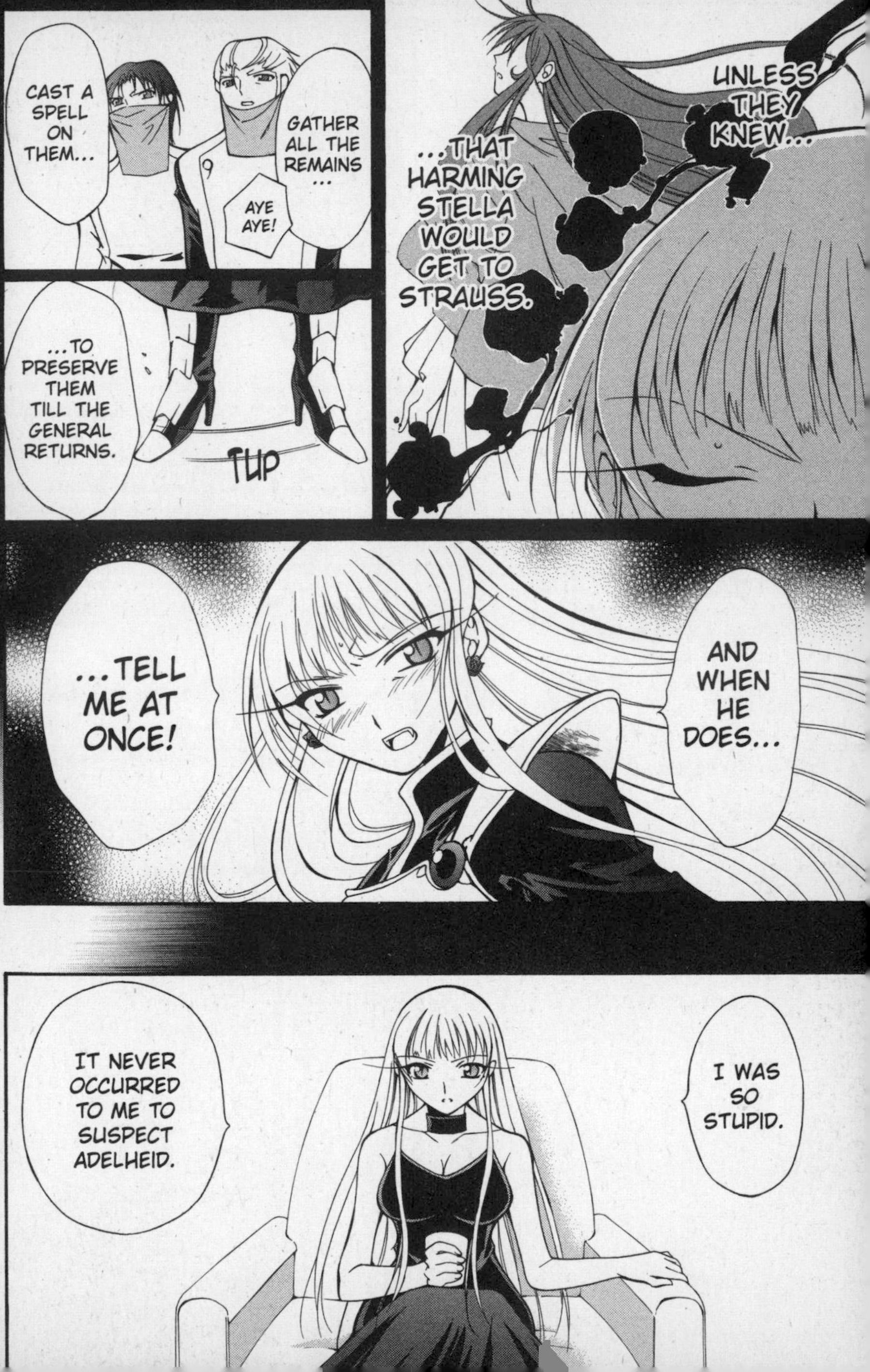
UNLESS THEY KNEW...
...THAT HARMING STELLA WOULD GET TO STRAUSS.
GATHER ALL THE REMAINS ...
AYE AYE!
CAST A SPELL ON THEM...
...TO PRESERVE THEM TILL THE GENERAL RETURNS.
TUP
AND WHEN HE DOES...
...TELL ME AT ONCE!
I WAS SO STUPID.
IT NEVER OCCURRED TO ME TO SUSPECT ADELHEID.

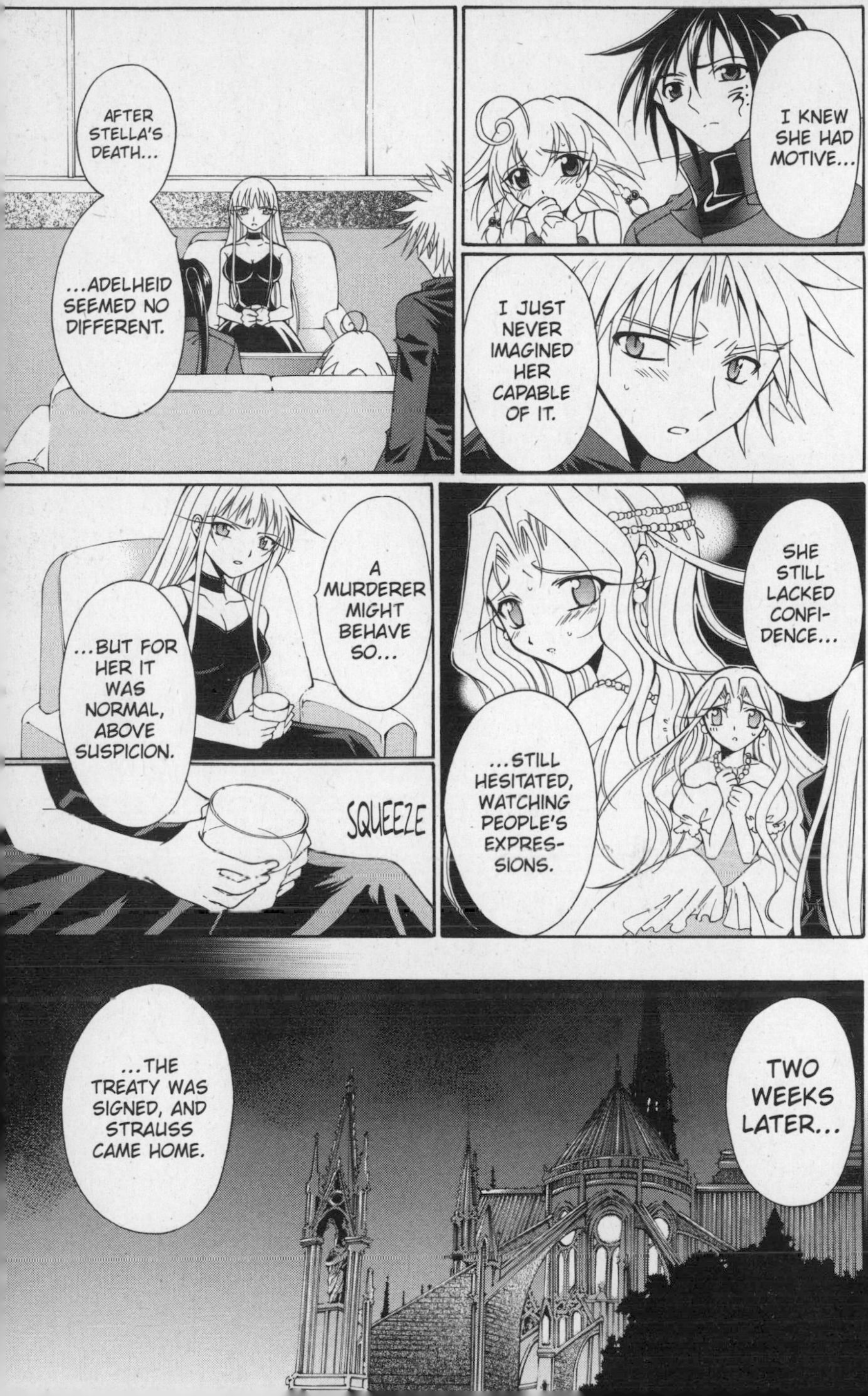
I KNEW SHE HAD MOTIVE...
I JUST NEVER IMAGINED HER CAPABLE OF IT.
AFTER STELLA'S DEATH...
...ADELHEID SEEMED NO DIFFERENT.
SHE STILL LACKED CONFI-DENCE...
...STILL HESITATED, WATCHING PEOPLE'S EXPRES-SIONS.
A MURDERER MIGHT BEHAVE SO...
...BUT FOR HER IT WAS NORMAL, ABOVE SUSPICION.
SQUEEZE
TWO WEEKS LATER...
...THE TREATY WAS SIGNED, AND STRAUSS CAME HOME.

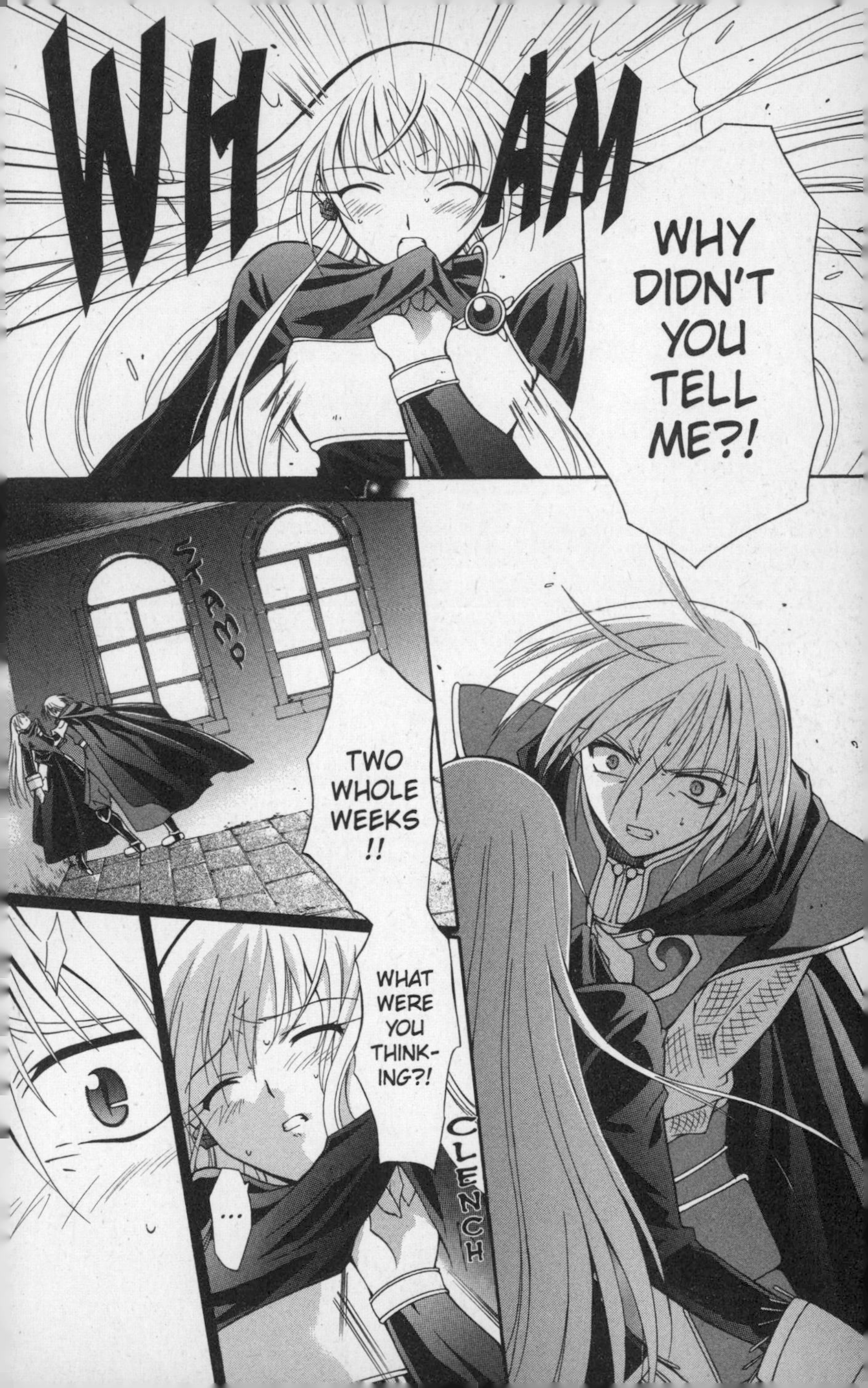
WHAM
WHY DIDN'T YOU TELL ME?!
TWO WHOLE WEEKS!!
WHAT WERE YOU THINKING?!
CLENCH
STAMP
...

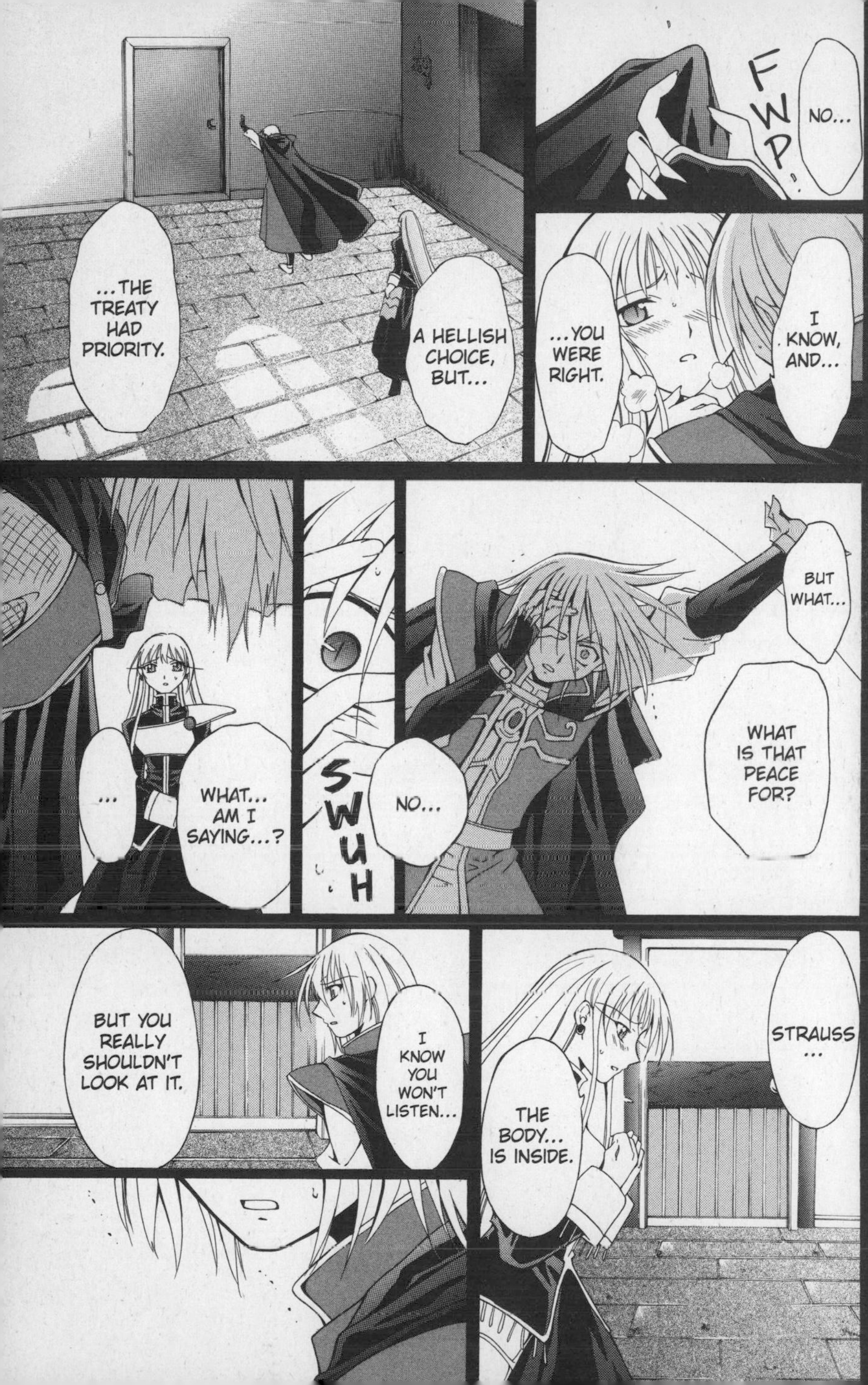
FWP
NO...
I KNOW, AND...
...YOU WERE RIGHT.
A HELLISH CHOICE, BUT...
...THE TREATY HAD PRIORITY.
BUT WHAT...
WHAT IS THAT PEACE FOR?
SWUH
NO...
WHAT... AM I SAYING...?
...
STRAUSS...
THE BODY... IS INSIDE.
I KNOW YOU WON'T LISTEN...
BUT YOU REALLY SHOULDN'T LOOK AT IT.

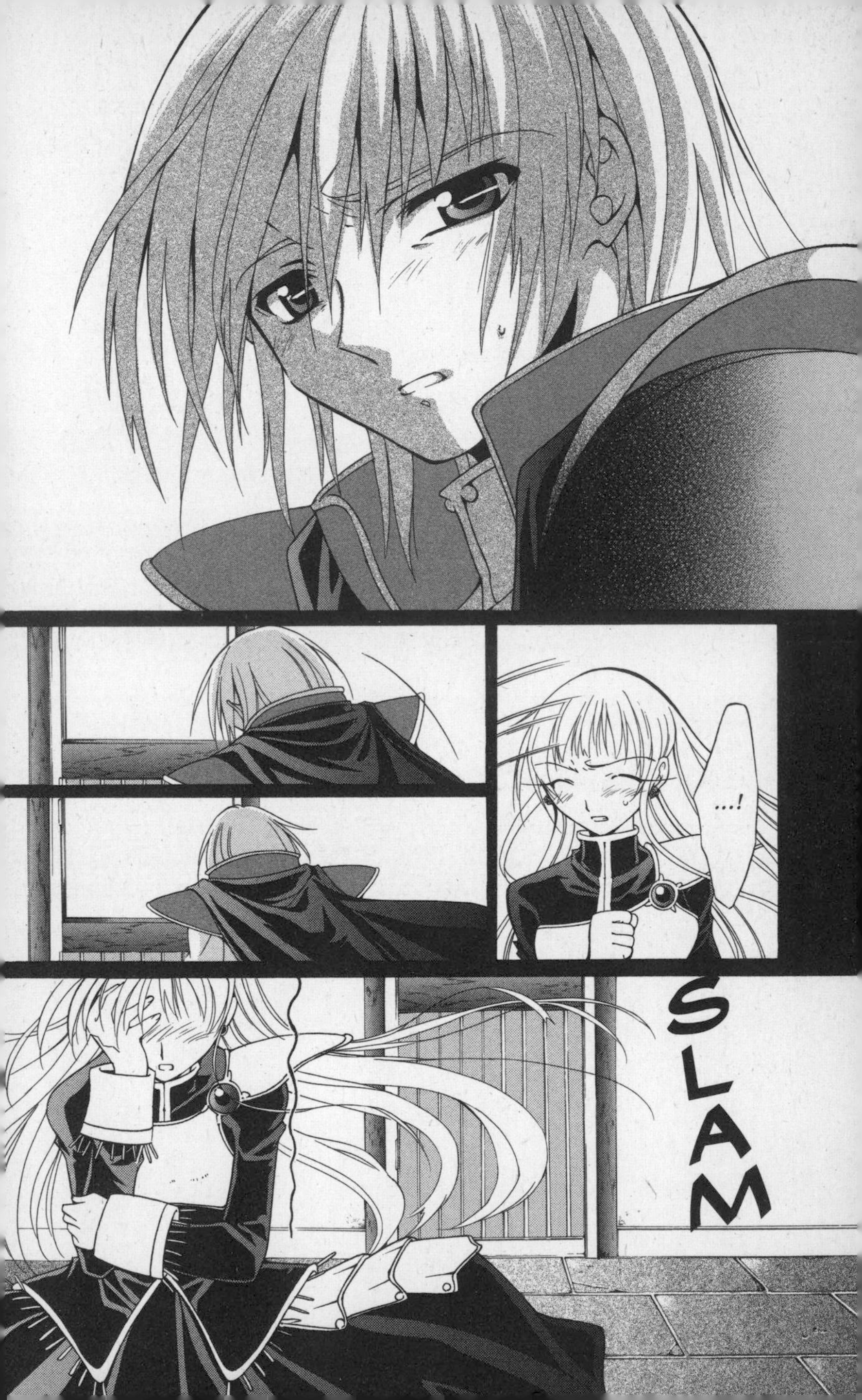
...!
SLAM

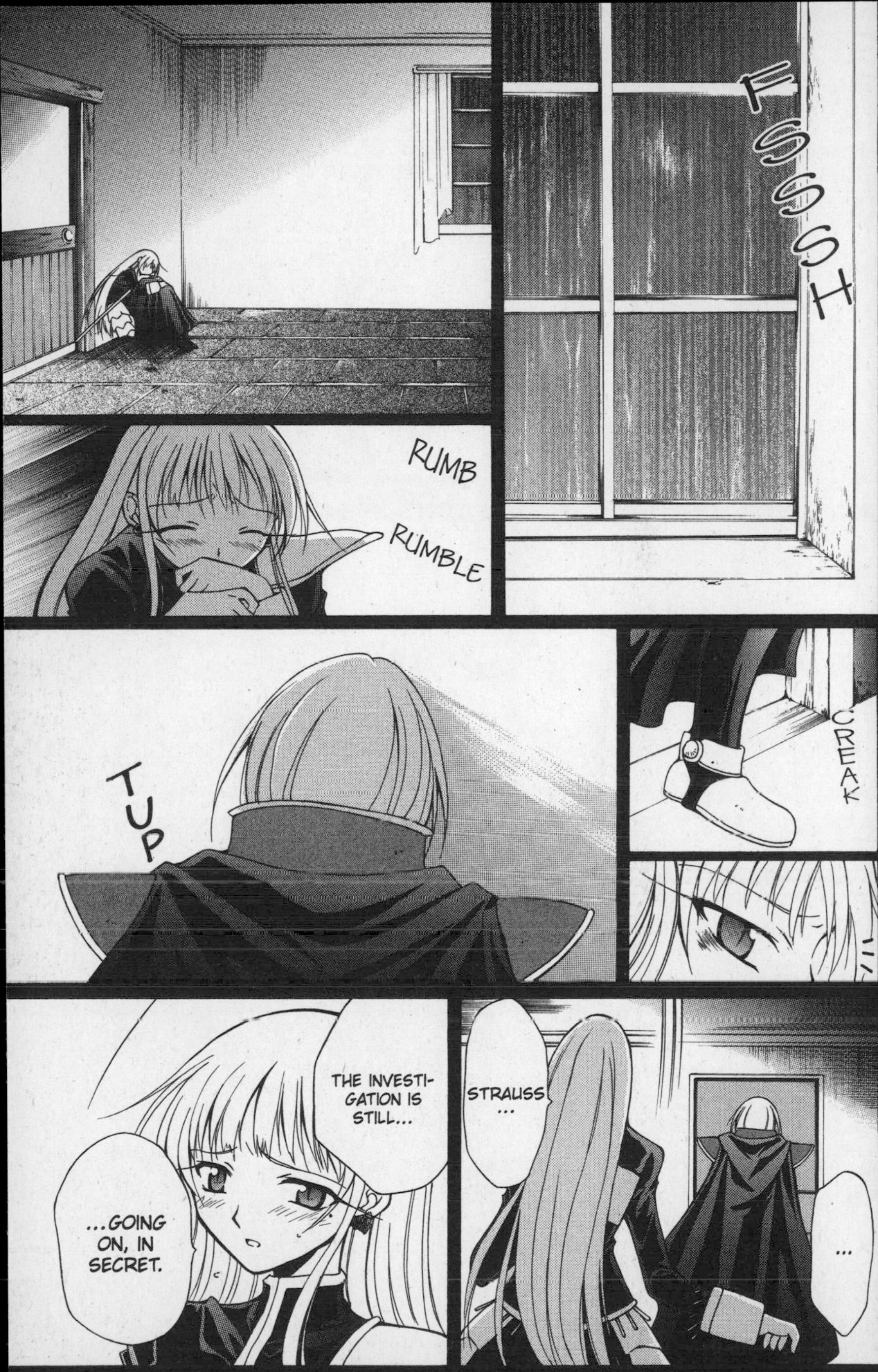
FSSSH
RUMB
RUMBLE
CREAK
TUP
STRAUSS ...
...
THE INVESTI-GATION IS STILL...
...GOING ON, IN SECRET.

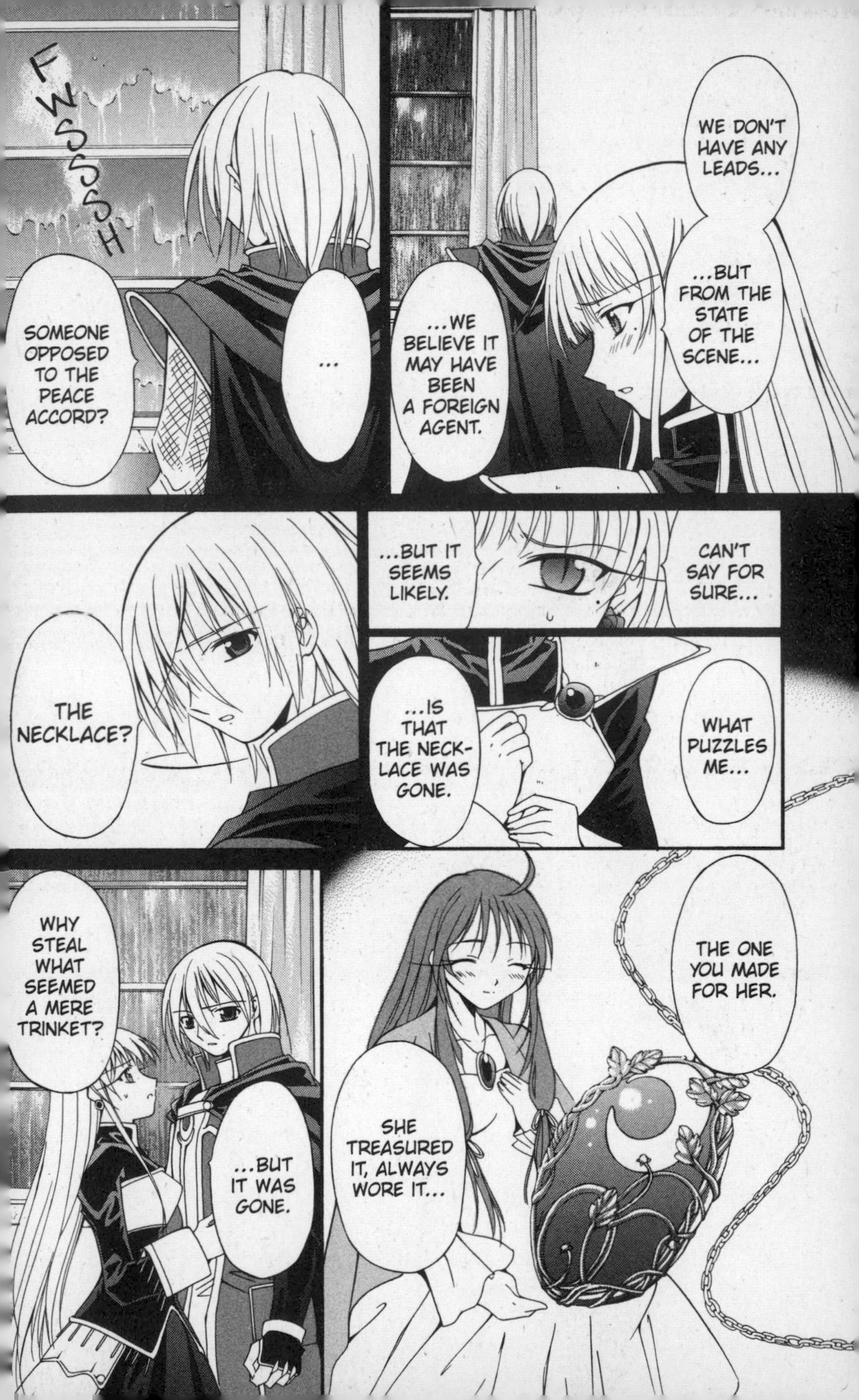
WE DON'T HAVE ANY LEADS...
...BUT FROM THE STATE OF THE SCENE...
...WE BELIEVE IT MAY HAVE BEEN A FOREIGN AGENT.
FWSSSH
...
SOMEONE OPPOSED TO THE PEACE ACCORD?
CAN'T SAY FOR SURE...
...BUT IT SEEMS LIKELY.
WHAT PUZZLES ME...
...IS THAT THE NECK-LACE WAS GONE.
THE NECKLACE?
THE ONE YOU MADE FOR HER.
SHE TREASURED IT, ALWAYS WORE IT...
...BUT IT WAS GONE.
WHY STEAL WHAT SEEMED A MERE TRINKET?

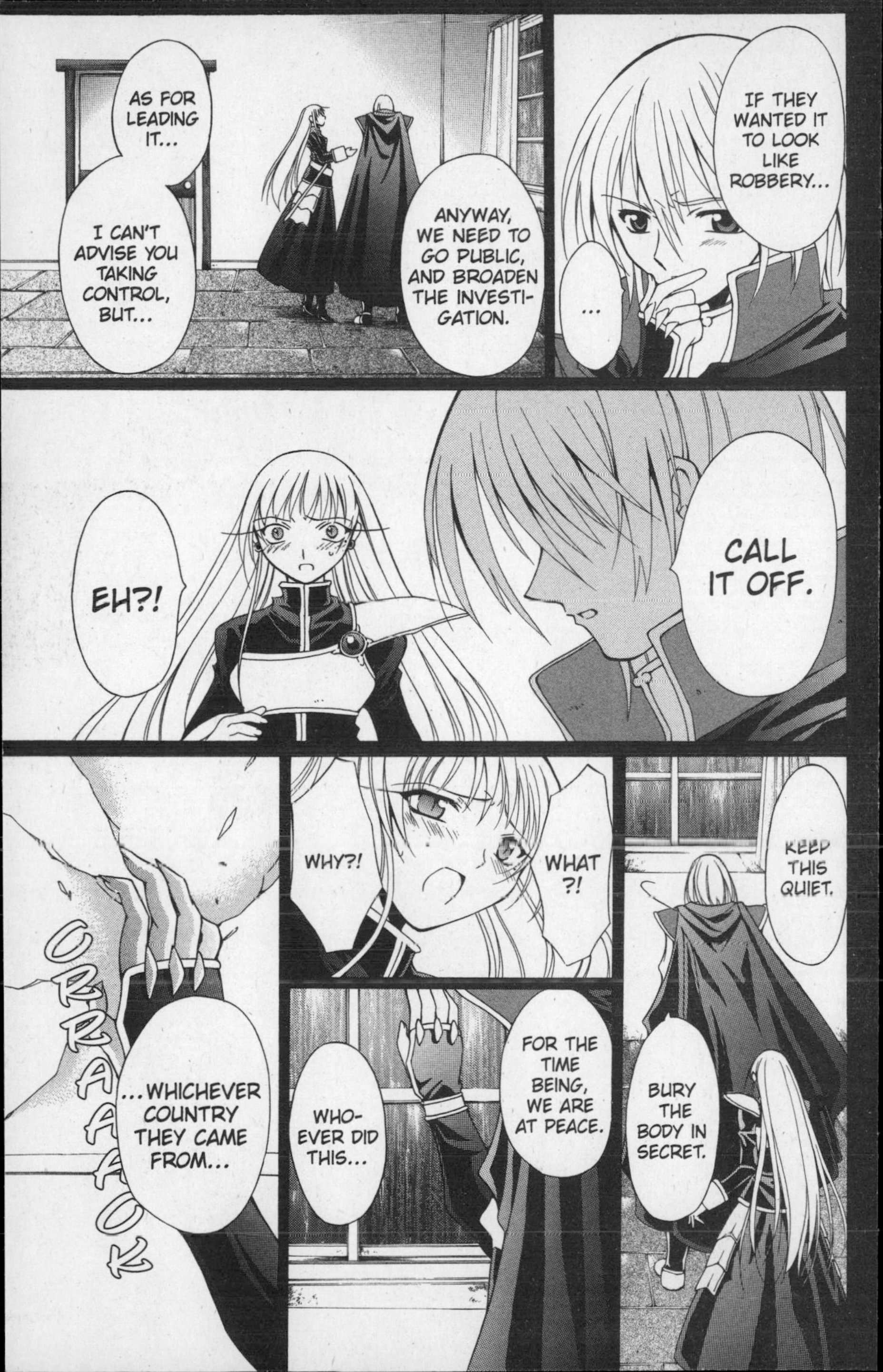
IF THEY WANTED IT TO LOOK LIKE ROBBERY...
...
ANYWAY, WE NEED TO GO PUBLIC, AND BROADEN THE INVESTI- GATION.
AS FOR LEADING IT...
I CAN'T ADVISE YOU TAKING CONTROL, BUT...
CALL IT OFF.
EH?!
KEEP THIS QUIET.
BURY THE BODY IN SECRET.
WHAT ?!
WHY?!
FOR THE TIME BEING, WE ARE AT PEACE.
WHO- EVER DID THIS...
...WHICHEVER COUNTRY THEY CAME FROM...
CRRAAACK

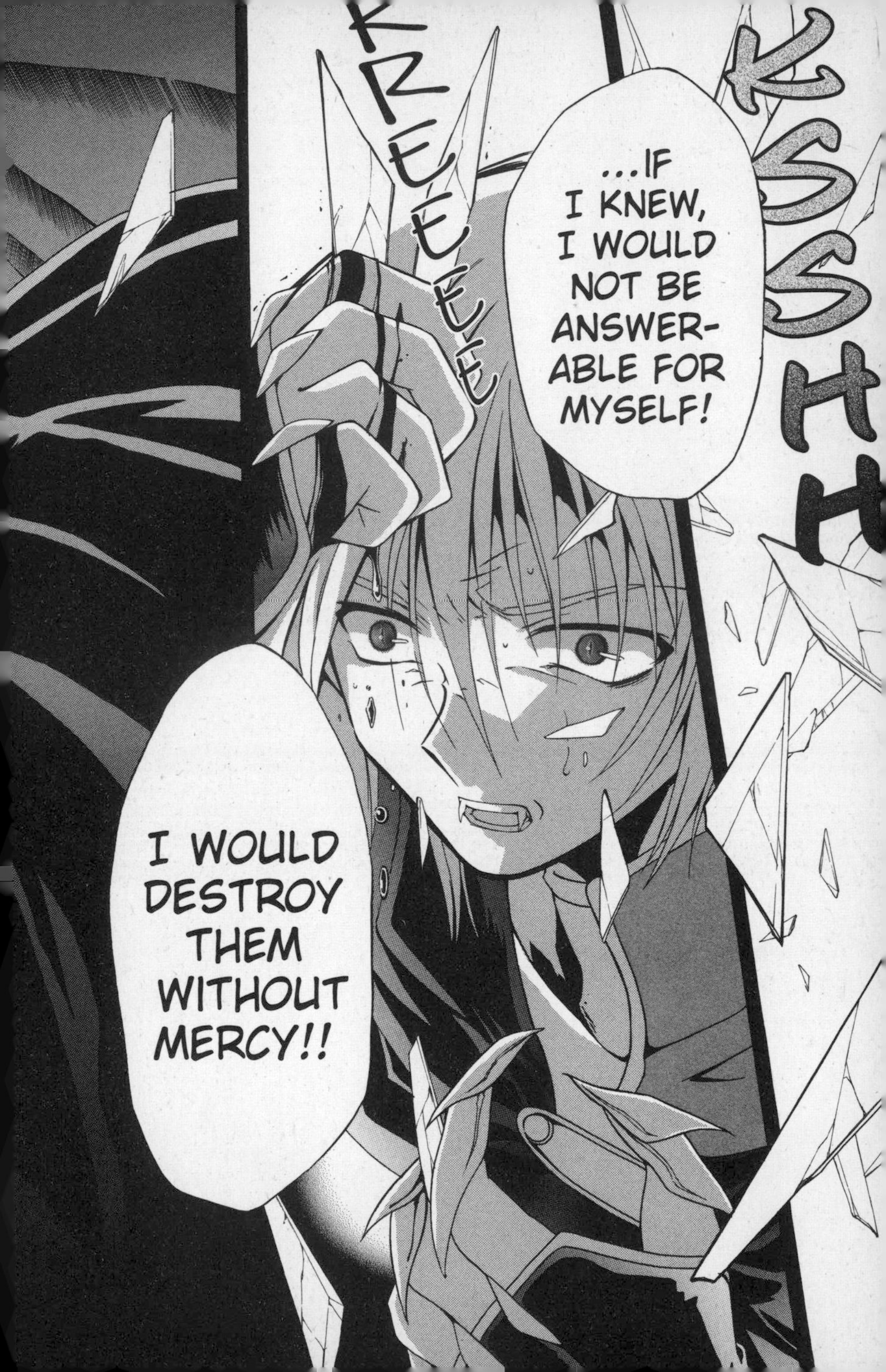
KSSHH
KREEEEE
...IF I KNEW, I WOULD NOT BE ANSWERABLE FOR MYSELF!
I WOULD DESTROY THEM WITHOUT MERCY!!

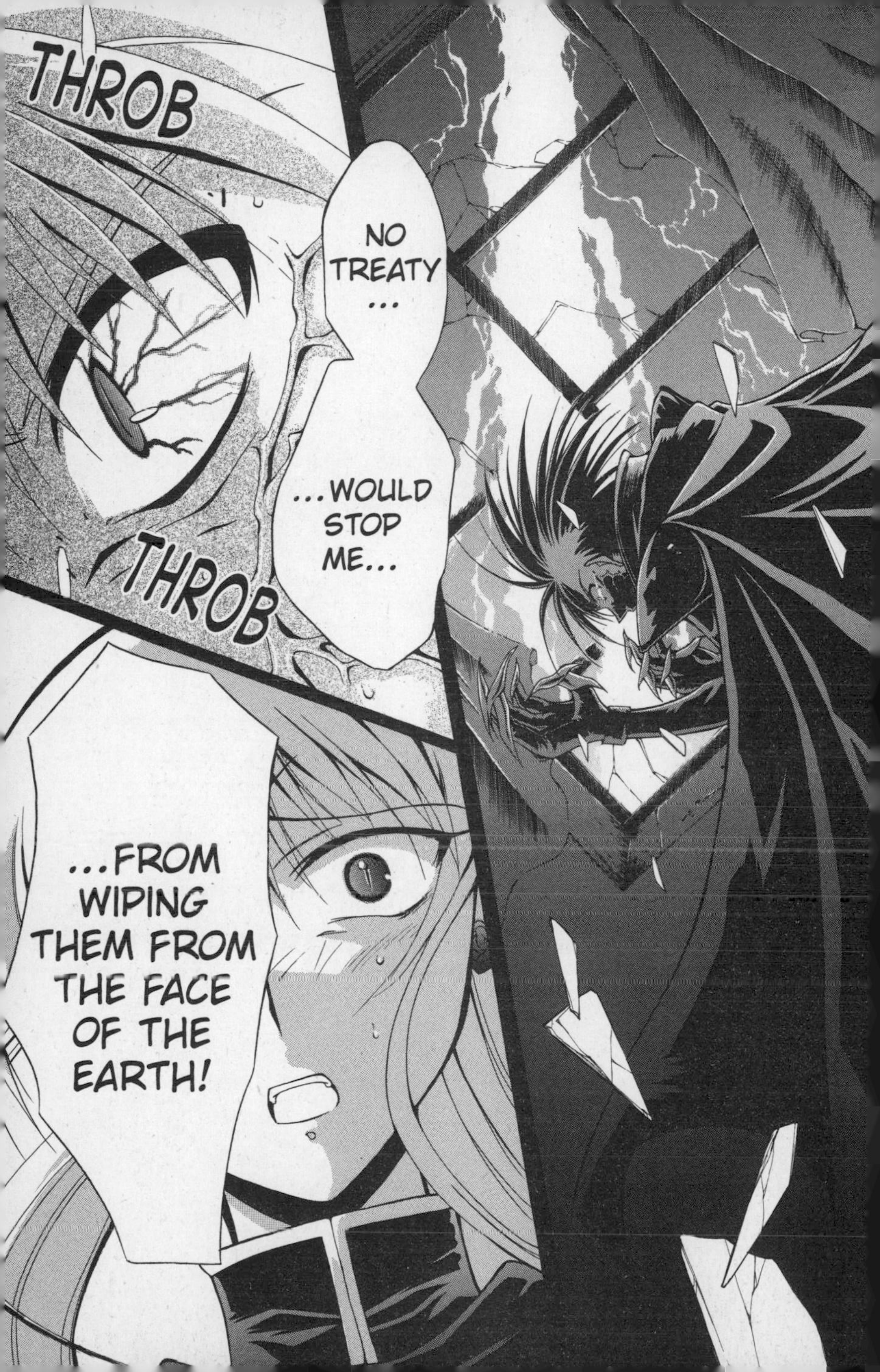
NO TREATY...
THROB
...WOULD STOP ME...
THROB
...FROM WIPING THEM FROM THE FACE OF THE EARTH!

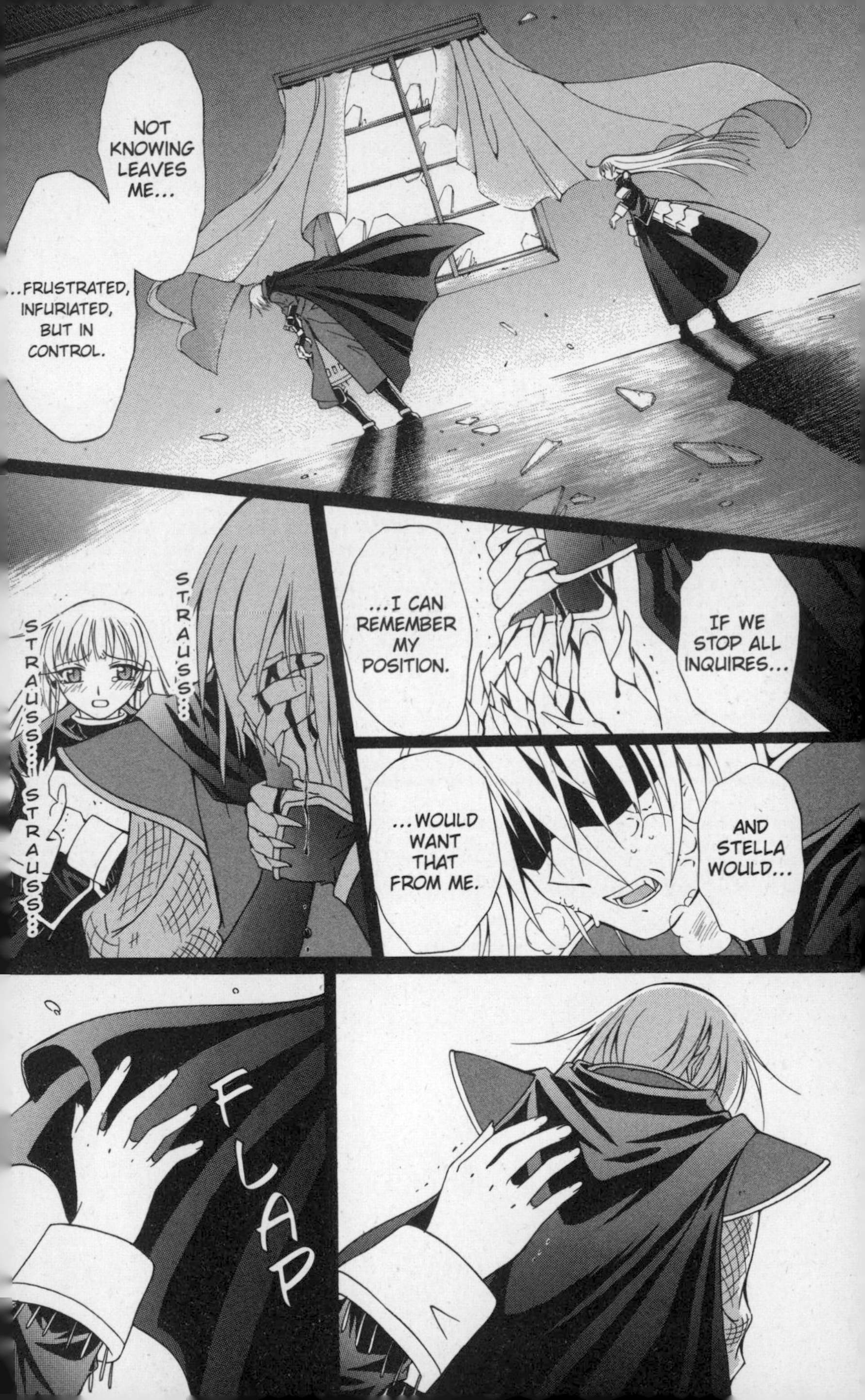
NOT KNOWING LEAVES ME...
...FRUSTRATED, INFURIATED, BUT IN CONTROL.
IF WE STOP ALL INQUIRES...
...I CAN REMEMBER MY POSITION.
AND STELLA WOULD...
...WOULD WANT THAT FROM ME.
STRAUSS...
STRAUSS...
STRAUSS...
FLAP

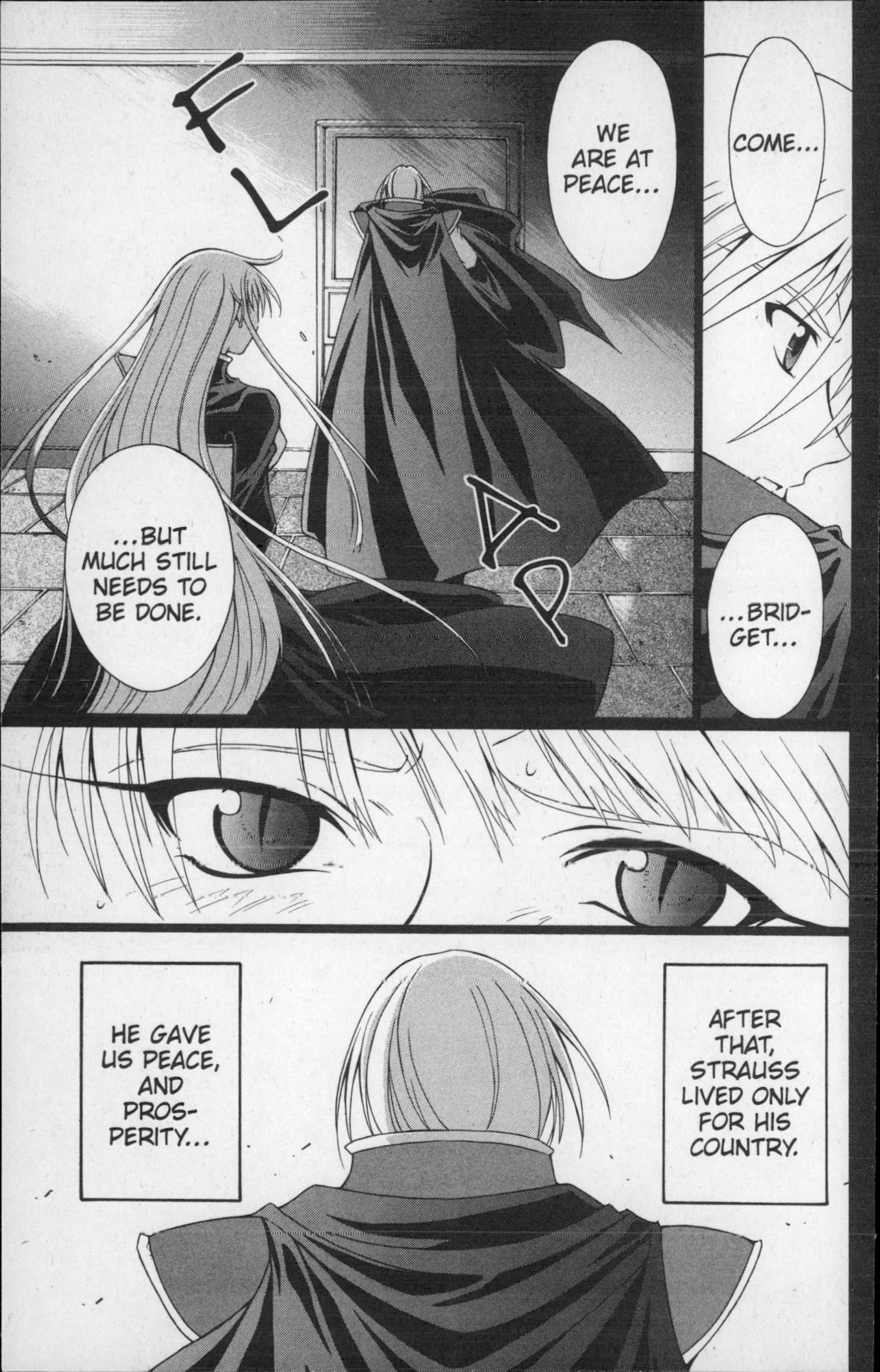
COME...
...BRID-GET...
WE ARE AT PEACE...
FLAP
...BUT MUCH STILL NEEDS TO BE DONE.
AFTER THAT, STRAUSS LIVED ONLY FOR HIS COUNTRY.
HE GAVE US PEACE, AND PROS-PERITY...

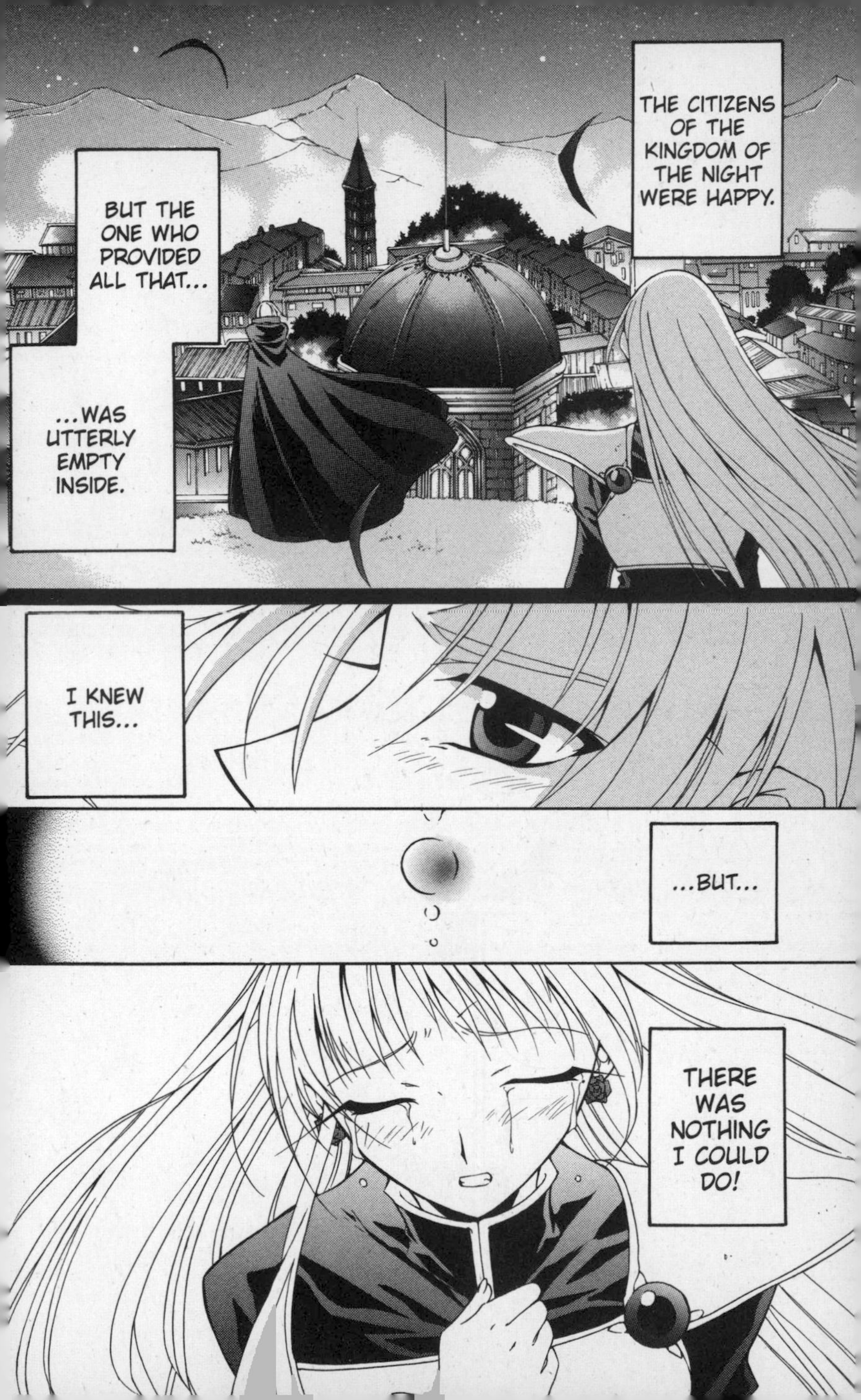
THE CITIZENS OF THE KINGDOM OF THE NIGHT WERE HAPPY.
BUT THE ONE WHO PROVIDED ALL THAT...
...WAS UTTERLY EMPTY INSIDE.
I KNEW THIS...
...BUT...
THERE WAS NOTHING I COULD DO!

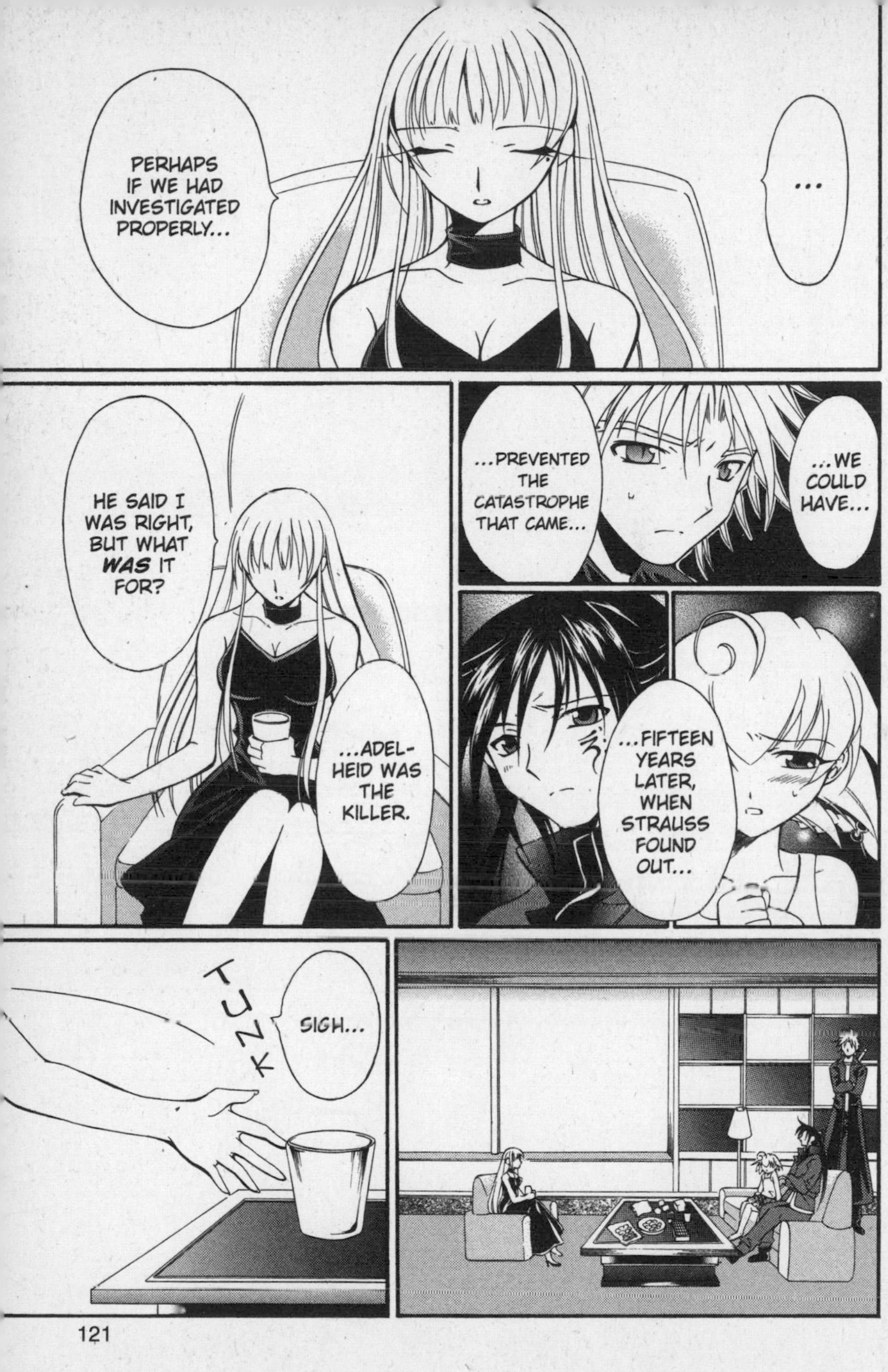
...
PERHAPS IF WE HAD INVESTIGATED PROPERLY...
...WE COULD HAVE...
...PREVENTED THE CATASTROPHE THAT CAME...
...FIFTEEN YEARS LATER, WHEN STRAUSS FOUND OUT...
...ADEL-HEID WAS THE KILLER.
HE SAID I WAS RIGHT, BUT WHAT *WAS* IT FOR?
SIGH...
TUNK

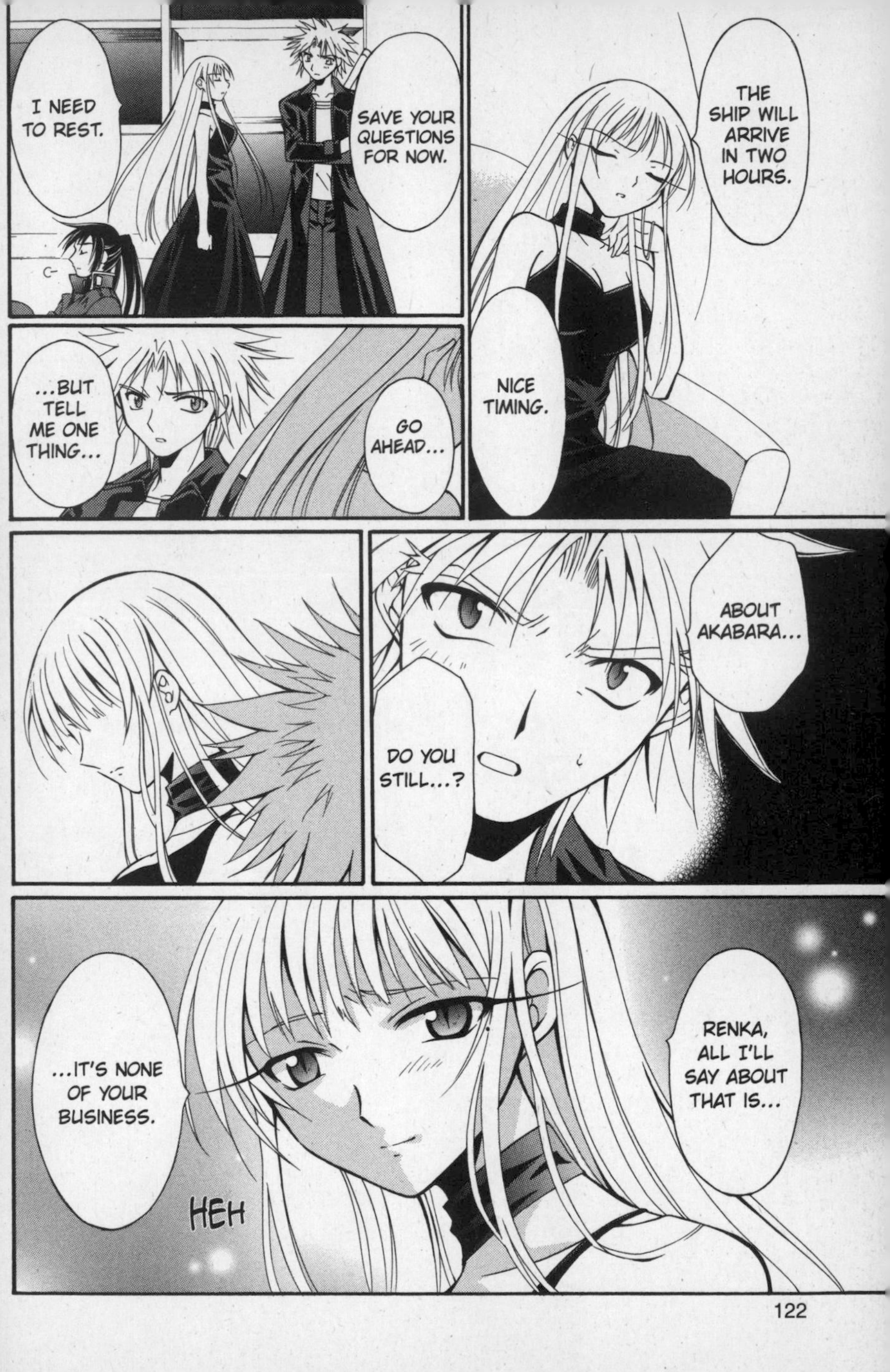
THE SHIP WILL ARRIVE IN TWO HOURS.
NICE TIMING.
SAVE YOUR QUESTIONS FOR NOW.
I NEED TO REST.
...BUT TELL ME ONE THING...
GO AHEAD...
ABOUT AKABARA...
DO YOU STILL...?
RENKA, ALL I'LL SAY ABOUT THAT IS...
...IT'S NONE OF YOUR BUSINESS.
HEH

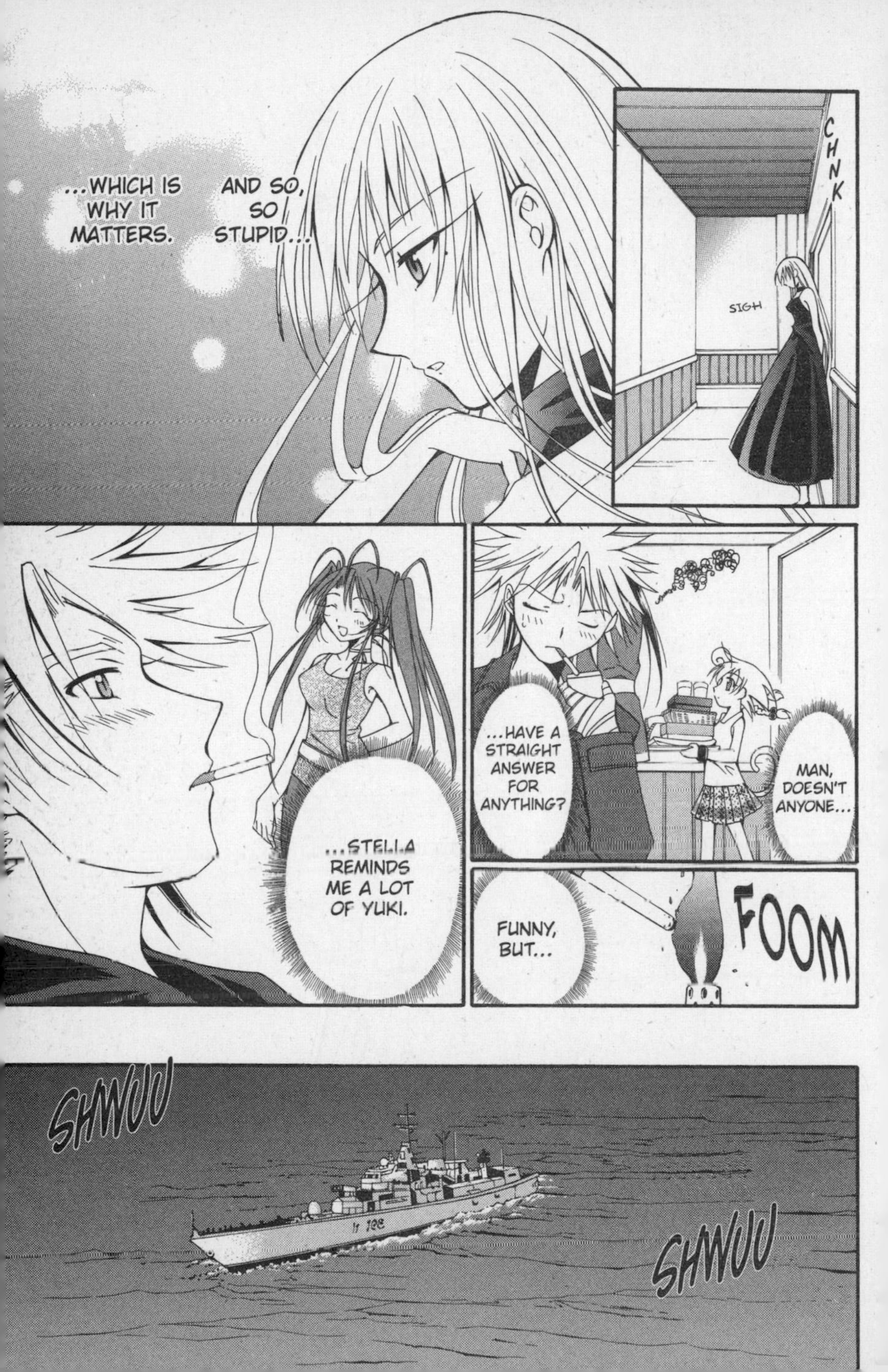
CHNK
SIGH
AND SO, SO STUPID...
...WHICH IS WHY IT MATTERS.
MAN, DOESN'T ANYONE...
...HAVE A STRAIGHT ANSWER FOR ANYTHING?
FOOM
FUNNY, BUT...
...STELLA REMINDS ME A LOT OF YUKI.
SHWUU
SHWUU

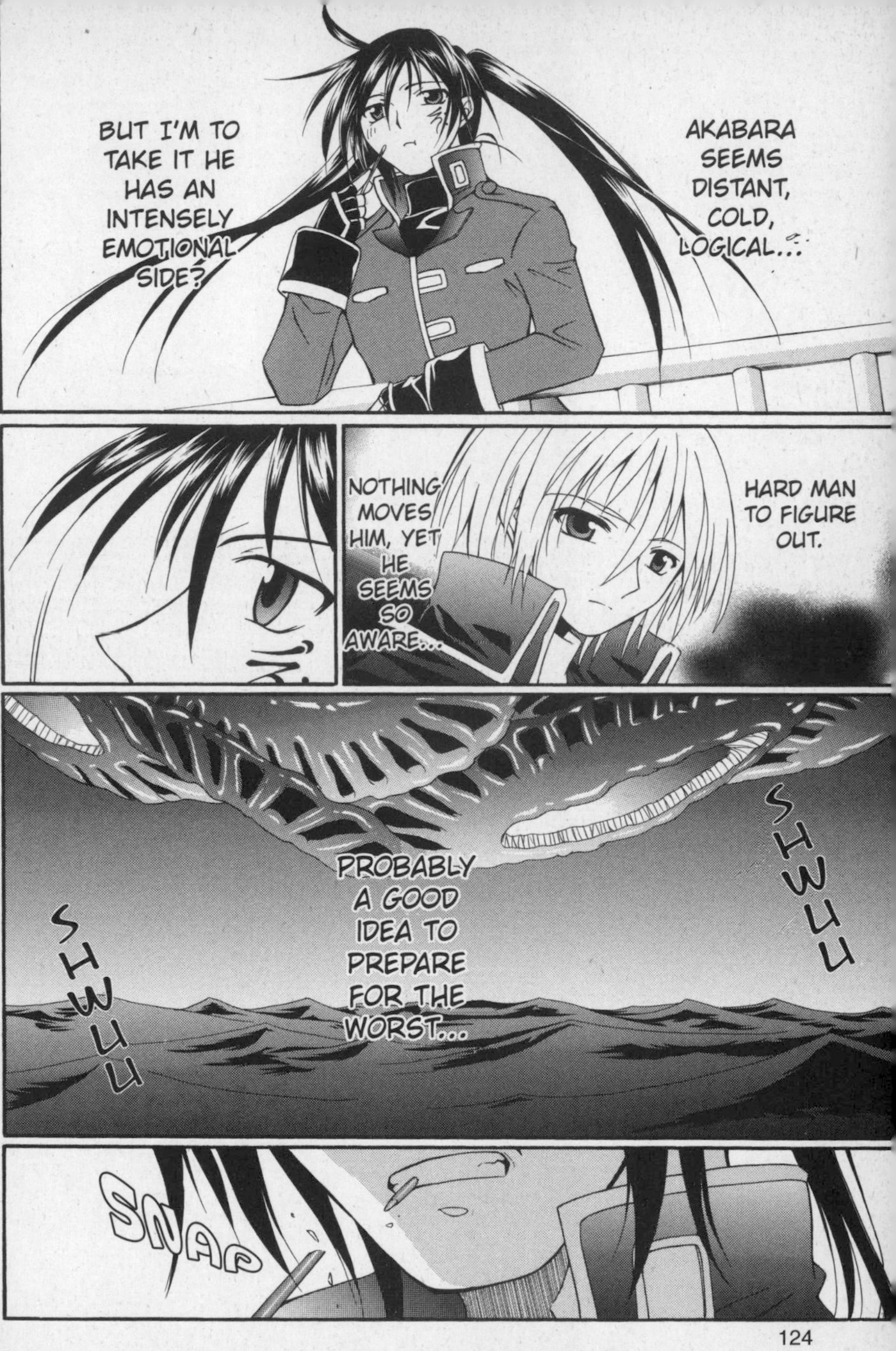
AKABARA SEEMS DISTANT, COLD, LOGICAL...
BUT I'M TO TAKE IT HE HAS AN INTENSELY EMOTIONAL SIDE?
HARD MAN TO FIGURE OUT.
NOTHING MOVES HIM, YET HE SEEMS SO AWARE...
SHWUU
PROBABLY A GOOD IDEA TO PREPARE FOR THE WORST...
SHWUU
SNAP

THE RECORD OF A

FALLEN VAMPIRE

THE RECORD OF A

FALLEN VAMPIRE

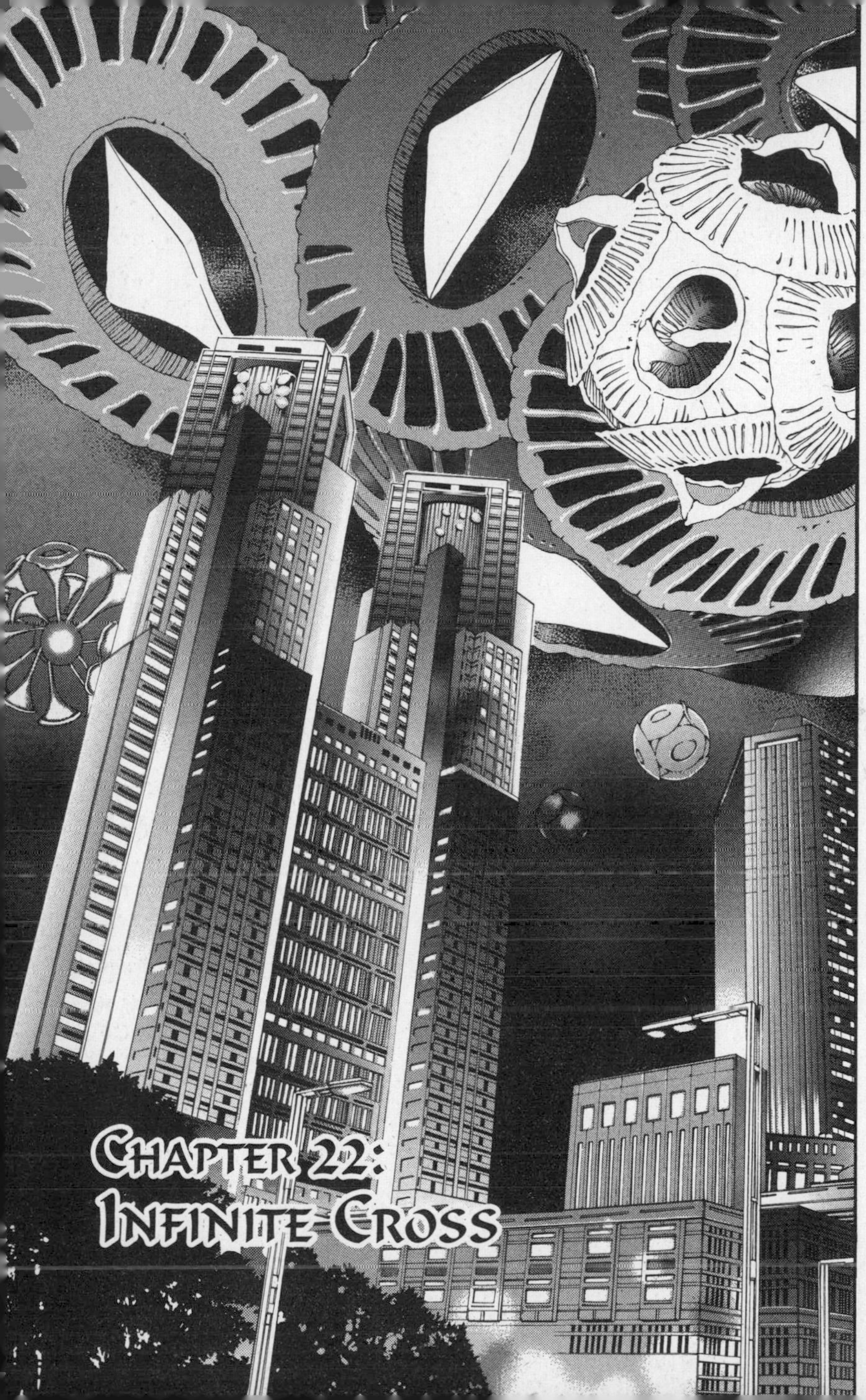
Chapter 22:
Infinite Cross

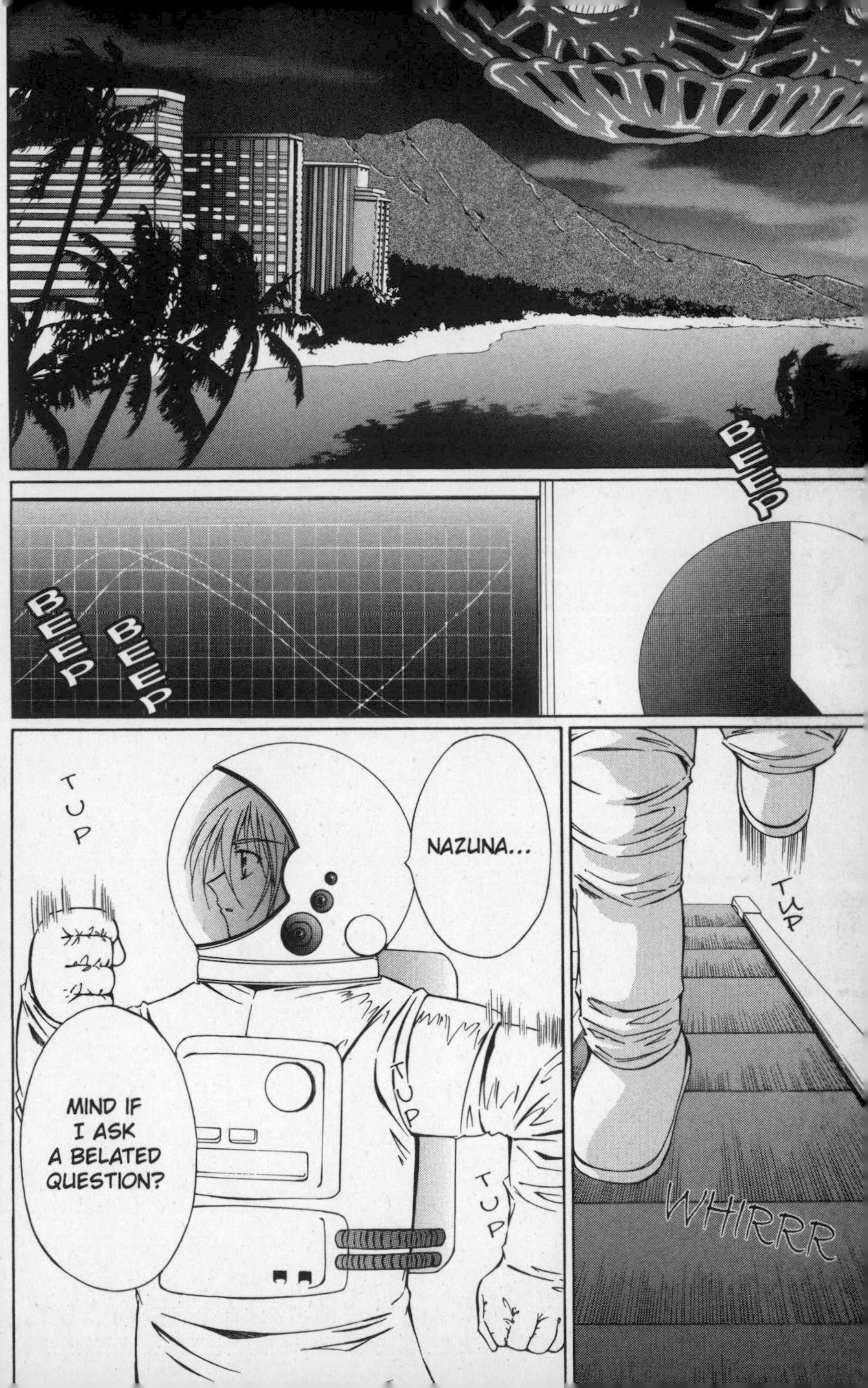
BEEP
BEEP
BEEP
TUP
WHIRRR
NAZUNA...
TUP
TUP
TUP
MIND IF I ASK A BELATED QUESTION?

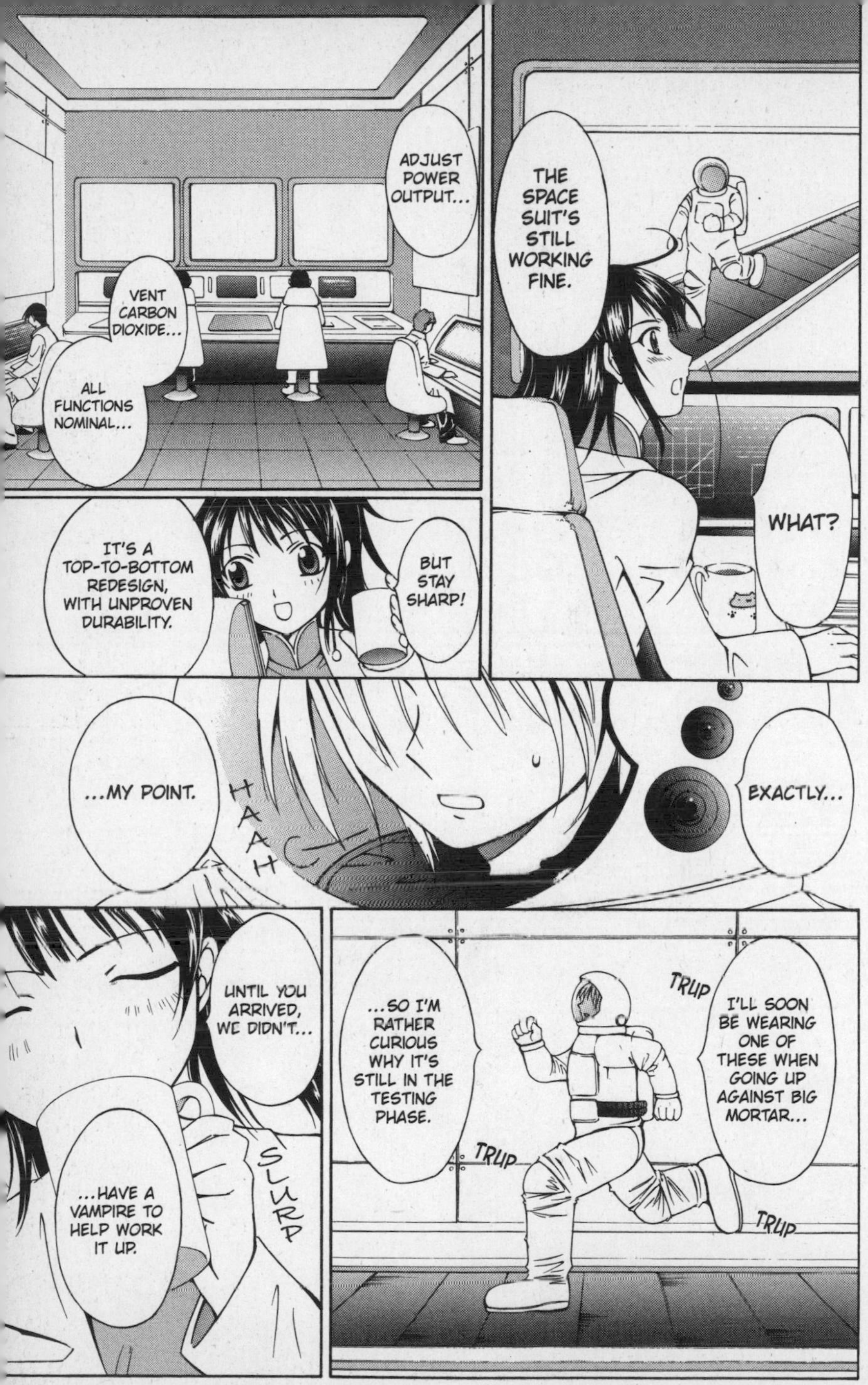
THE SPACE SUIT'S STILL WORKING FINE.
WHAT?
ADJUST POWER OUTPUT...
VENT CARBON DIOXIDE...
ALL FUNCTIONS NOMINAL...
BUT STAY SHARP!
IT'S A TOP-TO-BOTTOM REDESIGN, WITH UNPROVEN DURABILITY.
EXACTLY...
HAAAH
...MY POINT.
I'LL SOON BE WEARING ONE OF THESE WHEN GOING UP AGAINST BIG MORTAR...
TRUP
TRUP
TRUP
...SO I'M RATHER CURIOUS WHY IT'S STILL IN THE TESTING PHASE.
UNTIL YOU ARRIVED, WE DIDN'T...
SLURP
...HAVE A VAMPIRE TO HELP WORK IT UP.

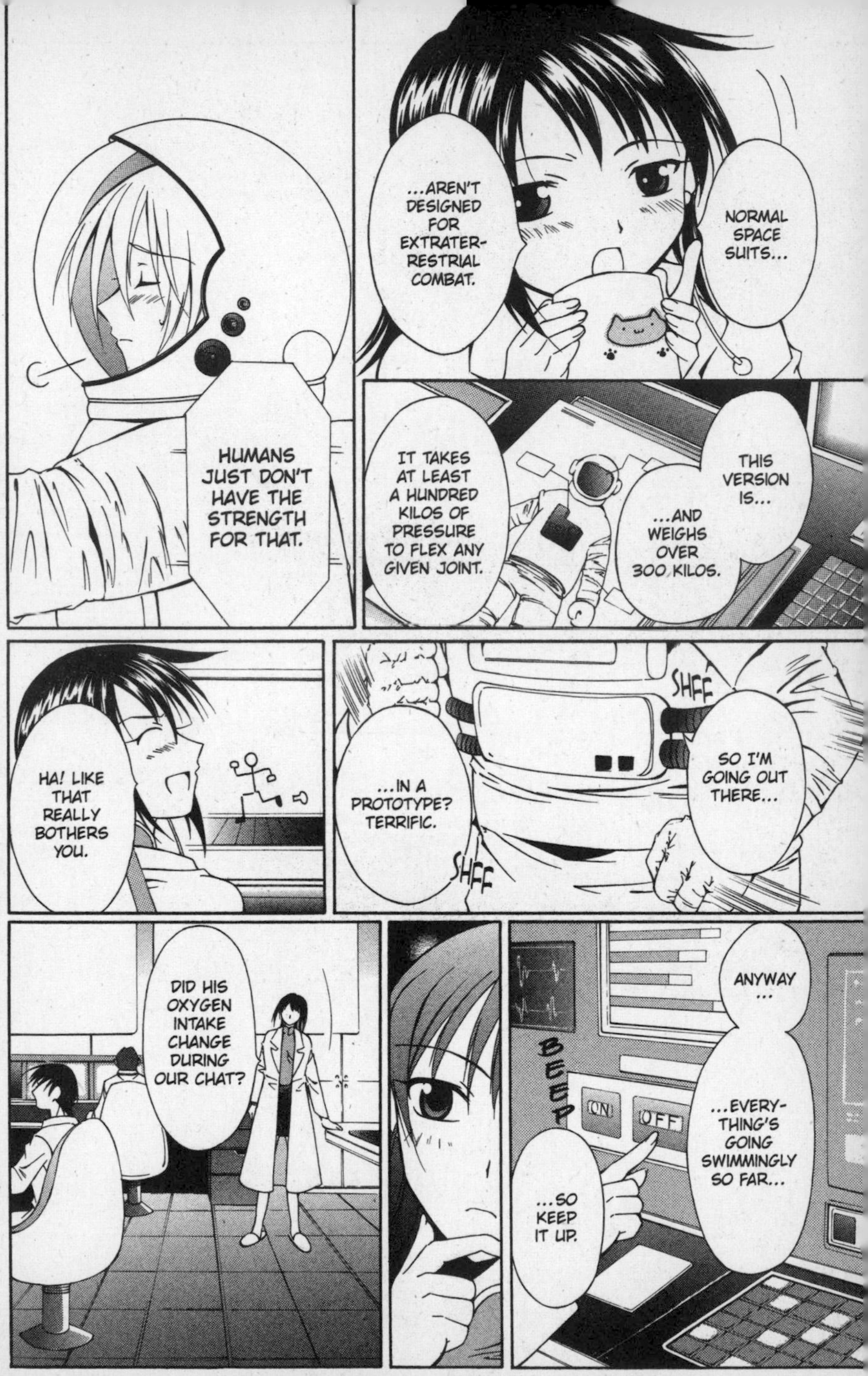
NORMAL SPACE SUITS...
...AREN'T DESIGNED FOR EXTRATER-RESTRIAL COMBAT.
THIS VERSION IS...
...AND WEIGHS OVER 300 KILOS.
IT TAKES AT LEAST A HUNDRED KILOS OF PRESSURE TO FLEX ANY GIVEN JOINT.
HUMANS JUST DON'T HAVE THE STRENGTH FOR THAT.
SHFF
SO I'M GOING OUT THERE...
...IN A PROTOTYPE? TERRIFIC.
SHFF
HA! LIKE THAT REALLY BOTHERS YOU.
ANYWAY...
...EVERY-THING'S GOING SWIMMINGLY SO FAR...
BEEP
ON
OFF
...SO KEEP IT UP.
DID HIS OXYGEN INTAKE CHANGE DURING OUR CHAT?

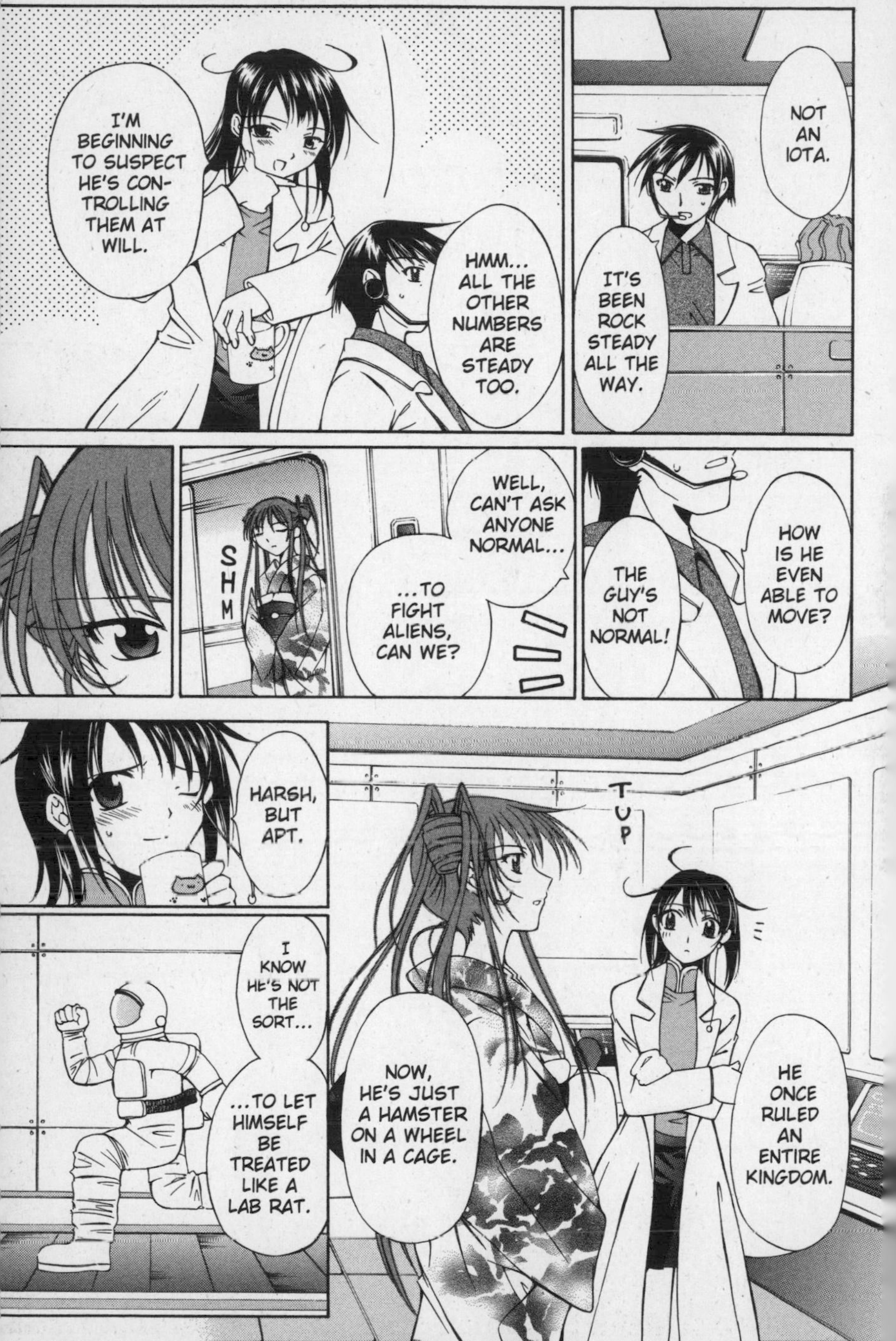
NOT AN IOTA.
IT'S BEEN ROCK STEADY ALL THE WAY.
HMM... ALL THE OTHER NUMBERS ARE STEADY TOO.
I'M BEGINNING TO SUSPECT HE'S CON-TROLLING THEM AT WILL.
HOW IS HE EVEN ABLE TO MOVE?
THE GUY'S NOT NORMAL!
WELL, CAN'T ASK ANYONE NORMAL...
...TO FIGHT ALIENS, CAN WE?
SHM
TUP
HE ONCE RULED AN ENTIRE KINGDOM.
NOW, HE'S JUST A HAMSTER ON A WHEEL IN A CAGE.
HARSH, BUT APT.
I KNOW HE'S NOT THE SORT...
...TO LET HIMSELF BE TREATED LIKE A LAB RAT.

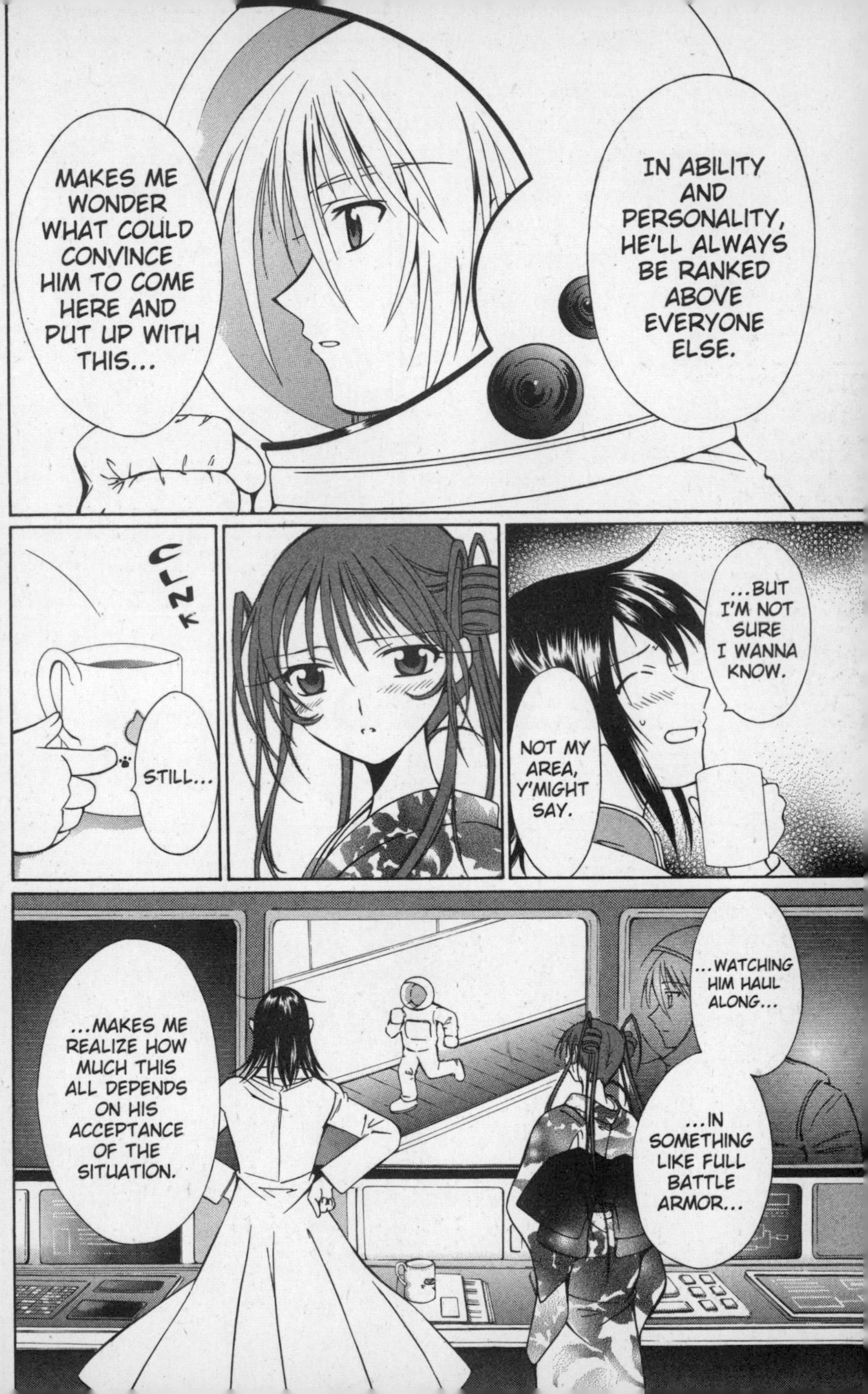
IN ABILITY AND PERSONALITY, HE'LL ALWAYS BE RANKED ABOVE EVERYONE ELSE.
MAKES ME WONDER WHAT COULD CONVINCE HIM TO COME HERE AND PUT UP WITH THIS...
...BUT I'M NOT SURE I WANNA KNOW.
NOT MY AREA, Y'MIGHT SAY.
CLNK
STILL...
...WATCHING HIM HAUL ALONG...
...IN SOMETHING LIKE FULL BATTLE ARMOR...
...MAKES ME REALIZE HOW MUCH THIS ALL DEPENDS ON HIS ACCEPTANCE OF THE SITUATION.

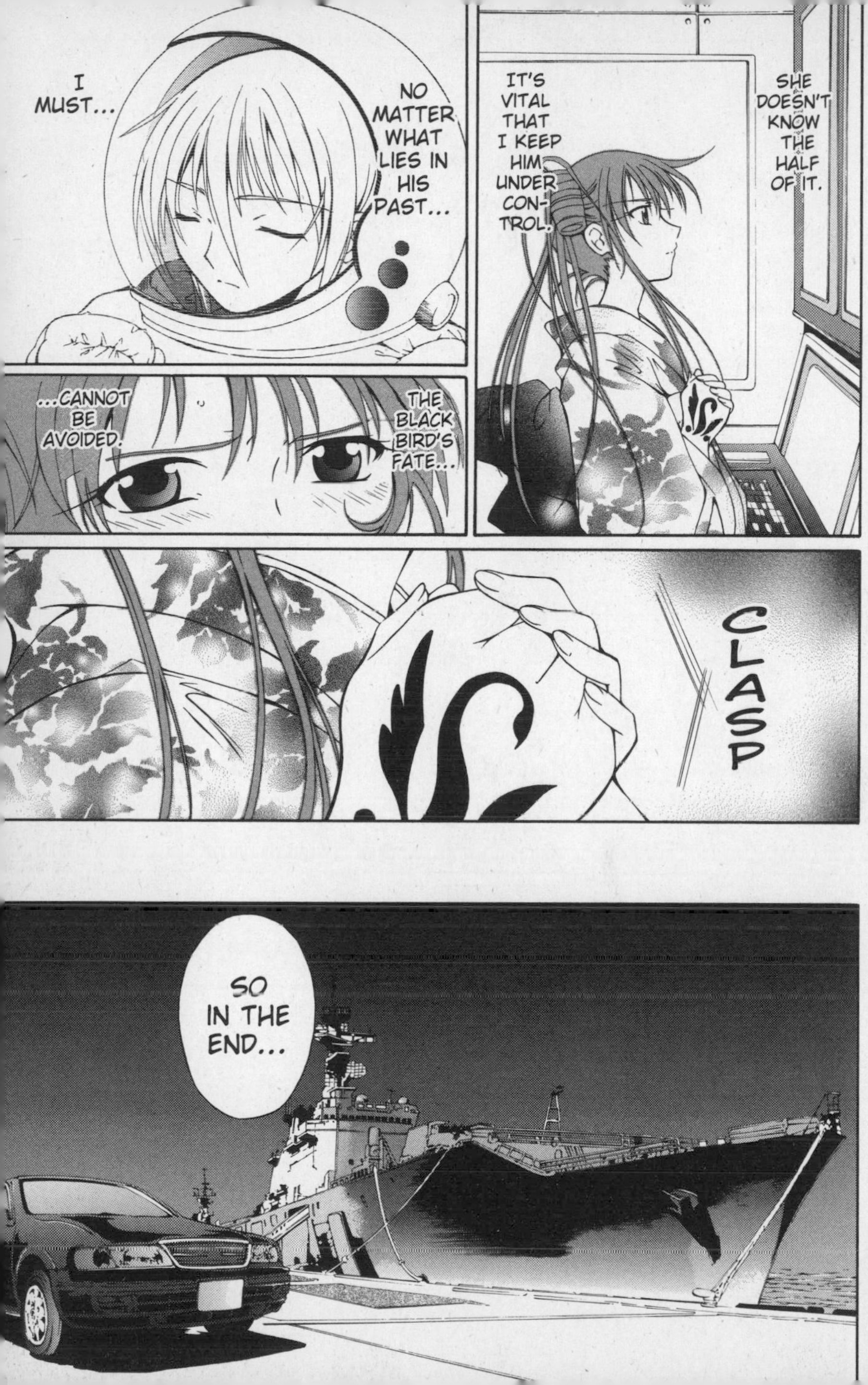
SHE DOESN'T KNOW THE HALF OF IT.
IT'S VITAL THAT I KEEP HIM UNDER CON-TROL.
NO MATTER WHAT LIES IN HIS PAST...
I MUST...
THE BLACK BIRD'S FATE...
...CANNOT BE AVOIDED.
CLASP
SO IN THE END...

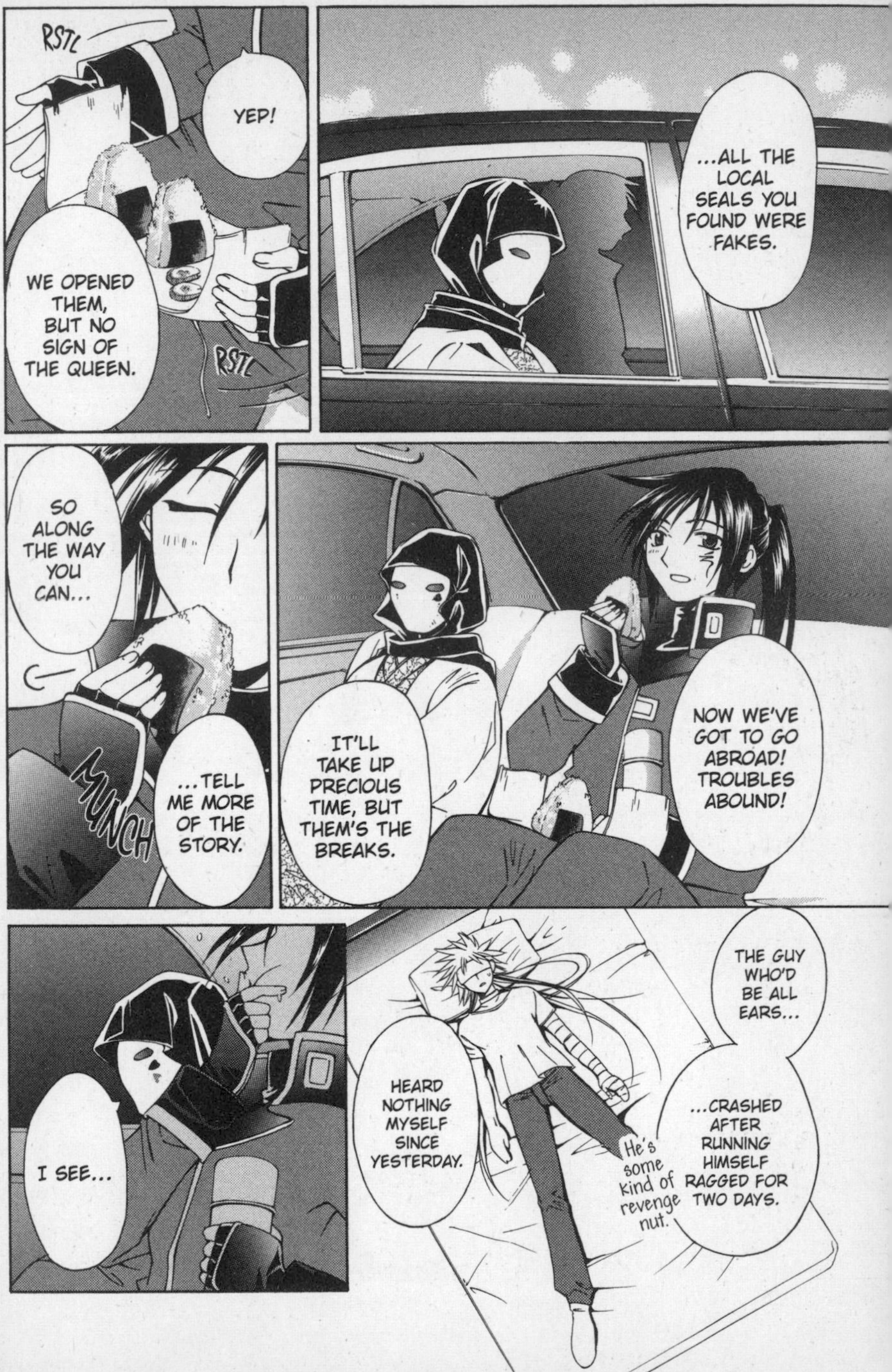
...ALL THE LOCAL SEALS YOU FOUND WERE FAKES.
RSTL
YEP!
WE OPENED THEM, BUT NO SIGN OF THE QUEEN.
RSTL
NOW WE'VE GOT TO GO ABROAD! TROUBLES ABOUND!
IT'LL TAKE UP PRECIOUS TIME, BUT THEM'S THE BREAKS.
SO ALONG THE WAY YOU CAN...
...TELL ME MORE OF THE STORY.
MUNCH
THE GUY WHO'D BE ALL EARS...
...CRASHED AFTER RUNNING HIMSELF RAGGED FOR TWO DAYS.
He's some kind of revenge nut.
HEARD NOTHING MYSELF SINCE YESTERDAY.
I SEE...

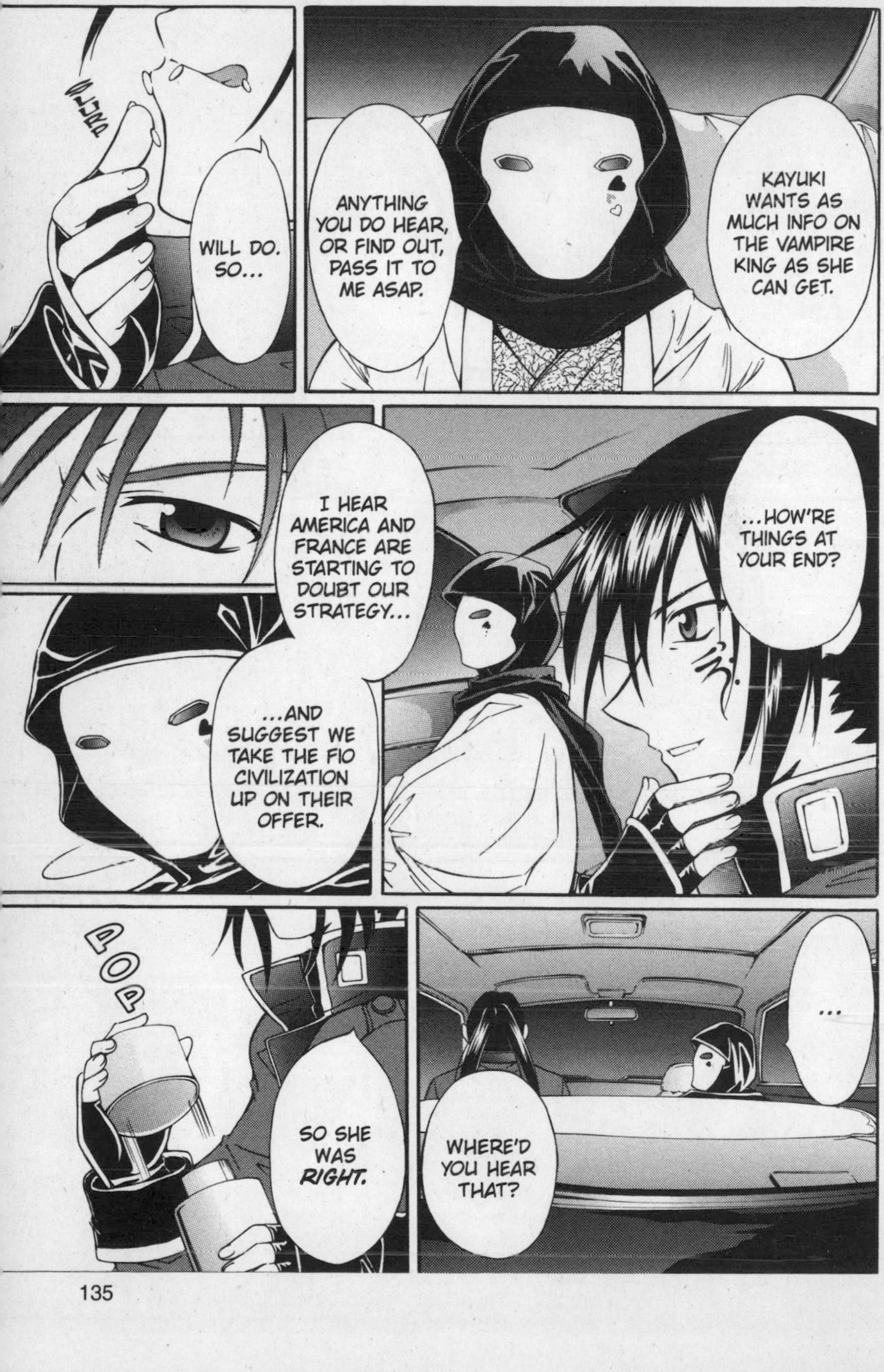
KAYUKI WANTS AS MUCH INFO ON THE VAMPIRE KING AS SHE CAN GET.
ANYTHING YOU DO HEAR, OR FIND OUT, PASS IT TO ME ASAP.
SLURP
WILL DO. SO...
...HOW'RE THINGS AT YOUR END?
I HEAR AMERICA AND FRANCE ARE STARTING TO DOUBT OUR STRATEGY...
...AND SUGGEST WE TAKE THE FIO CIVILIZATION UP ON THEIR OFFER.
...
WHERE'D YOU HEAR THAT?
POP
SO SHE WAS *RIGHT*.

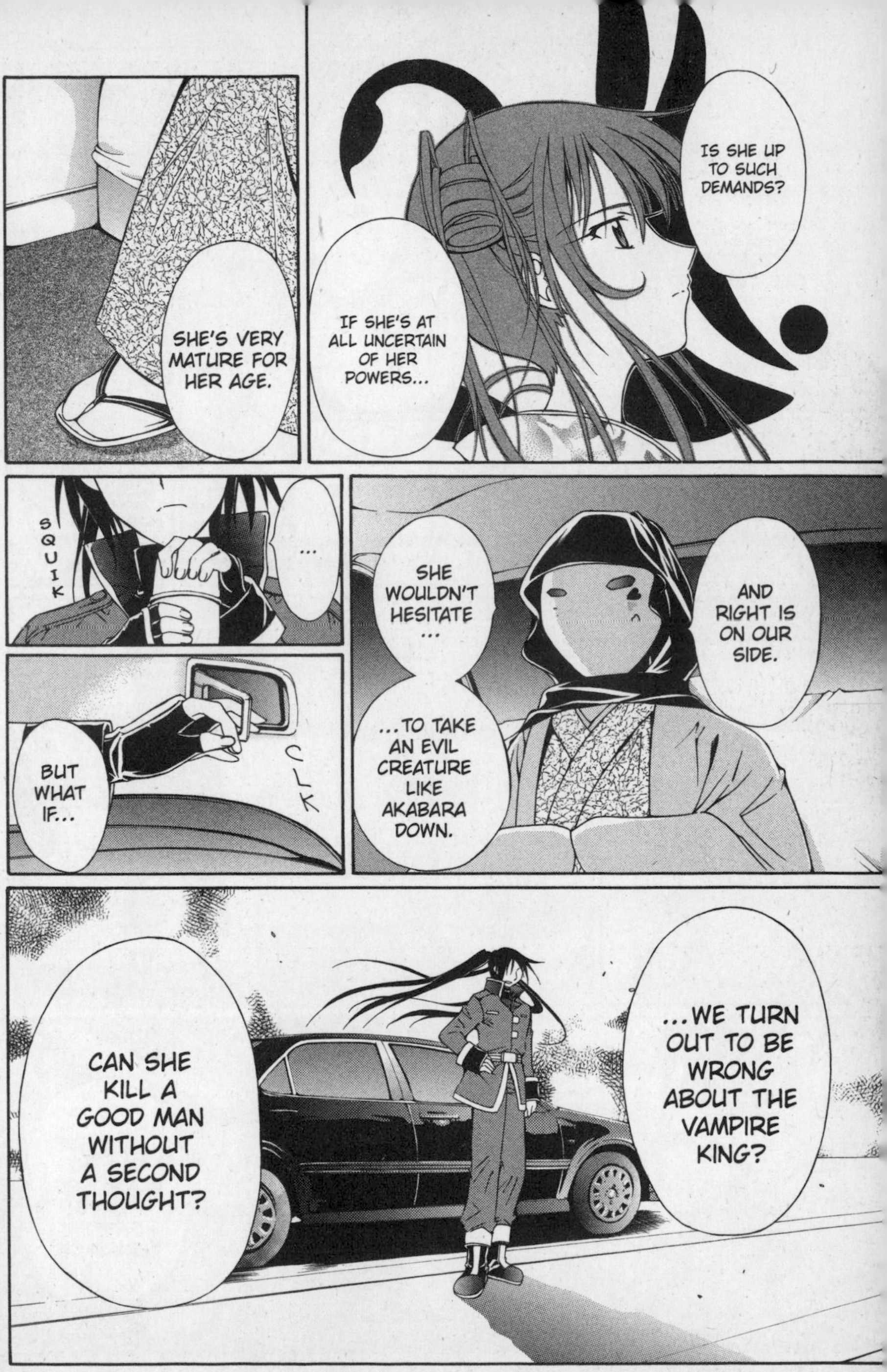
IS SHE UP TO SUCH DEMANDS?
IF SHE'S AT ALL UNCERTAIN OF HER POWERS...
SHE'S VERY MATURE FOR HER AGE.
AND RIGHT IS ON OUR SIDE.
SHE WOULDN'T HESITATE ...
...TO TAKE AN EVIL CREATURE LIKE AKABARA DOWN.
...
SQUIK
CLK
BUT WHAT IF...
...WE TURN OUT TO BE WRONG ABOUT THE VAMPIRE KING?
CAN SHE KILL A GOOD MAN WITHOUT A SECOND THOUGHT?

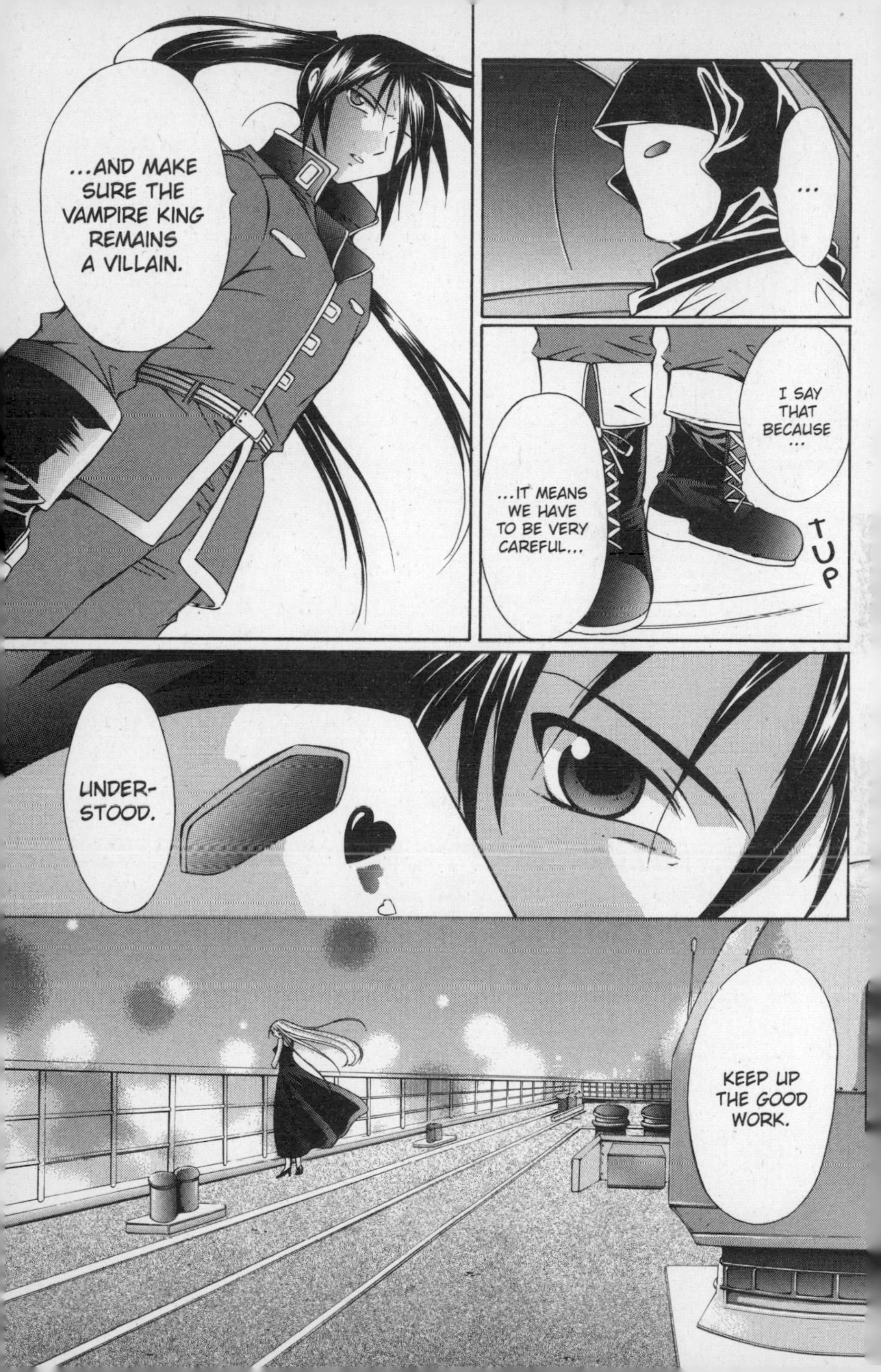
...
I SAY THAT BECAUSE ...
...IT MEANS WE HAVE TO BE VERY CAREFUL...
TUP
...AND MAKE SURE THE VAMPIRE KING REMAINS A VILLAIN.
UNDER-STOOD.
KEEP UP THE GOOD WORK.

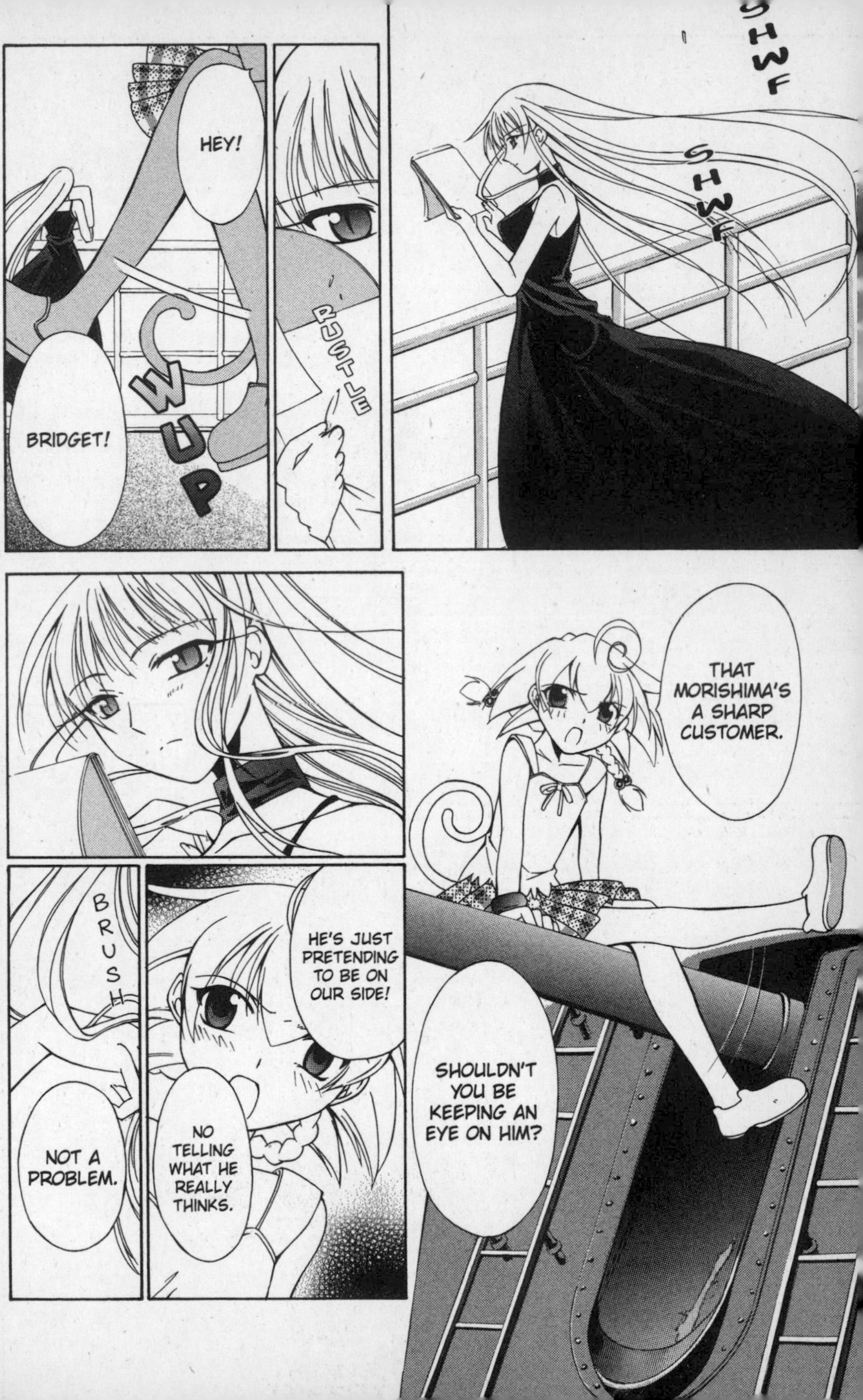
SHWF
SHWF
RUSTLE
HEY!
WUP
BRIDGET!
THAT MORISHIMA'S A SHARP CUSTOMER.
SHOULDN'T YOU BE KEEPING AN EYE ON HIM?
HE'S JUST PRETENDING TO BE ON OUR SIDE!
NO TELLING WHAT HE REALLY THINKS.
BRUSH
NOT A PROBLEM.

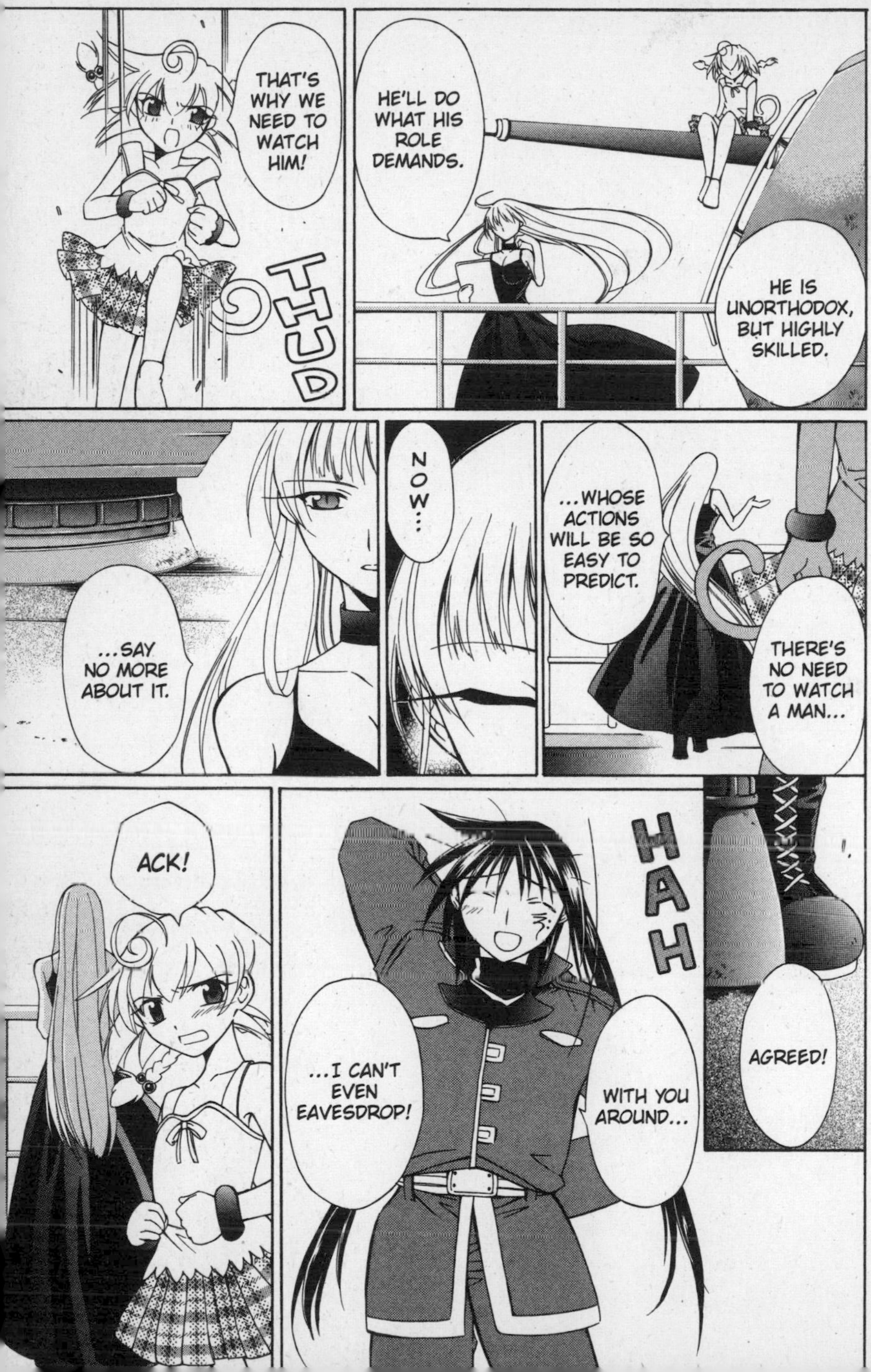
HE IS UNORTHODOX, BUT HIGHLY SKILLED.
HE'LL DO WHAT HIS ROLE DEMANDS.
THAT'S WHY WE NEED TO WATCH HIM!
THUD
THERE'S NO NEED TO WATCH A MAN...
...WHOSE ACTIONS WILL BE SO EASY TO PREDICT.
NOW...
...SAY NO MORE ABOUT IT.
AGREED!
HAH
WITH YOU AROUND...
...I CAN'T EVEN EAVESDROP!
ACK!

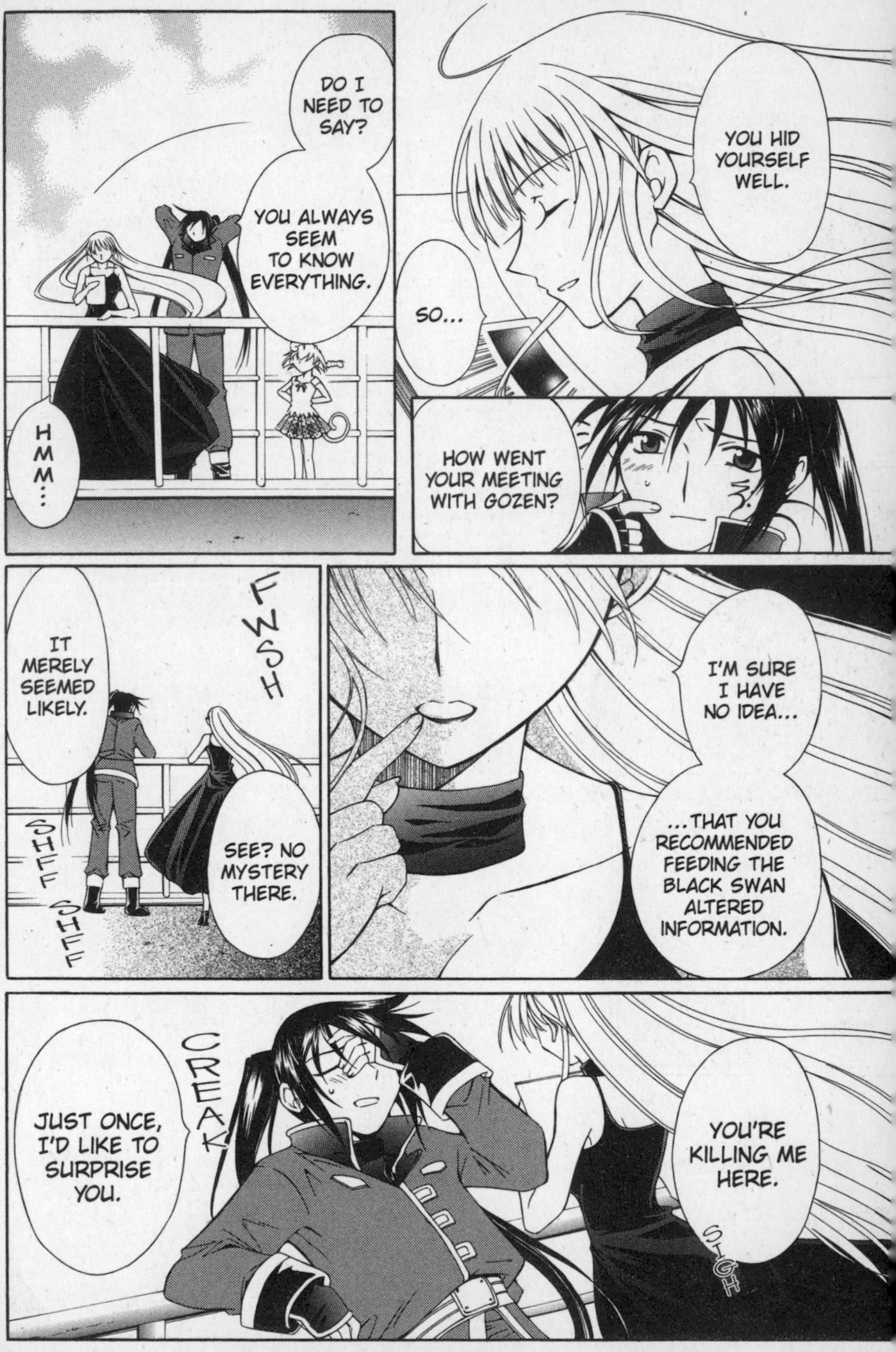
YOU HID YOURSELF WELL.
SO...
HOW WENT YOUR MEETING WITH GOZEN?
DO I NEED TO SAY?
YOU ALWAYS SEEM TO KNOW EVERYTHING.
HMM...
I'M SURE I HAVE NO IDEA...
...THAT YOU RECOMMENDED FEEDING THE BLACK SWAN ALTERED INFORMATION.
FWSH
IT MERELY SEEMED LIKELY.
SEE? NO MYSTERY THERE.
SHEFF SHEFF
YOU'RE KILLING ME HERE.
SIGH
CREAK
JUST ONCE, I'D LIKE TO SURPRISE YOU.

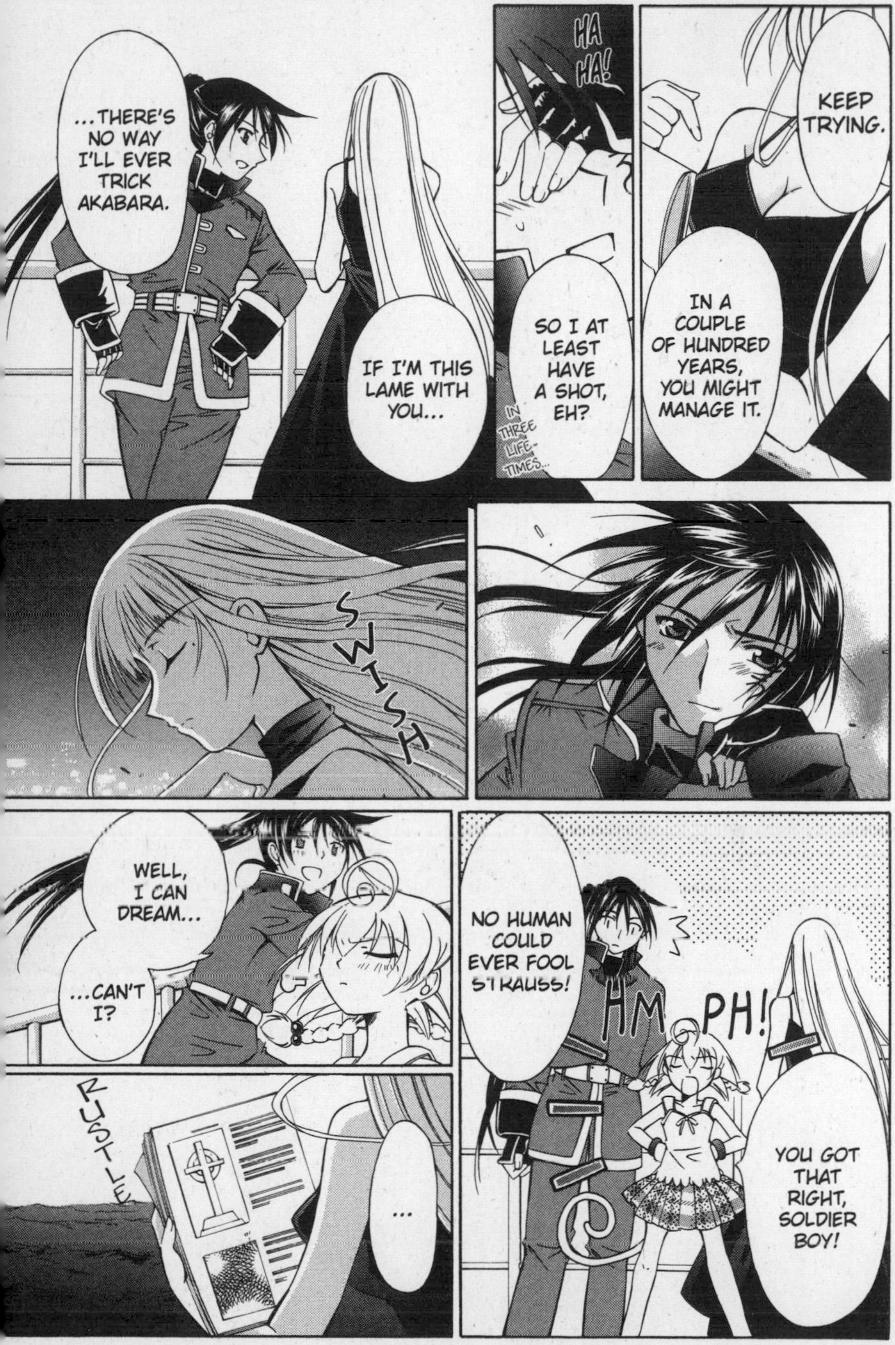
KEEP TRYING.
IN A COUPLE OF HUNDRED YEARS, YOU MIGHT MANAGE IT.
HA HA!
SO I AT LEAST HAVE A SHOT, EH?
IN THREE LIFE-TIMES...
IF I'M THIS LAME WITH YOU...
...THERE'S NO WAY I'LL EVER TRICK AKABARA.
SWISH
NO HUMAN COULD EVER FOOL STRAUSS!
HMPH!
YOU GOT THAT RIGHT, SOLDIER BOY!
WELL, I CAN DREAM...
...CAN'T I?
RUSTLE
...

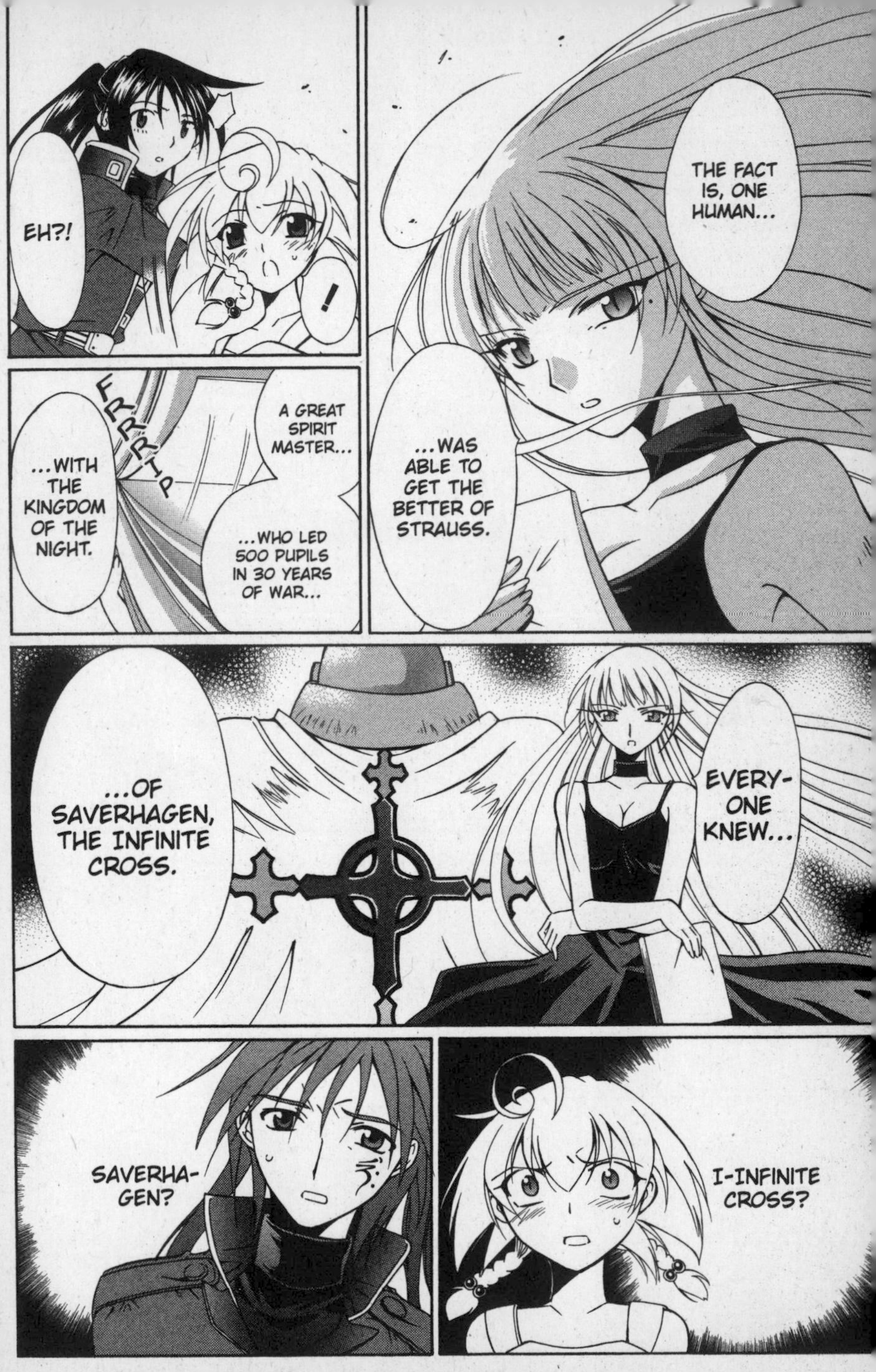
THE FACT IS, ONE HUMAN...
...WAS ABLE TO GET THE BETTER OF STRAUSS.
!
EH?!
A GREAT SPIRIT MASTER...
...WHO LED 500 PUPILS IN 30 YEARS OF WAR...
FRRRIP
...WITH THE KINGDOM OF THE NIGHT.
EVERY-ONE KNEW...
...OF SAVERHAGEN, THE INFINITE CROSS.
I-INFINITE CROSS?
SAVERHA-GEN?

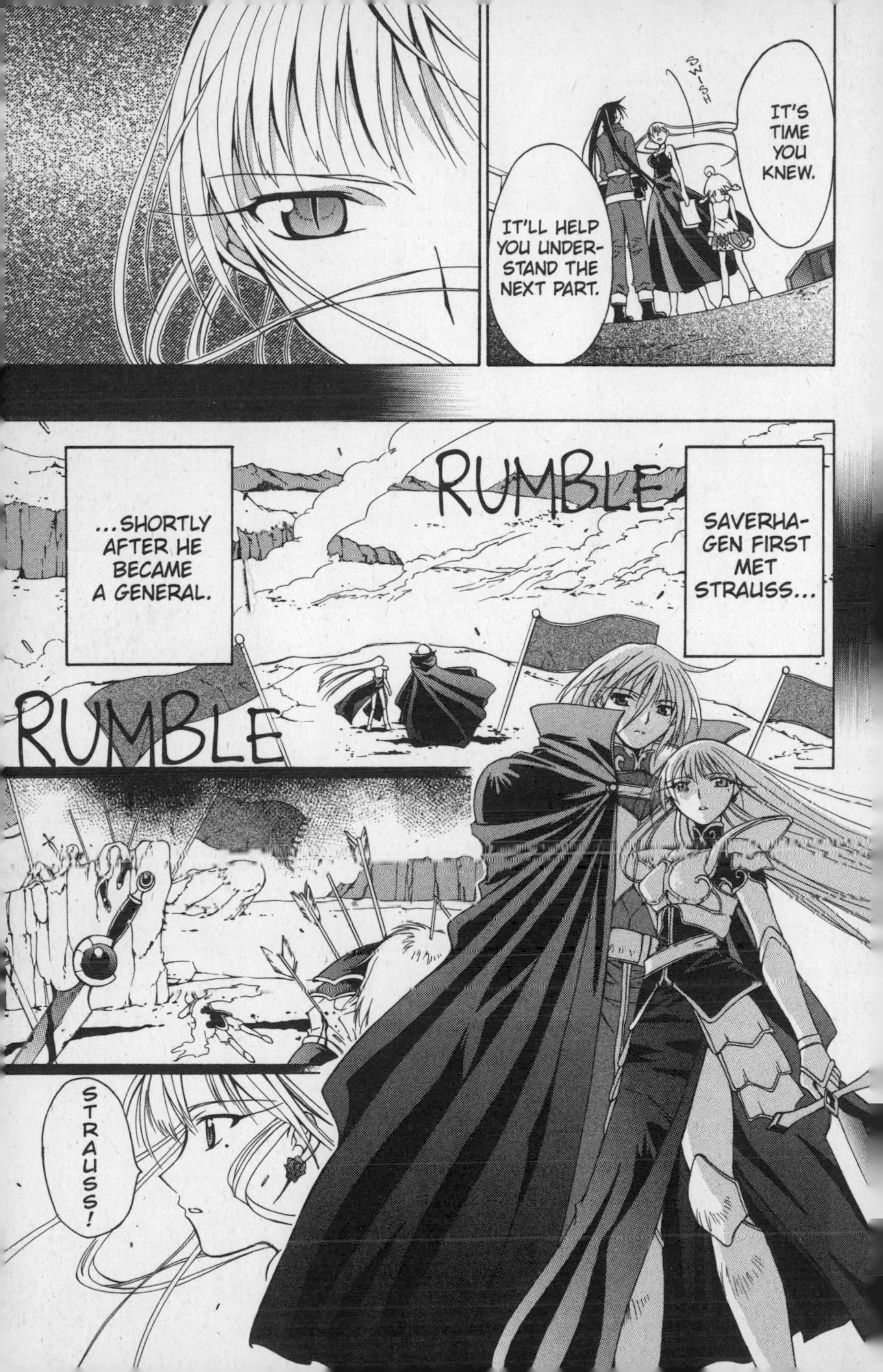
SWISH
IT'S TIME YOU KNEW.
IT'LL HELP YOU UNDERSTAND THE NEXT PART.
SAVERHAGEN FIRST MET STRAUSS...
RUMBLE
...SHORTLY AFTER HE BECAME A GENERAL.
RUMBLE
STRAUSS!

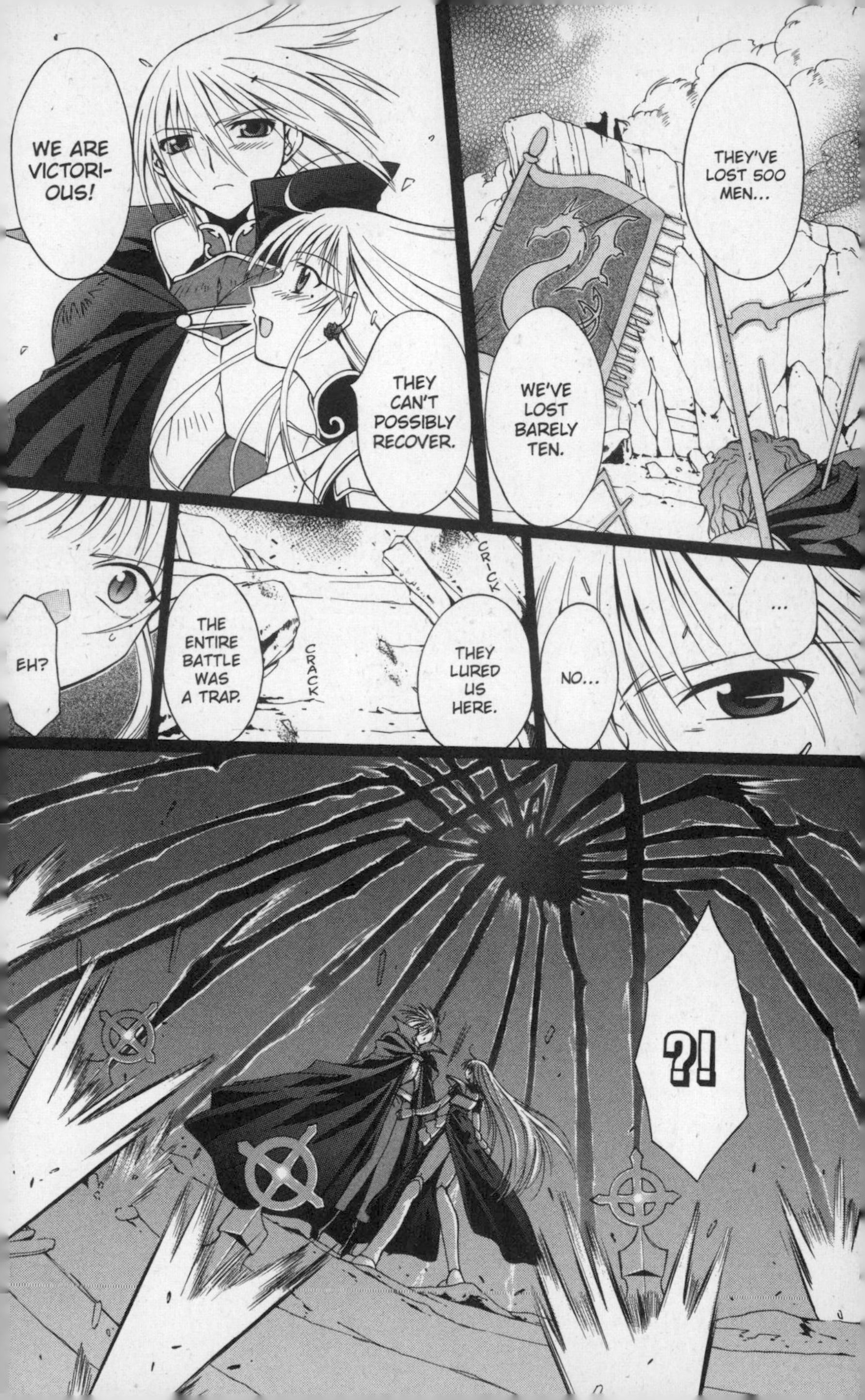
THEY'VE LOST 500 MEN...
WE'VE LOST BARELY TEN.
WE ARE VICTORI-OUS!
THEY CAN'T POSSIBLY RECOVER.
...
NO...
CRICK
THEY LURED US HERE.
CRACK
THE ENTIRE BATTLE WAS A TRAP.
EH?
?!

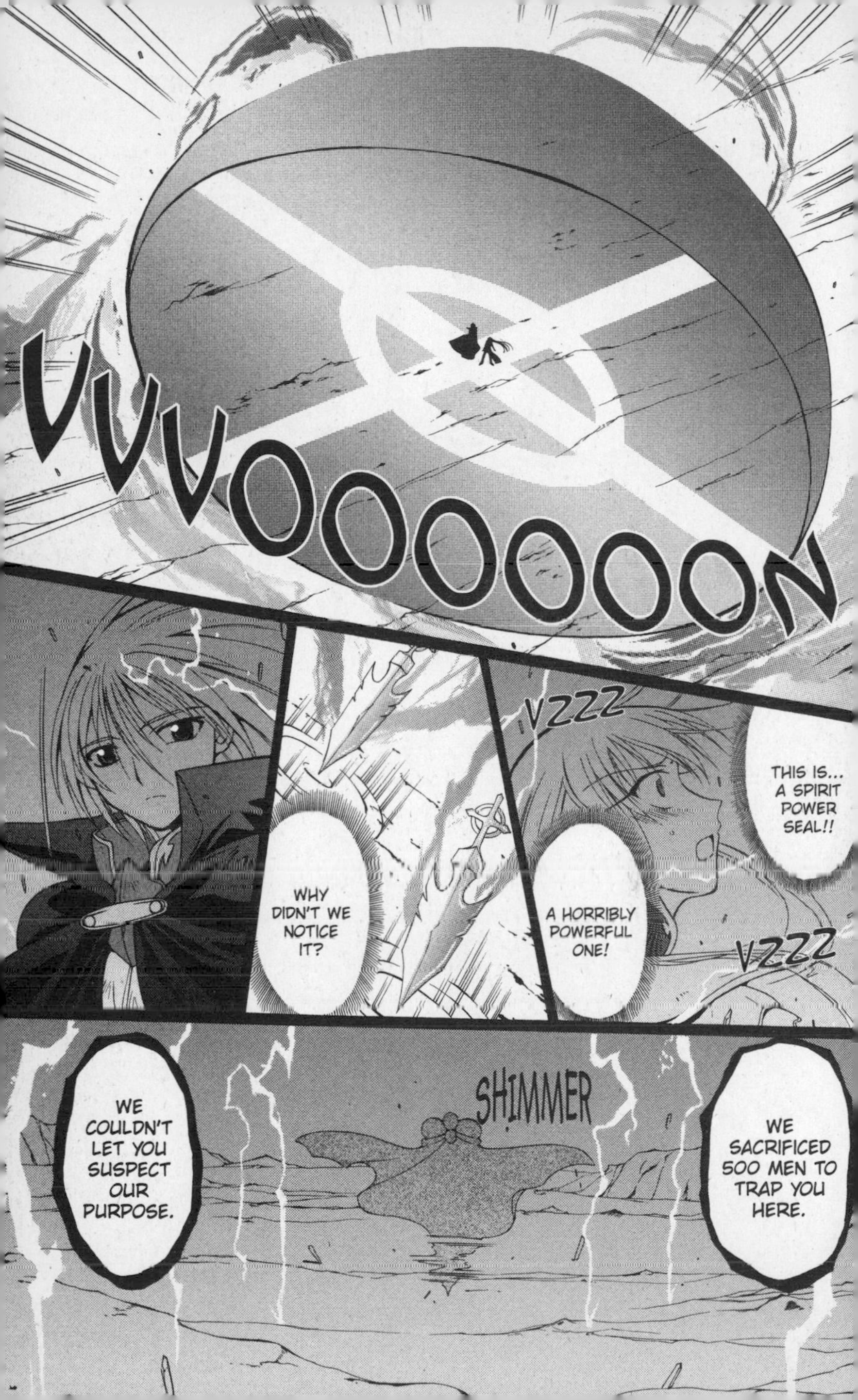
VVVOOOOOOON
VZZZ
THIS IS... A SPIRIT POWER SEAL!!
A HORRIBLY POWERFUL ONE!
VZZZ
WHY DIDN'T WE NOTICE IT?
WE SACRIFICED 500 MEN TO TRAP YOU HERE.
SHIMMER
WE COULDN'T LET YOU SUSPECT OUR PURPOSE.

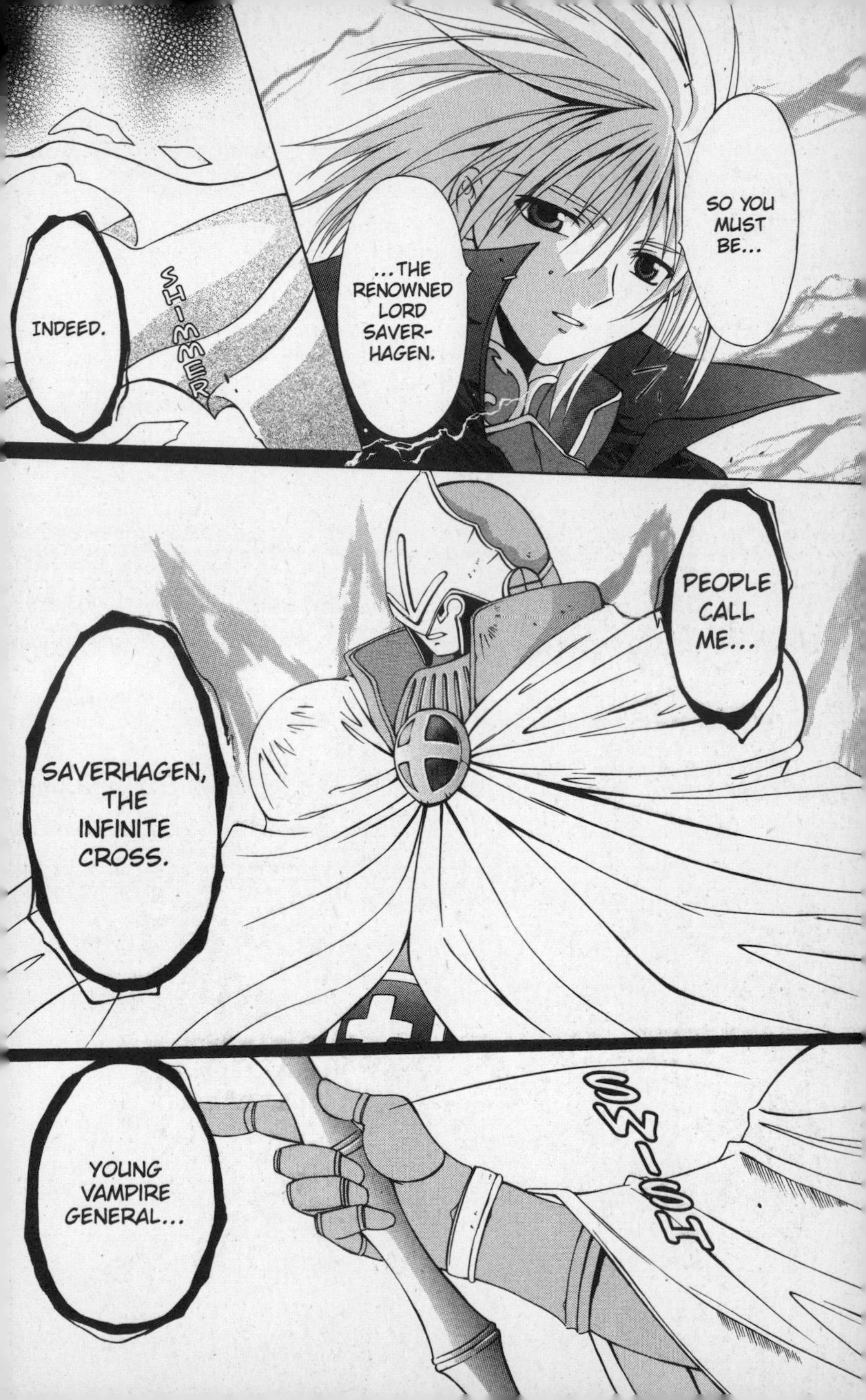
SO YOU MUST BE...
...THE RENOWNED LORD SAVERHAGEN.
SHIMMER
INDEED.
PEOPLE CALL ME...
SAVERHAGEN, THE INFINITE CROSS.
YOUNG VAMPIRE GENERAL...

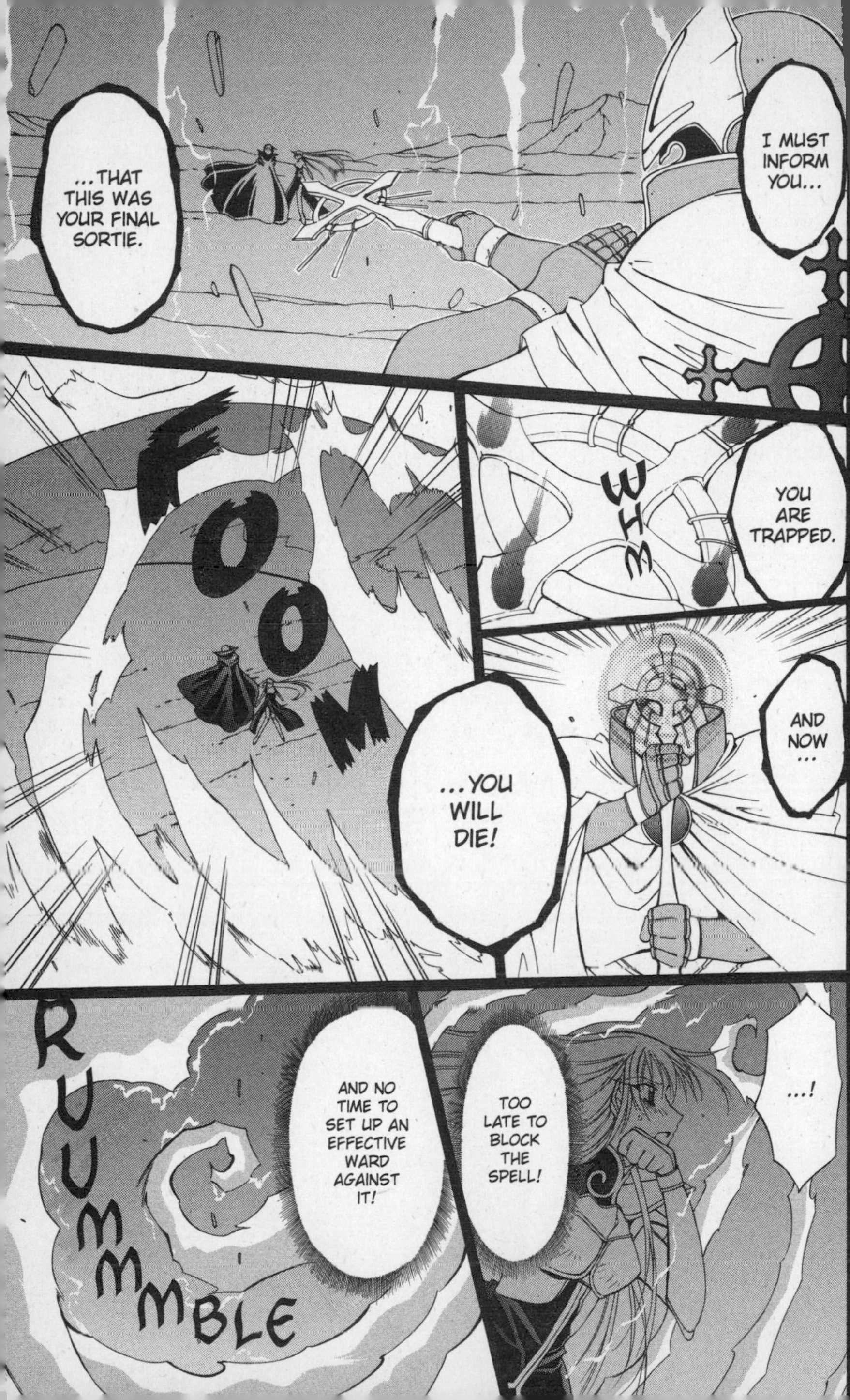
I MUST INFORM YOU...
...THAT THIS WAS YOUR FINAL SORTIE.
WHM
YOU ARE TRAPPED.
AND NOW...
...YOU WILL DIE!
FOOOM
...!
TOO LATE TO BLOCK THE SPELL!
AND NO TIME TO SET UP AN EFFECTIVE WARD AGAINST IT!
RUMMMBLE

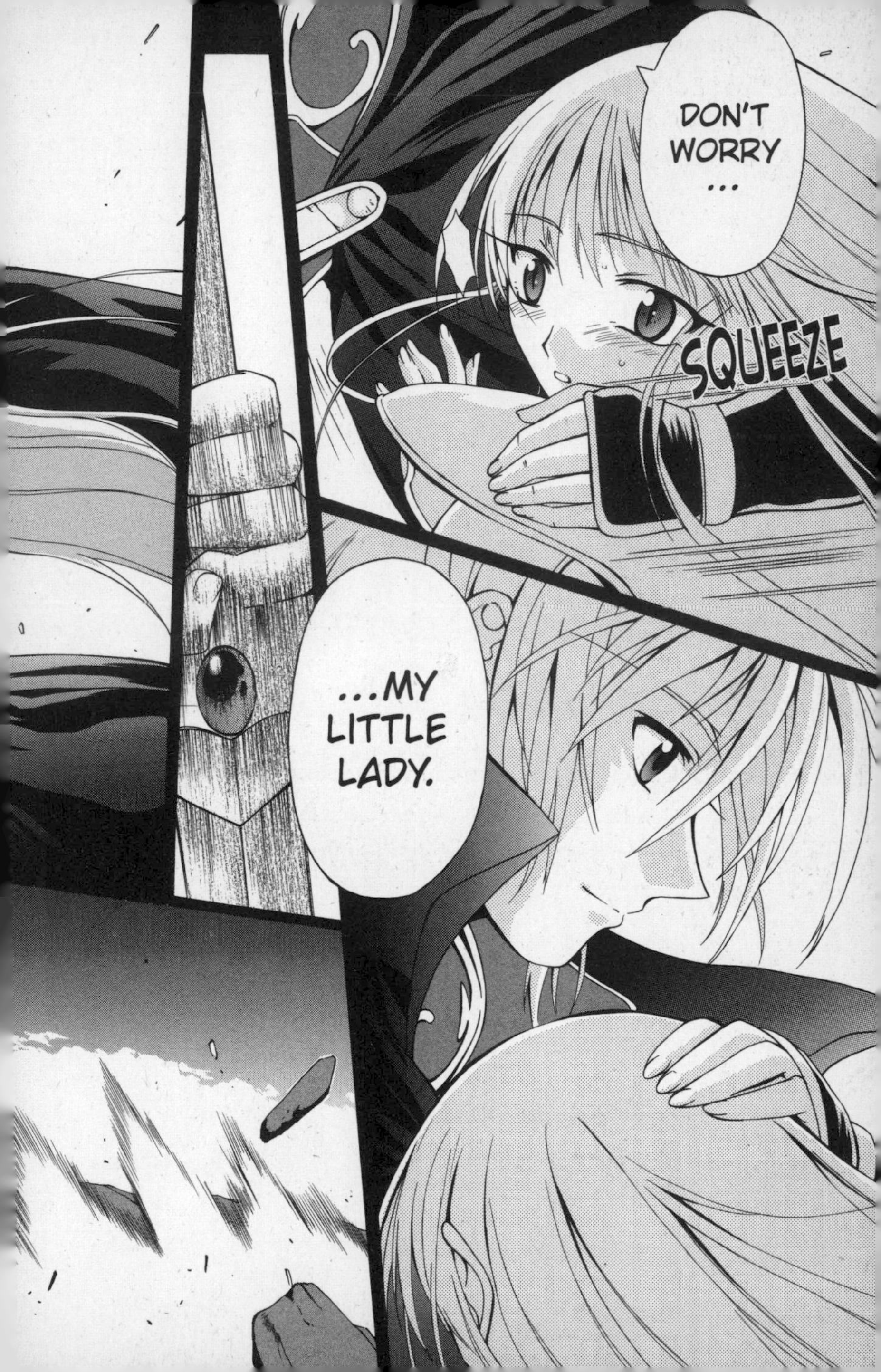
DON'T WORRY ...
SQUEEZE
...MY LITTLE LADY.

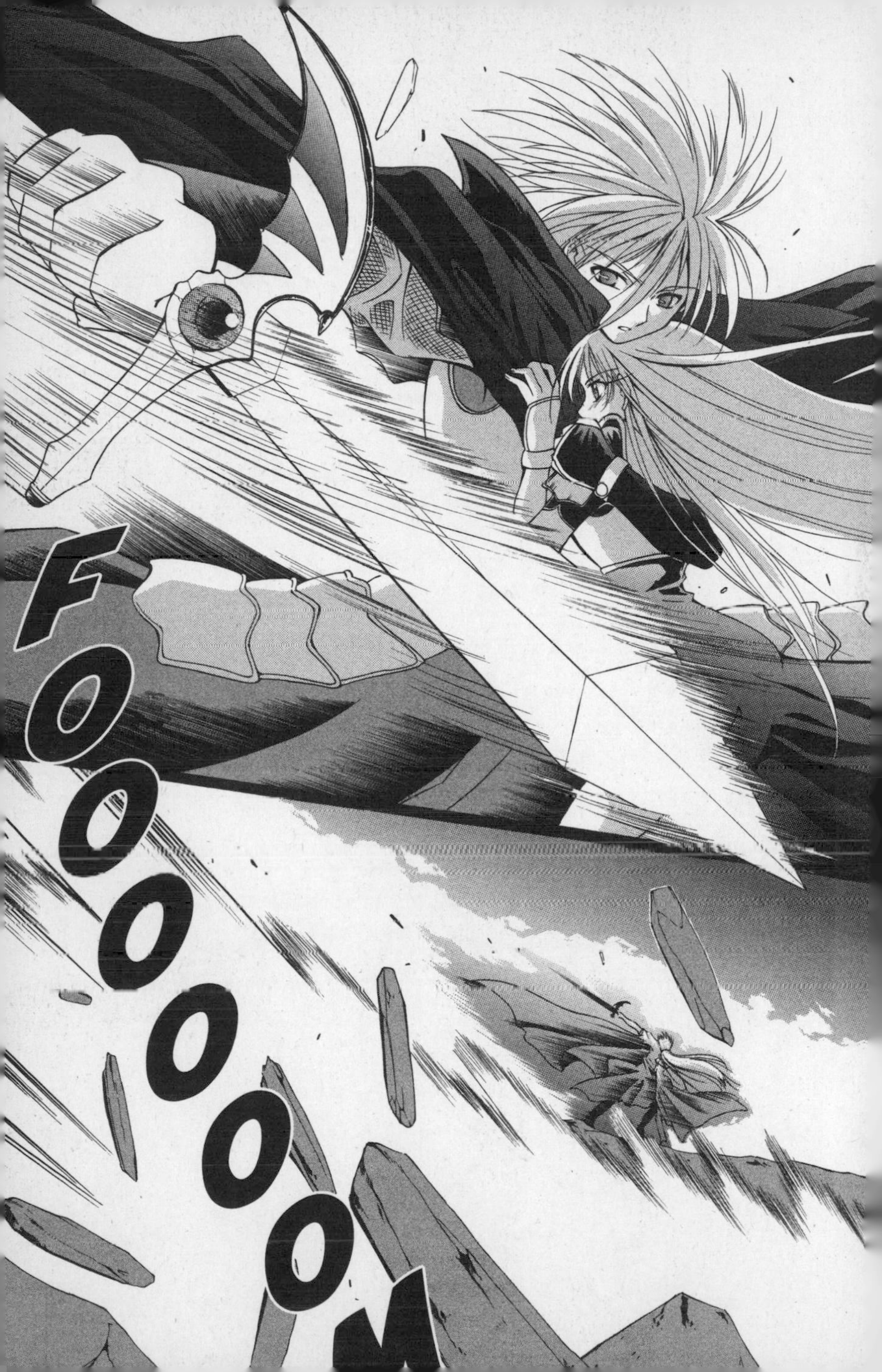
FOOOOOOM

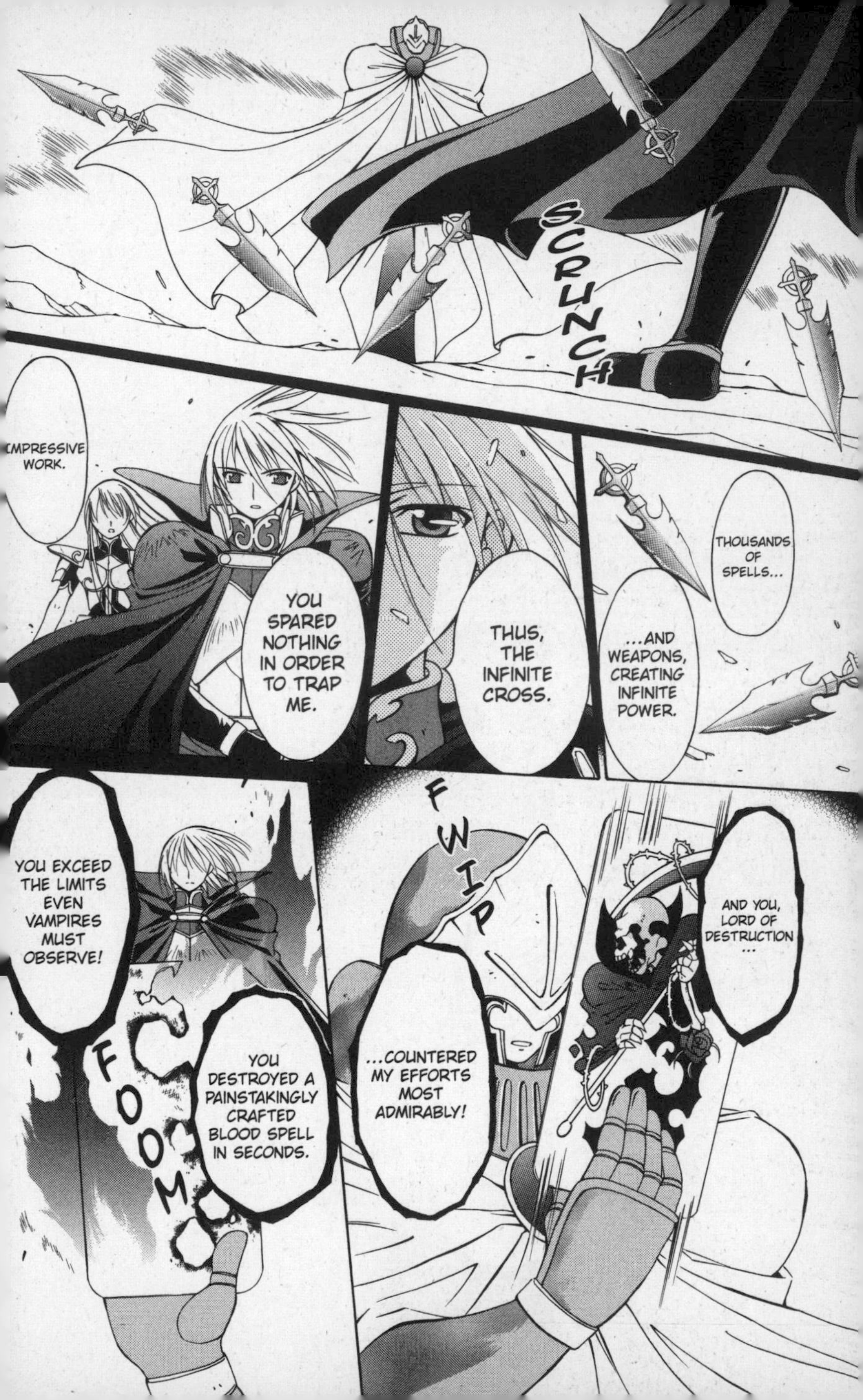
SCRUNCH
THOUSANDS OF SPELLS...
...AND WEAPONS, CREATING INFINITE POWER.
THUS, THE INFINITE CROSS.
MPRESSIVE WORK.
YOU SPARED NOTHING IN ORDER TO TRAP ME.
FWIP
AND YOU, LORD OF DESTRUCTION...
...COUNTERED MY EFFORTS MOST ADMIRABLY!
FOOM
YOU DESTROYED A PAINSTAKINGLY CRAFTED BLOOD SPELL IN SECONDS.
YOU EXCEED THE LIMITS EVEN VAMPIRES MUST OBSERVE!

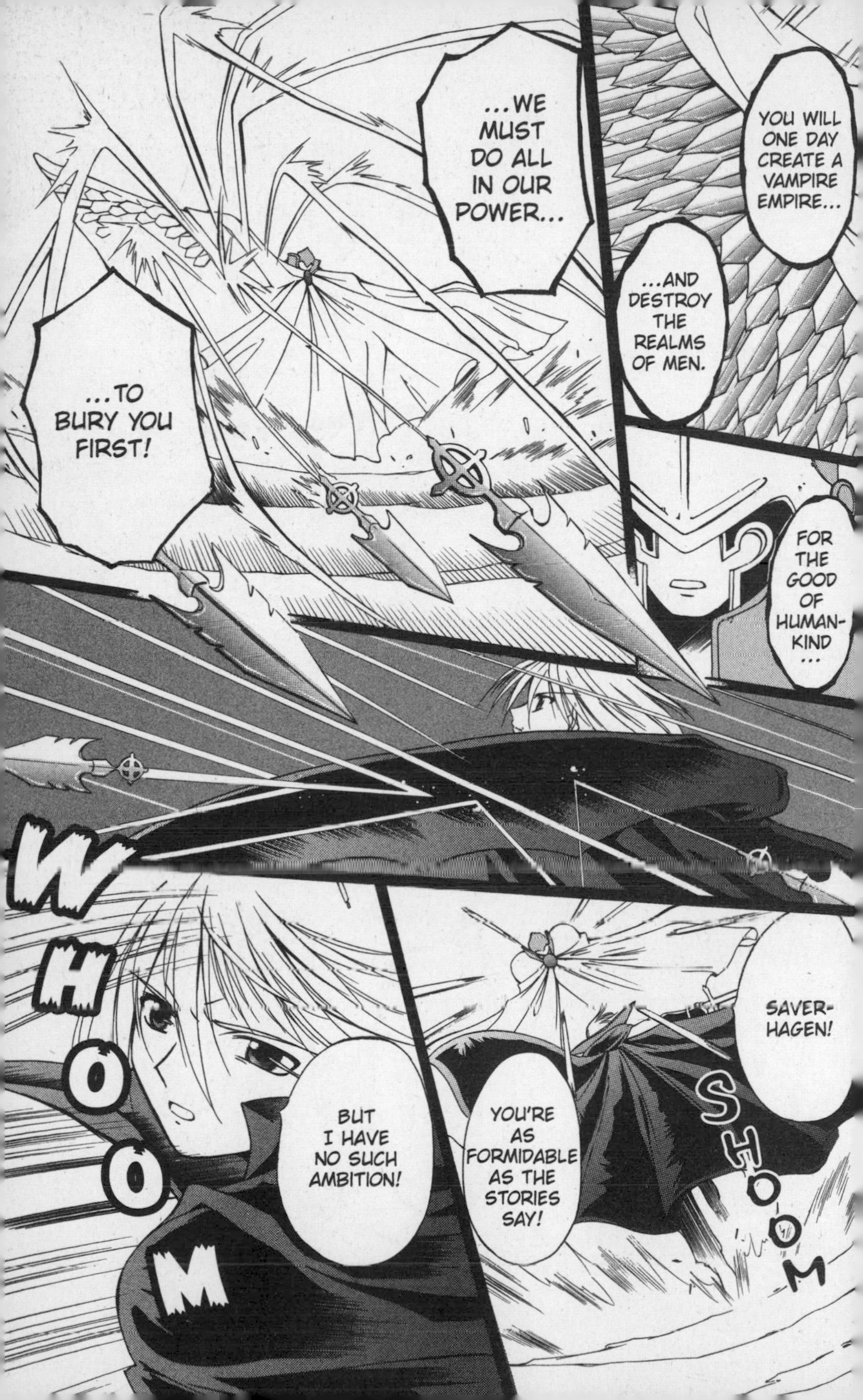
YOU WILL ONE DAY CREATE A VAMPIRE EMPIRE...
...AND DESTROY THE REALMS OF MEN.
FOR THE GOOD OF HUMAN-KIND...
...WE MUST DO ALL IN OUR POWER...
...TO BURY YOU FIRST!
SAVER-HAGEN!
SHOOOM
YOU'RE AS FORMIDABLE AS THE STORIES SAY!
BUT I HAVE NO SUCH AMBITION!
WHOOM

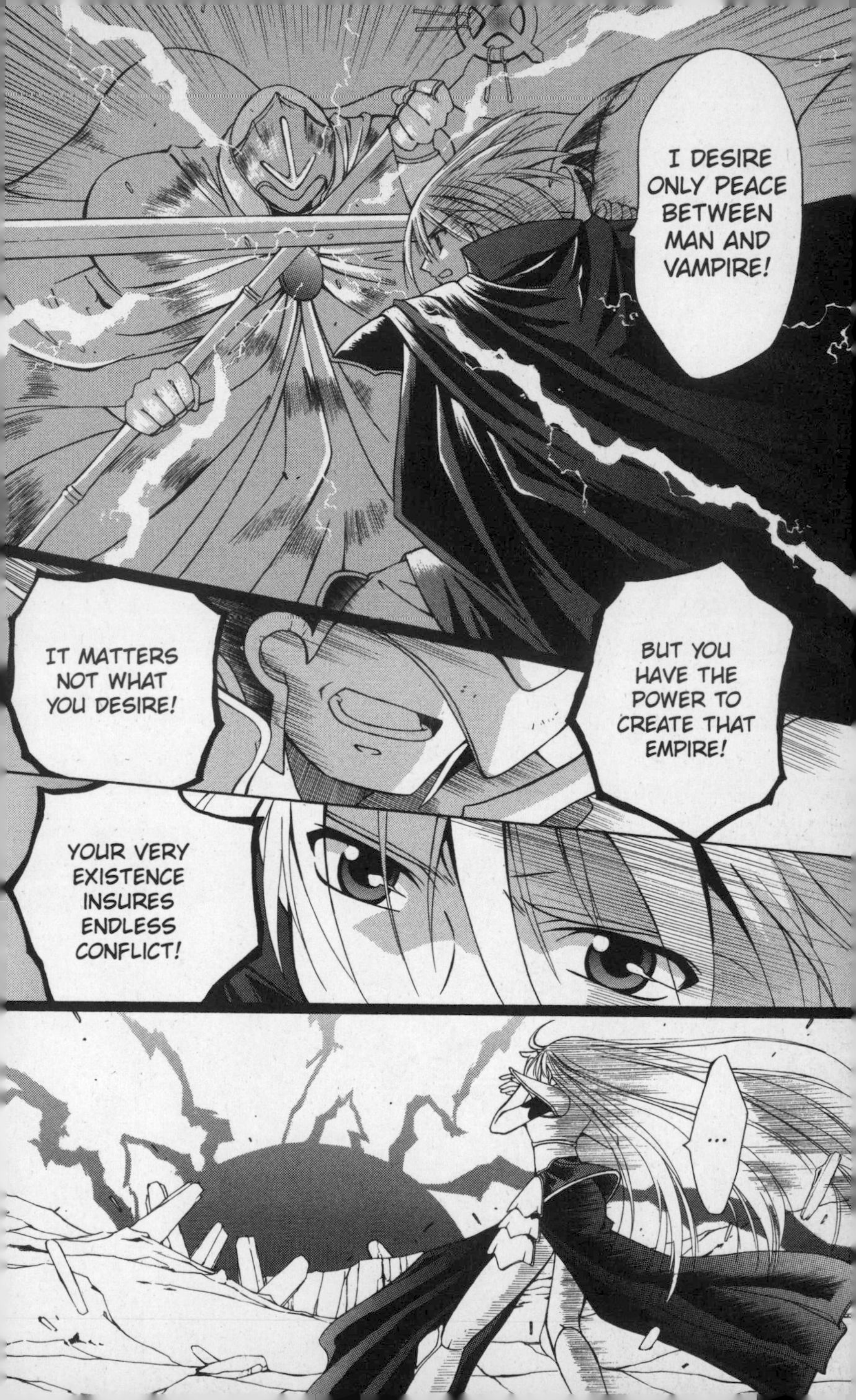
I DESIRE ONLY PEACE BETWEEN MAN AND VAMPIRE!
BUT YOU HAVE THE POWER TO CREATE THAT EMPIRE!
IT MATTERS NOT WHAT YOU DESIRE!
YOUR VERY EXISTENCE INSURES ENDLESS CONFLICT!
...

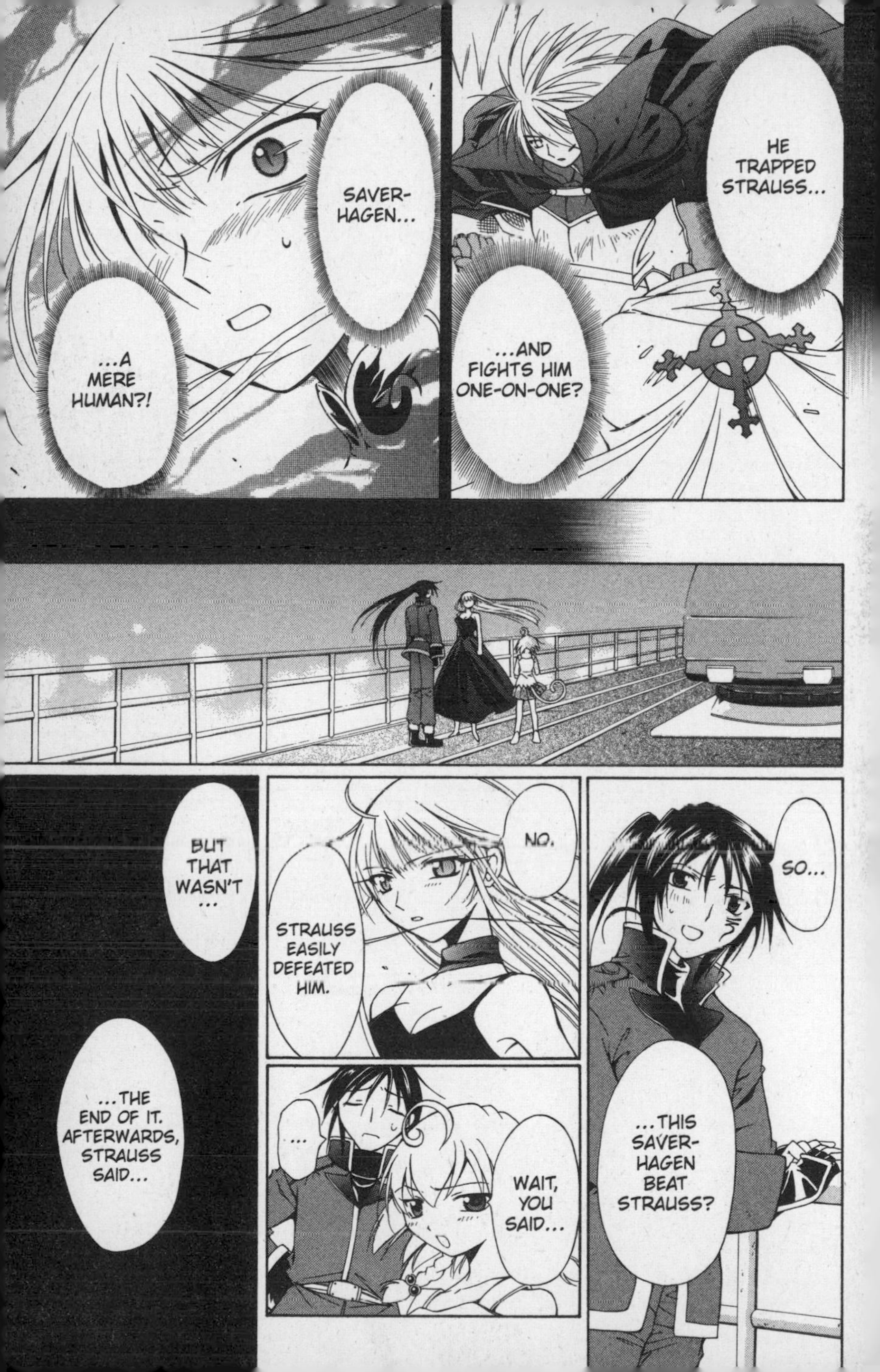
HE TRAPPED STRAUSS...
...AND FIGHTS HIM ONE-ON-ONE?
SAVER-HAGEN...
...A MERE HUMAN?!
SO...
...THIS SAVER-HAGEN BEAT STRAUSS?
NO.
STRAUSS EASILY DEFEATED HIM.
WAIT, YOU SAID...
...
BUT THAT WASN'T ...
...THE END OF IT. AFTERWARDS, STRAUSS SAID...

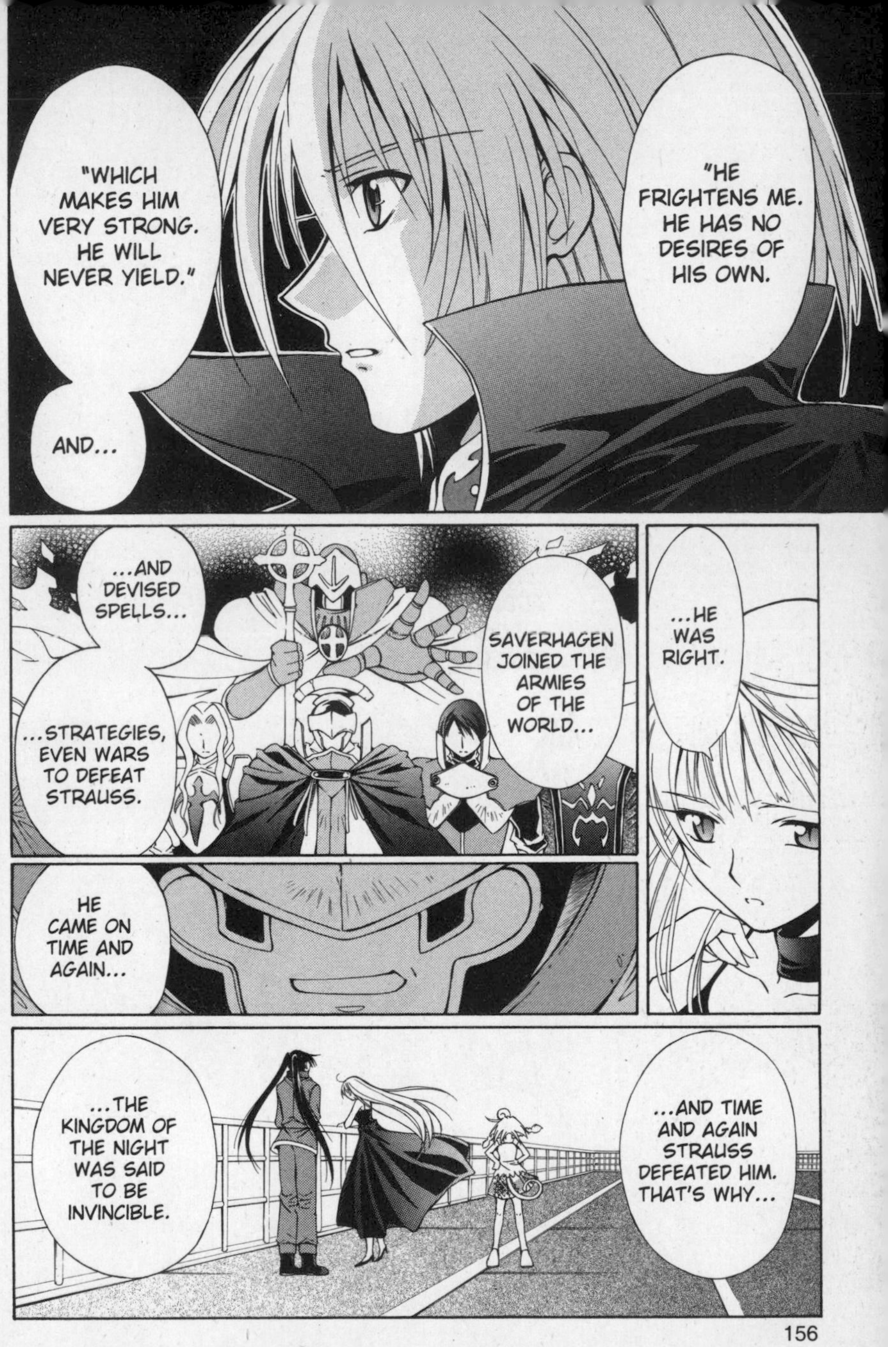
"HE FRIGHTENS ME. HE HAS NO DESIRES OF HIS OWN.
"WHICH MAKES HIM VERY STRONG. HE WILL NEVER YIELD."
AND...
...HE WAS RIGHT.
SAVERHAGEN JOINED THE ARMIES OF THE WORLD...
...AND DEVISED SPELLS...
...STRATEGIES, EVEN WARS TO DEFEAT STRAUSS.
HE CAME ON TIME AND AGAIN...
...AND TIME AND AGAIN STRAUSS DEFEATED HIM. THAT'S WHY...
...THE KINGDOM OF THE NIGHT WAS SAID TO BE INVINCIBLE.

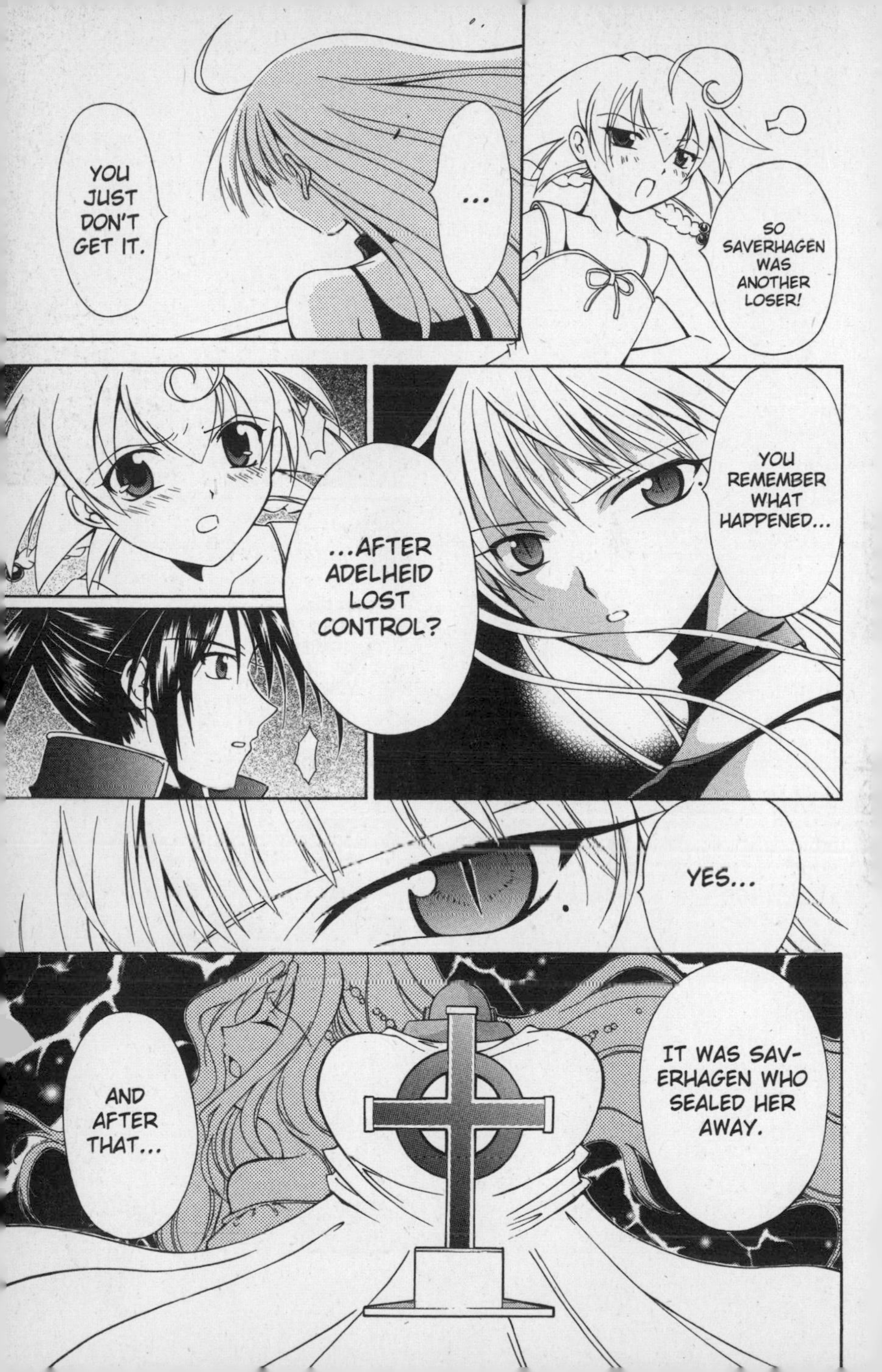
SO SAVERHAGEN WAS ANOTHER LOSER!
...
YOU JUST DON'T GET IT.
YOU REMEMBER WHAT HAPPENED...
...AFTER ADELHEID LOST CONTROL?
YES...
IT WAS SAV-ERHAGEN WHO SEALED HER AWAY.
AND AFTER THAT...

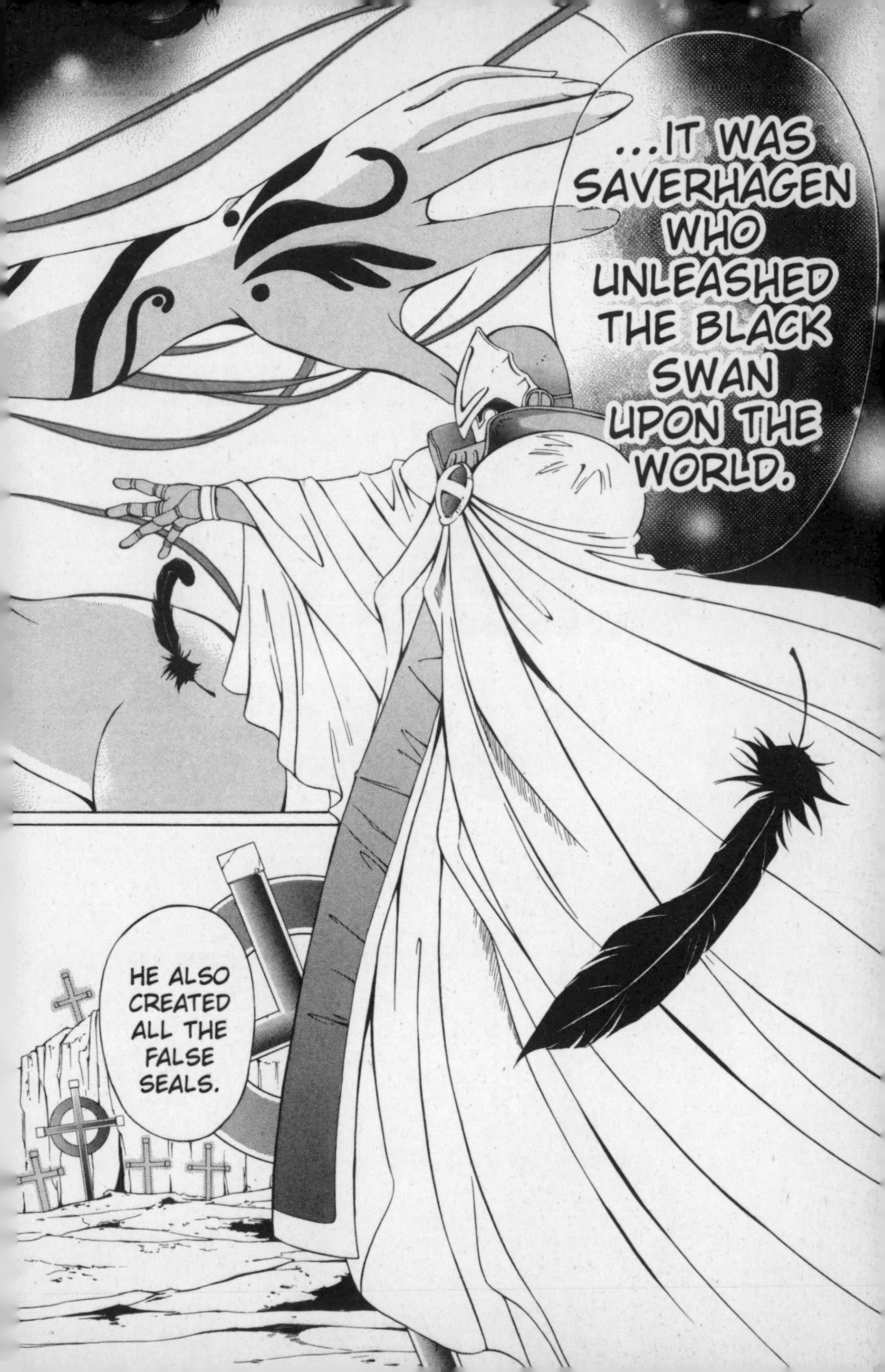
...IT WAS SAVERHAGEN WHO UNLEASHED THE BLACK SWAN UPON THE WORLD.
HE ALSO CREATED ALL THE FALSE SEALS.

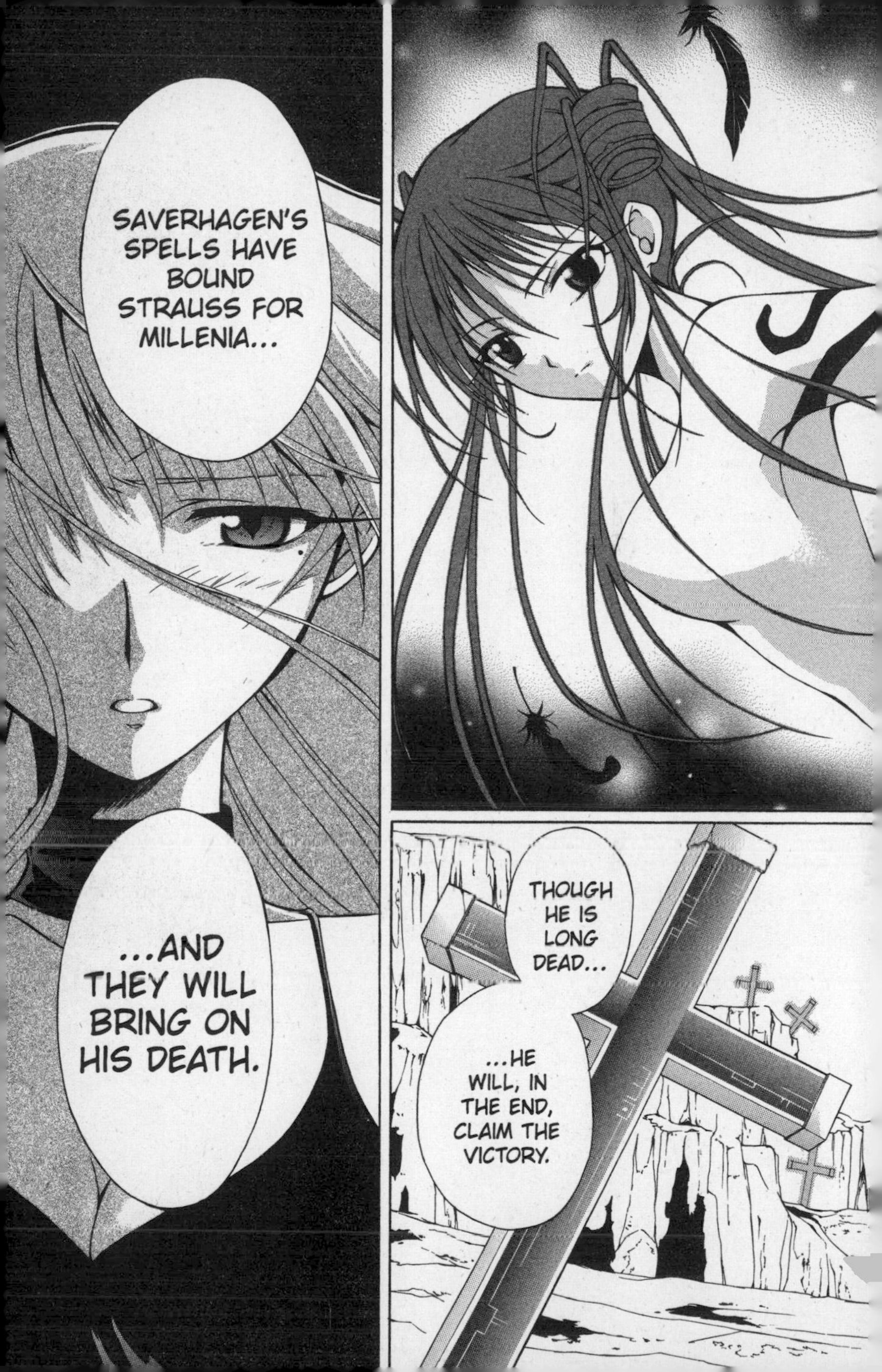
THOUGH HE IS LONG DEAD...
...HE WILL, IN THE END, CLAIM THE VICTORY.
SAVERHAGEN'S SPELLS HAVE BOUND STRAUSS FOR MILLENIA...
...AND THEY WILL BRING ON HIS DEATH.

THE RECORD OF A

FALLEN VAMPIRE

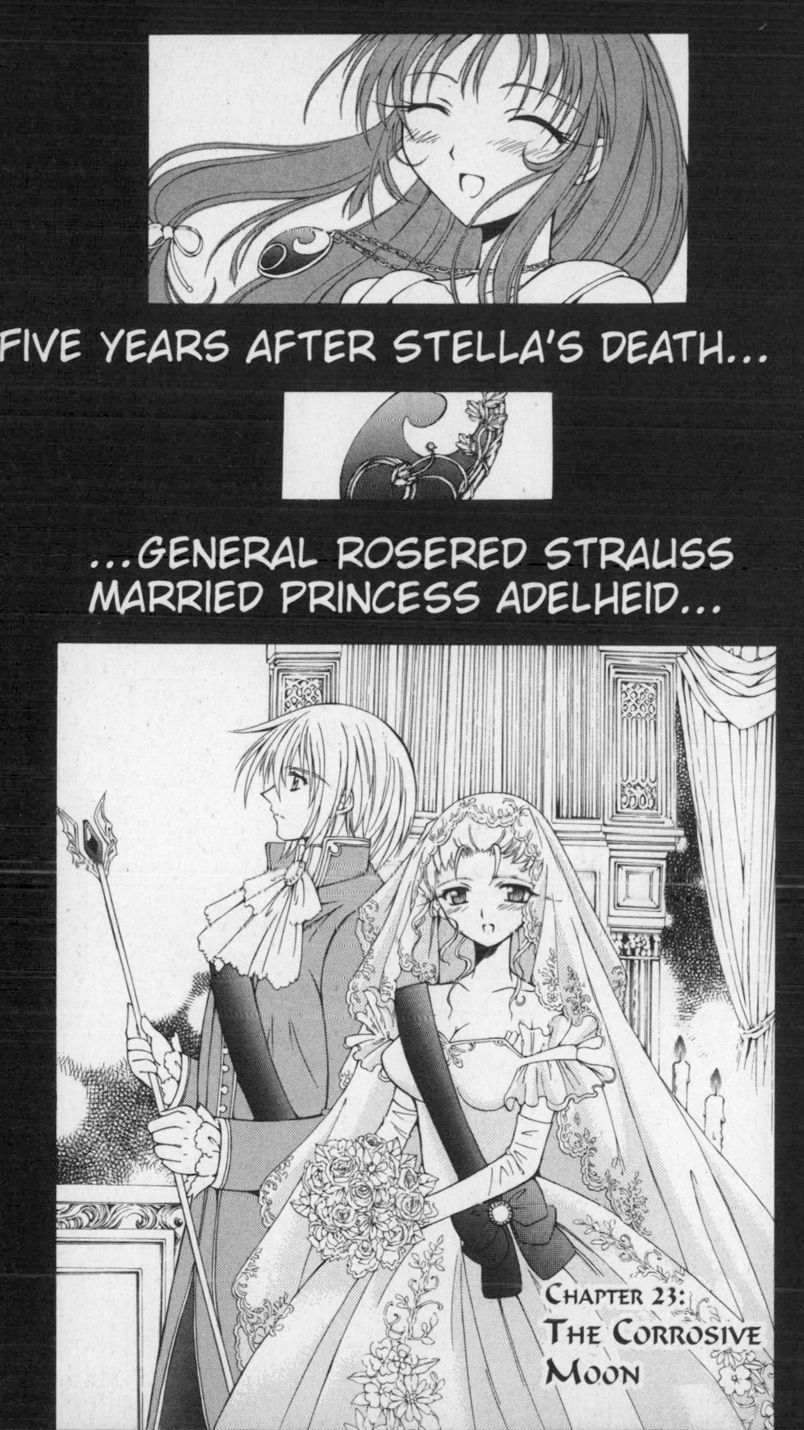
FIVE YEARS AFTER STELLA'S DEATH...
...GENERAL ROSERED STRAUSS MARRIED PRINCESS ADELHEID...
CHAPTER 23: THE CORROSIVE MOON

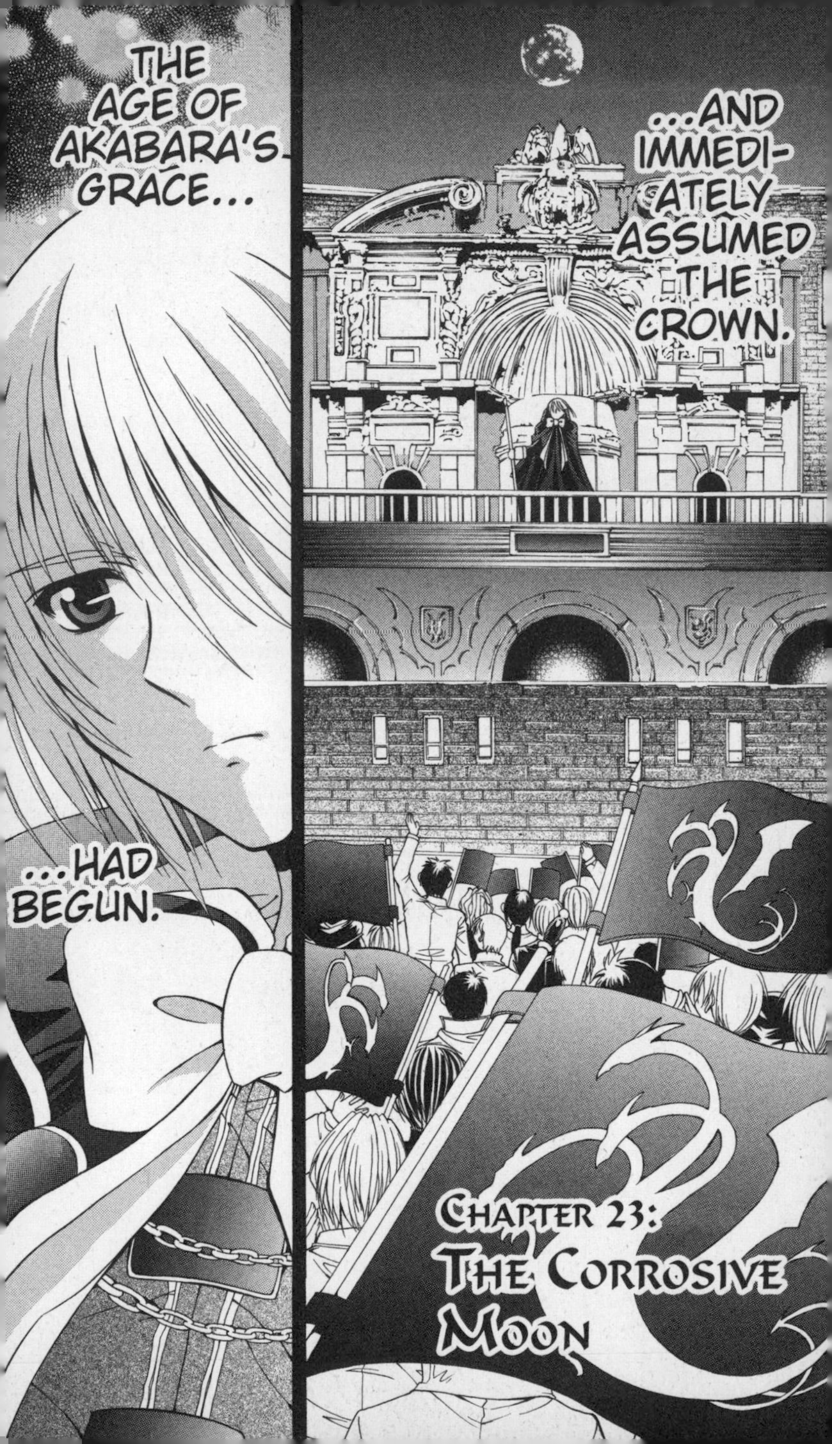
...AND IMMEDI-ATELY ASSUMED THE CROWN.
CHAPTER 23: THE CORROSIVE MOON
THE AGE OF AKABARA'S GRACE...
...HAD BEGUN.

FOR THE NINE YEARS STRAUSS RULED...
...THE COUNTRIES BORDERING OURS FEARED HIM.
THEY SCHEMED AGAINST US, AND EVEN WITHIN
THE KINGDOM...
...PEOPLE BEGAN TO SEE STRAUSS' POWER
AS A PROBLEM.

WITHIN A YEAR, THE BORDERING COUNTRIES
FORMED AN ALLIANCE.

THE ELDERS OF THE KINGDOM OF THE NIGHT...
...DECIDED THAT STRAUSS HAD TO BE
ELIMINATED.

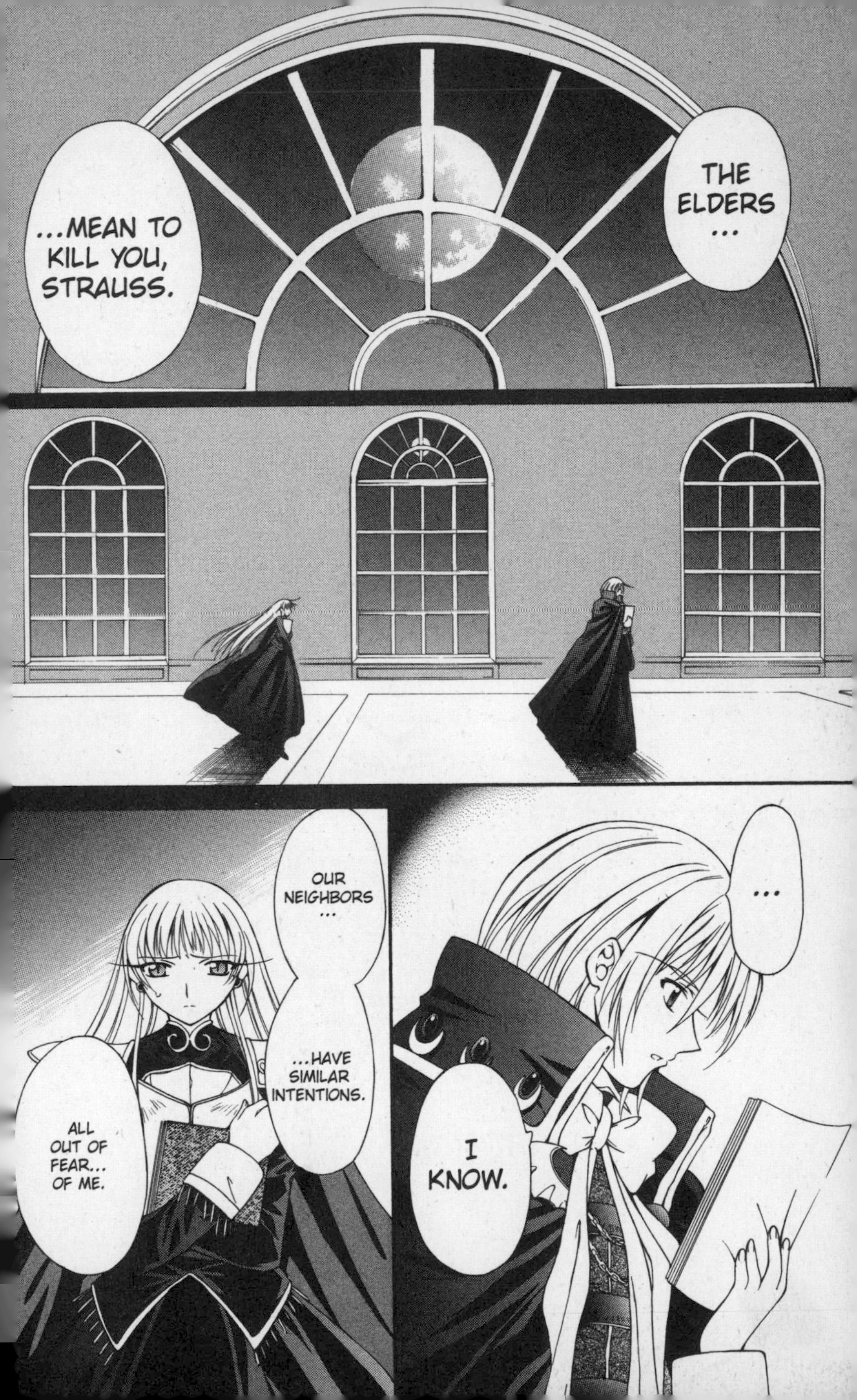
THE ELDERS ...
...MEAN TO KILL YOU, STRAUSS.
...
I KNOW.
OUR NEIGHBORS ...
...HAVE SIMILAR INTENTIONS.
ALL OUT OF FEAR... OF ME.

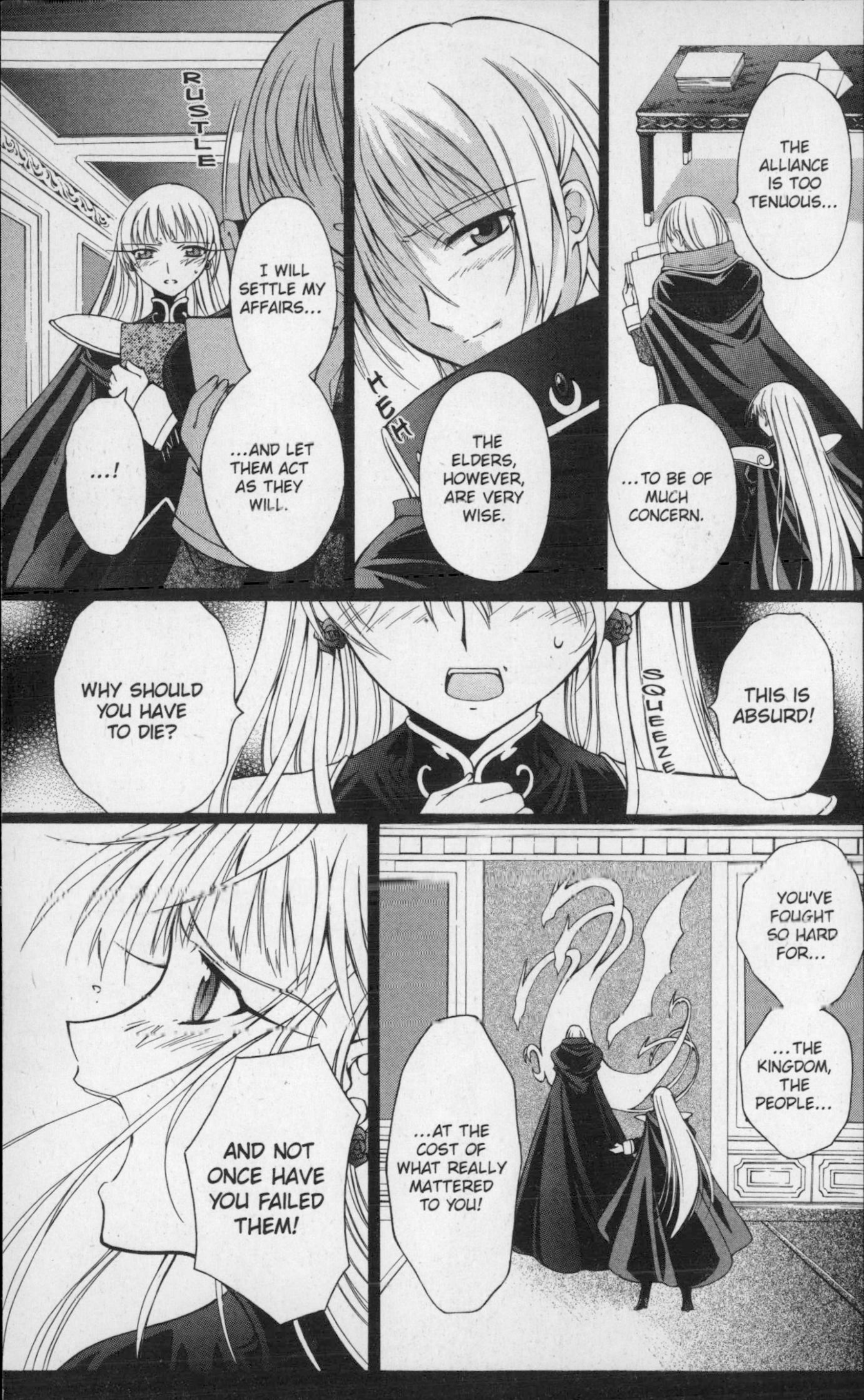
THE ALLIANCE IS TOO TENUOUS...
...TO BE OF MUCH CONCERN.
HEH
THE ELDERS, HOWEVER, ARE VERY WISE.
RUSTLE
I WILL SETTLE MY AFFAIRS...
...AND LET THEM ACT AS THEY WILL.
...!
THIS IS ABSURD!
SQUEEZE
WHY SHOULD YOU HAVE TO DIE?
YOU'VE FOUGHT SO HARD FOR...
...THE KINGDOM, THE PEOPLE...
...AT THE COST OF WHAT REALLY MATTERED TO YOU!
AND NOT ONCE HAVE YOU FAILED THEM!

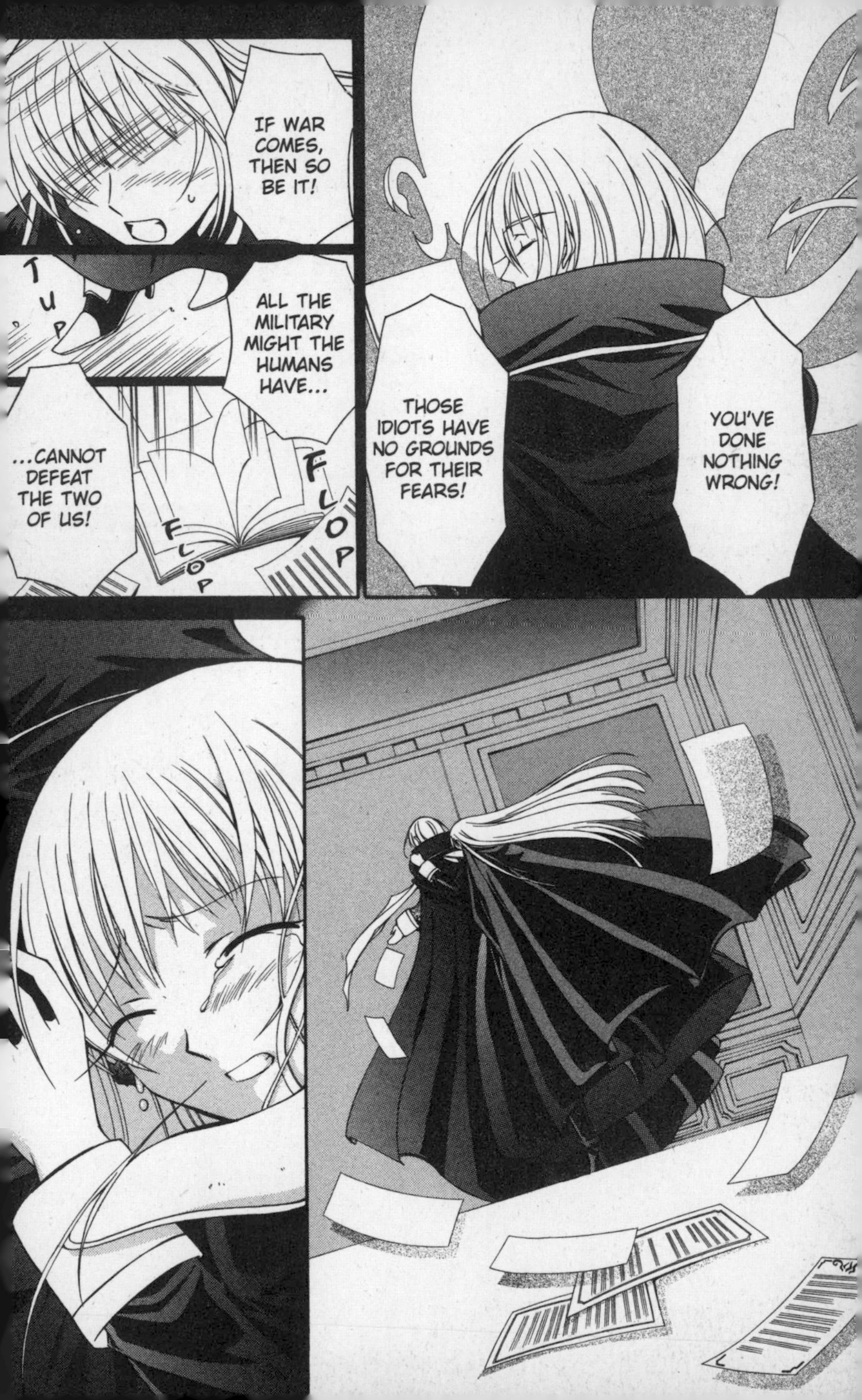
YOU'VE DONE NOTHING WRONG!
THOSE IDIOTS HAVE NO GROUNDS FOR THEIR FEARS!
IF WAR COMES, THEN SO BE IT!
TUP
ALL THE MILITARY MIGHT THE HUMANS HAVE...
FLOP
FLOP
...CANNOT DEFEAT THE TWO OF US!

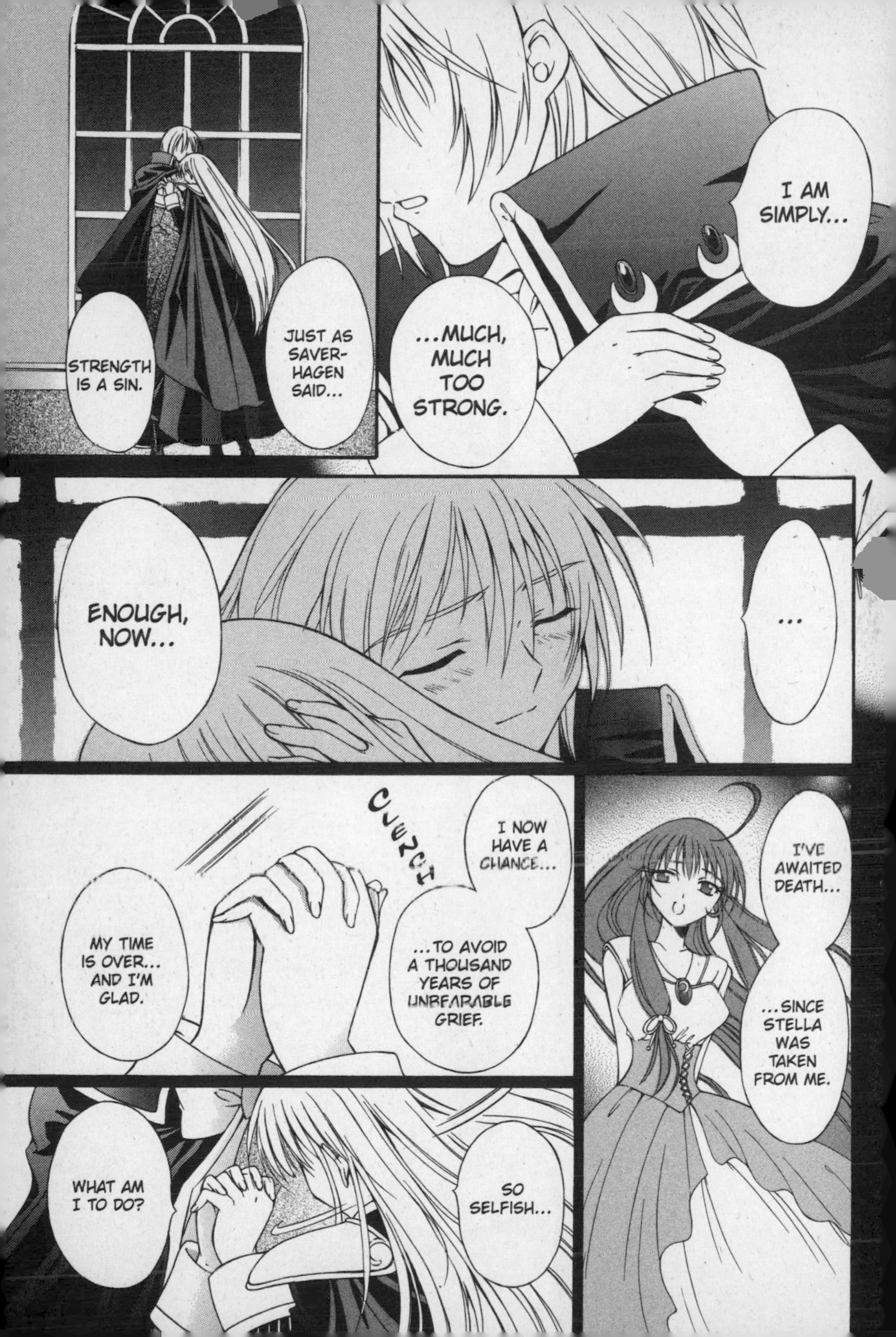
I AM SIMPLY...
...MUCH, MUCH TOO STRONG.
JUST AS SAVER-HAGEN SAID...
STRENGTH IS A SIN.
...
ENOUGH, NOW...
I'VE AWAITED DEATH...
...SINCE STELLA WAS TAKEN FROM ME.
I NOW HAVE A CHANCE...
CLENCH
...TO AVOID A THOUSAND YEARS OF UNBEARABLE GRIEF.
MY TIME IS OVER... AND I'M GLAD.
SO SELFISH...
WHAT AM I TO DO?

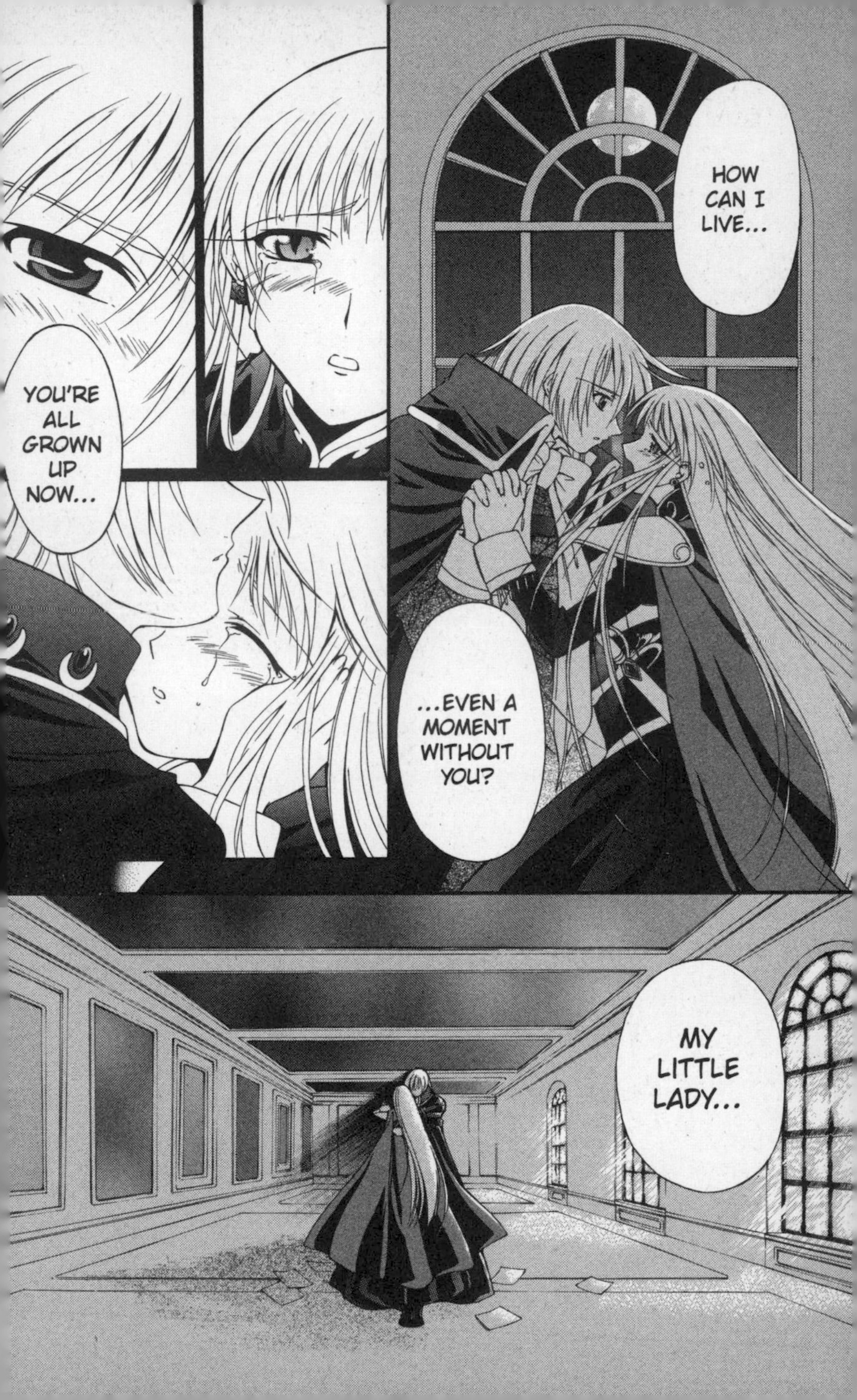
HOW CAN I LIVE...
...EVEN A MOMENT WITHOUT YOU?
YOU'RE ALL GROWN UP NOW...
MY LITTLE LADY...

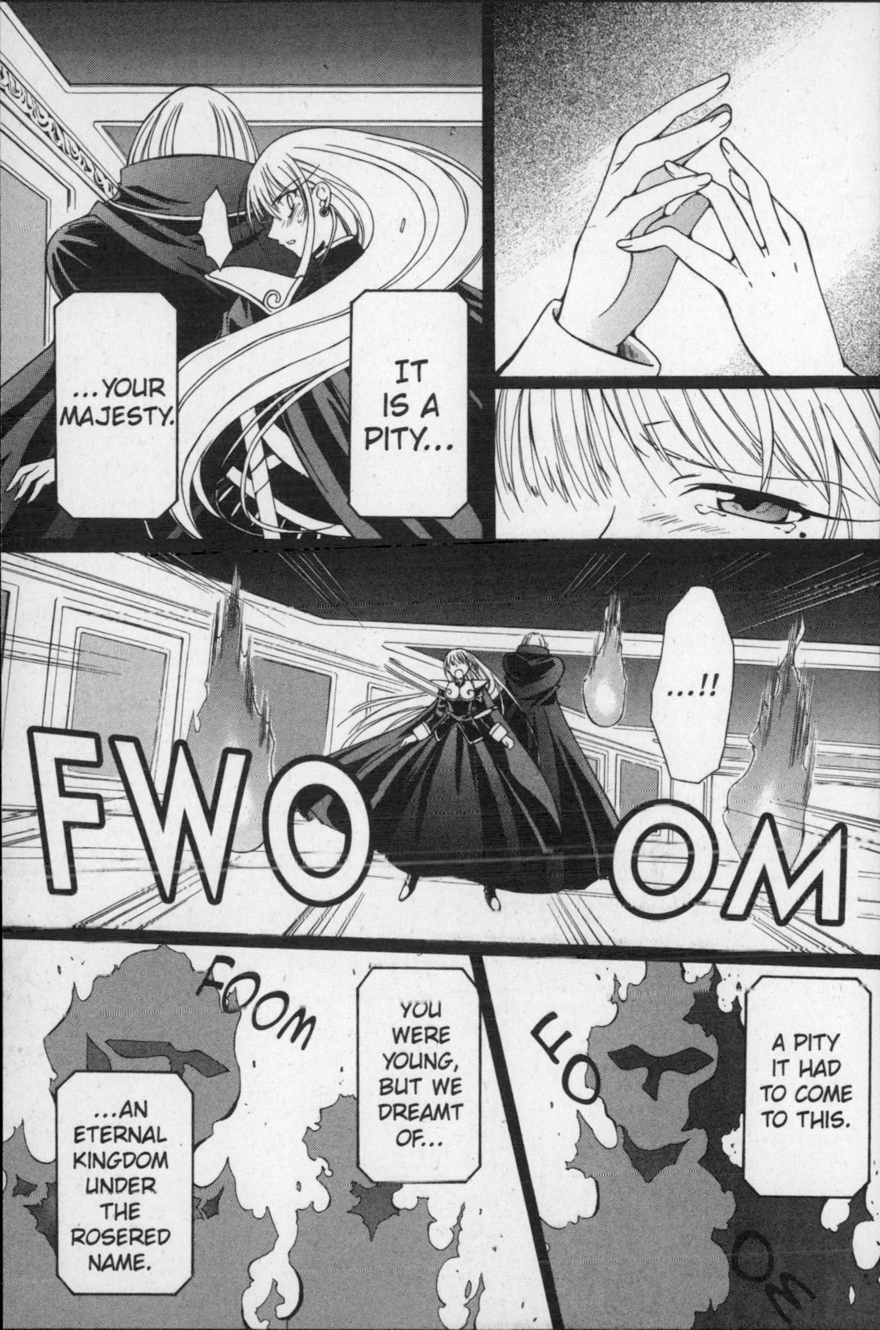
IT IS A PITY...
...YOUR MAJESTY.
...!!
FWOOM
A PITY IT HAD TO COME TO THIS.
YOU WERE YOUNG, BUT WE DREAMT OF...
FOOM
...AN ETERNAL KINGDOM UNDER THE ROSERED NAME.

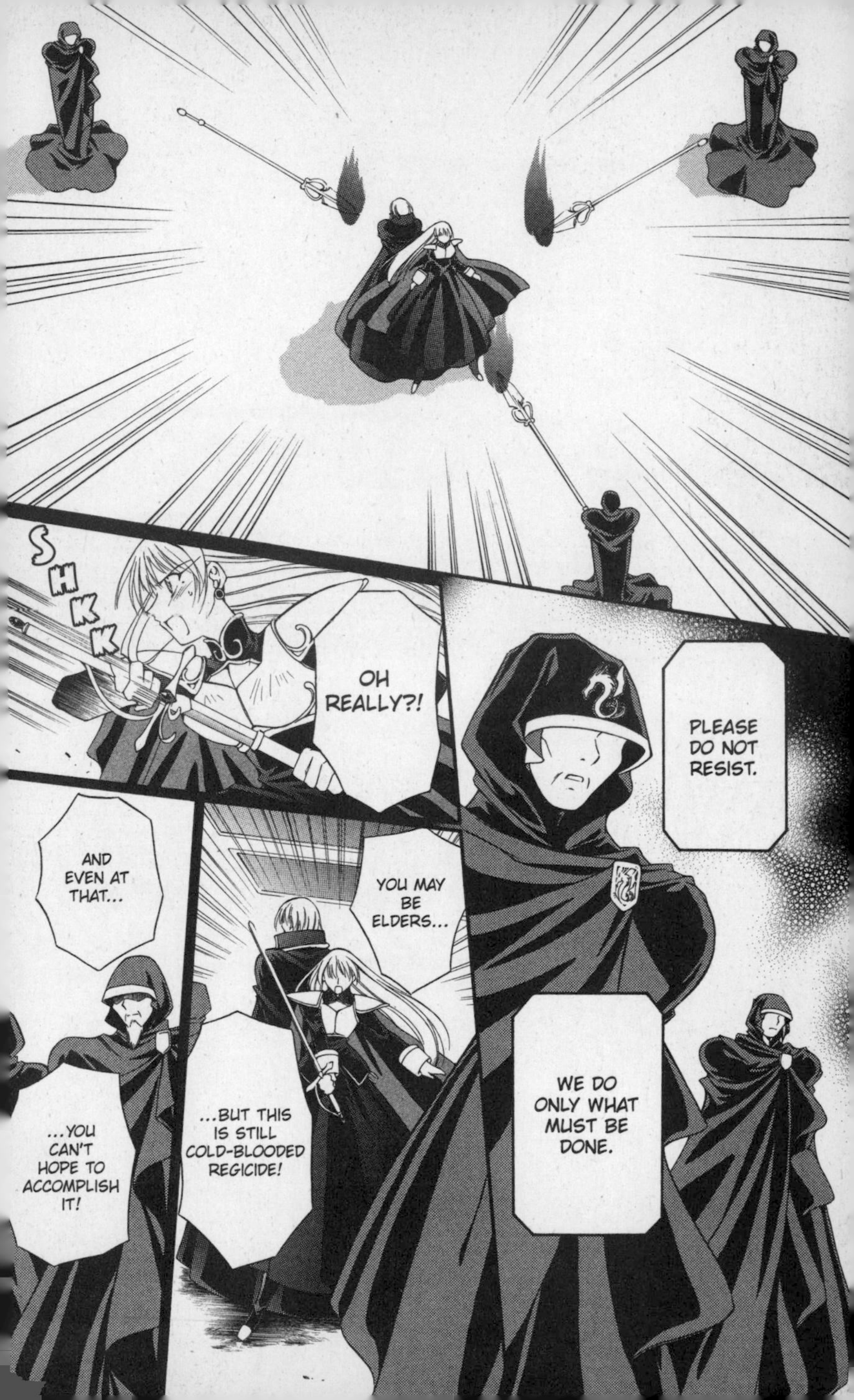
PLEASE DO NOT RESIST.
WE DO ONLY WHAT MUST BE DONE.
SHKK
OH REALLY?!
YOU MAY BE ELDERS...
...BUT THIS IS STILL COLD-BLOODED REGICIDE!
AND EVEN AT THAT...
...YOU CAN'T HOPE TO ACCOMPLISH IT!

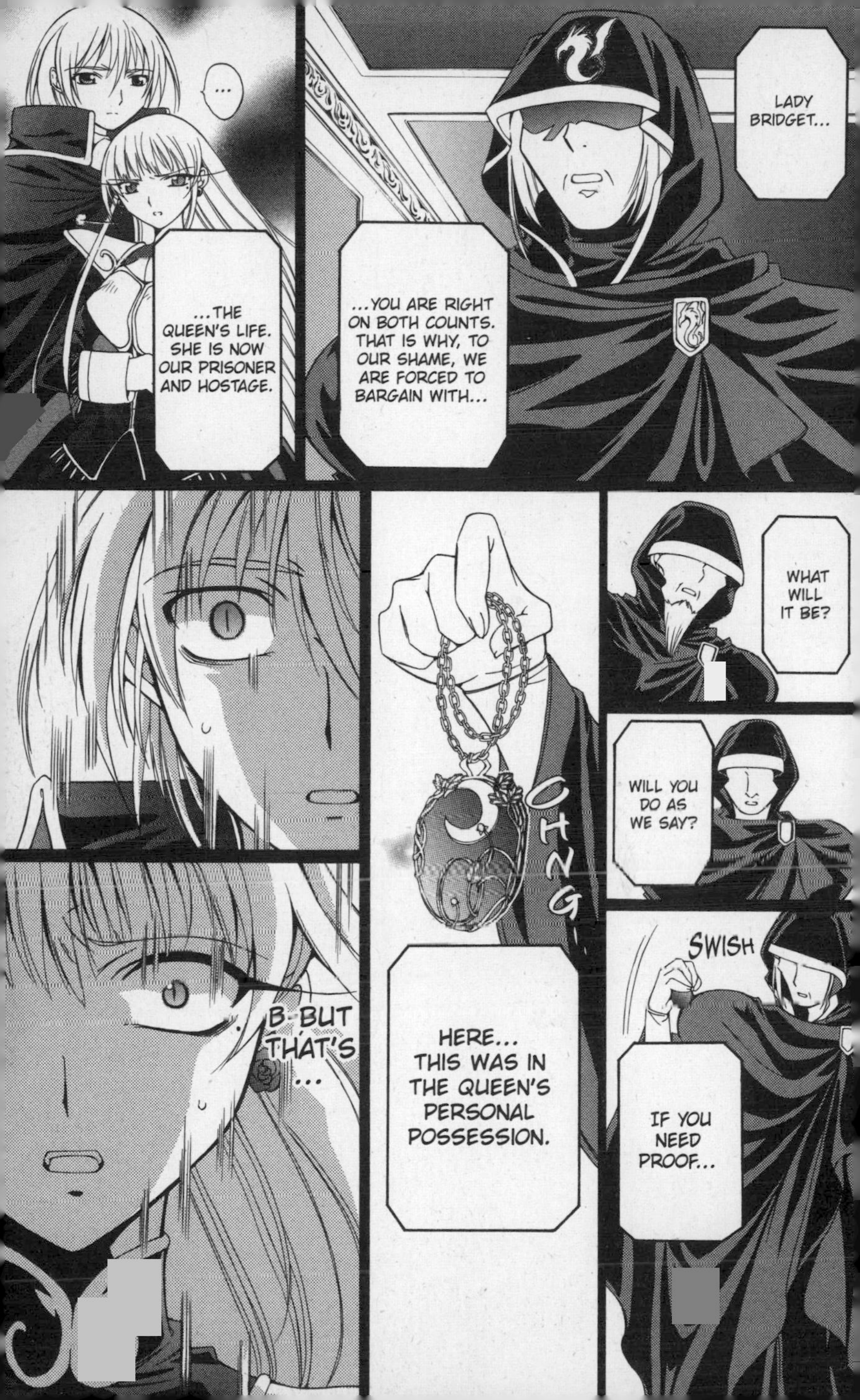
LADY BRIDGET...
...YOU ARE RIGHT ON BOTH COUNTS. THAT IS WHY, TO OUR SHAME, WE ARE FORCED TO BARGAIN WITH...
...
...THE QUEEN'S LIFE. SHE IS NOW OUR PRISONER AND HOSTAGE.
WHAT WILL IT BE?
WILL YOU DO AS WE SAY?
SWISH
IF YOU NEED PROOF...
CHNG
HERE... THIS WAS IN THE QUEEN'S PERSONAL POSSESSION.
B-BUT THAT'S...

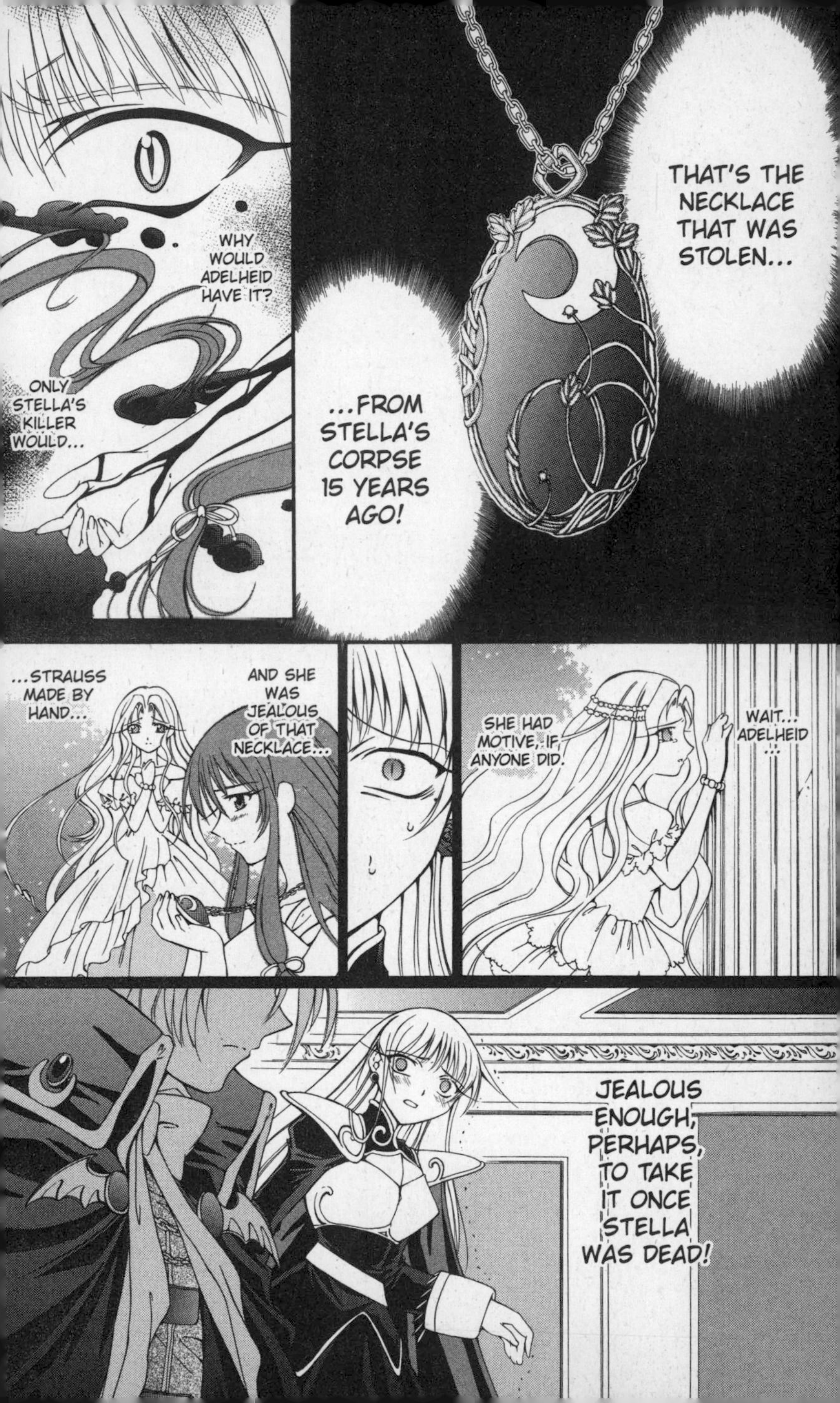
THAT'S THE NECKLACE THAT WAS STOLEN...
...FROM STELLA'S CORPSE 15 YEARS AGO!
WHY WOULD ADELHEID HAVE IT?
ONLY STELLA'S KILLER WOULD...
WAIT... ADELHEID ...
SHE HAD MOTIVE, IF ANYONE DID.
AND SHE WAS JEALOUS OF THAT NECKLACE...
...STRAUSS MADE BY HAND...
JEALOUS ENOUGH, PERHAPS, TO TAKE IT ONCE STELLA WAS DEAD!

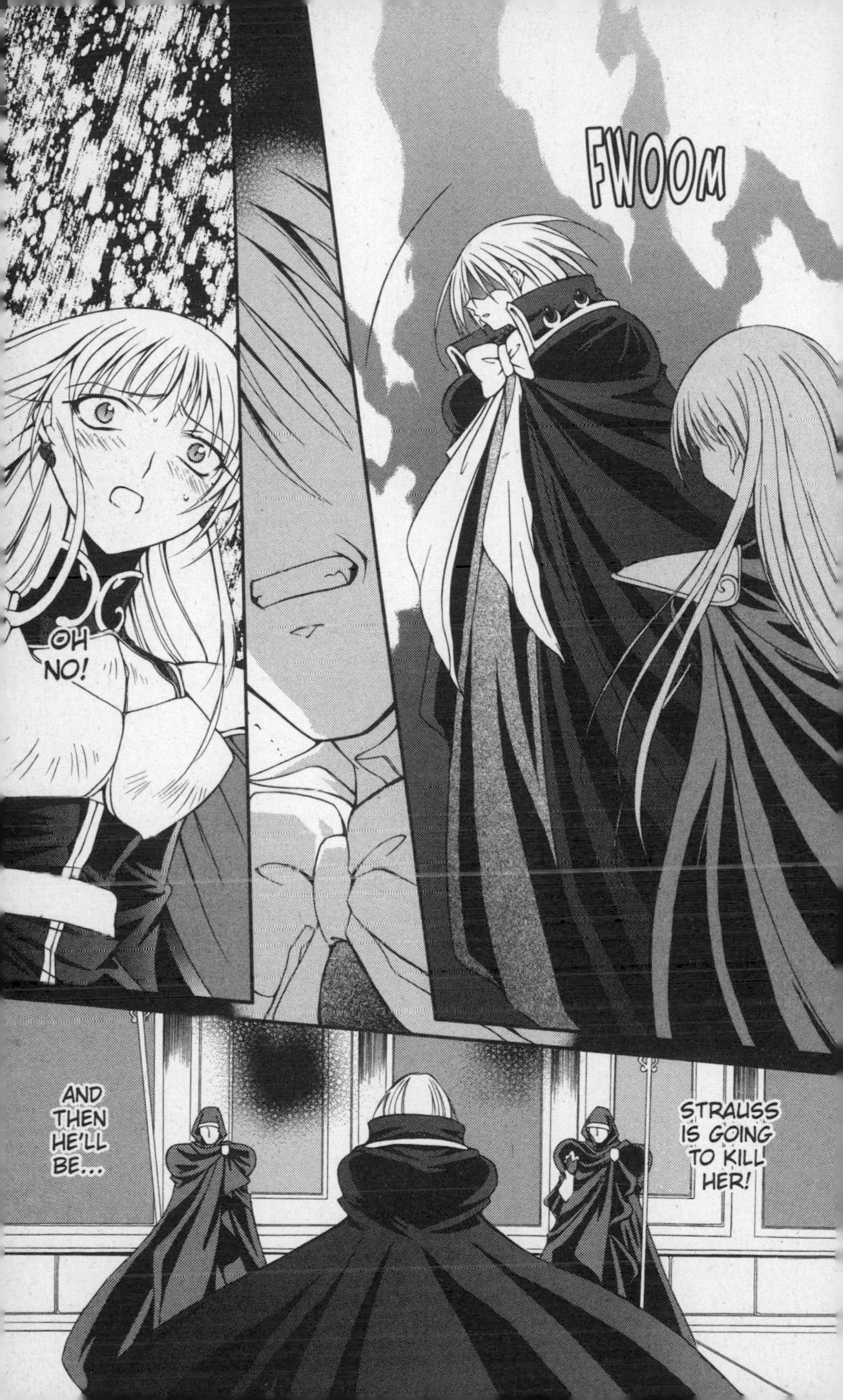
FWOOM
OH NO!
STRAUSS IS GOING TO KILL HER!
AND THEN HE'LL BE...

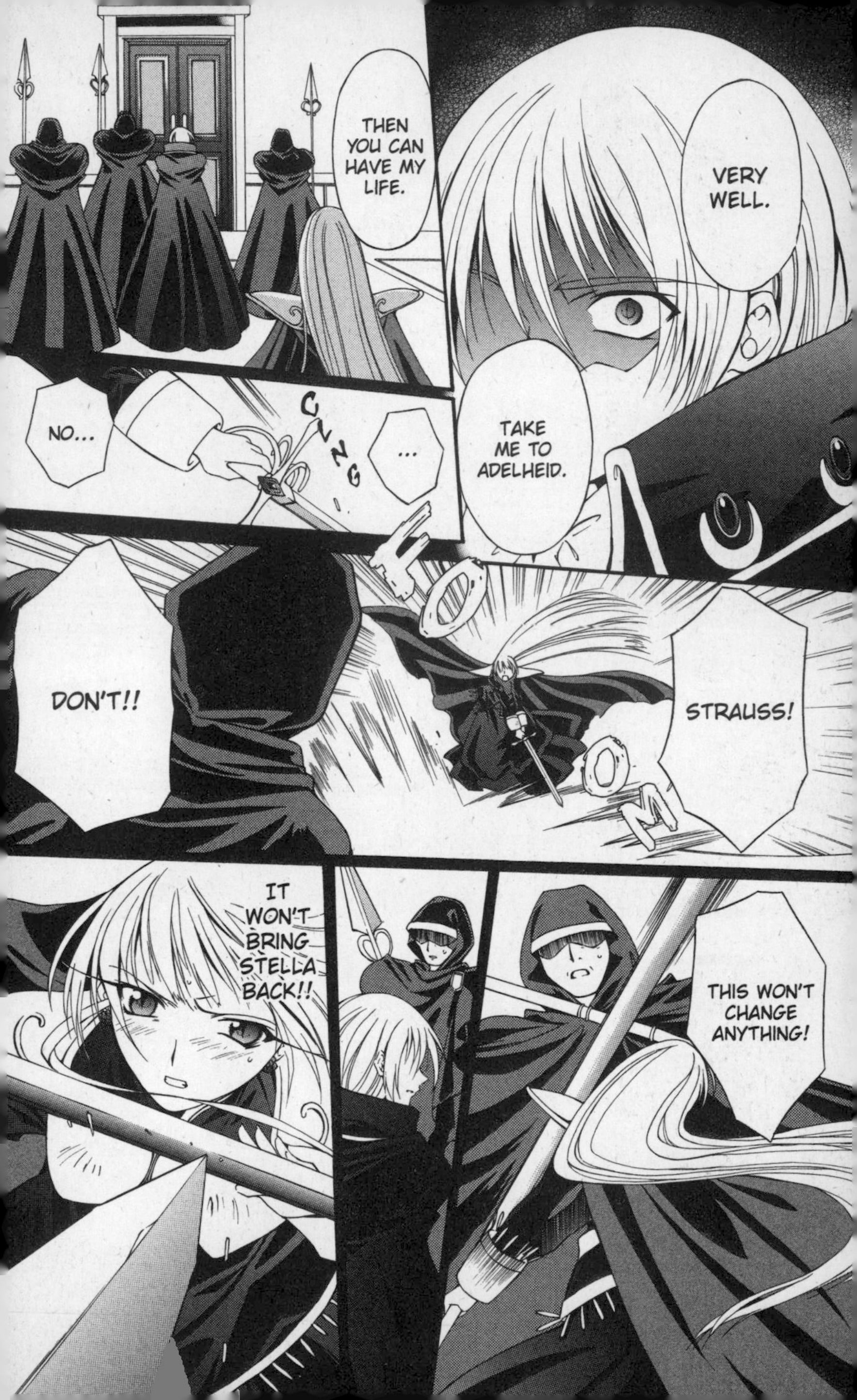
VERY WELL.
TAKE ME TO ADELHEID.
THEN YOU CAN HAVE MY LIFE.
...
CLNG
NO...
STRAUSS!
DON'T!!
THIS WON'T CHANGE ANYTHING!
IT WON'T BRING STELLA BACK!!

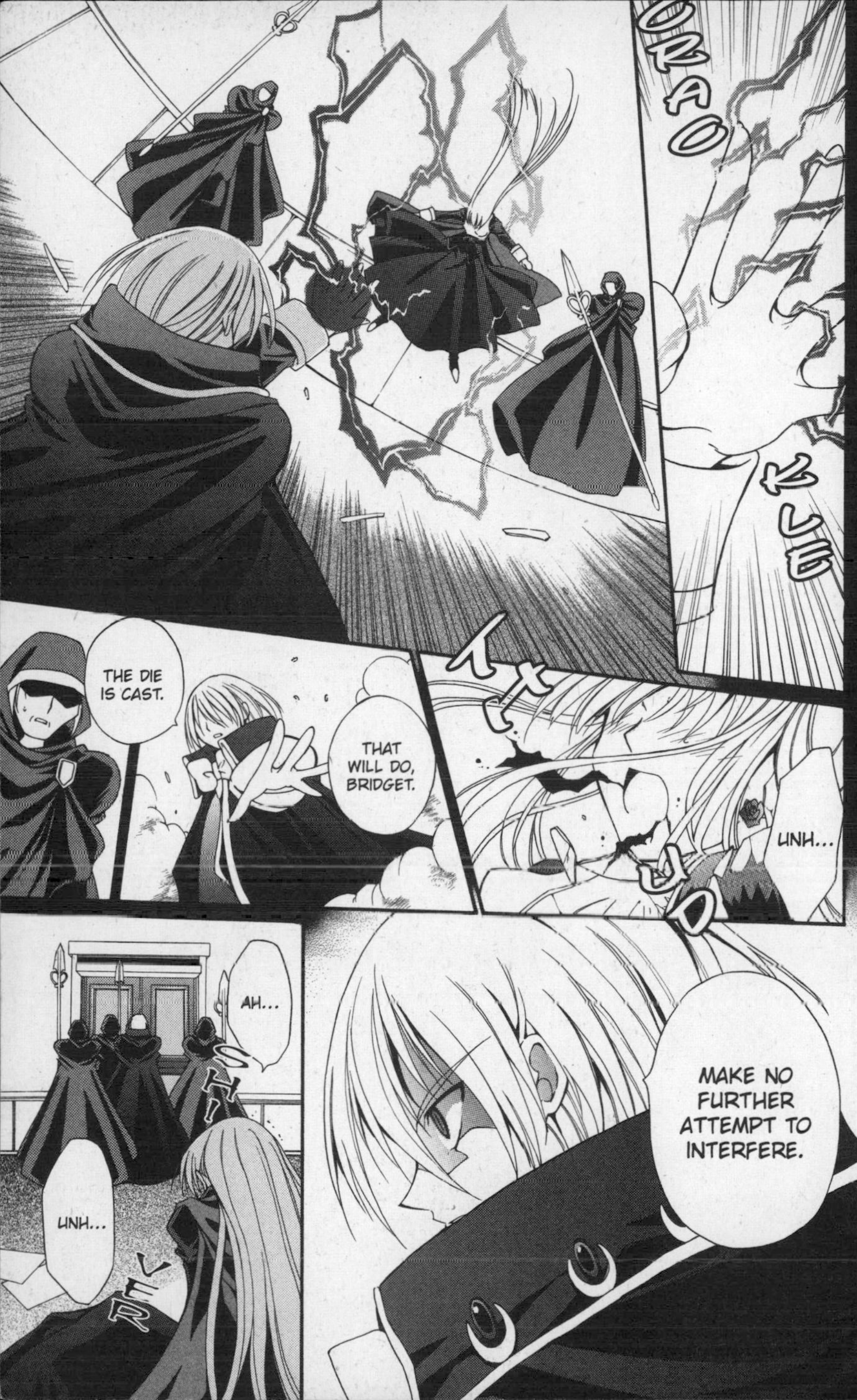
UNH...
THAT WILL DO, BRIDGET.
THE DIE IS CAST.
MAKE NO FURTHER ATTEMPT TO INTERFERE.
AH...
UNH...

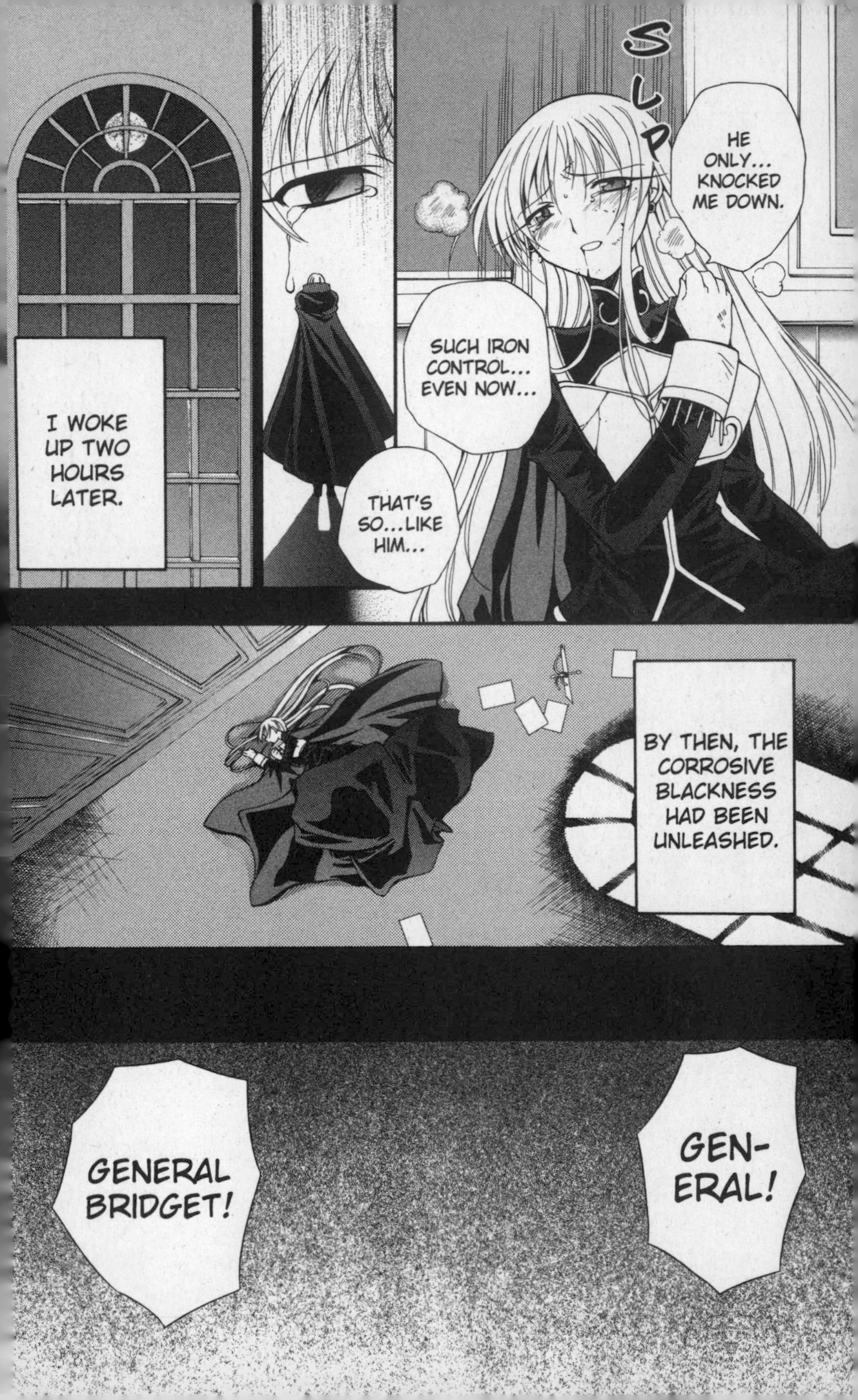

SLP
HE ONLY... KNOCKED ME DOWN.
SUCH IRON CONTROL... EVEN NOW...
THAT'S SO...LIKE HIM...
I WOKE UP TWO HOURS LATER.
BY THEN, THE CORROSIVE BLACKNESS HAD BEEN UNLEASHED.
GEN-ERAL!
GENERAL BRIDGET!

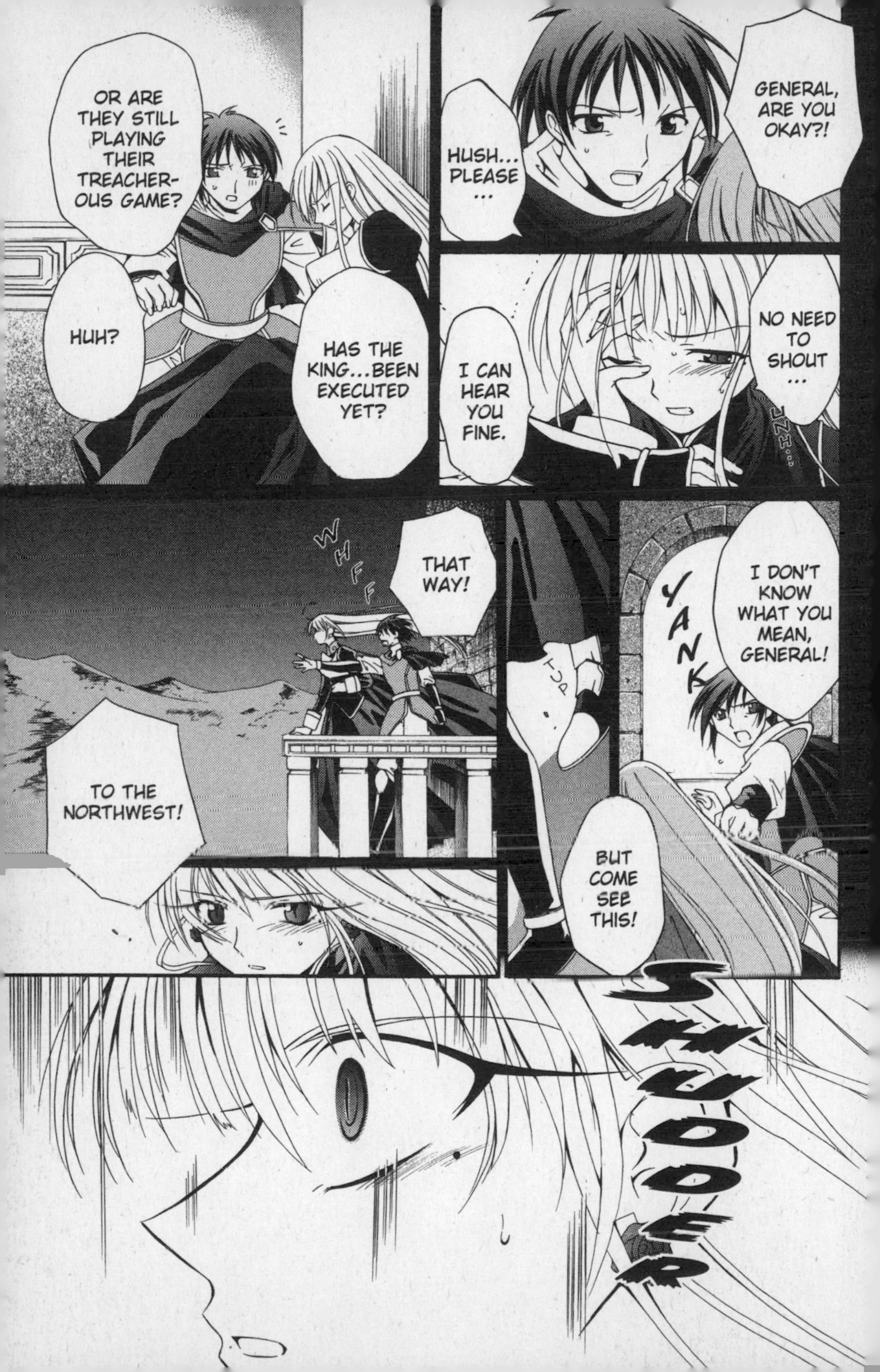
GENERAL, ARE YOU OKAY?!
HUSH... PLEASE ...
NO NEED TO SHOUT ...
UNH...
I CAN HEAR YOU FINE.
HAS THE KING...BEEN EXECUTED YET?
OR ARE THEY STILL PLAYING THEIR TREACHER-OUS GAME?
HUH?
I DON'T KNOW WHAT YOU MEAN, GENERAL!
YANK
TUP
BUT COME SEE THIS!
THAT WAY!
WHFF
TO THE NORTHWEST!
SHUDDER

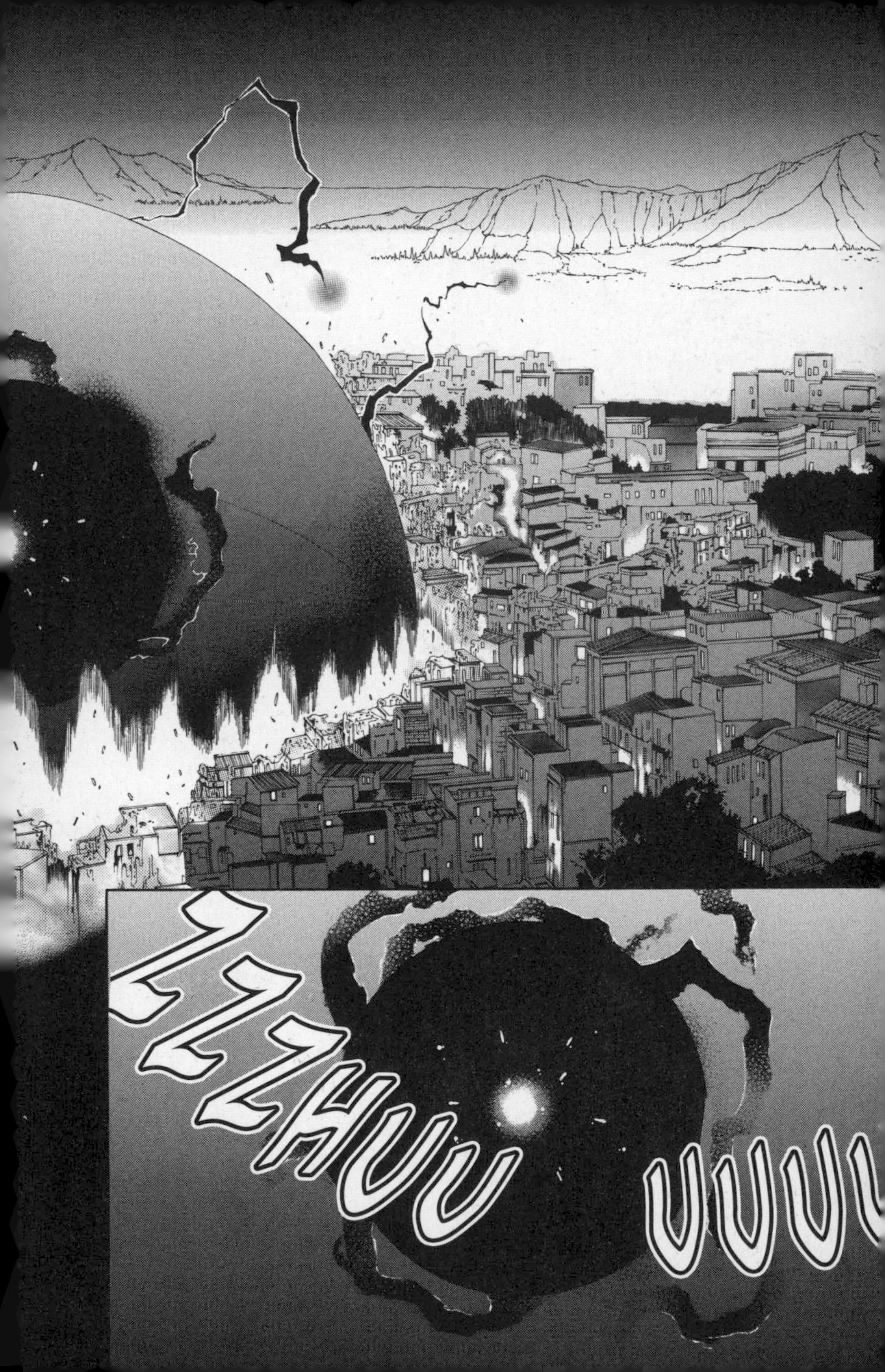
ZZZHUU UUUU

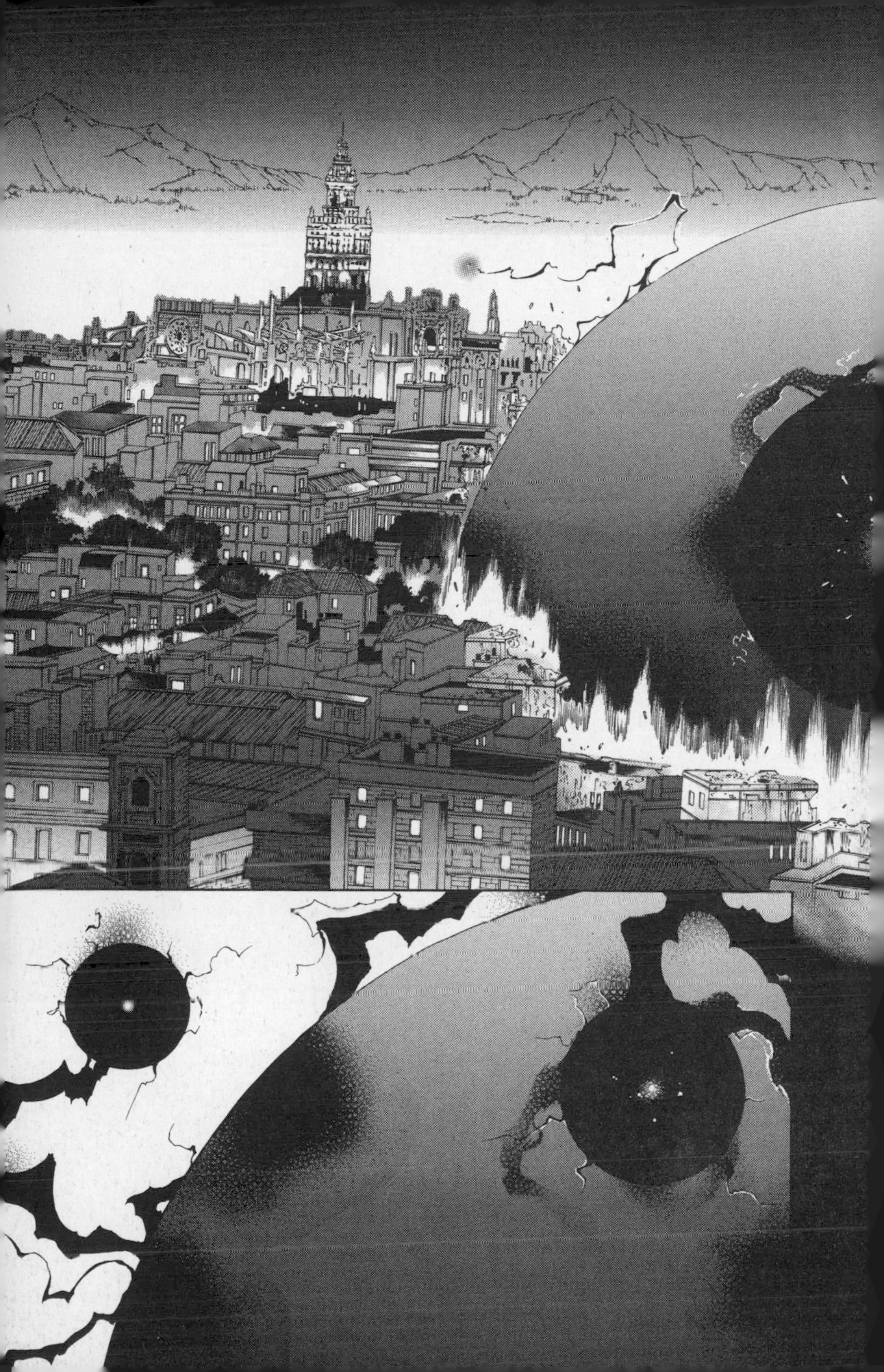

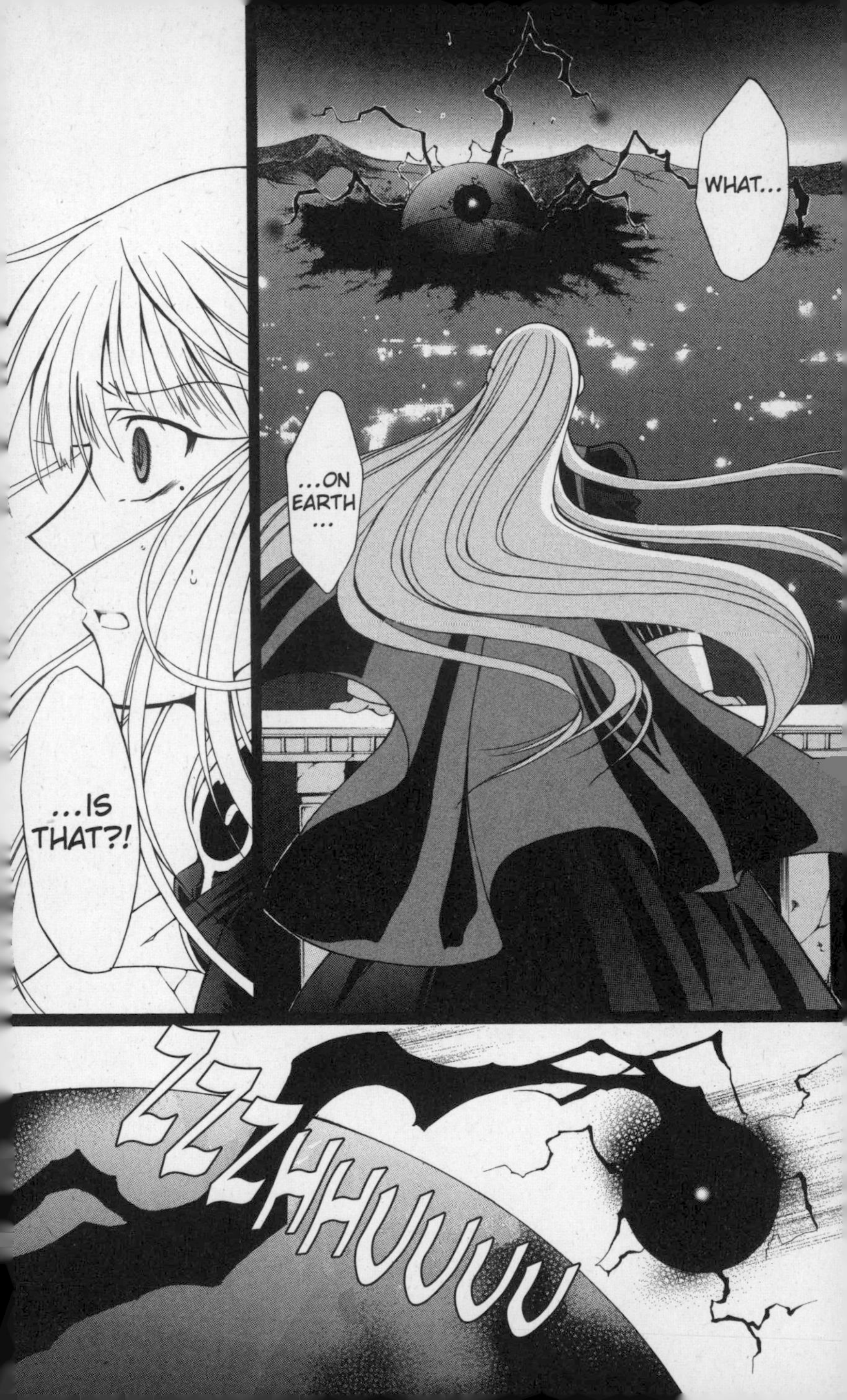
WHAT...
...ON EARTH...
...IS THAT?!
ZZZHHUUUUU

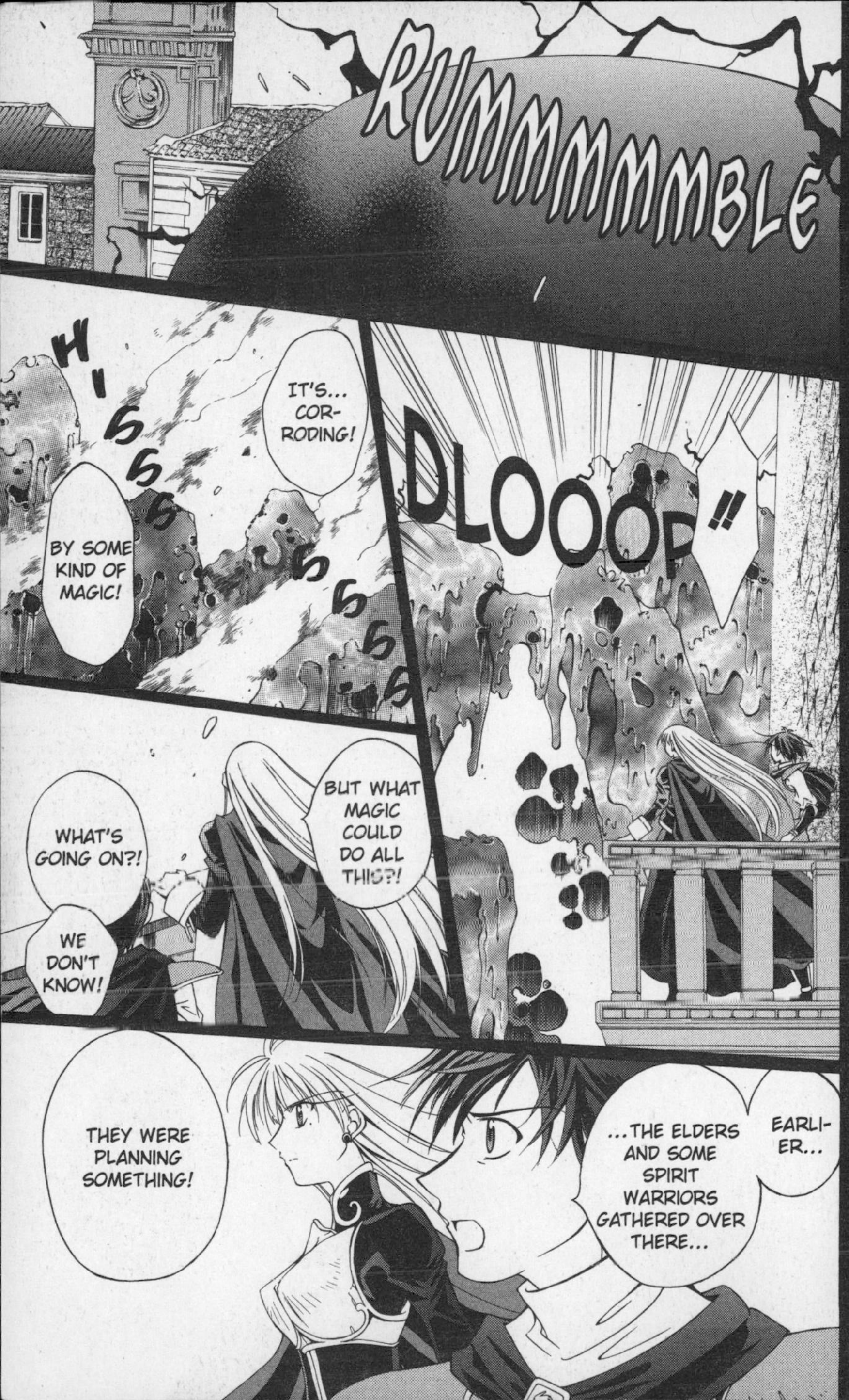
RUMMMMMMBLE
DLOOOP!!
IT'S... COR-RODING!
BY SOME KIND OF MAGIC!
HISSSSSSSSS
BUT WHAT MAGIC COULD DO ALL THIS?!
WHAT'S GOING ON?!
WE DON'T KNOW!
EARLI-ER...
...THE ELDERS AND SOME SPIRIT WARRIORS GATHERED OVER THERE...
THEY WERE PLANNING SOMETHING!

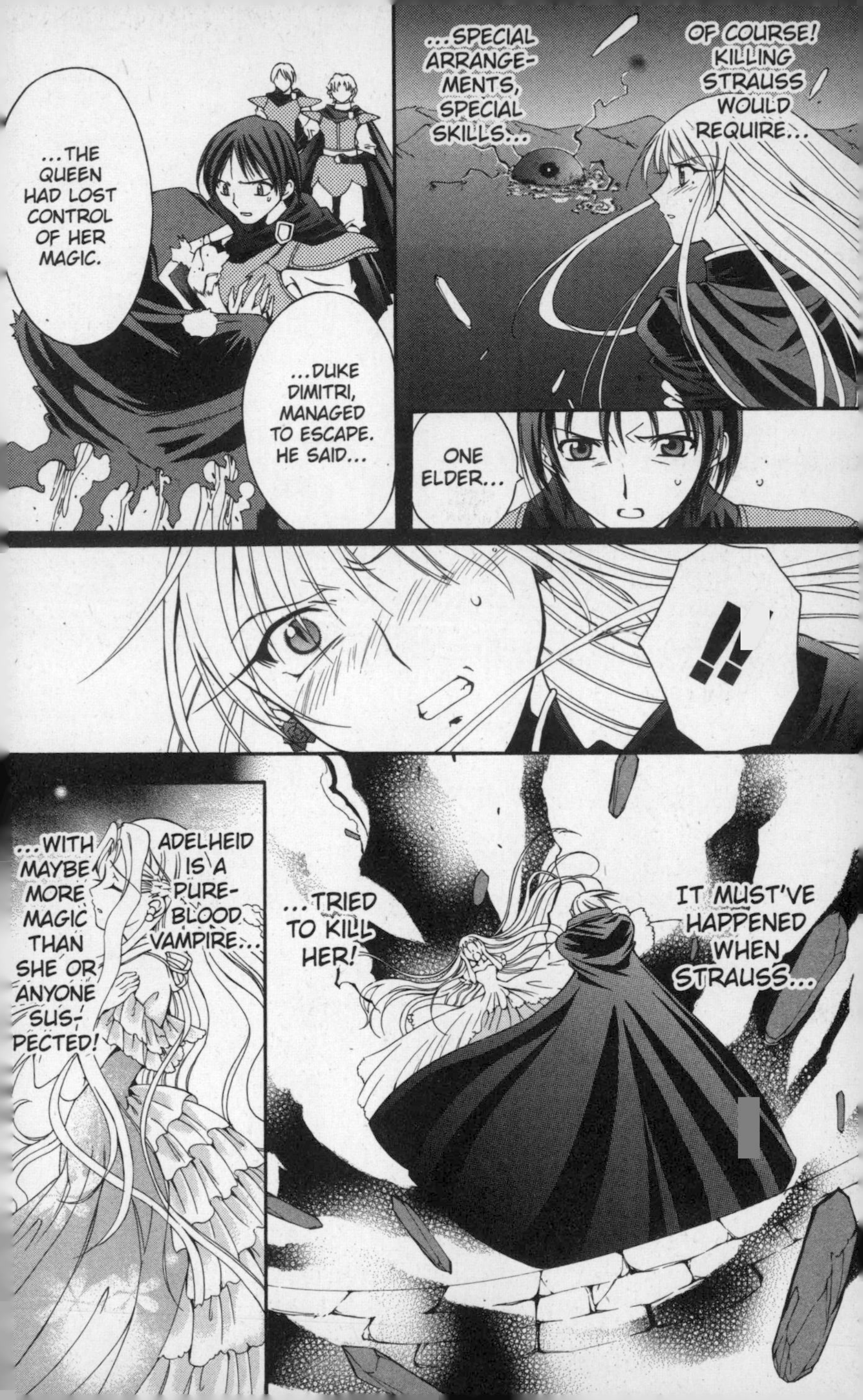
OF COURSE! KILLING STRAUSS WOULD REQUIRE...
...SPECIAL ARRANGEMENTS, SPECIAL SKILLS...
ONE ELDER...
...DUKE DIMITRI, MANAGED TO ESCAPE. HE SAID...
...THE QUEEN HAD LOST CONTROL OF HER MAGIC.
!!
IT MUST'VE HAPPENED WHEN STRAUSS...
...TRIED TO KILL HER!
ADELHEID IS A PURE-BLOOD VAMPIRE...
...WITH MAYBE MORE MAGIC THAN SHE OR ANYONE SUSPECTED!

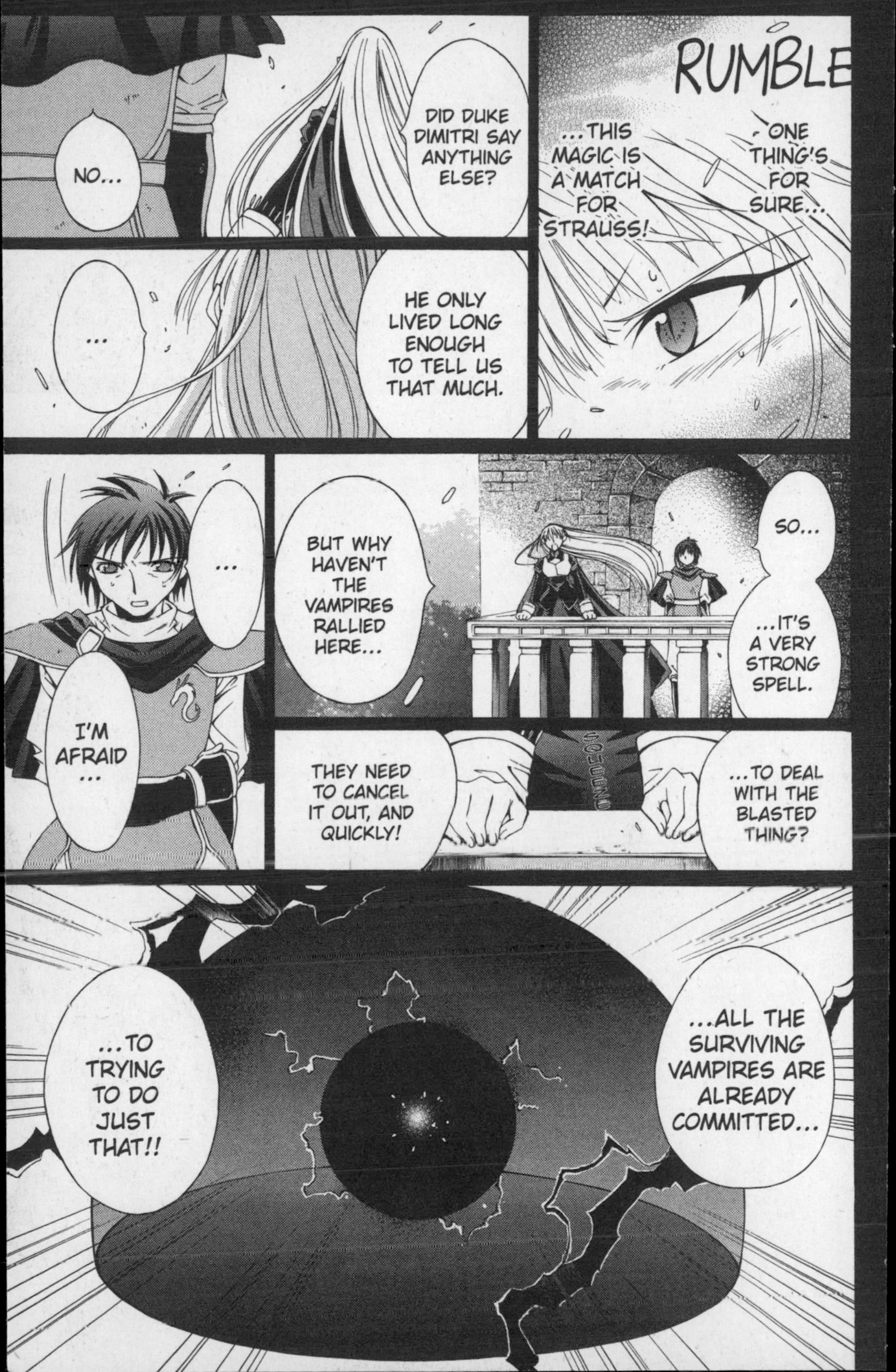
RUMBLE
ONE THING'S FOR SURE...
...THIS MAGIC IS A MATCH FOR STRAUSS!
DID DUKE DIMITRI SAY ANYTHING ELSE?
NO...
HE ONLY LIVED LONG ENOUGH TO TELL US THAT MUCH.
...
SO...
...IT'S A VERY STRONG SPELL.
BUT WHY HAVEN'T THE VAMPIRES RALLIED HERE...
...TO DEAL WITH THE BLASTED THING?
THEY NEED TO CANCEL IT OUT, AND QUICKLY!
...
I'M AFRAID ...
...ALL THE SURVIVING VAMPIRES ARE ALREADY COMMITTED...
...TO TRYING TO DO JUST THAT!!

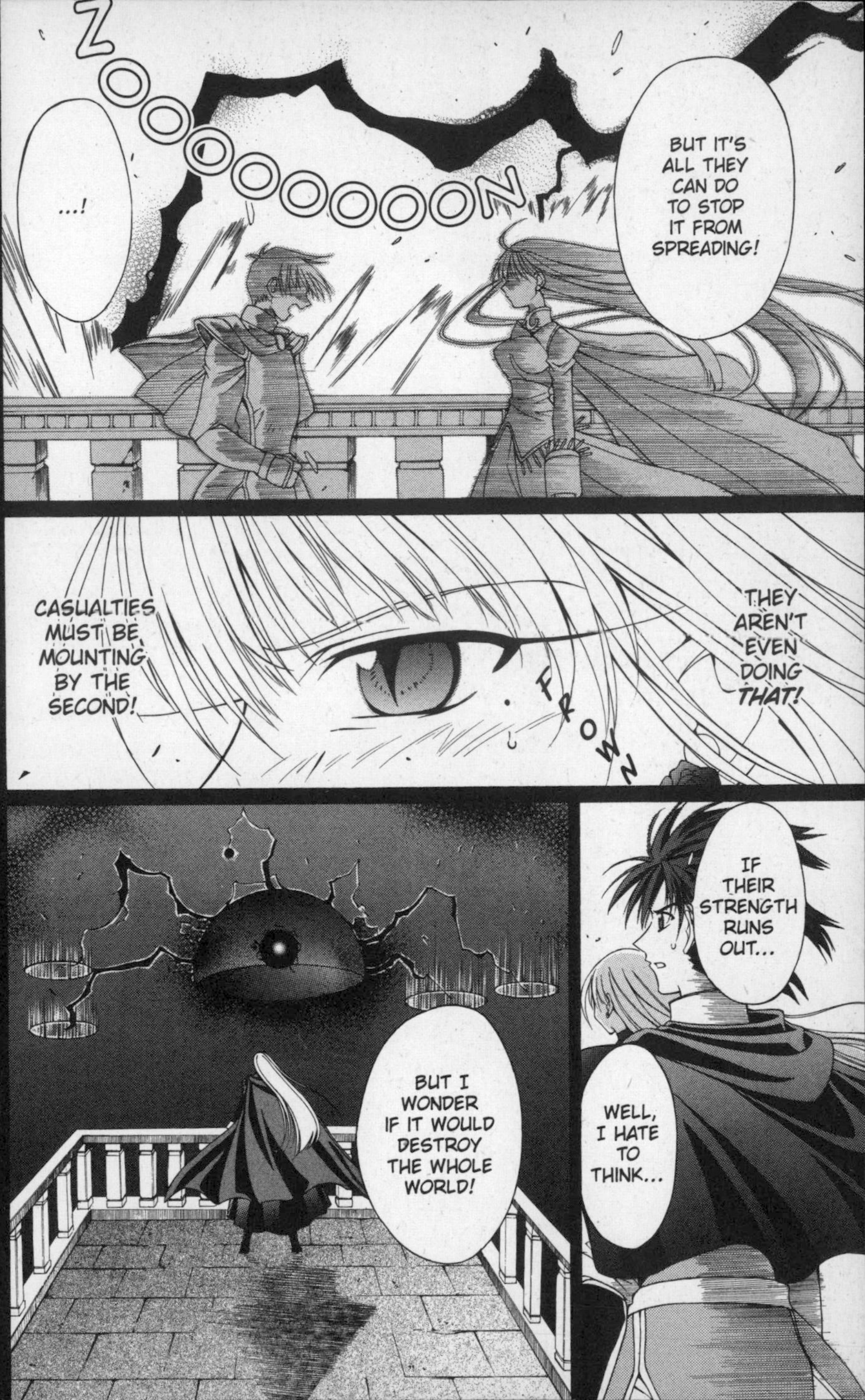
BUT IT'S ALL THEY CAN DO TO STOP IT FROM SPREADING!
ZOOOOOOOON
...!
THEY AREN'T EVEN DOING THAT!
FROWN
CASUALTIES MUST BE MOUNTING BY THE SECOND!
IF THEIR STRENGTH RUNS OUT...
WELL, I HATE TO THINK...
BUT I WONDER IF IT WOULD DESTROY THE WHOLE WORLD!

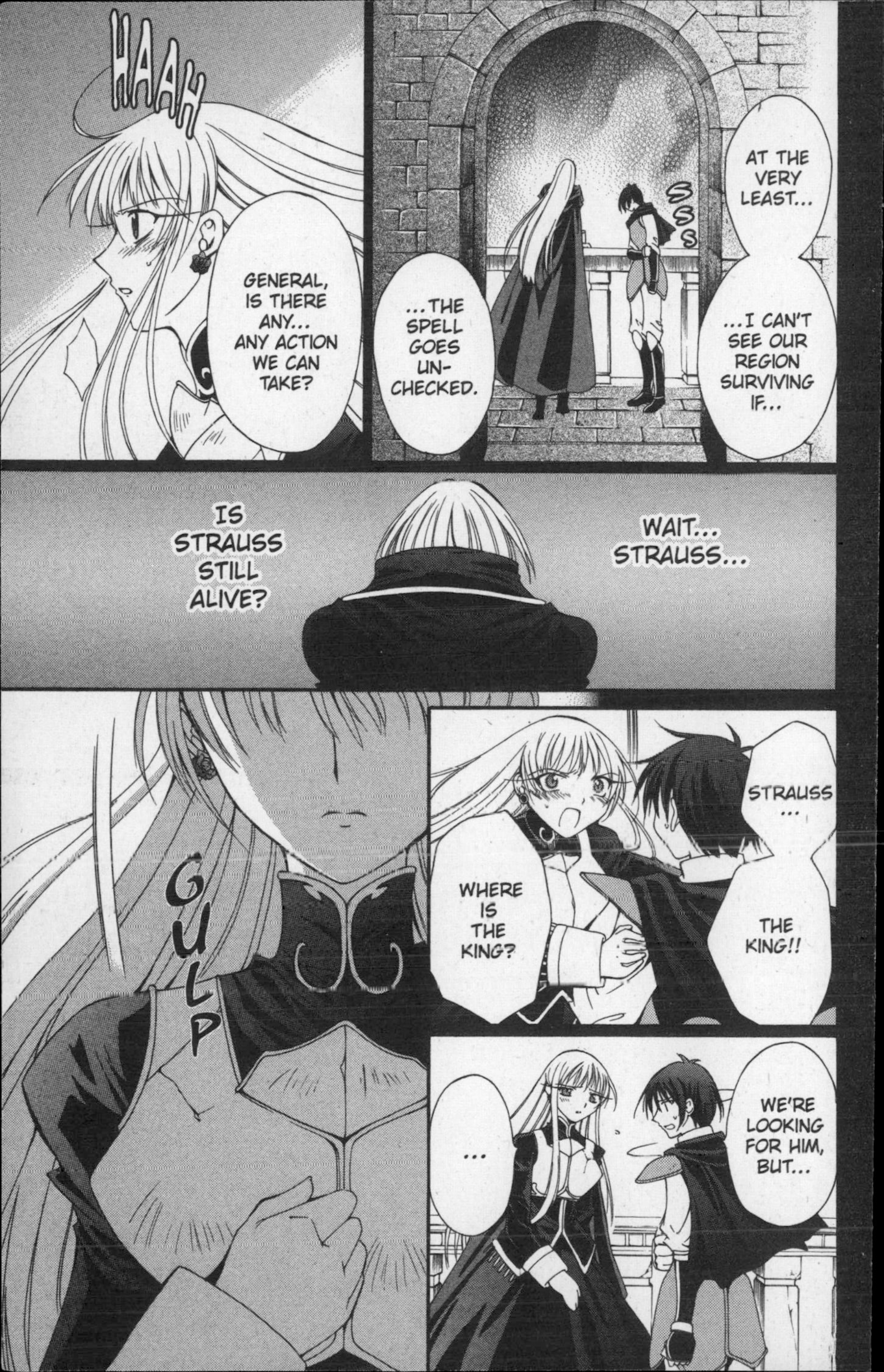
AT THE VERY LEAST...
SSS
...I CAN'T SEE OUR REGION SURVIVING IF...
...THE SPELL GOES UN-CHECKED.
HAAH
GENERAL, IS THERE ANY... ANY ACTION WE CAN TAKE?
WAIT... STRAUSS...
IS STRAUSS STILL ALIVE?
STRAUSS...
THE KING!!
WHERE IS THE KING?
WE'RE LOOKING FOR HIM, BUT...
...
GULP

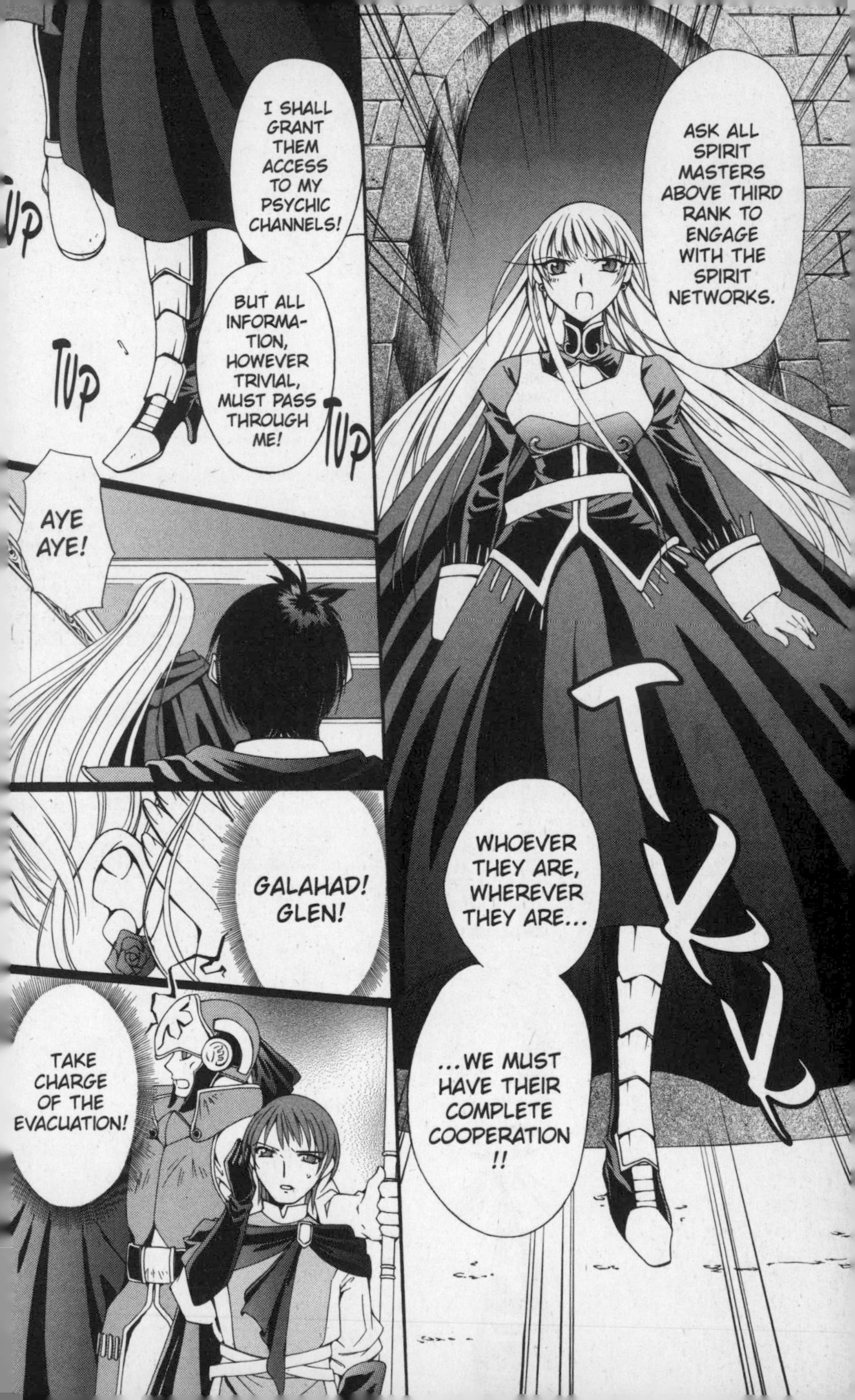
ASK ALL SPIRIT MASTERS ABOVE THIRD RANK TO ENGAGE WITH THE SPIRIT NETWORKS.
WHOEVER THEY ARE, WHEREVER THEY ARE...
...WE MUST HAVE THEIR COMPLETE COOPERATION !!
I SHALL GRANT THEM ACCESS TO MY PSYCHIC CHANNELS!
BUT ALL INFORMATION, HOWEVER TRIVIAL, MUST PASS THROUGH ME!
TUP
TUP
TUP
AYE AYE!
GALAHAD! GLEN!
TAKE CHARGE OF THE EVACUATION!

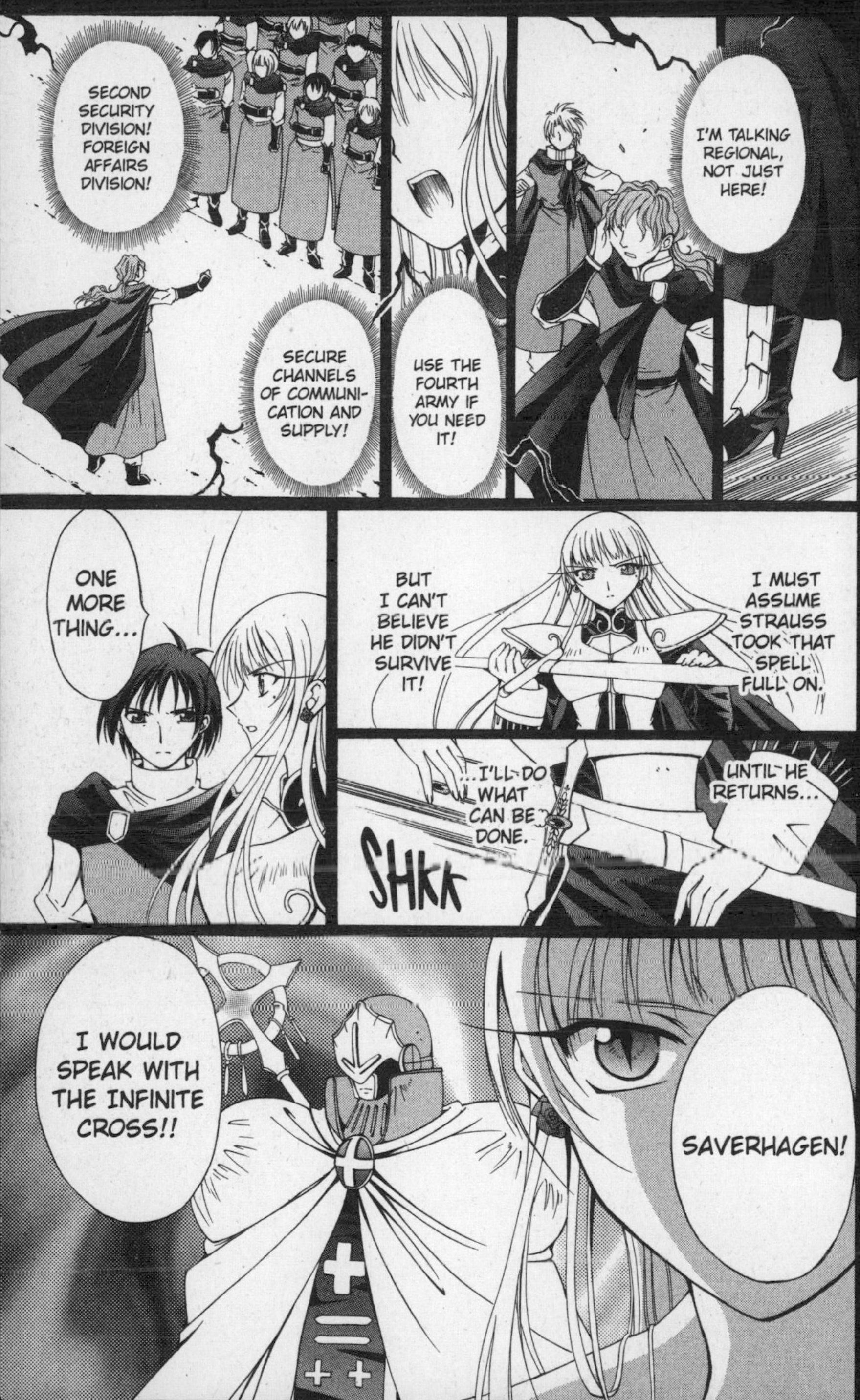
I'M TALKING REGIONAL, NOT JUST HERE!
USE THE FOURTH ARMY IF YOU NEED IT!
SECOND SECURITY DIVISION! FOREIGN AFFAIRS DIVISION!
SECURE CHANNELS OF COMMUNI-CATION AND SUPPLY!
I MUST ASSUME STRAUSS TOOK THAT SPELL FULL ON.
BUT I CAN'T BELIEVE HE DIDN'T SURVIVE IT!
UNTIL HE RETURNS...
...I'LL DO WHAT CAN BE DONE.
SHKK
ONE MORE THING...
SAVERHAGEN!
I WOULD SPEAK WITH THE INFINITE CROSS!!

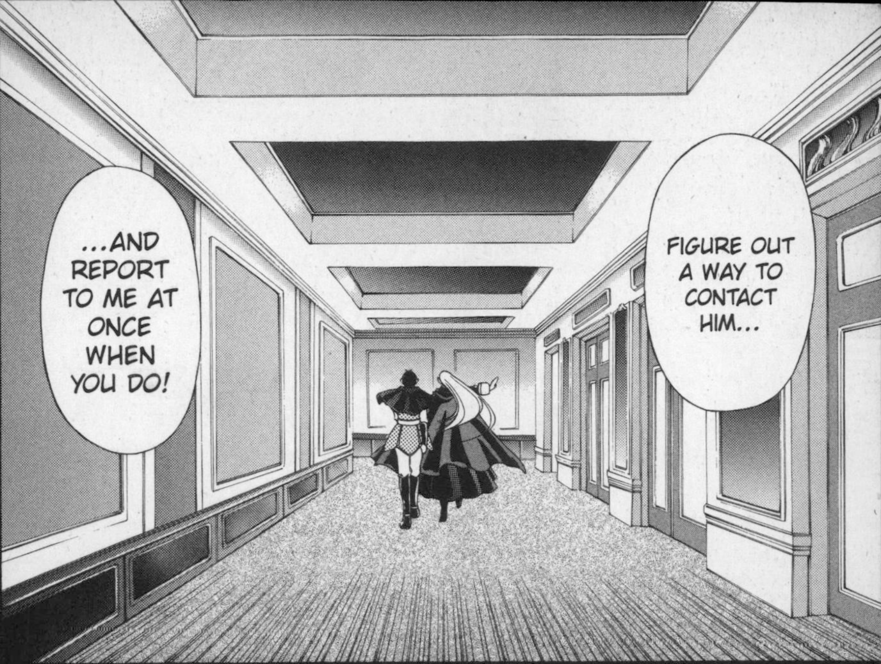
FIGURE OUT A WAY TO CONTACT HIM...
...AND REPORT TO ME AT ONCE WHEN YOU DO!

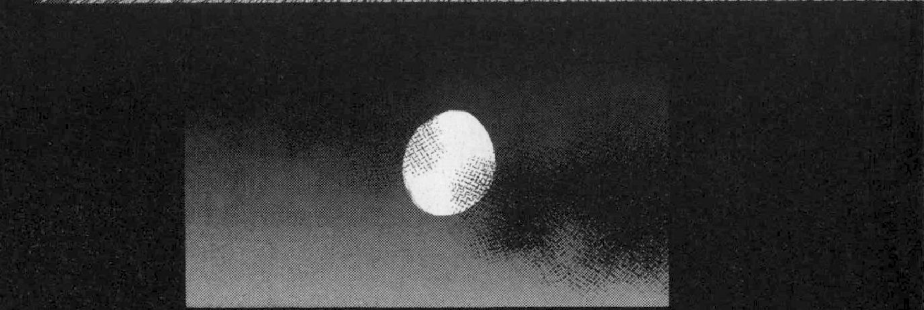

DAY TWO

THREE HUNDRED HUMAN SPIRIT MASTERS
JOIN THE VAMPIRES...
...TO TRY TO CONTROL THE CORROSION, BUT THEY FAIL.
CASUALTIES ACROSS THE CONTINENT NUMBER
MORE THAN 6,000.

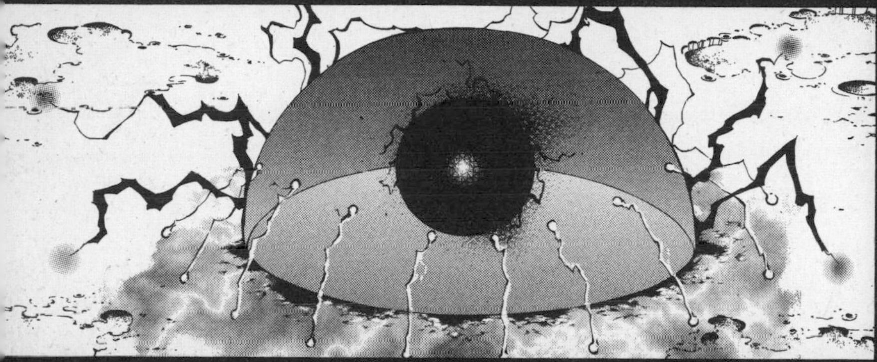

DAY THREE

THE NUMBER OF DEAD CONTINUES TO RISE,
PASSING 10,000.
SAVERHAGEN JOINS THE BATTLE...

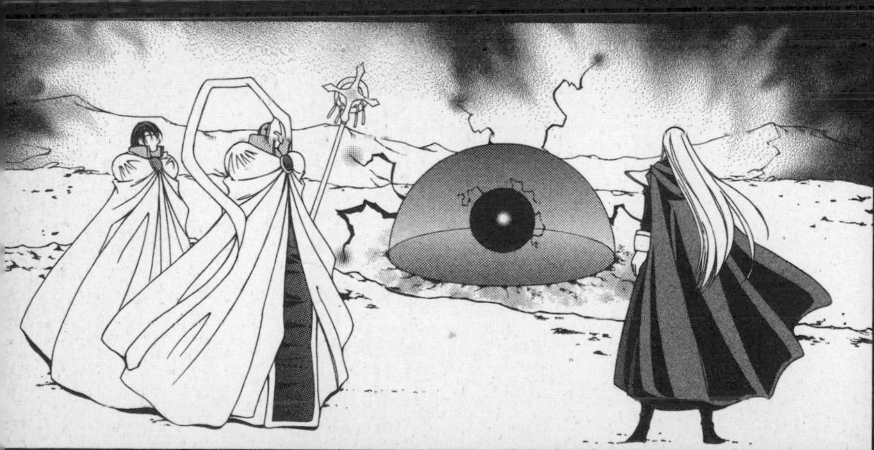

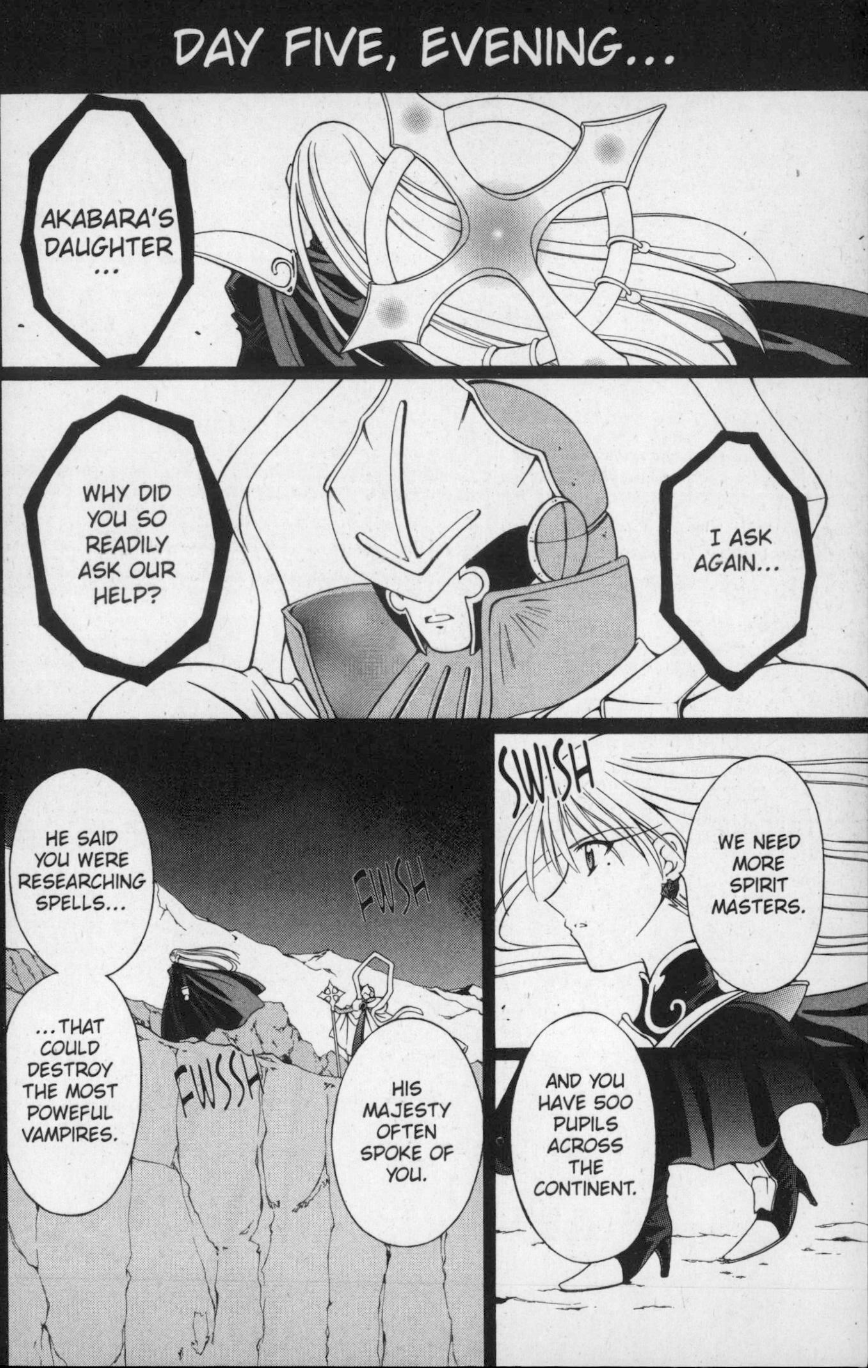
DAY FIVE, EVENING...
AKABARA'S DAUGHTER ...
I ASK AGAIN...
WHY DID YOU SO READILY ASK OUR HELP?
SWISH
WE NEED MORE SPIRIT MASTERS.
AND YOU HAVE 500 PUPILS ACROSS THE CONTINENT.
FWSH
HIS MAJESTY OFTEN SPOKE OF YOU.
HE SAID YOU WERE RESEARCHING SPELLS...
...THAT COULD DESTROY THE MOST POWEFUL VAMPIRES.
FWSSH

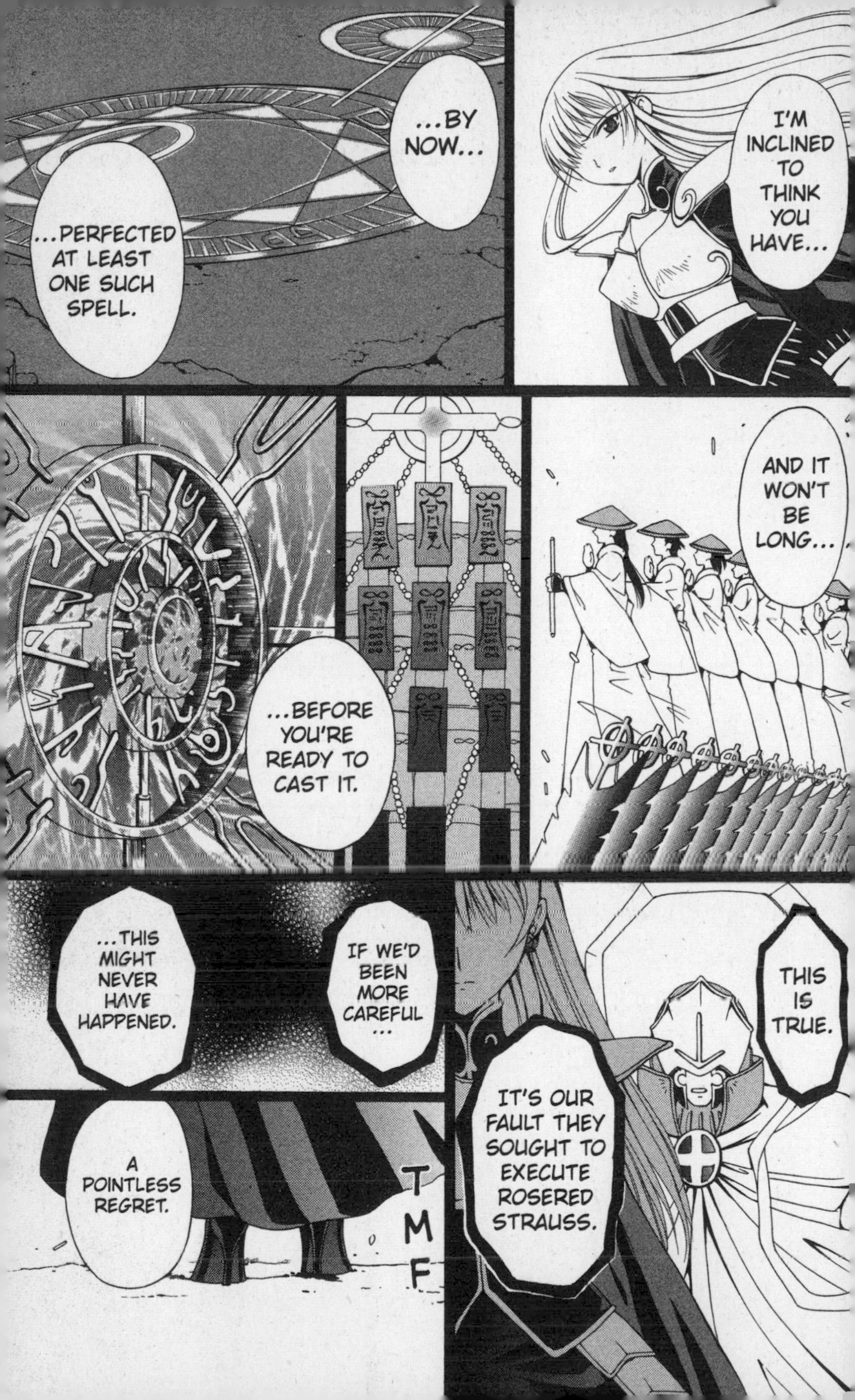
I'M INCLINED TO THINK YOU HAVE...
...BY NOW...
...PERFECTED AT LEAST ONE SUCH SPELL.
AND IT WON'T BE LONG...
...BEFORE YOU'RE READY TO CAST IT.
THIS IS TRUE.
IT'S OUR FAULT THEY SOUGHT TO EXECUTE ROSERED STRAUSS.
IF WE'D BEEN MORE CAREFUL...
...THIS MIGHT NEVER HAVE HAPPENED.
A POINTLESS REGRET.
TMF

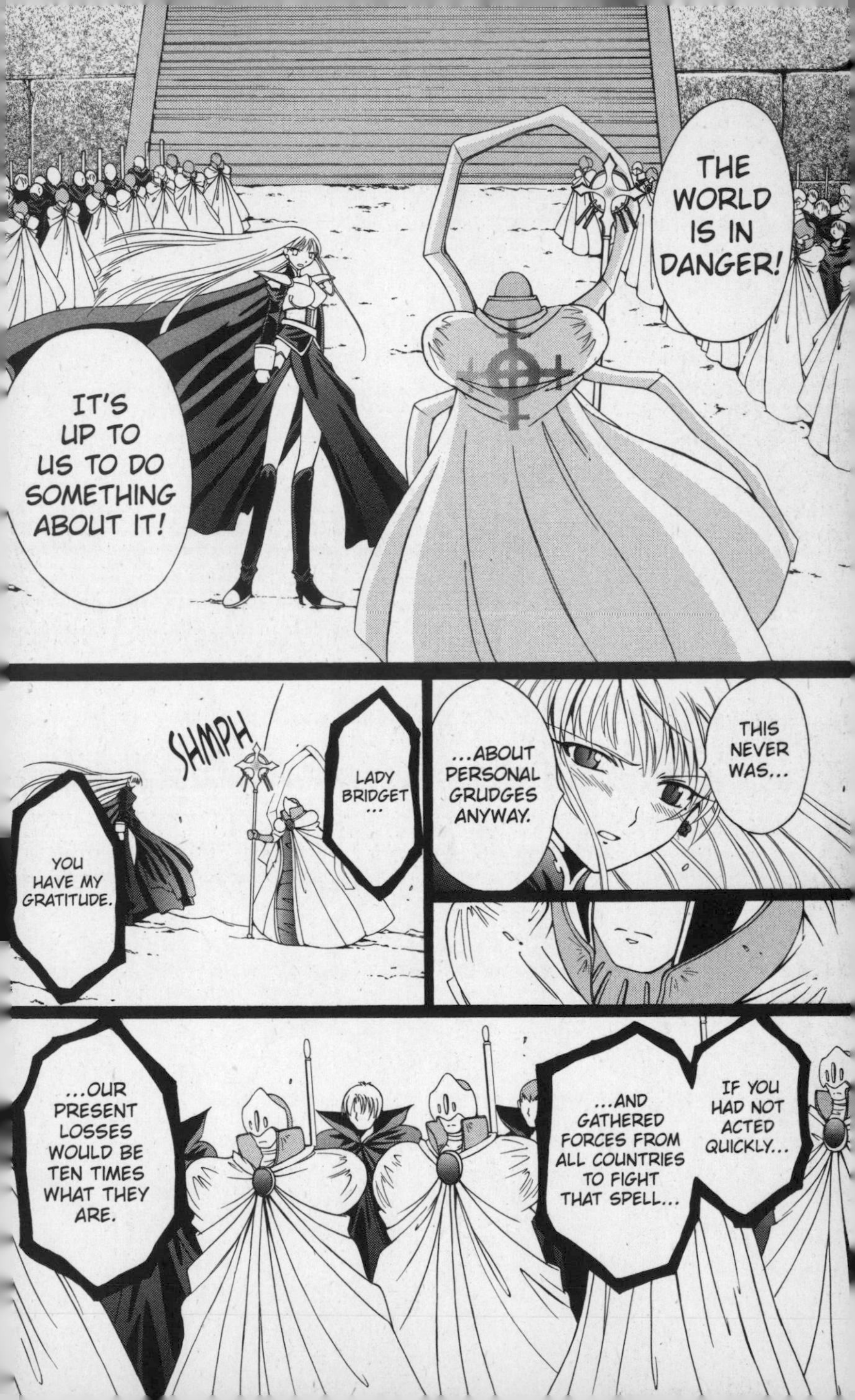
THE WORLD IS IN DANGER!
IT'S UP TO US TO DO SOMETHING ABOUT IT!
THIS NEVER WAS...
...ABOUT PERSONAL GRUDGES ANYWAY.
SHMPH
LADY BRIDGET...
YOU HAVE MY GRATITUDE.
IF YOU HAD NOT ACTED QUICKLY...
...AND GATHERED FORCES FROM ALL COUNTRIES TO FIGHT THAT SPELL...
...OUR PRESENT LOSSES WOULD BE TEN TIMES WHAT THEY ARE.

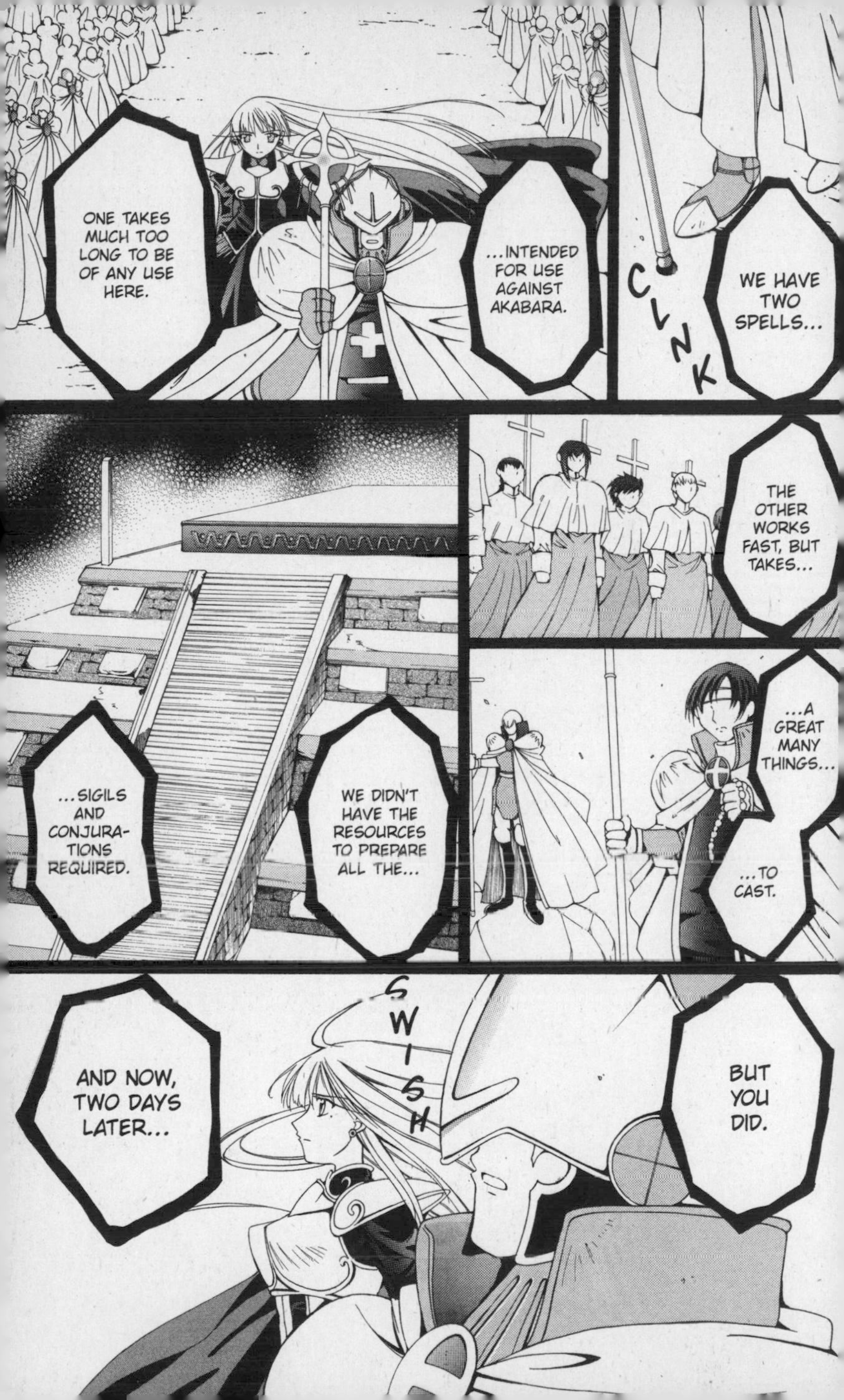
WE HAVE TWO SPELLS...
CLNK
...INTENDED FOR USE AGAINST AKABARA.
ONE TAKES MUCH TOO LONG TO BE OF ANY USE HERE.
THE OTHER WORKS FAST, BUT TAKES...
...A GREAT MANY THINGS...
...TO CAST.
WE DIDN'T HAVE THE RESOURCES TO PREPARE ALL THE...
...SIGILS AND CONJURA-TIONS REQUIRED.
BUT YOU DID.
SWISH
AND NOW, TWO DAYS LATER...

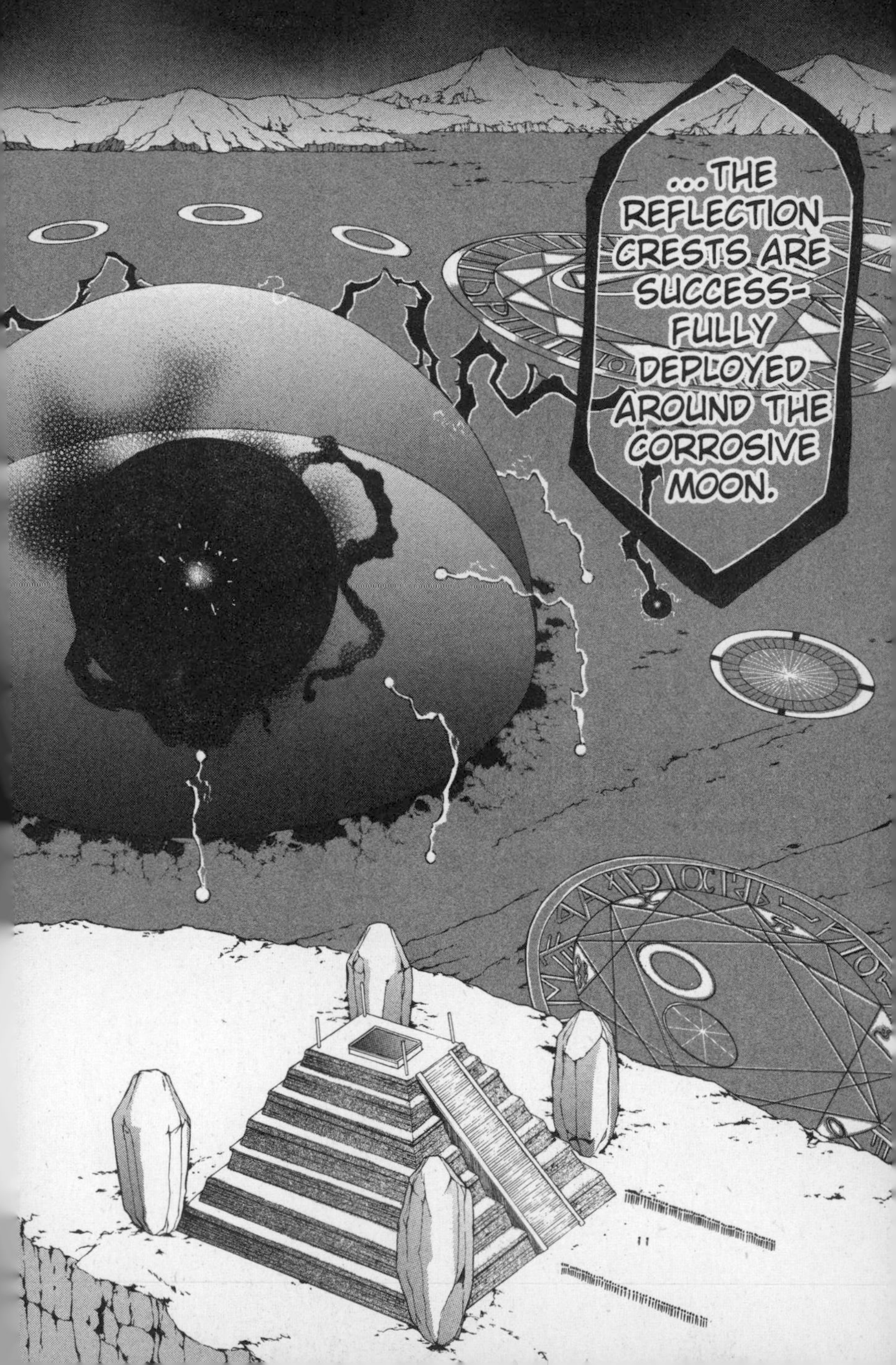
...THE REFLECTION CRESTS ARE SUCCESS-FULLY DEPLOYED AROUND THE CORROSIVE MOON.

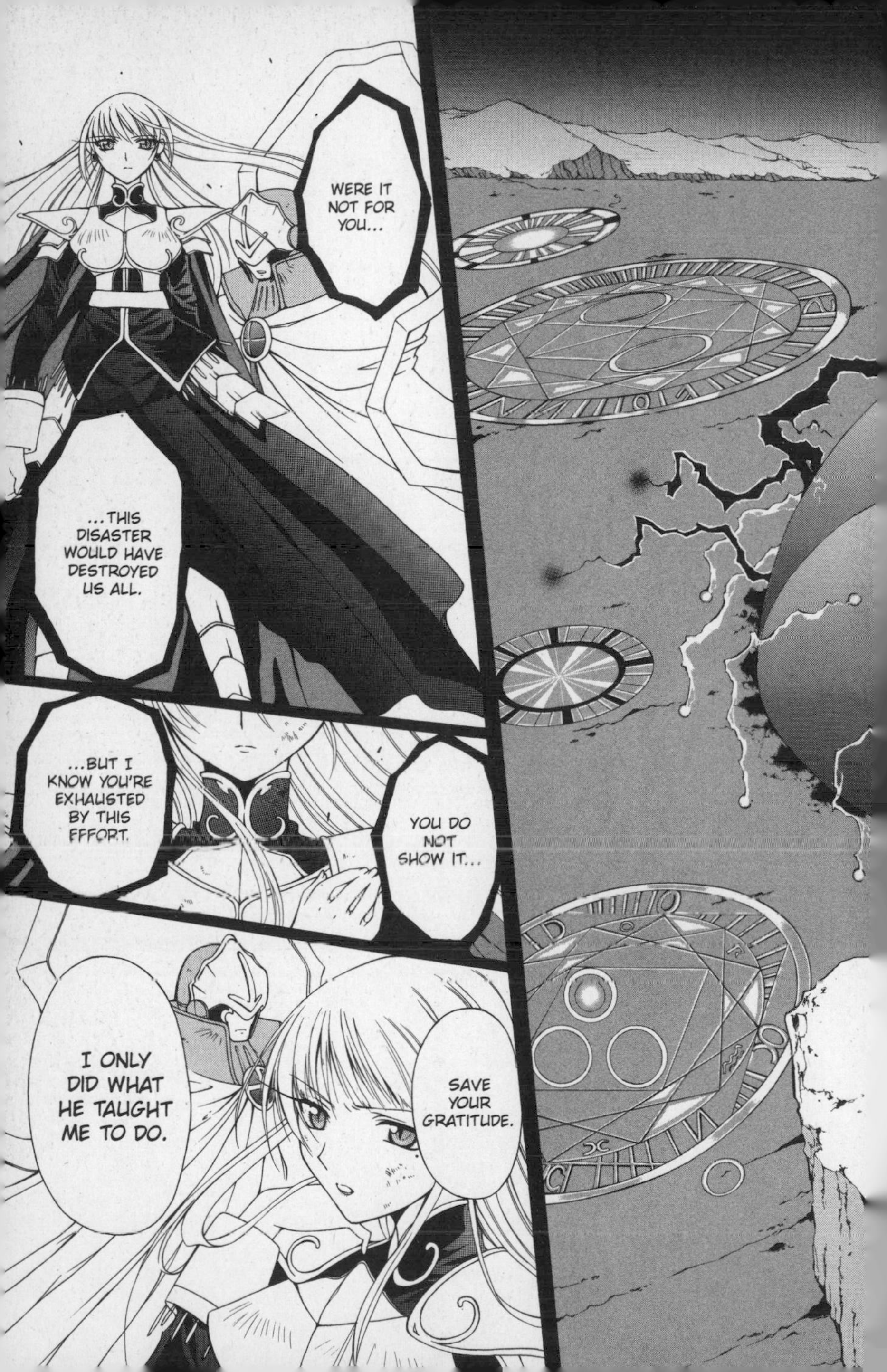
WERE IT NOT FOR YOU...
...THIS DISASTER WOULD HAVE DESTROYED US ALL.
YOU DO NOT SHOW IT...
...BUT I KNOW YOU'RE EXHAUSTED BY THIS EFFORT.
SAVE YOUR GRATITUDE.
I ONLY DID WHAT HE TAUGHT ME TO DO.

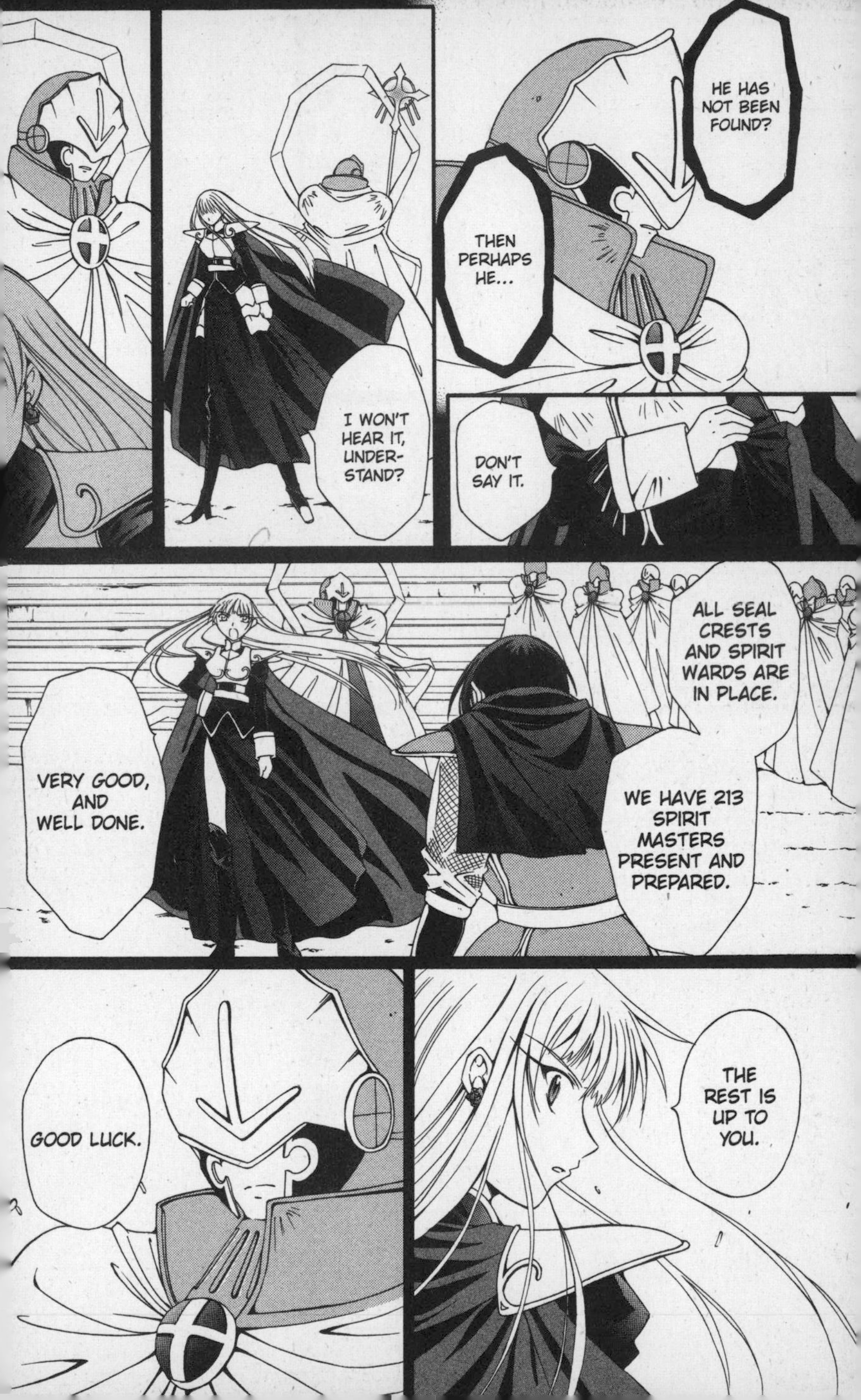
HE HAS NOT BEEN FOUND?
THEN PERHAPS HE...
DON'T SAY IT.
I WON'T HEAR IT, UNDER-STAND?
ALL SEAL CRESTS AND SPIRIT WARDS ARE IN PLACE.
WE HAVE 213 SPIRIT MASTERS PRESENT AND PREPARED.
VERY GOOD, AND WELL DONE.
THE REST IS UP TO YOU.
GOOD LUCK.

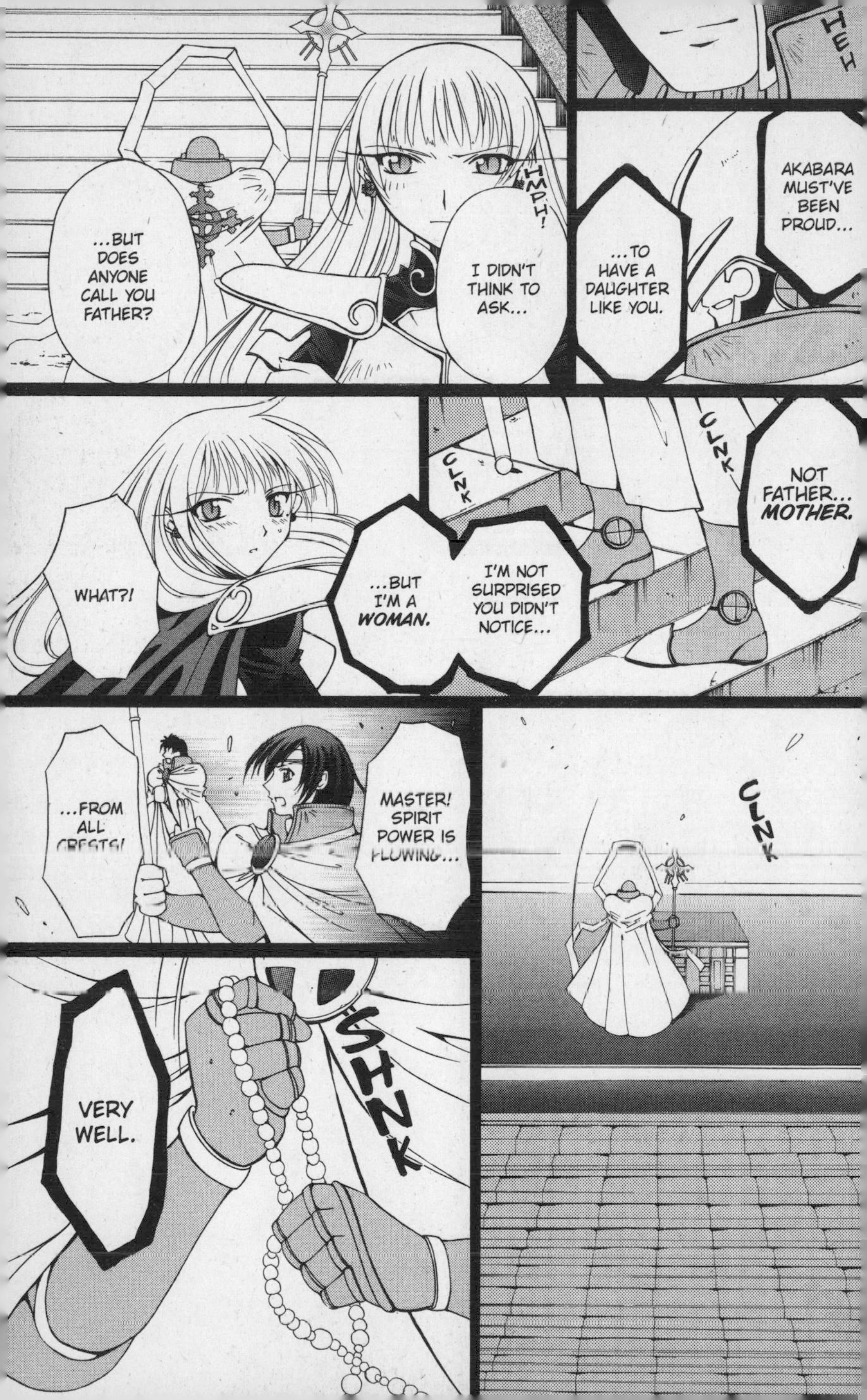
HEH
AKABARA MUST'VE BEEN PROUD...
...TO HAVE A DAUGHTER LIKE YOU.
HMPH!
I DIDN'T THINK TO ASK...
...BUT DOES ANYONE CALL YOU FATHER?
CLNK
CLNK
NOT FATHER... *MOTHER.*
I'M NOT SURPRISED YOU DIDN'T NOTICE...
...BUT I'M A *WOMAN.*
WHAT?!
CLNK
MASTER! SPIRIT POWER IS FLOWING...
...FROM ALL CRESTS!
SHNK
VERY WELL.

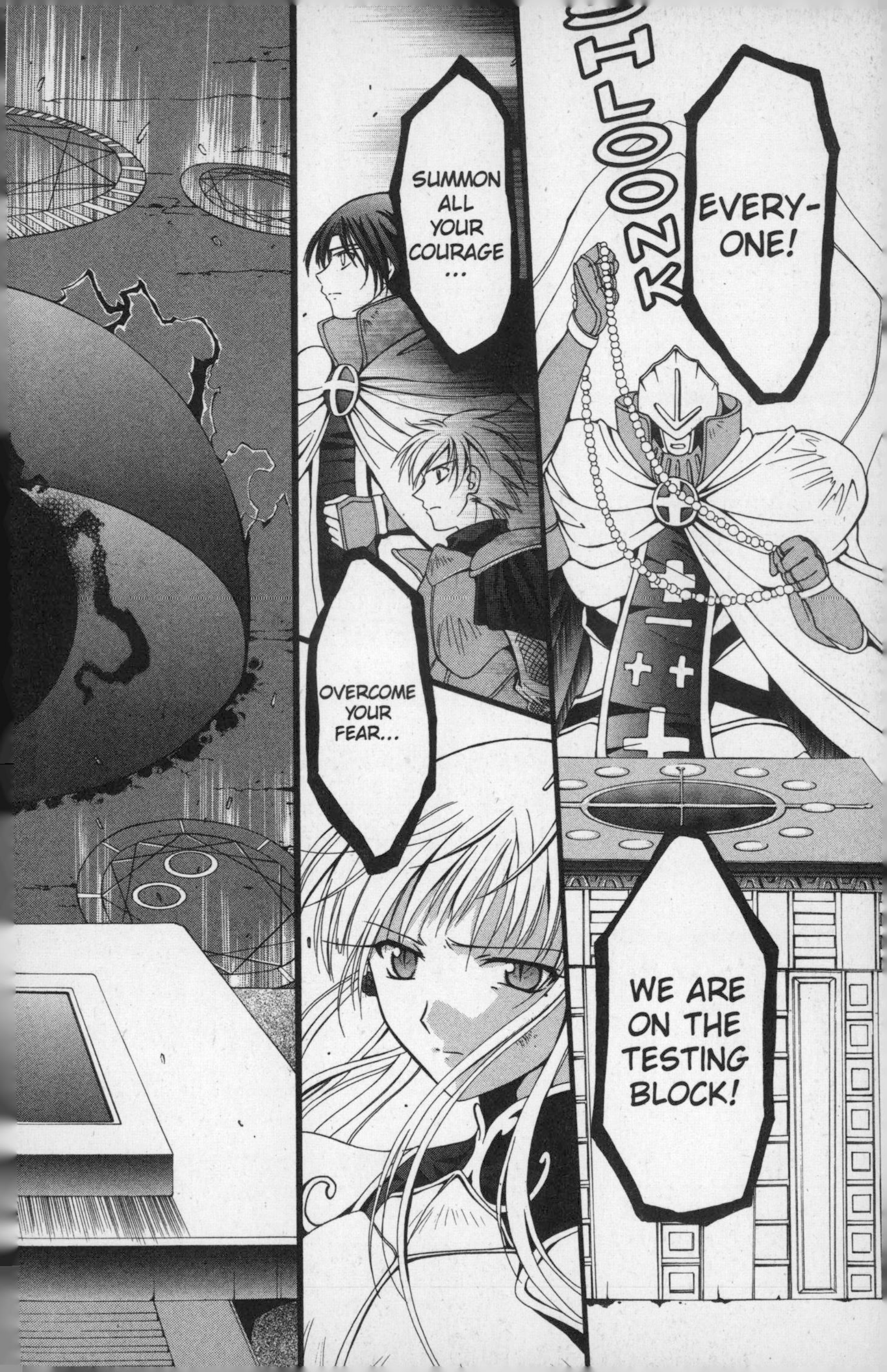
KNOOLH
EVERY-ONE!
WE ARE ON THE TESTING BLOCK!
SUMMON ALL YOUR COURAGE...
OVERCOME YOUR FEAR...

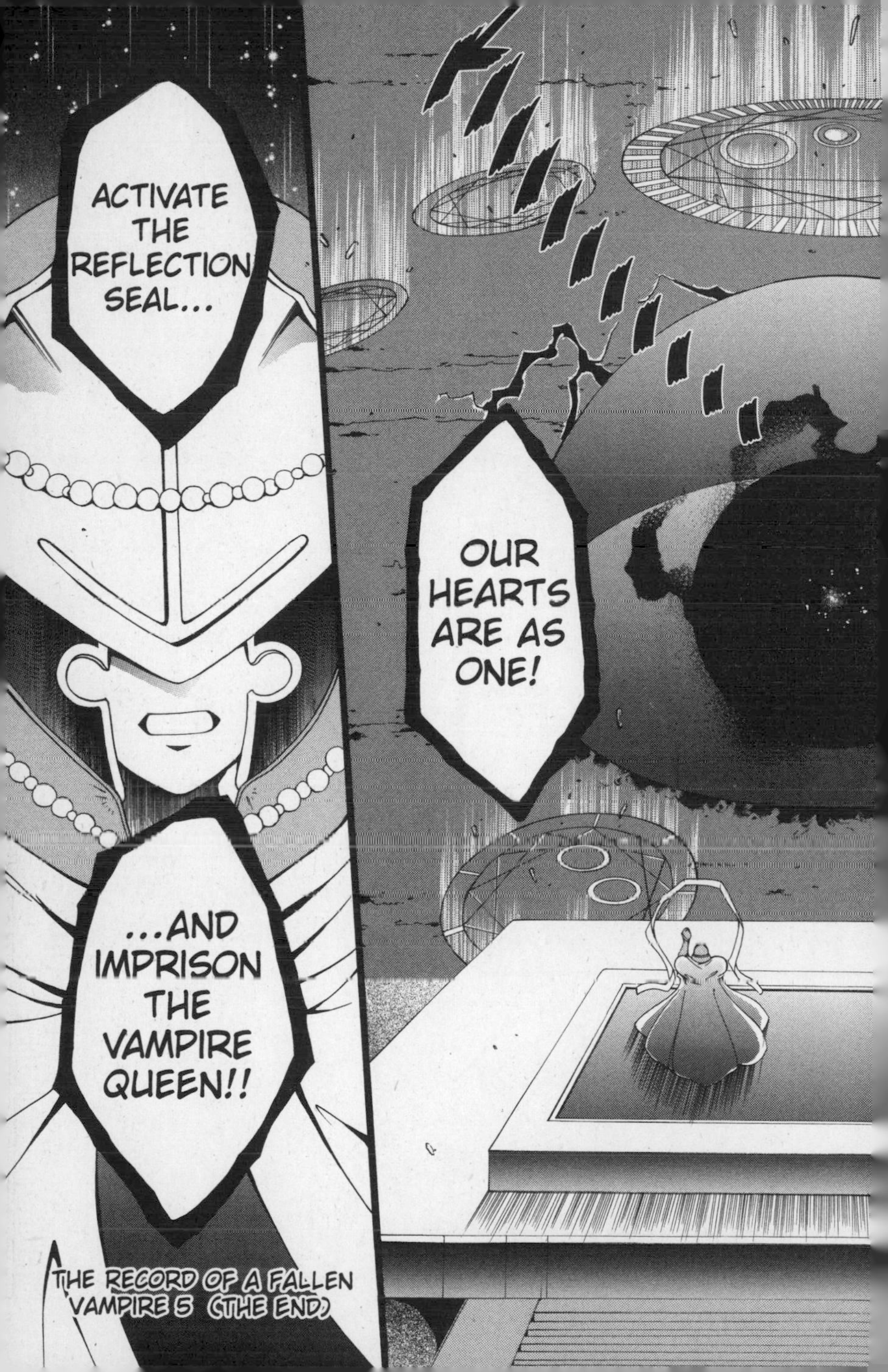
OUR HEARTS ARE AS ONE!
ACTIVATE THE REFLECTION SEAL...
...AND IMPRISON THE VAMPIRE QUEEN!!
THE RECORD OF A FALLEN VAMPIRE 5 (THE END)

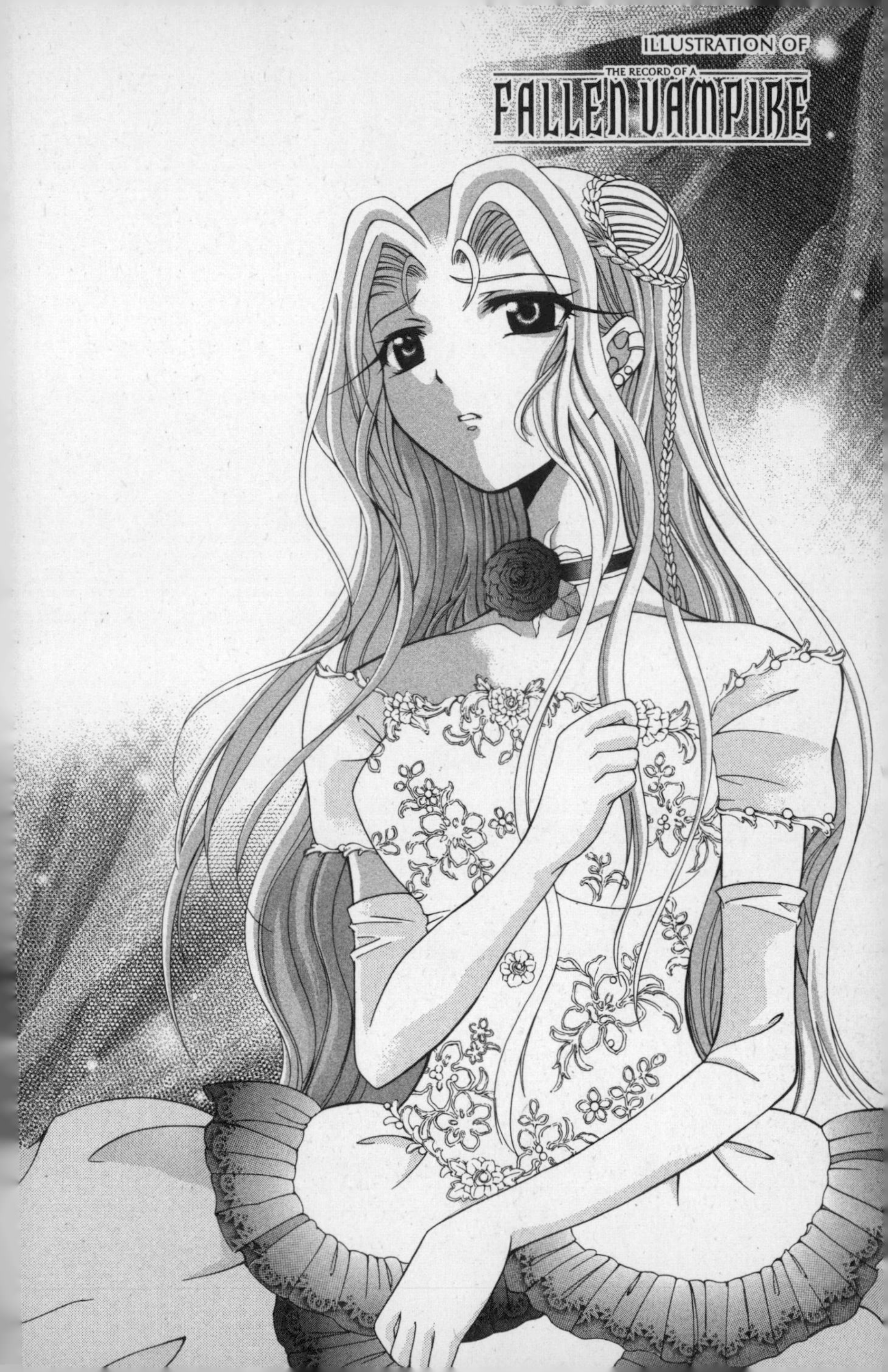
ILLUSTRATION OF
THE RECORD OF A
FALLEN VAMPIRE

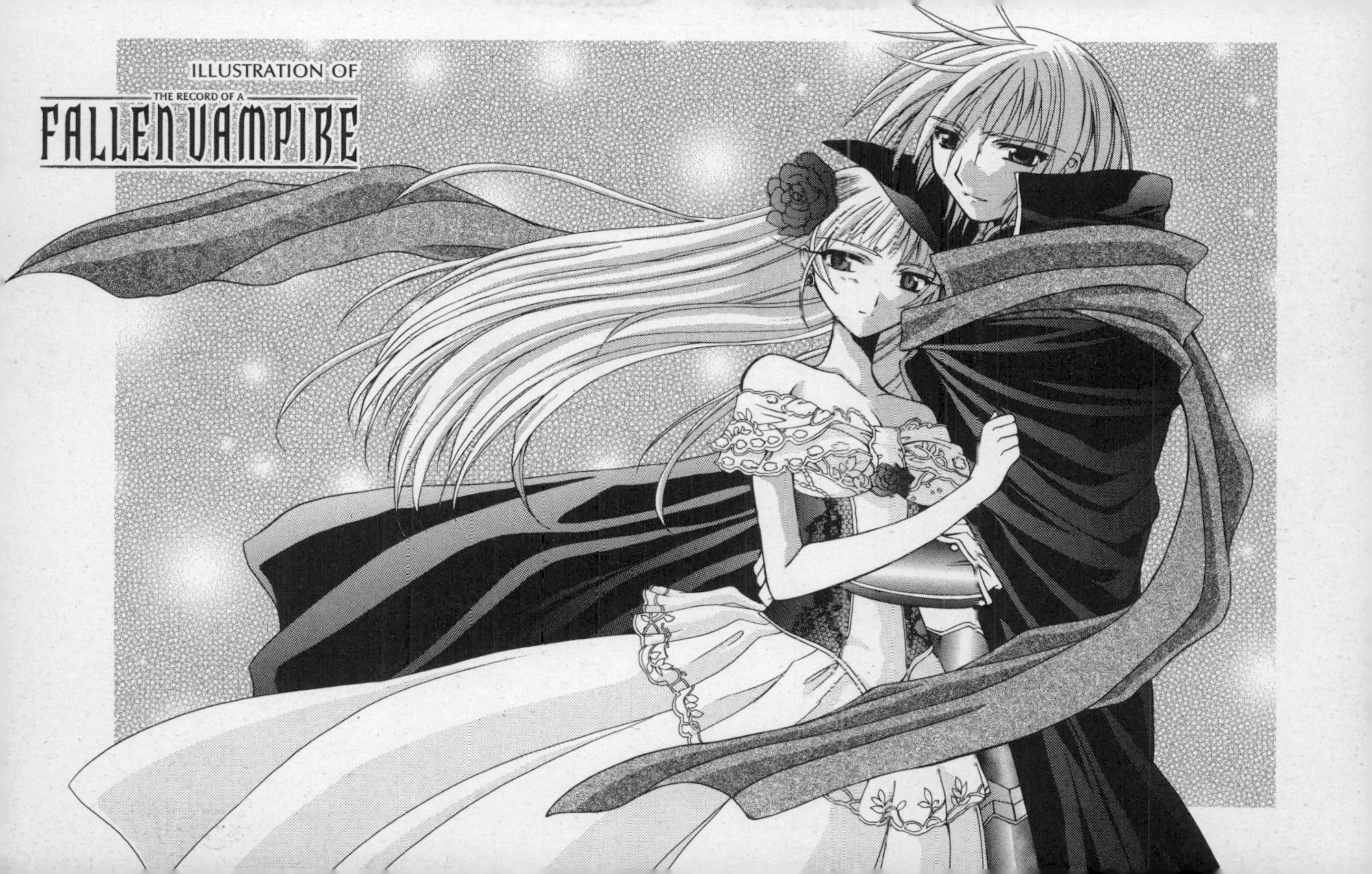
ILLUSTRATION OF
THE RECORD OF A
FALLEN VAMPIRE

RECORD OF A FALLEN VAMPIRE VOLUME 5!

ALL THE CHAPTERS THIS TIME ARE FOCUSED ON THE PAST, AND I GOT REALLY WORKED UP DRAWING THEM! CASTLES! SHIPS! SPACE SUITS! BIG MORTAR! THE CORROSIVE MOON! ALL KINDS OF THINGS THAT ARE HARD TO DRAW. SO... THIS LONG FLASHBACK IS ALL TOLD FROM BRIDGET'S POINT OF VIEW, AND WE GET TO SEE HOW SHE REMEMBERS STRAUSS.

STRAUSS IN THE PRESENT... IT'S ALWAYS HARD TO TELL WHAT HE'S THINKING (HE DOES HIS BEST NOT TO LET HIS FEELINGS SHOW), AND I'VE BEEN VERY CAREFUL TO DRAW HIM THAT WAY. THAT'S VERY HARD TO DO AND IS A REAL TEST OF MY SKILLS. HE TAKES MORE OUT OF ME THAN ANY OTHER CHARACTER. BUT IN THE FLASHBACK, HE WAS VERY EASY TO DRAW. HE WAS LIKE A NORMAL HUMAN, DISPLAYING LOVE, ANGER AND SADNESS. WHEN HE WAS WITH STELLA, I COULD EVEN MAKE HIM LOOK LIKE A COMPLETE IDIOT.

DRAWING STRAUSS WHEN HE WAS HAPPY... IT WAS LIKE A DREAM COME TRUE.

BUT HAPPINESS IS FLEETING,
AND THE STORY QUICKLY
BECAME ONE OF ANGUISH
AND DESPAIR.

I HOPE WE MEET AGAIN
IN VOLUME 6.

    - YURI KIMURA

SPECIAL THANKS

MARUKO ASAGAYA
TEPPEI TAKUMI
CHIKA HANAZAWA
AKIRA KIMURA

EDITOR: NOBUAKI YUMURA

"SUNA NO KISHIBE" - FROM
AKINO ARAI'S ALBUM *EDEN*

AND TO EVERYONE WHO
READ THIS!

AUTHOR'S AFTERWORD

I SAW A MOVIE—MADE IN THE 21ST CENTURY—IN WHICH, AT THE BEGINNING, A CHARACTER WAS GIVEN A TOUGH-LOOKING CHARM; THEN, IN THE MIDDLE, HE PULLED IT OUT AND LOOKED AT IT AND, NEAR THE END, WAS SHOT IN THE CHEST BY AN ARROW.

ANYONE WITH ANY EXPERIENCE AT ALL WOULD NATURALLY ASSUME HE WAS PROTECTED WHEN THE ARROW HIT THE TOUGH-LOOKING CHARM. INSTEAD, THE CHARACTER JUST DIED.

HAD IT ACTUALLY SAVED HIM, THAT WOULD HAVE BEEN A CLICHÉ, BUT IN THAT CASE, WHAT WAS THE POINT OF MAKING SUCH A BIG DEAL ABOUT THE TOUGH CHARM?

HERE I AM STARTING ANOTHER POINTLESS RAMBLE. I AM KYO SHIRODAIRA, AND THIS IS VOLUME 5. WHAT'S MY POINT? IF YOU INTRODUCE AN ITEM OR AN ASPECT OF THE SETTING AS IF IT MEANS SOMETHING, IT HAS TO EVENTUALLY MEAN SOMETHING, OR YOU'RE IN TROUBLE.

A SERIALIZED MANGA TENDS TO FIND THE STORY GOING IN DIFFERENT DIRECTIONS THAN ORIGINALLY INTENDED, AS NEW IDEAS COME IN AND TAKE THE STORY WITH THEM, OCCASIONALLY CREATING THINGS THAT DON'T QUITE MATCH UP WITH EVENTS EARLY ON IN THE SERIES. SOMETIMES ITEMS OR BITS OF THE SETTING INTRODUCED EARLY ON END UP NOT BEING AS IMPORTANT AS ORIGINALLY INTENDED.

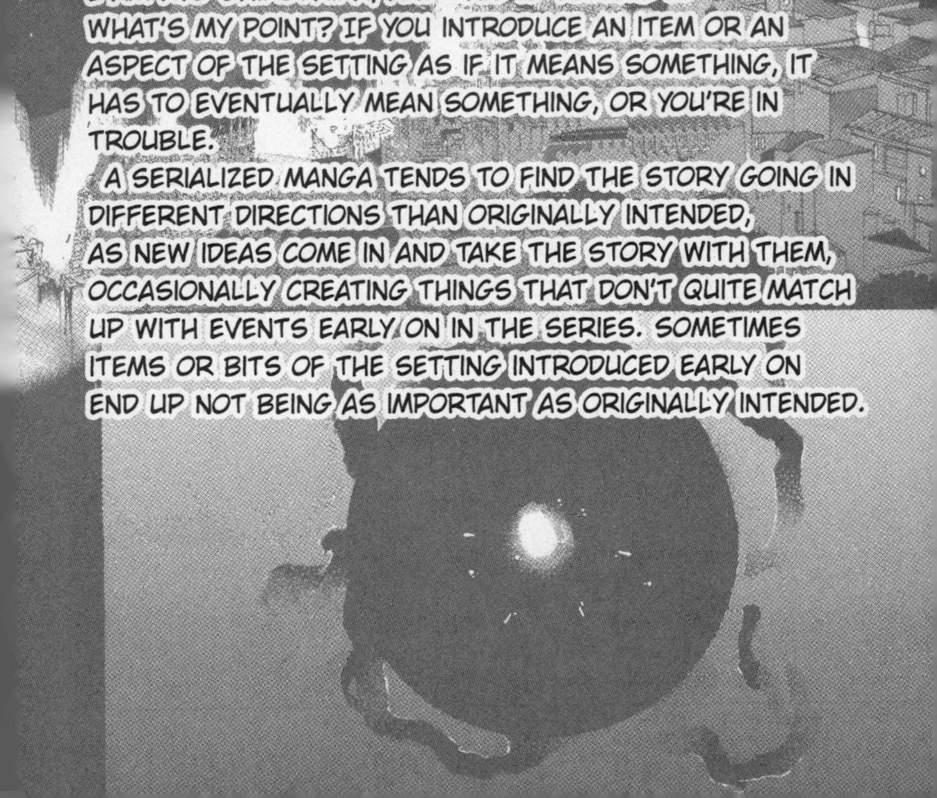

IF IT'S JUST AN OFFHAND LINE OF DIALOGUE, THEN IT CAN BE IGNORED, BUT THERE'S NO WAY TO TURN BACK THE CLOCK AND DELETE AN ITEM INTRODUCED WITH GREAT SIGNIFICANCE, EVEN IF THE MEANING IT ORIGINALLY HELD HAS LONG SINCE BEEN LOST.

SOMETIMES ALL YOU CAN DO IS LEAVE IT BE, BUT THAT ALWAYS MAKES ME AGITATED, AND I DO MY BEST TO FIND A NEW MEANING FOR IT SO I CAN PRETEND I ALWAYS MEANT IT TO TURN OUT THAT WAY.

THERE ARE A NUMBER OF THINGS LIKE THAT IN *THE RECORD OF A FALLEN VAMPIRE*. I EXPECT THERE WILL BE MORE IN FUTURE VOLUMES. STELLA'S NECKLACE IS ONE OF THESE. I HAD NO IDEA IT WOULD EVER BE SO IMPORTANT IN A FLASHBACK. WHEN THE SERIES STARTED, I HAD NOT EVEN COME UP WITH HER CHARACTER...

SO I'M PRETTY BAD AT PREDICTING THE FUTURE, AND THE MORE I WRITE, THE MORE LITTLE TRICKS AND TWISTS I HAVE TO ADD TO REPAIR THE DAMAGE I'VE DONE. I HOPE I MANAGE TO HAVE IT ALL MAKE SENSE.

WITH GREAT EFFORT, BRIDGET'S FLASHBACK DRAWS TO A CLOSE, AND WE MOVE FORWARD WITH THE PLANS TO FIGHT BIG MORTAR. THE MISSING LINK BETWEEN PAST AND PRESENT, QUEEN ADELHEID, WILL SOON BE REVIVED.

I PRAY WE WILL MEET AGAIN IN VOLUME 6.

- KYO SHIRODAIRA

THE RECORD OF A FALLEN VAMPIRE
VOL. 5
VIZ MEDIA EDITION

STORY BY: **KYO SHIRODAIRA**   ART BY: **YURI KIMURA**

Translation & Adaptation...**Andrew Cunningham**
Touch-up Art & Lettering...**HudsonYards**
Cover Design...**Courtney Utt**
Interior Design...**Ronnie Casson**
Editor...**Gary Leach**

Editor in Chief, Books...**Alvin Lu**
Editor in Chief, Magazines...**Marc Weidenbaum**
VP, Publishing Licensing...**Rika Inouye**
VP, Sales & Product Marketing...**Gonzalo Ferreyra**
VP, Creative...**Linda Espinosa**
Publisher...**Hyoe Narita**

VAMPIRE JYUJIKAI vol.5 © 2005 Kyo Shirodaira, Yuri Kimura/
SQUARE ENIX. All rights reserved. First published in Japan in 2005
by SQUARE ENIX CO., LTD. English translation rights arranged with
SQUARE ENIX CO., LTD. and VIZ Media, LLC.

The stories, characters and incidents mentioned in this
publication are entirely fictional.

No portion of this book may be reproduced or transmitted
in any form or by any means without written permission
from the copyright holders.

Printed in the U.S.A.

Published by VIZ Media, LLC
P.O. Box 77010
San Francisco, CA 94107

10 9 8 7 6 5 4 3 2 1
First printing, May 2009

LeRoy Collins Leon Co.
Public Library System
200 West Park Avenue
Tallahassee, FL 32301

YA F SHI   FTB
1487 0938
Shirodaira, Kyo, 1974-

The record of a fallen

                    4-9-09 - SDW

YA F SHI   FTB
1487 0938
Shirodaira, Kyo, 1974-

store.viz.com

ENTAL ADVISORY
RECORD OF A FALLEN VAMPIRE is rated T for Teen and is
mmended for ages 13 and up. Contains strong language and
asy violence.
ratings.viz.com